权威·前沿·原创

皮书系列为
"十二五""十三五"国家重点图书出版规划项目

法律声明

"皮书系列"(含蓝皮书、绿皮书、黄皮书)之品牌由社会科学文献出版社最早使用并持续至今,现已被中国图书市场所熟知。"皮书系列"的LOGO( )与"经济蓝皮书""社会蓝皮书"均已在中华人民共和国国家工商行政管理总局商标局登记注册。"皮书系列"图书的注册商标专用权及封面设计、版式设计的著作权均为社会科学文献出版社所有。未经社会科学文献出版社书面授权许可,任何使用与"皮书系列"图书注册商标、封面设计、版式设计相同或者近似的文字、图形或其组合的行为均系侵权行为。

经作者授权,本书的专有出版权及信息网络传播权为社会科学文献出版社享有。未经社会科学文献出版社书面授权许可,任何就本书内容的复制、发行或以数字形式进行网络传播的行为均系侵权行为。

社会科学文献出版社将通过法律途径追究上述侵权行为的法律责任,维护自身合法权益。

欢迎社会各界人士对侵犯社会科学文献出版社上述权利的侵权行为进行举报。电话:010-59367121,电子邮箱:fawubu@ssap.cn。

社会科学文献出版社

城市生活质量蓝皮书

BLUE BOOK OF
QUALITY OF LIFE IN CITIES

中国城市生活质量报告（2016）

REPORT ON THE QUALITY OF LIFE IN CHINESE CITIES (2016)

预期稳定　挑战犹存

张连城　张　平　杨春学
郎丽华　赵家章　张自然 ／著

中国经济实验研究院

社会科学文献出版社
SOCIAL SCIENCES ACADEMIC PRESS (CHINA)

图书在版编目(CIP)数据

中国城市生活质量报告.2016,预期稳定　挑战犹存/张连城等著. -- 北京：社会科学文献出版社，2017.2
（城市生活质量蓝皮书）
ISBN 978-7-5201-0282-7

Ⅰ.①中… Ⅱ.①张… Ⅲ.①城市-生活质量-指数-研究报告-中国-2016　Ⅳ.①D669.3

中国版本图书馆CIP数据核字（2016）第322056号

城市生活质量蓝皮书
中国城市生活质量报告（2016）
——预期稳定　挑战犹存

著　　者 /	张连城　张　平　杨春学　郎丽华　等
出 版 人 /	谢寿光
项目统筹 /	恽　薇　王楠楠
责任编辑 /	王楠楠
出　　版 /	社会科学文献出版社·经济与管理出版分社（010）59367226 地址：北京市北三环中路甲29号院华龙大厦　邮编：100029 网址：www.ssap.com.cn
发　　行 /	市场营销中心（010）59367081　59367018
印　　装 /	北京季蜂印刷有限公司
规　　格 /	开　本：787mm×1092mm　1/16 印　张：21.25　字　数：290千字
版　　次 /	2017年2月第1版　2017年2月第1次印刷
书　　号 /	ISBN 978-7-5201-0282-7
定　　价 /	89.00元

皮书序列号 / B-2013-292

本书如有印装质量问题，请与读者服务中心（010-59367028）联系

版权所有　翻印必究

"城市生活质量蓝皮书"编委会

张连城　张　平　杨春学
郎丽华　赵家章　张自然

本年度报告执笔人

张连城　张　平　杨春学　郎丽华　赵家章
张自然　王　银　赫宇彪　陈建先　王　钰

组织和策划本次调研的人员

张　平　张连城　杨春学　纪　宏　刘霞辉
郎丽华　徐　雪　王　诚　张晓晶　田新民
袁富华　张自然　赵家章　王　银　蔡　斌

中国经济实验研究院简介

改革开放以来，特别是社会主义市场经济体制建立以来，中国经济发展已经进入一个崭新的阶段。中国已经成为世界第二大经济体，人均国民收入已经达到中等收入国家的水平；同时，中国改革正在从"浅水区"进入"深水区"，改革所面临的形势将更为艰巨和复杂，中国改革必须从"摸着石头过河"的"实践试错"向着利用现代手段进行政策模拟和评估的"实验试错"转变。与此同时，从学科发展的角度看，经济学发展到今天，科学研究正在向协同研究和交叉学科研究的方向发展。这在客观上要求我国的高等院校、研究机构要打破学科界限、打破单位界限，整合一切可利用的资源，精诚合作，不断创新，才有可能应对中国社会所面临的新挑战。在这种背景下，经过长期调研、论证和精心准备，首都经济贸易大学与中国社会科学院经济研究所合作，共同成立了"中国经济实验研究院"。

早在2006年，首都经济贸易大学与中国社会科学院经济研究所就组建了"中国经济增长与周期研究中心"，并且联合香港经济导报社从2007年开始，成功举办了6届"中国经济增长与周期论坛"。目前，该论坛已经成为国内研究宏观经济的著名学者进行学术交流的重要平台。2010年，首都经济贸易大学与中国社会科学院经济研究所又组建了"中国城市生活质量研究中心"，经过对城市生活质量指数体系的深入研究和几个月的调研，在2011年举办的第五届"中国经济增长与周期论坛"上，首次发布了中国30个省会城市的生活质量指数，在国内引起了很大的反响，并引

起了国际同行和世界银行等国际机构的关注。中国经济实验研究院就是在上述研究机构的基础上成立的。

目前，中国经济实验研究院设有"中国经济增长与周期研究中心""中国城市生活质量研究中心""数量经济研究中心""WTO研究中心"，并且设有经济运行与国际贸易实验室、经济预警实验室、经济数据处理与计算机仿真实验室和数字化调查中心。

中国经济实验研究院成立以后，在对原有机构和实验室进行整合的基础上，拟设如下机构：

1. 中国经济实验研究院专家委员会；

2. 中国经济增长与周期研究中心；

3. 中国城市生活质量研究中心；

4. 数量经济研究中心；

5. 博士后流动站；

6. 中国经济增长与周期论坛；

7. 北京经济转型发展研究中心；

8. 经济运行与经济预警实验室、计算机仿真实验室。

中国经济实验研究院成立以后，近期的主要任务如下。

第一，进一步深入开展中国经济增长与经济周期的研究，继续办好"中国经济增长与周期论坛"，并且将逐步实现国际化。

第二，进一步扩大生活质量指数研究的覆盖面，使其逐步从省会城市扩展到全国中等城市、从国内扩展到国际，同时实现指数发布的常态化。此外，生活质量只是经济增长质量的一部分内容，中国经济实验研究院将逐步把经济增长质量纳入自己的研究视野，争取获得一批高质量的科研成果。

第三，不断拓展经济实验研究的范围，开展经济改革实验、政策效应实验、经济增长压力实验等，为中国改革、政府机构及相关部门提供可量化的决策支持，并且努力服务社会。

第四，成立具有国际化特色的研究生指导团队，同时开展与国外大学的紧密合作，共同指导硕士和博士研究生，招收博士后，为首都经济贸易大学的人才队伍建设做出贡献。

第五，中国经济实验研究院目前与国外20多所高校有着紧密的合作关系，并将以此为基础，开展广泛的国际合作和国际学术交流，共同进行科学研究，协同创新，构造研究院的国际化特色。

中国经济实验研究院的宗旨是：推动经济实验研究，繁荣经济科学，为推进我国的经济体制改革、提高经济增长质量、促进经济发展服务。中国经济实验研究院的目标是：在未来，经过我们的不懈努力，争取把中国经济实验研究院建设成为这一领域的具有国际一流水平的高度开放的研究机构。

主要著者简介

张连城 首都经济贸易大学研究生毕业，2004年在美国新英格兰大学进修。现为首都经济贸易大学教授、博士生导师、中国经济实验研究院院长。在首都经济贸易大学（北京经济学院）任教30余载。1998~2002年担任首都经济贸易大学经济系副主任，2002~2012年担任首都经济贸易大学经济学院院长，并在2009~2011年兼任研究生部主任。大学任教期间，1981~1985年先后兼任中国经济学团体联合会机关报《全国经济学团体通信》和《经济学周报》编辑部主任、记者部主任、研究发展部主任。1985~1987年在国家经济体制改革研究所兼任城市经济体制改革办公室副主任并从事研究工作。目前在多家学会兼任副会长、常会理事。

主要研究领域：经济增长、经济周期与宏观经济政策。在该领域发表了近百篇学术论文，出版了10余部专著、教材、译著，其中5项科研成果获教育部、北京市哲学社会科学优秀科研成果一、二等奖。由于自身的学术成就，2011年被国务院批准为享受政府特殊津贴的专家，2016年被评为北京市有突出贡献的专家。1986年以来，曾主持多项社科基金课题，目前主持国家社会科学基金重大项目"正确处理经济平稳较快发展、调整经济结构、管理通胀预期的关系研究"（12 & ZD038），担任我国经济理论界"现代外国经济学大系"丛书的主编工作，领导国家级经济学特色专业、国家级经济学国际化人才培养实验区、国家级经济学核心课程教学团队的建设工作。

张　平　中国社会科学院经济研究所副所长、研究员，中国社会科学院研究生院教授、博士生导师。参加和主持了多项与世界银行、亚洲开发银行、世界劳工组织等的国际合作，以及社科基金重点课题和国家交办的课题。负责中国社会科学院重大课题"中国经济增长的前沿"、国家社会科学基金重大招标课题"我国经济结构战略性调整和增长方式转变"以及"加快经济结构调整与促进经济自主协调发展研究"等课题。分别于1995年、2005年获孙冶方经济科学奖。出版专著若干部，在《经济研究》和其他核心刊物上发表或合作发表了几十篇论文，共计百余万字。

杨春学　1962年11月生于云南新平，彝族。1979~1986年就读于云南大学经济系，获学士和硕士（经济学）学位。1986~1992年执教于云南财经大学（原云南财贸学院），讲授西方经济学、发展经济学和国际金融；1992年考入中国社会科学院研究生院，1995年获博士学位。之后，一直在中国社会科学院经济研究所从事研究工作，并于1998年起在中国社会科学院研究生院讲授中级经济学课程。其间，2001年9月至2002年9月在云南经济贸易委员会挂职，任主任助理。研究领域：经济思想史、当代西方经济学说、某些现实经济问题的政治经济学。出版著作《经济人与社会秩序分析》，发表论文《利他主义经济学的追求》《和谐社会的政治经济学基础》等。

郎丽华　吉林通化人，经济学博士，教授，博士生导师，任首都经济贸易大学经济学院院长、校学位委员会委员、经济学院学位委员会主任、学术委员会副主任、世界贸易组织研究中心副主任，以及北京国际贸易学会副会长、中国服务贸易专家委员会副主任委员等职。研究领域：国际贸易理论与政策、国际贸易战略、世界经济。长期从事国际经济与贸易的教学科研工作，为本科生、研究生、留学生讲授

"国际经济学"、"国际贸易理论与政策"等课程，是北京市精品课程"国际贸易"、国家级双语示范课"国际经济学"的主讲教师，国家级双语示范课程"国际商务"的项目负责人，国家级经济学国际化人才培养实验区、北京市经济学国际化人才培养模式创新实验区主要负责人。1990年以来，先后在《人民日报》《经济研究》《世界经济》《管理世界》《经济学动态》《经济管理与研究》等报纸和杂志上发表数十篇学术论文。主持并参与北京市哲学社会科学规划项目、北京市教育委员会社会科学研究计划项目、国家社科基金重大项目等研究工作。

摘　要

　　中国经济实验研究院城市生活质量研究中心2016年继续对35个城市生活质量进行跟踪调查，通过测算得出2016年城市生活质量的主观满意度指数和客观社会经济数据指数。本次调查仍然采用随机尾号调查方法，保证样本空间分布的合理性和随机性，产生有效随机样本14193个。调查显示，2016年，全国35个城市生活质量主观满意度指数平均值为55.82，比2015年略有提高，处于满意区间。2016年35个城市的主观满意度指数全部超过了满意和不满意的临界点——50。在生活质量客观指数即社会经济数据指数方面，东部城市仍旧高于中西部城市，但同时部分城市存在主客观指数的反差。2016年，35个城市客观社会经济数据指数平均值为54.75，比2015年的55.84有所降低。专项调查显示，35个城市的居民均认为空气质量是影响生活质量的最大因素，其次是物价、食品安全和交通状况；35个城市居民预期未来一两年内房价将呈现下跌趋势；对就业前景的预期处于基本乐观区间。本次调查给我们的启示是：当前，中国经济仍旧处于转型与改革的攻坚阶段，经济与社会发展面临的挑战与风险犹存。在客观生活质量指数与上年相比有所下降的情况下，主观满意度指数保持了基本稳定。但是，当前我们仍面临着生活质量提高方面的巨大挑战：居高不下的生活成本、过快的生活节奏、不确定的房地产价格以及令人担忧的就业前景。在未来的经济与社会发展转型过程中，中央以

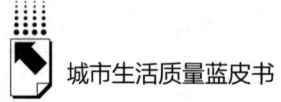

及地方各级政府要继续致力于推进民生体系建设,稳定经济增长,实现居民生活质量的进一步提升。

关键词:城市生活质量 主观满意度指数 客观指数 房价预期 就业预期

目 录

Ⅰ 总报告

B.1 2016年城市生活质量调查 …………………………………………… 001
    一　引言 ……………………………………………………………… 001
    二　主要结论 ………………………………………………………… 002
    三　框架安排 ………………………………………………………… 003
B.2 城市生活质量研究综述 …………………………………………………… 005
    一　生活质量研究历程 ……………………………………………… 005
    二　生活质量的概念 ………………………………………………… 006
    三　生活质量相关理论 ……………………………………………… 008
    四　政府质量与居民生活质量的关系 ……………………………… 009
    五　生活质量指标体系 ……………………………………………… 013

Ⅱ 观测篇

B.3 对2016年城市生活质量调查的说明 …………………………………… 016
B.4 2016年中国35个城市生活质量指数 …………………………………… 019
B.5 中国35个城市生活质量的细分指数 …………………………………… 028

Ⅲ 专项调查篇

B.6 房价预期专项调查 …………………………………… 118
B.7 最关注因素调查：空气质量居首位，物价跃居第二………… 123
B.8 就业满意度调查 …………………………………………… 127

Ⅳ 结论篇

B.9 结论与启示 ………………………………………………… 132

参考文献 ……………………………………………………………… 146

总 报 告

B.1
2016年城市生活质量调查

一 引言

中国经济实验研究院城市生活质量研究中心2016年3~5月对中国35个城市生活质量进行了调查，本次调查是2011年后的第六次年度调查。我们通过统计分析和计算得出了评价2016年中国城市生活质量的主观满意度指数和客观指数（QLICC），该指数体系在2016年第十届中国经济增长与周期论坛上发布。本次主观满意度调查历时两个多月，共产生有效随机样本14193个，整体主观指数的标准误差为0.179。此外，在主观满意度的电话调查中，除了继续对城市住房价格预期和居民最关注因素进行调查外，还增加了居民对就业问题预期的调查。城市生活质量的客观指数即社会经济数据指数，是根据国家权

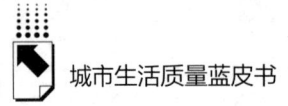

威机构发布的35个城市的社会经济数据计算得出的,从而保证了该指数的客观性和权威性。

二 主要结论

调查显示,2016年,全国35个城市生活质量主观满意度指数平均值为55.82,比2015年略有提高,处于满意区间。2016年35个城市的主观满意度指数全部超过了满意和不满意的临界点——50。城市生活质量主观满意度指数的5个分指数平均值情况如下:生活水平满意度指数为60.44、生活成本满意度指数为39.74、人力资本满意度指数为62.20、社会保障满意度指数为60.66、生活感受满意度指数为56.05。与2015年相比,5个分指数均有所提高。但其中的生活成本满意度分指数仍处于不满意区间。此外,生活感受满意度分指数中的生活节奏细分指数,35个城市的平均值为44.07,仍处于不满意区间。

生活质量主观满意度指数排名前10位的城市是:宁波(1)、杭州(2)、昆明(3)、南宁(4)、重庆(5)、成都(6)、大连(7)、济南(8)、西宁(9)、呼和浩特(10)。排名后10位的城市是:贵阳(26)、南京(27)、郑州(28)、福州(29)、上海(30)、深圳(31)、长春(32)、西安(33)、兰州(34)、厦门(35)。

生活质量客观指数即社会经济数据指数显示,东部城市仍旧高于中西部城市,但同时部分城市存在主客观指数的反差。2016年,35个城市客观社会经济数据指数平均值为54.75,比2015年的55.84有所降低。得分在50以上的城市有32个,比2015年多1个。5个客观分指数的平均值分别是:生活成本客观指数为58.74、生活感受客观指数为57.54、人力资本客观指数为56.98、社会保障客观指数为50.43、生活水平客观指数为50.07。与2015年相比,生活水平、人力资本、社会保障客观分指数有所下降,生活成本、生活感受客观分指数有所上升。

生活质量客观指数排名前10位的城市是：北京（1）、深圳（2）、南京（3）、广州（4）、杭州（5）、上海（6）、昆明（7）、武汉（8）、西安（9）、贵阳（10）。排名后10位的城市是：合肥（26）、哈尔滨（27）、南昌（28）、海口（29）、兰州（30）、南宁（31）、福州（32）、重庆（33）、西宁（34）、郑州（35）。

在对35个城市生活质量主观满意度和客观指数调查的基础上，2016年进行了三项专项调查。影响居民生活质量因素的调查结果显示，在给定的四个选项中，35个城市的居民均认为空气质量是影响生活质量的最重要因素（46.33%），其次是物价（23.94%），排在第三位和第四位的分别是食品安全（20.87%）和交通状况（8.86%）。与2015年的调查结果有所不同，2016年城市居民对物价的关注超过了对食品安全的关注。房价预期的专项调查显示：35个城市预期房价指数平均值为40.16，比2015年的平均值43.86还要低，表明居民预期未来一两年内房价将呈现下跌趋势。2016年新增的就业前景预期调查显示：35个城市对就业前景预期的平均值为57.41，所有城市得分均超过了50，尽管分值不高，但仍处于对就业前景基本乐观的区间。

当前，中国经济仍旧处于转型与改革的攻坚阶段，经济与社会发展面临的挑战与风险犹存。在生活质量客观指数与上年相比有所下降的情况下，主观满意度指数保持了基本稳定。但是，当前我们仍面临居民生活质量提高方面的巨大挑战：居高不下的生活成本、过快的生活节奏、不确定的房地产价格以及令人担忧的就业前景。在未来的经济与社会发展转型过程中，中央以及地方各级政府要继续致力于推进民生体系建设，稳定经济增长，实现居民生活质量的进一步提升。

三 框架安排

本书的第二篇报告是城市生活质量研究综述。从生活质量研究历

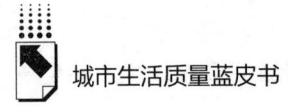

程、生活质量概念、生活质量相关理论、生活质量指标体系等几个方面，对生活质量相关研究进行梳理、归纳。

第三篇报告是对2016年城市生活质量调查的说明。主要包括主观数据调查的技术说明、客观数据指标的设计、客观数据的来源。

第四篇报告介绍了2016年中国35个城市的生活质量指数，包括主观满意度指数和客观指数的排序和说明。为了便于分析各城市生活质量的动态变化，本部分将各个城市生活质量总指数评分和排序列出，并与前几次调查获取的指数进行比较。同时，我们分别给出了2012~2016年主客观指数的直方图，以及35个城市主客观指数的柱状图。

第五篇报告是2016年中国35个城市生活质量指数的细分指数。该报告分别列出了35个城市生活质量的细分指数及排序情况，给出了35个城市生活质量一级指标的雷达图；同时给出了城市生活质量细分指数的直方图和柱状图，以便对城市生活质量指数进行动态比较。

本书第三部分"专项调查篇"是针对三项专项调查的说明，包括房价预期专项调查、居民最关注因素调查以及新增的关于就业满意度的调查。

本书第四部分"结论篇"是本次调查的主要结论、启示以及政策建议。

B.2
城市生活质量研究综述

改革开放以来，随着经济的不断增长，人们对生活质量的追求发生了深刻的变化，由追求生存质量向追求多层次、全方位的生活质量转变。提高人们的生活质量不仅是"以人为本"的科学发展观的重要体现，也是全面建设小康社会的重要目标之一。因此，研究生活质量问题就显得格外重要。而研究生活质量问题需要厘清概念、理论脉络和现实依据，这就要求我们对以前的文献进行梳理。

一 生活质量研究历程

居民生活质量是个世界性的问题。该领域的研究主要集中在以美国为首的发达国家。苏联也对生活质量研究做出了自己的贡献。霍夫曼和苏特纳于1976年、斯沙莱和安德罗于1980年对各个国家的生活质量研究现状与成果进行了比较及综述。

现代生活质量研究起源于美国，与发展经济学的兴起密切相关。随着历史的变迁、社会环境的改变以及人们对福利认知的深入，生活质量研究也不断推进，研究范围越来越广，研究问题也越来越深。1933年，以威廉·奥格博为首的社会学家开始关注生活质量研究，并出版了《近期美国社会动向》一书。Gurin等于1957年首次对美国民众进行了社会质量调查，分析了他们的精神状态和幸福感觉。值得提出的是，制度学派代表人物Galbraith于1958年在其著作中首次定义了"生活质量"。在此之后，生活质量的概念不断丰富和完善。Bauer

于 1966 年在《社会指标》一书中正式使用了"生活质量"这一术语。生活质量研究开始从社会指标里脱离出来，作为一个专门的领域被学者关注，指人们对经济、社会及其生活环境的一种心理感觉。Rostow 于 1971 年在《政治和增长阶段》一书中把"生活质量"纳入理论研究框架。他认为，追求生活质量是人类社会发展的最终阶段。显然，这里的生活质量更加强调人们在物质需求得到满足之后精神上的幸福感。进入 20 世纪 90 年代，Perroux、Milesi、Cummins 等认为经济发展的最终目标是提高人类的福利。

20 世纪 70 年代国内开始对生活质量进行初步的研究。80 年代后，该领域有了大规模的调研和经验性分析。90 年代后，国家统计局和相关部门制定了指标体系和量化标准，明确了小康社会的生活质量标准。进入 21 世纪以来，一些高校和研究机构开始设定生活质量研究中心，出版了生活质量调查报告，生活质量研究也进入了新的发展阶段。

二 生活质量的概念

"生活质量"是个内涵非常丰富的概念，既有主观内容，又有客观存在。美国经济学家 Galbraith 是最早系统性研究生活质量问题的学者。他发现，美国较高的经济水平并没有给居民带来相应的社会和精神上的幸福感及满足感。随后，Galbraith 和 Ball 在 1960 年首次提出了"生活质量"这一术语。从此以后，学术界开始研究和关注生活质量问题。经过半个多世纪的发展，生活质量仍然没有统一和公认的概念。不同的群体对生活质量的了解和要求各不相同。对于低收入群体来讲，其最基本的温饱问题尚未解决，生活质量的概念就可以界定为生存质量或生命质量，生活质量的好坏取决于物质层面；而对于高收入群体，生活质量的概念被界定为优质的生活，生活质量的评价标准

更加偏重于精神层面。

在一些经济学者看来，偏好的差异性导致了对生活质量理解的差异性。对于低收入群体，生活物质较少，边际效用就较高，提高物质水平能够提高总效用，从而使幸福感上升。相反，对于高收入群体，生活物质的边际效用较低，而精神产品的边际效用较高，因此增加精神产品能够提高这些阶层的幸福感。在一些社会学者看来，物质层面的生活质量是一种需求（need），而精神层面的生活质量是一种欲望（desire）。前者满足人最基本的生存和生理需求，后者满足人的理想、信念、尊重等高层次多方面的欲望。处于需求阶段的人们，即使存在高层次生活的欲望，但由于缺乏物质层面的支持，这些欲望也无法实现。只有在物质层面的需求得到满足以后，欲望才有可能得到满足。需求和欲望并没有清晰的界限，完全可能同时出现在同一个人的身上。但两者又有所区别，不能混淆。Veehoven 于 1991 年指出，需求是一种天性，原则上有限，是一个绝对概念；而欲望是精神上的产物，是无止境的，是个相对概念。

目前来看，生活质量研究存在两种模式。一种模式为斯堪的纳维亚模式。该模式注重客观生活条件，生活质量被看成是个人对资源的支配能力。如 Rostow 于 1971 年把生活质量定义为"居民生活的自然环境的美化和社会环境的改善"。另一种模式是美国模式，该模式强调主观生活质量。

综上所述，生活质量是个集合的概念，包含有形的物质生活，也包含无形的精神生活。本报告作者比较认同周长城于 2001 年提出的定义。他把生活质量定义为"社会提高国民生活的充分程度和国民生活需求的满足程度，是建立在一定物质条件基础上的，社会全体对自身及其自身社会环境的认同感"。

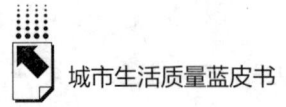

三 生活质量相关理论

生活质量研究是一门跨学科和多学科交叉的学问，涉及经济学、社会学、心理学、人口和资源环境学等多种学科。不同的学科对生活质量的研究角度和侧重点也各不相同，形成了各自的概念、方法以及理论体系。这些理论体系丰富和扩展了生活质量研究的范围。

（一）经济学角度

经济学强调在约束条件下资源的最优配置。应用于生活质量研究领域，经济学研究的是如何运用有效的资源实现行为主体生活质量最大化的问题。在经济学理论中，消费者行为目标是实现效用的最大化。效用是一种心理感受，指的是消费者从商品消费中获得的幸福感和满足感。因此，效用和生活质量之间存在正相关关系。在收入约束的情况下，消费者在物质性产品和精神性产品之间进行选择，按照等边际原则，提高自己的生活质量。而生产者在约束条件下实现利润最大化，从而提高自己的生活质量。政府通过产权和税收等制度安排，实现社会福利的最大化。福利的增加能够促进整个社会生活质量的提高。1976年，B. C. Liu 就尝试把生活质量纳入微观分析框架。Jester 等于1981年把有形资源和无形资源结合起来，考虑到资源的分配和生活质量的最大化问题。1986年，厉以宁在《社会主义政治经济学》中把福利经济学理论引入生活质量研究中，他认为生活质量的高低与福利水平挂钩，在实际收入不发生改变的情况下，通过改善自然和社会环境等手段实现帕累托改进，提升了整个社会的生活质量水平。

（二）社会心理学角度

社会心理学的代表人物有 Campbell、Schiller、Geisen、林南等社

会学家。Campbell 于 1981 年强调用心理学人来分析人的幸福感受。区别于经济学人假设，心理学人或自我强调需求减少过程能够提升幸福感，但需求得不到满足时，自我幸福感被赋予负值。Schiller 于 1974 年认为生活质量存在于自我评价以及与他人的相互关系上。生活质量具有主观性、复杂性和相互性。Geisen 认为生活质量是自我感受的一部分。自我感受随自我与社会的相互关系变化而变化。林南于 1987 年把生活质量定义为"对于生活及其各方面的评价与总结"，强调自我对经济社会环境的满意程度。生活质量包含三个层面：生活满意度、精神幸福感和反馈性公益行为。

（三）生态学角度

Milbrath 是从生态学角度分析生活质量的代表性人物。他认为，生活质量不是独立于生态系统之外，而是生态系统的一部分，是构建生态容貌的一个重要因素。自然环境的改变能够带来生活质量的改变，同样的，生活质量的升级也能促进自然环境的改善。生活质量是个动态过程，不是一成不变的。由此可以看出，生态学观点注重事物之间的相互联系，生活质量和环境的其他因素之间是彼此联系和互相影响的。

四　政府质量与居民生活质量的关系

长期以来，学术界关注了经济因素和社会因素对居民生活质量的影响。经济因素包括经济增长、收入差距、通货膨胀、失业率等；社会因素主要包括性别、年龄、婚姻、阶层等（Dolan 等，2008）。近年来，一些文献发现政府质量也是影响生活质量的重要变量（陈刚和李树，2012；张克中和何凌云，2012）。政府质量是个多维的概念，包括政府效率、法治水平、政府社会治理水平、公共物品供给状况、财产权利保护、腐败状况等。

（一）政府质量对居民生活质量的直接作用机制

政府执行人们赋予的权力，管理社会公共事务，掌握着资源和公共政策制定的权力，目标是提高国民的福利水平，提高客观和主观生活质量水平。政府在多大程度上满足居民主客观生活质量的需求是评价政府质量的一个重要标准。

Helliwell 和 Huang 于 2008 年把政府质量分为政府的民主质量和技术质量，两者直接影响居民的生活质量状况。一方面，高水平的政府民主质量能够提高居民生活质量。Frey 和 Stutzer 2002 年的研究表明，瑞典居民的主观生活质量与该国的民主程度显著正相关。在良好的民主社会里，居民能够充分地参与政策决策过程，从而获得"程序效用"，增强幸福感受。此外，执政的代理人由居民选举产生，执政理念和居民的理念较为吻合，这种共鸣也会提升居民的主观生活质量。另一方面，良好的政府技术质量对居民生活质量也有积极的影响。Tavits 2008 年以欧洲国家的个人层面和国家层面为研究样本，发现腐败显著影响了居民的生活质量，腐败问题越严重，居民幸福感越低；反之亦然。在一个腐败多发的国家里，公共物品只提供给价高者或者有关系的人，而排除了其他人，从而降低了总体生活质量；而参与腐败交易的行为人也失去了独立性，变得不幸福。腐败还会恶化人际关系，从而降低居民的主观感受。

相对于不同收入和发展阶段的国家，政府质量对居民生活质量的影响也存在差异。Helliwell 和 Huang 以及 Otter 2008 年指出，政府技术质量对于发展水平和收入水平较低的国家更为重要，而政府的民主质量对于发达、收入水平较高的国家更为重要。当国家处于发展中阶段时，居民对政府技术质量提出更高的要求，希望政府提供稳定的社会环境、完善的制度和良好的公共物品等。比如，对于东南亚大部分发展中国家的居民而言，医疗条件和住房条件改善所带来的幸福感远高于民主程度提

高所带来的幸福感。行政效率的提高、法治的进步、公平公正的社会环境、稳定的政治环境为居民主观和客观生活质量的提升提供了良好的物质及制度保障。随着经济的不断增长、收入水平的提高，人们基本的生活需求得到满足，政治民主和参与需求随之上升，此时政府民主质量对居民生活质量发挥着越来越重要的作用。良好的政府民主质量可以保障人们参与政治过程，从而提高"政治效用"，人们的幸福感也会增强。

政府的技术质量和民主质量从不同方面影响居民的生活质量。好的治理本身就是居民幸福感的来源（张克中和何凌云，2012）。良好的政府质量为居民生活质量提供了优良的经济、社会政治环境和完善的制度保障，让居民生活更有安全感和幸福感。

（二）政府质量对居民生活质量的间接作用机制

政府质量是个复杂和多维的概念，标准也不尽相同。早期的文献认为政府质量取决于腐败程度的高低。世界银行从以下方面评价政府质量水平：公民表达与政府问责、政治稳定与低暴力、政府效能、管理质量、法治水平。"自由之家"（Freedom House）侧重于公民自由和政府权力的大小。哥德堡大学关注政府的公正性。尽管研究者们对政府质量的评价标准存在不同（Holmberg 等，2009），但在政府质量指标选取方面意见较为一致，主要选取政府效率、腐败、法治水平等（La Porta 等，1999；Treisman, 2002）。总体而言，政府效率的提高、腐败程度的下降和公正公平的制度能够提升居民的主观生活质量（Helliwell and Huang, 2008；Kim and Kim, 2011；等等）。

政府质量影响居民的生活质量存在五种间接作用机制。第一，良好的政府质量促进了经济增长，从而提高了居民生活质量。一方面，政府应用强大的行政权力推进制度改革，从而促进发展。张五常在2009年曾指出，中国经济的高速发展主要原因是中国政府通过强而有力的权力，推动了财税分权改革，带来了激烈的"县域竞争"，促进

了地区经济增长。张德荣2013年发现，改革的制度红利是我国经济增长的一个重要推动力。另一方面，政府通过提高治理成本，以求维持社会稳定。在经济增长到一定阶段之后，增长速度放缓，深层次的矛盾不断累积，社会不稳定因素上升。政府不得不提高治理成本，导致社会总成本上升，进一步阻碍经济的增长。North 1981年发现，政府质量能够很好地解释欧洲国家1000年以来的兴衰更替。Mauro 1995年也指出，政府质量是国家间经济增长存在差异的重要原因。而经济增长直接影响居民的客观生活质量。邢占军2011年发现，经济增长是提高我国居民主观生活质量的重要原因。经济增长能提高居民的收入水平，改善居民的物质生活，人们对未来充满了乐观的预期，从而提高了居民的生活质量。

第二，政府质量影响收入分配和不平等程度，从而影响居民生活质量。腐败盛行的政府加剧了收入不平等。一个政府越腐败，寻租行为越盛行，税收和支出结构扭曲，加剧了收入分配的不公平程度（Alesina等，2004）。而且，腐败进一步加剧了机会的不平等，不同群体间流动性降低，导致阶层固化，不利于生活稳定（Alesina等，2005）。社会不公平和收入不平等的加剧不利于生活质量的提升，幸福感也会随之降低。我国相关研究发现，良好的政府质量显著减少了收入分配不平等现象（陈刚，2011），收入不平等的缩小增强了居民的幸福感（何立新和潘春阳，2011）。

第三，良好的政府质量通过完善的司法制度，增强了居民的幸福感。一方面，良好的政府拥有完善和高效的司法体系，可保证程序正义、结果正义，居民获得了"程序效用"（Procedural Utility），生活质量也得以提高。另一方面，完善的司法制度可以强化居民的人身安全和财产权利，提高居民的安全感，进而增加居民的幸福感（Bjornskov等，2010）。

第四，政府质量对社会信任制度产生影响，从而影响了居民的生

活质量。在一个信任度高的社会里，人际关系更为和谐，从而给居民带来较高的生活质量（Helliwell and Putnam, 2004）。而且，信任制度可以培育和创造更多的社会资本，有助于降低市场交易成本和解决"搭便车"的问题，从而提高居民的生活质量（Hudson, 2006）。相反，Rothstein and Eek 认为，如果一个政府腐败盛行，市场参与者都在"寻租"，那么社会信任难以形成，社会资本的创造也会受到抑制，居民的幸福就难以达成，生活质量也会下降。

第五，政府质量影响财政支出结构，从而影响居民生活质量。政府质量的优劣反映在政府支出行为和结构上，而支出结构能够显著影响居民的幸福感。Hessami 2010 年以及 Kotakorpi 和 Laamanen 2010 年的研究发现，教育支出和医疗卫生支出都有利于提高居民的生活质量。在腐败程度高的政府里，由于教育和医疗卫生领域的寻租机会较少，而军工领域的寻租机会较多，为了获得更多的利益，政府可能减少对教育和医疗卫生的支出，而增加对军工的支出，从而降低居民的生活质量（Mauro, 1998）。中国财政在教育和医疗卫生方面投入较低，而在行政管理方面投入过高，财政支出结构扭曲，不利于居民幸福感的提升。陈刚和李树（2010）发现，政府质量提高确实能够显著提高社会性支出及其效率，而这能够改善居民的生活质量。

政府质量通过多种机制影响居民的生活质量。这些机制表明，良好的政府质量能够提高居民生活质量，增强居民的幸福感。相反，低劣的政府质量不利于居民生活质量的改善。因此，政府质量是促进居民生活质量提高的重要源头，改善政府质量能够显著提高居民生活质量。

五 生活质量指标体系

（一）国外研究情况

生活质量指标体系的研究可概括为三种模式：扩展 GDP 账户模

式、社会指标模式和心理主观模式。

1. 扩展GDP账户模式

传统的GDP核算体系存在一些缺陷。GDP并不是衡量一个社会福利大小的完美指标，如它不能衡量孩子的健康水平、教育质量、诗歌之美。为了弥补GDP的缺陷，一些学者提出了扩展GDP账户模式，包括"真实进步指数"和"可持续经济福利指数"等。该模式以GDP为基本评价单位，通过考察个体消费和资本账户来形成生活质量的指标体系。该模式不仅能够反映人们生活幸福、环境状况改善和教育水平提升等生活质量的提高，也能反映出贫富差距、环境恶化等所导致的生活质量下降。

2. 社会指标模式

从20世纪60年代至80年代，西方国家掀起了"社会指标运动"。"社会指标运动"关注居民生活质量，包括经济、社会、政治等多重指标，涉及住房、教育、医疗、环境、社会治安等方面，也有政治自由和言论自由等指标。北欧各国把生活水平划分为两大指标：物质生活质量指标和生活进步指标。联合国也提出了"人类发展指标"等。

3. 心理主观模式

心理主观模式更加注重居民的精神生活质量，重视个体的心理感受。古瑞1957年首次运用该模式，侧重个体精神疾病分析。此后学者对该模式进行了扩展，既关注个人情感和心理健康状况，也开始重视个人对社会的认同感和归属感。代表人物包括坎贝尔和林南教授，他们从情感、认知和行为三个层面来分析生活质量，设置了满意度、幸福感和社会积极性三个指标。

（二）国内研究情况

中国自20世纪70年代开始对生活质量做初步探讨，80年代出现了一波研究高峰，代表人物有厉以宁和卢汉龙等。厉以宁1986年

提出生活质量是反映人们生活和福利状况的一个标志。卢汉龙与美国林南教授合作，从情感、认知和行为3个层次衡量居民生活质量状态（林南和卢汉龙，1987）。卢淑华和韦鲁英的生活质量指标不仅包括衣、食、住、行客观指标，也包括满意度和幸福感主观指标。周长城从四个方面区别生活质量，分别是环境的承载能力、生命的效用、个体的生存能力和个体对生活的评价（周长城等，2001）。罗萍等（2000）设计了八大因素38个具体指标来衡量居民生活质量，八大因素包括收入状况、消费结构、住房条件、婚姻家庭、社会服务、健康状况、文化教育和经济环境。赵彦云、王作成（2003）借鉴IMD的指标体系，构建了包含11个因素的生活质量指标体系，这些因素包含经济发展水平、收入分配状况、消费水平、交通条件、信息化水平、健康保障水平、就业保障状况、教育水平、社会安全、城市化情况、居民生活水平。纪竹荪（2003）从5个方面来测算生活质量，分别是物质生活水平、精神文化生活、社会生活、个人身心健康和情感生活及个性发展空间、国民生活质量改善。张润清、谢艳辉（2004）研究了农村居民的生活质量状况，设定了物质生活质量和精神生活质量两大指标，物质生活质量指标由人均GDP、非农业劳动力比重、受教育程度、每万人拥有医生数、平均寿命、人口自然增长率、恩格尔系数等9项指标构成；精神生活质量指标包括政府农村政策满意度、个人生活条件满意度、婚姻状况满意度等7项指标。贾海薇（2005）建立了工作生活质量评价指标体系，对高校教师的生活质量状况进行了研究。王予东等（2001）研究了针对老年人的调查表，研究了老年人的生活质量状况。廖湘岳和贺春临（2002）从安全感、控制感、和谐感和自主感四个维度来衡量居民的生活质量。

观 测 篇

B.3
对2016年城市生活质量调查的说明

为了保证调查结果的连续性和可比性，2015年我们在调查方法、指标体系设置以及样本的选取方面基本延续了前面三年的做法，同时在局部做了细微的调整和完善。

一 对本次调查的整体说明

中国经济实验研究院城市生活质量研究中心于2016年3~5月对中国35个城市生活质量进行了调查，本次调查是自2011年起的第六次年度调查。我们通过统计分析和计算得出了评价2016年中国城市生活质量的主观满意度指数和客观指数（QLICC），该指数体系在2016年第十届中国经济增长与周期论坛上发布。本次主观满意度调查历时两个多月，

共产生有效随机样本14193个，整体主观指数的标准误差为0.179。此外，在主观满意度的电话调查中，除了继续对城市住房价格预期和居民最关注因素进行调查外，还增加了居民对就业问题预期的调查。

二 主客观指标体系的构建和专项调查

根据我们的理解和中国的实际情况，2011年，中国经济实验研究院创建了中国城市生活质量指数体系，即QLICC体系。这个体系包括两部分：主观满意度指数体系和客观指数（社会经济数据指数）体系。2016年，主观满意度指数体系和客观指数体系的构建延续了2012年以来的做法（见表1和表2）。

表1 中国城市生活质量主观满意度指数体系

满意度指数（主观指数）	主观问题	答案赋值				
		100	75	50	25	0
生活水平满意度指数	收入现状（50%）	很满意	满意	一般	不满意	很不满意
	收入预期（50%）	很乐观	乐观	一般	不乐观	很不乐观
生活成本满意度指数	生活成本	很低	低	一般	高	很高
人力资本满意度指数	人力资本	很满意	满意	一般	不满意	很不满意
社会保障满意度指数	医疗和养老保障（50%）	很满意	满意	一般	不满意	很不满意
	城市安全状况（50%）	很满意	满意	一般	不满意	很不满意
生活感受满意度指数	生活节奏（50%）	很慢	慢	一般	快	很快
	生活便利（50%）	很便利	便利	一般	不便利	很不便利

此外，在2016年的主观满意度电话调查中，除了继续对城市住房价格预期和城市居民最关注因素进行调查外，还新增了城市居民对

就业问题的满意度调查，试图了解互联网消费对城市居民生活质量的影响。专项调查的结果仍旧不被纳入QLICC体系，但这三项专项调查的结果可以进一步佐证居民对生活质量的满意度。

表2 中国城市生活质量客观指数体系

社会经济数据指数（客观指数）	一级指标	二级指标	对城市生活质量的影响
生活水平客观指数	收入水平	消费率（消费/收入）	+
		人均财富（包含人均储蓄和人均住房财富）	+
		人均可支配收入	+
	生活改善指数	人均消费增长	+
		人均财富增长	+
		人均可支配收入增长	+
生活成本客观指数	生活成本指数	房屋销售价格指数	−
		通货膨胀率	−
		房价收入比	−
人力资本客观指数	人力资本指数	教育提供指数（包含万人学校数和万人教师数）	+
		教育文化娱乐消费支出比	+
社会保障客观指数	社会保障指数	社保覆盖率	+
		基本医疗保险覆盖率	+
		失业保险覆盖率	+
生活感受客观指数	生活便利指数	交通提供能力（包含人均铺装道路面积、万人拥有公共电汽车数量、万人出租车数量）	+
		万人影剧院数	+
		医疗提供能力（包含万人床位数、万人医院数、万人拥有医生数）	+
	生态环境指数	人均绿地面积	+
		空气质量	+
	收入差距感受指数	基尼系数	−

注：本栏目中的"+"为正影响，"−"为负影响。

B.4
2016年中国35个城市生活质量指数

根据中国城市生活质量指标体系进行调查，得出了中国2016年35个城市生活质量指数以及排序情况，并结合2012年以来的调查结果进行比较分析。

一 生活质量主观满意度微升，上升速率下降

调查结果显示，如表1所示，2016年全国35个城市生活质量主观满意度指数加权平均值为55.82，自2011年开展调查以来，呈现持续上升态势，保持在满意区间。但由于满意区间的答案赋值为50~75，因此仍处于基本满意的水平。2012~2016年，全国生活质量主观满意度指数加权平均值分别为50.88、50.87、51.57、55.38、55.82。排名靠后的城市的生活质量满意度指数分值也逐渐上升，2012年贵阳市的得分最低，为47.33；2013年兰州市的得分最低，为48.57；2014年深圳市得分最低，为49.51；2015年兰州市的得分最低，为53.30；2016年得分最低的是厦门市，得分为53.98。这意味着：2015~2016年35个城市生活质量主观满意度指数得分全部超过50，也就是说连续两年被调查的35个城市的生活质量满意度全部进入了满意区间。

表 1　2016 年中国 35 个城市生活质量主观满意度指数

城市	2016 年			2015 年		2014 年		2013 年		2012 年	
	得分	排序	上升位次	得分	排序	得分	排序	得分	排序	得分	排序
宁波市	57.36	1	2	57.24	3	52.63	8	52.17	7	52.51	7
杭州市	56.75	2	-1	57.58	1	52.83	4	52.05	10	54.04	2
昆明市	56.63	3	2	57.03	5	49.63	34	48.73	33	48.72	32
南宁市	56.59	4	14	55.24	18	50.00	32	49.81	28	49.60	27
重庆市	56.56	5	12	55.26	17	52.69	7	51.01	19	52.28	11
成都市	56.51	6	7	55.46	13	52.14	10	51.40	13	52.13	12
大连市	56.42	7	5	55.49	12	50.61	26	50.10	26	50.37	18
济南市	56.41	8	3	55.73	11	52.57	9	53.68	1	53.78	4
西宁市	56.40	9	16	54.72	25	51.94	13	52.21	6	51.57	14
呼和浩特市	56.38	10	17	54.64	27	50.62	25	50.37	22	50.14	22
太原市	56.30	11	23	53.32	34	50.90	23	49.90	27	49.38	29
武汉市	56.23	12	4	55.34	16	50.45	28	49.07	32	49.95	24
合肥市	56.19	13	-7	56.85	6	51.94	12	52.34	5	53.20	5
海口市	56.09	14	-10	57.09	4	51.83	16	51.80	11	50.05	23
南昌市	56.00	15	-1	55.41	14	51.31	21	50.35	23	48.41	33
银川市	55.99	16	16	53.81	32	51.90	15	51.07	18	52.29	10
哈尔滨市	55.95	17	-8	56.59	9	51.05	22	49.79	29	48.78	31
广州市	55.91	18	3	55.00	21	50.05	31	49.21	31	49.74	25
乌鲁木齐市	55.89	19	10	54.48	29	50.76	24	50.38	21	50.23	21
沈阳市	55.80	20	-5	55.40	15	52.85	3	51.25	16	49.73	26
石家庄市	55.74	21	1	54.95	22	51.75	18	52.17	8	53.86	3
青岛市	55.73	22	-3	55.18	19	53.06	1	53.05	2	52.31	8
北京市	55.64	23	5	54.49	28	51.78	17	50.16	24	49.47	28
长沙市	55.63	24	0	54.89	24	50.37	29	50.15	25	50.29	19
天津市	55.61	25	5	54.22	30	52.81	6	51.35	14	52.07	13
贵阳市	55.61	26	7	53.77	33	49.94	33	49.58	30	47.33	35
南京市	55.39	27	-20	56.70	7	51.43	20	51.70	12	50.75	16
郑州市	55.25	28	-8	55.03	20	50.25	30	51.28	15	50.76	15
福州市	55.20	29	-6	54.92	23	51.90	14	52.06	9	52.60	6
上海市	55.20	30	-20	55.74	10	51.94	11	50.53	20	50.24	20
深圳市	54.67	31	0	54.06	31	49.51	35	48.68	34	49.16	30
长春市	54.48	32	-24	56.60	8	52.88	2	52.34	4	54.51	1
西安市	54.47	33	-7	54.65	26	50.58	27	51.16	17	50.40	17
兰州市	54.07	34	1	53.30	35	51.50	19	48.57	35	47.95	34
厦门市	53.98	35	-33	57.57	2	52.82	5	53.00	3	52.30	9
平均值	55.82			55.38		51.57		50.87		50.88	

从35个城市生活质量主观满意度指数排序情况的变化看，2012年以来连续5年排名始终处于前10位的城市只有杭州市和宁波市；连续5年处于后10位的城市为贵阳市和深圳市。5年以来，首次进入前10位的城市分别为南宁市、大连市和呼和浩特市。与2015年相比，排名上升最快的3个城市为太原市、呼和浩特市、西宁市，分别上升了23位、17位和16位，下滑最快的4个城市为厦门市、长春市、上海市和南京市，分别下滑了33位、24位、20位和20位。北京市的生活质量满意度排名从2012年到2016年的位次分别为：28、24、17、28、23，一直位于中下区间。

2016年城市生活质量主观满意度指数的5个分指数加权平均值分别为：人力资本，62.20；社会保障，60.66；生活水平，60.44；生活感受，56.05；生活成本，39.74。与2015年相比，35个城市的5个分指数加权平均值均有微升。5个分指数中得分最高的是人力资本满意度指数，得分最低的是生活成本满意度指数。

由图1的主观满意度总指数直方图可见，整体主观满意度上升是由35个城市主观满意度指数得分不断升高且分布逐步集中带来的。

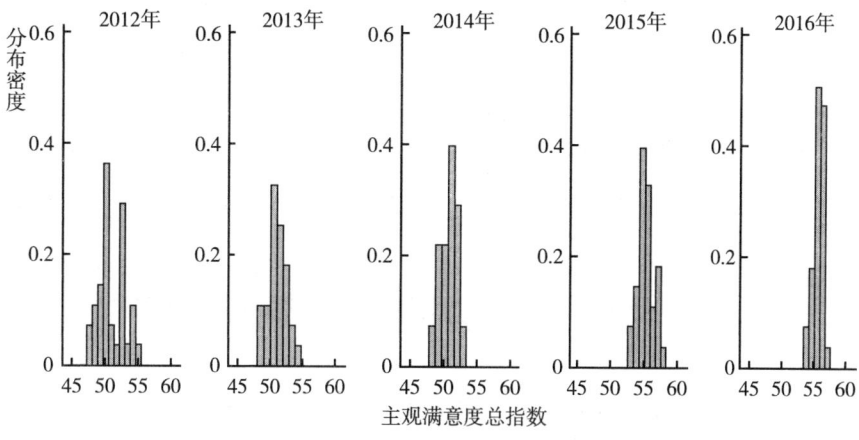

图1 2012~2016年35个城市主观满意度总指数直方图

从统计分析的结果也可以清楚地看出这种变化趋势。2012年，主观满意度总指数得分最高的是长春市（54.51），得分最低的是贵阳市（47.33），两者相差7.18，所有35个城市的主观满意度总指数得分的标准差为1.81；2013年，得分最高的是济南市（53.68），得分最低的是兰州市（48.57），两者相差5.11，35个城市得分的标准差为1.31；2014年，得分最高的是青岛市（53.06），得分最低的是深圳市（49.51），两者相差3.55，35个城市得分的标准差为1.05；2015年，得分最高的是杭州市（57.58），得分最低的是兰州市（53.30），两者相差4.28，35个城市得分的标准差为1.15；2016年，得分最高的是宁波市（57.36），得分最低的是厦门市（53.98），两者相差3.38，35个城市得分的标准差为0.76。可见，最高分变化不大，但最低分却上升较快。2016年所有城市的主观满意度上升幅度最大，城市间主观满意度指数得分的标准差已经由2012的1.81缩小到0.76。

从每个城市的情况看，2012~2016年大部分城市的生活质量主观满意度指数是不断上升的。如图2所示，生活质量主观满意度指数一直处于上升态势的城市有北京市、贵阳市、呼和浩特市、南昌市、青岛市、沈阳市、太原市、乌鲁木齐市、兰州市和南宁市；波动上升的有长沙市、成都市、大连市、福州市、广州市、济南市、宁波市、深圳市、石家庄市、天津市、武汉市、西宁市、银川市、郑州市和重庆市。而至2016年略有回落的有长春市、哈尔滨市、海口市、杭州市、合肥市、昆明市、南京市、上海市、西安市和厦门市。

二 经济承压，客观生活质量指数下降

与往年一样，2016年城市生活质量客观指数是通过统计和计算35个城市官方公布的20个客观经济指标得出的，计算结果如表2所示。

2016年中国35个城市生活质量指数

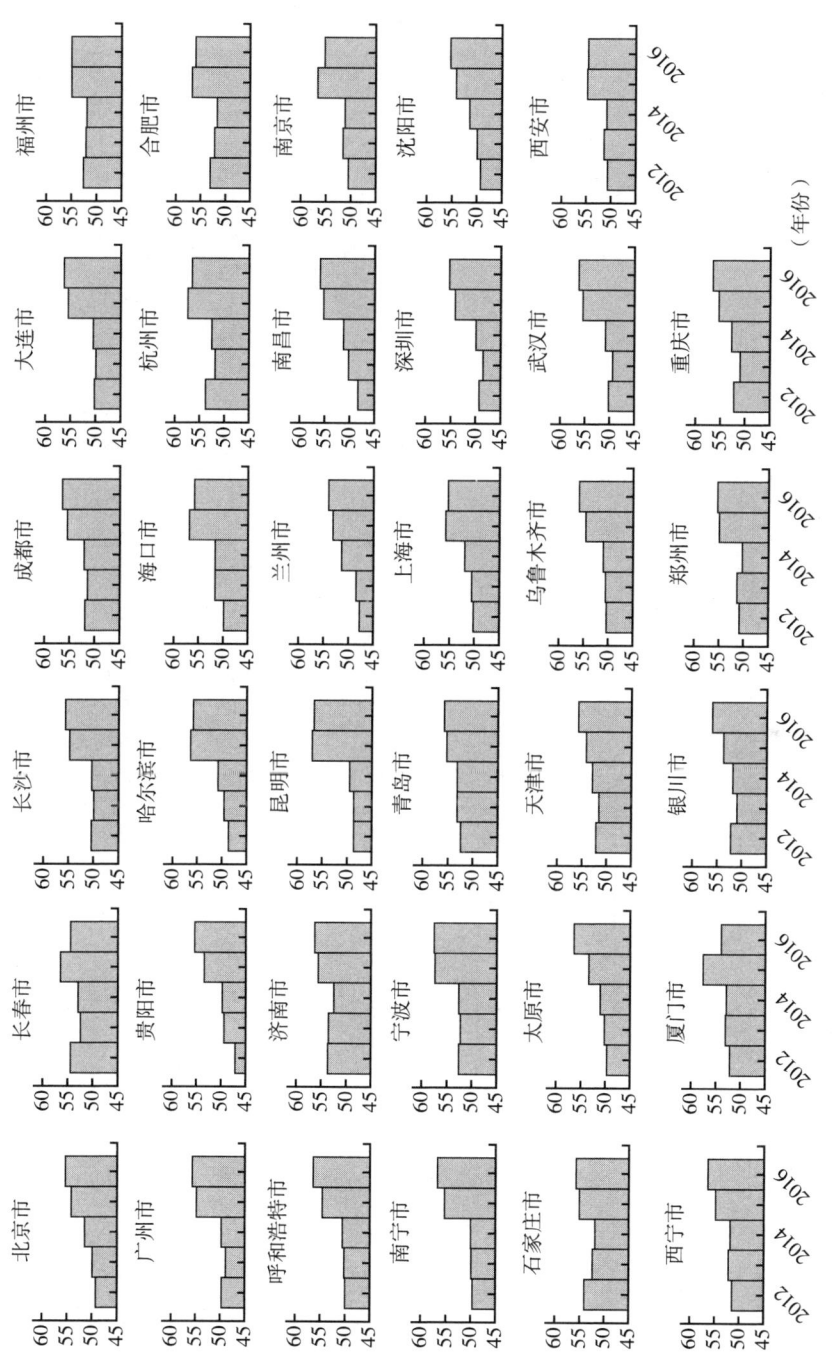

图 2　2012~2016 年 35 个城市生活质量主观满意度指数

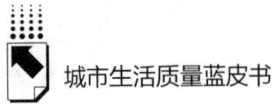

表2 2012~2016年中国35个城市生活质量客观指数

城市	2016年			2015年		2014年		2013年		2012年	
	得分	排序	上升位次	得分	排序	得分	排序	得分	排序	得分	排序
北京市	64.42	1	0	67.41	1	68.78	1	69.80	1	68.72	1
深圳市	64.00	2	5	59.87	7	63.25	4	63.93	5	64.24	3
南京市	62.79	3	-1	63.37	2	65.52	3	66.65	3	62.38	5
广州市	60.76	4	1	61.08	5	66.39	2	66.85	2	64.87	2
杭州市	59.60	5	-1	61.70	4	59.49	13	59.54	12	59.09	8
上海市	58.93	6	0	59.95	6	61.30	7	61.78	8	62.72	4
昆明市	58.23	7	1	59.69	8	60.61	10	58.05	15	54.08	14
武汉市	57.95	8	1	58.87	9	60.33	12	58.93	13	56.61	10
西安市	57.93	9	-6	62.39	3	61.61	5	64.65	4	61.59	6
贵阳市	57.20	10	4	56.92	14	56.46	18	52.45	29	50.98	25
呼和浩特市	57.17	11	0	58.16	11	60.99	9	62.22	6	59.55	7
沈阳市	57.04	12	0	57.22	12	60.41	11	59.99	10	56.59	11
银川市	55.72	13	0	57.19	13	56.77	17	57.68	16	52.45	18
宁波市	54.88	14	1	55.70	15	61.11	8	61.47	9	55.21	12
长春市	54.49	15	1	55.22	16	57.63	15	59.64	11	52.29	19
石家庄市	54.03	16	4	54.00	20	54.44	25	54.78	24	50.49	28
厦门市	53.91	17	2	54.32	19	61.58	6	61.89	7	58.86	9
乌鲁木齐市	53.74	18	3	53.53	21	54.42	26	54.59	26	49.73	32
长沙市	53.56	19	-9	58.48	10	59.15	14	58.36	14	53.53	16
太原市	53.53	20	6	52.15	26	51.62	31	55.45	21	52.15	20
青岛市	53.16	21	-4	55.03	17	55.87	21	54.76	25	54.05	15
大连市	52.69	22	-4	54.38	18	56.15	19	55.64	20	52.00	21
济南市	52.50	23	1	52.72	24	56.10	20	56.84	17	53.22	17
成都市	52.48	24	-2	53.35	22	54.89	23	55.96	19	51.15	24
天津市	52.35	25	5	51.25	30	55.48	22	55.42	22	54.30	13
合肥市	52.23	26	-1	52.69	25	56.83	16	56.73	18	50.92	26
哈尔滨市	52.03	27	1	51.45	28	53.80	28	51.86	30	50.44	29
南昌市	51.99	28	-5	52.88	23	51.29	32	53.03	27	49.03	34
海口市	51.64	29	0	51.28	29	53.72	29	51.50	31	51.17	23
兰州市	50.73	30	1	51.22	31	54.79	24	55.22	23	50.08	31
南宁市	50.25	31	1	49.79	32	52.93	30	50.00	33	50.69	27
福州市	50.12	32	-5	51.55	27	53.96	27	52.66	28	51.37	22
重庆市	49.17	33	2	47.93	35	51.04	33	47.83	35	49.40	33
西宁市	48.19	34	-1	49.08	33	50.15	34	49.29	34	45.21	35
郑州市	46.93	35	-1	48.68	34	48.39	35	50.54	32	50.26	30
平均值	54.75			55.84		57.87		57.75		54.56	

从整体上看，如表2中的平均值所示，从2012年到2016年，全国35个监测城市生活质量客观指数均值分别为54.56、57.75、57.87、55.84、54.75。从动态角度观察，虽然生活质量客观指数在2016年仍位于满意区间，但继2015年由升转降后，2016年继续回落。

横向比较而言，北京连续5年位列榜首。连续5年排名前10位的城市还有深圳市、南京市、广州市、上海市、西安市；连续5年排名后10位的城市有哈尔滨市、南宁市、西宁市、郑州、重庆市。5年来，贵阳市首次进入前10名；下降幅度最大的是长沙市，其于2015年首次进入前10名后，于2016年快速滑落至第19名。另外，2015年中国35个城市居民生活质量客观指数得分低于50的有郑州市、南宁市、西宁市和重庆市，但2016年南宁市的城市生活质量客观指数得分回升至50.25，最低的是郑州（46.93）。根据QLICC体系的答案赋值标准，生活质量客观指数得分低于临界点50意味着进入了不满意区间，即从客观指标的计算来看，重庆、西宁和郑州3个城市的生活质量是令人不满意的。图3为2012~2016年35个城市生活质量客观指数直方图。

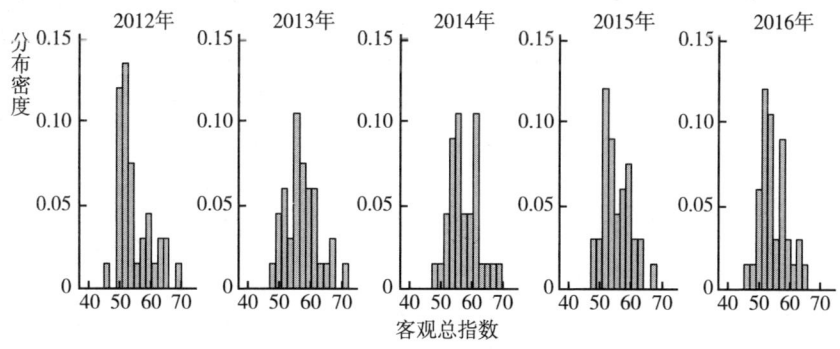

图3　2012~2016年35个城市生活质量客观指数直方图

分城市看，在35个城市中，生活质量客观指数连续3年呈现持续小幅下降的城市有北京市、南京市、广州市、上海市；此外，还有呼和浩特市、宁波市、长春市、厦门市、成都市、济南市、兰州市，占比近1/3，而贵阳市的生活质量客观指数得分连续5年呈现上升态势，从2012年的50.98增至2016年的57.20（见图4）。

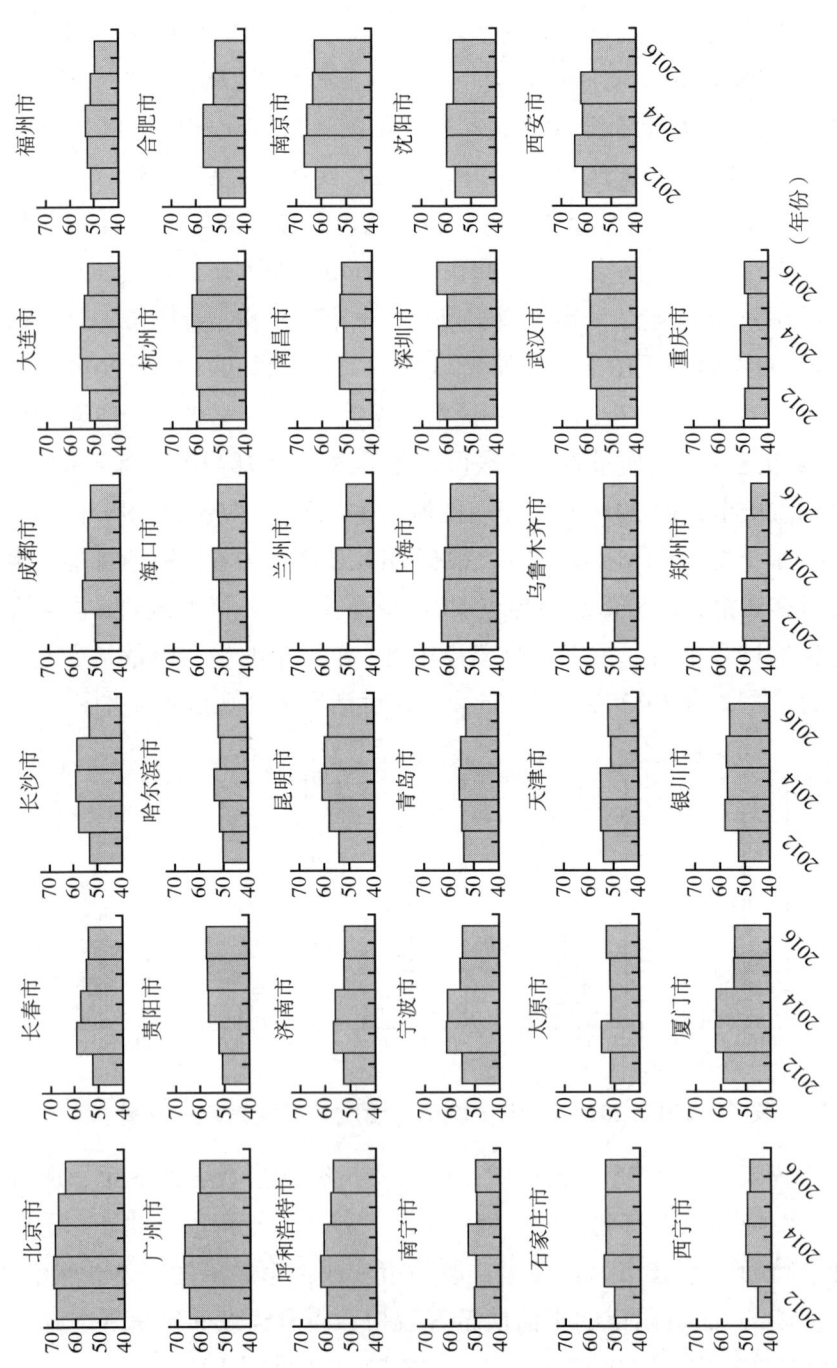

图 4　2012~2016 年 35 个城市生活质量客观指数

从统计分析的结果看，2012~2016年客观总指数得分最高的一直是北京市（得分分别为68.72、69.80、68.78、67.41、64.42），得分最低的依次分别是西宁市（45.21）、重庆市（47.83）、郑州市（48.39）、重庆市（47.93）、郑州市（46.93），各年份最高分和最低分两者相差依次分别为23.51、21.97、20.39、19.48和17.49，对应的标准差分别为5.32、5.22、4.68、4.55和4.22。可见，最高分和最低分都呈总体下降的态势，但分差却在逐渐减小。35个城市中大多数城市的客观指数虽在2013~2014年略有好转，但到2015~2016年又有所回落。

B.5
中国35个城市生活质量的细分指数

35个城市生活质量主观满意度指数和客观指数（社会经济数据指数）的得分高低及排序情况，均可以从各自的细分指数中得到解释。[①] 本部分将把描述城市生活质量指数的主观满意度指数和客观指数的各个细分指数进行对比分析。

一 生活水平指数

生活水平指数包括生活水平满意度指数和客观指数（社会经济数据指数）。前者根据电话调查并结合答案赋值得到，后者是通过对35个城市的社会经济指标计算得出的。

（一）生活水平满意度指数

根据QLICC体系，生活水平满意度指数是由收入现状满意度指数和收入预期满意度指数加权平均构成的。表1是2012~2016年35个城市生活水平满意度的调查结果。从表1可以看到，2016年35个城市生活水平满意度指数得分均超过了满意与不满意区间的临界点50，且有23个城市的得分超过60。2012~2016年，全国35个城市生活水

[①] 与前面几次调查一样，支撑35个城市生活质量总指数的细分指数包括生活水平指数、生活成本指数、人力资本指数、社会保障指数和生活感受指数。每个细分指数都包括主观满意度指数和客观指数（社会经济数据指数）。

平满意度指数加权平均值分别为 51.28、52.51、54.32、60.07、60.44，连续 5 年都在满意区间内，且满意度总体上呈上升趋势；上升速度分别为 2.4%、3.4%、10.6% 和 0.6%，呈现出先快后慢的变化趋势。

表 1　2012~2016 年中国 35 个城市生活水平满意度指数

城市	2016 年			2015 年		2014 年		2013 年		2012 年	
	得分	排序	上升位次	得分	排序	得分	排序	得分	排序	得分	排序
宁波市	62.06	1	0	63.16	1	54.58	12	54.62	6	52.77	8
北京市	61.99	2	10	60.43	12	58.68	1	52.19	22	50.37	23
南宁市	61.62	3	27	58.58	30	51.89	31	51.48	28	51.47	16
昆明市	61.55	4	-1	62.28	3	52.91	23	52.84	17	52.32	11
大连市	61.33	5	19	59.74	24	52.84	24	50.28	32	50.69	22
重庆市	61.26	6	21	59.00	27	56.63	2	52.11	24	52.64	9
海口市	61.21	7	-5	62.78	2	56.03	4	56.46	1	54.75	3
杭州市	61.11	8	-2	62.04	6	54.97	10	54.10	10	56.49	1
成都市	61.11	9	13	59.91	22	55.02	8	53.30	15	51.39	18
合肥市	60.88	10	-6	62.27	4	53.99	17	54.14	9	55.76	2
济南市	60.84	11	6	60.27	17	54.28	16	54.29	8	51.43	17
呼和浩特市	60.81	12	20	58.14	32	54.43	14	54.31	7	50.36	24
哈尔滨市	60.81	13	-5	61.31	8	52.27	27	49.86	33	48.89	30
西宁市	60.75	14	6	60.04	20	51.99	30	55.00	4	52.31	12
南京市	60.60	15	-4	60.65	11	52.69	26	52.34	19	49.23	29
广州市	60.59	16	-7	61.09	9	52.77	25	52.32	20	50.97	21
青岛市	60.50	17	-7	60.97	10	55.37	6	55.81	2	52.59	10
南昌市	60.49	18	3	60.00	21	53.48	21	52.18	23	48.27	32
太原市	60.31	19	6	59.25	25	51.84	32	50.42	30	48.27	33
天津市	60.26	20	14	57.89	34	54.98	9	52.24	21	51.27	19
郑州市	60.14	21	5	59.08	26	50.98	35	48.00	35	52.86	7
长沙市	60.10	22	-8	60.31	14	54.53	13	53.44	14	50.29	25
乌鲁木齐市	60.01	23	-8	60.29	15	54.90	11	54.10	11	50.99	20
深圳市	59.98	24	-11	60.41	13	53.49	20	51.65	26	52.08	14
福州市	59.94	25	-2	59.76	23	54.40	15	54.64	5	53.76	4
武汉市	59.75	26	-7	60.07	19	53.25	22	50.39	31	49.95	26
上海市	59.75	27	-9	60.16	18	56.60	3	52.59	18	51.65	15
石家庄市	59.63	28	3	58.46	31	51.69	33	51.79	25	53.38	6
长春市	59.38	29	-22	61.64	7	55.32	7	53.07	16	53.74	5
贵阳市	59.14	30	5	57.58	35	53.61	19	53.74	13	49.40	28

续表

城市	2016年			2015年		2014年		2013年		2012年	
	得分	排序	上升位次	得分	排序	得分	排序	得分	排序	得分	排序
沈阳市	58.85	31	-2	58.89	29	53.65	18	51.54	27	46.95	34
兰州市	58.74	32	1	58.04	33	51.42	34	49.72	34	46.88	35
银川市	58.22	33	-17	60.29	16	52.16	29	51.10	29	49.74	27
厦门市	57.66	34	-29	62.26	5	55.78	5	55.69	3	52.18	13
西安市	57.58	35	-7	58.94	28	52.26	28	53.88	12	48.79	31
平均值	60.44			60.07		54.32		52.51		51.28	

从生活水平满意度指数的直方图看，35个城市的得分整体升高并有所集中，分数分布最集中的区间从50~55逐渐转为55~65（见图1）。

从统计分析中也可以看出，35个城市的生活水平满意度指数差距不断缩小。2012年，生活水平满意度指数得分最高的是杭州市（56.49），得分最低的是兰州市（46.88），两者相差9.61，35个城市生活水平满意度指数得分的标准差为2.21；2013年，得分最高的是海口市（56.46），得分最低的是郑州市（48.00），两者相差8.46，35个城市得分的标准差为1.88；2014年，得分最高的是北京市（58.68），得分最低的是郑州市（50.98），两者相差7.70，35个城市得分的标准差为1.70；2015年，得分最高的是宁波市（63.16），得分最低的是贵阳市（57.58），两者相差5.58，35个城市得分的标准差为1.42；2016年，得分最高的是宁波市（62.06），得分最低的是西安市（57.58），两者相差4.48，35个城市得分的标准差为1.09。最高分和最低分的差距逐年缩小，从2012年的9.61减少至2016年的4.48，差值减少超过50%。标准差也不断缩小，由2012年的2.21下降至2016年的1.09，减少也超过50%。最高分与最低分相比，最低分的上升速度快于最高分的上升速度。

2016年生活水平满意度指数得分排前10位的城市分别是：宁波（1）、北京（2）、南宁（3）、昆明（4）、大连（5）、重庆（6）、海口

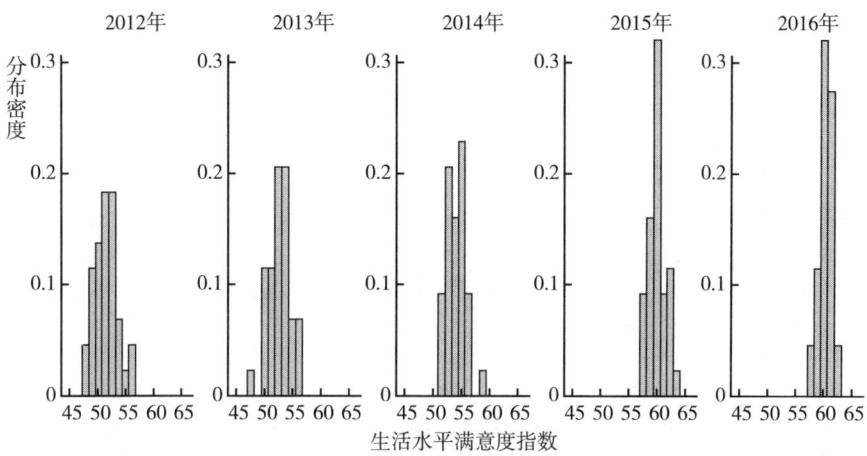

图 1　2012~2016 年 35 个城市生活水平满意度指数直方图

(7)、杭州(8)、成都(9)、合肥(10),其中有 5 个东部城市、1 个中部城市、4 个西部城市。排名后 10 位的城市分别是:武汉(26)、上海(27)、石家庄(28)、长春(29)、贵阳(30)、沈阳(31)、兰州(32)、银川(33)、厦门(34)、西安(35),其中有 4 个东部城市、2 个中部城市、4 个西部城市。海口、杭州连续 5 年均排名前 10 位,连续 5 年排名后 10 位的城市是兰州。从排名前 10 位和后 10 位的城市分布看,东部城市生活水平满意度指数整体上有与西部城市持平的趋势。

排名前 10 位的城市中,北京、南宁、大连、重庆、成都的排名与 2015 年相比有了较大幅度的上升,其中按上升位数排序依次是南宁(+27)、重庆(+21)、大连(+19)、成都(+13)、北京(+10)。排名后 10 位的城市中武汉、上海、长春、沈阳、银川、厦门、西安排名与 2015 年相比发生不同程度的下降,下降位数分别为武汉(-7)、上海(-9)、长春(-22)、沈阳(-2)、银川(-17)、厦门(-29)、西安(-7)。

分城市看,如图 2 所示,连续 4 年得分均上升的城市有北京、南宁、成都、呼和浩特、南昌、太原、天津和兰州 8 个城市。与 2015 年相比,尽管 2016 年的平均值略高于 2015 年的平均值 60.07,但只

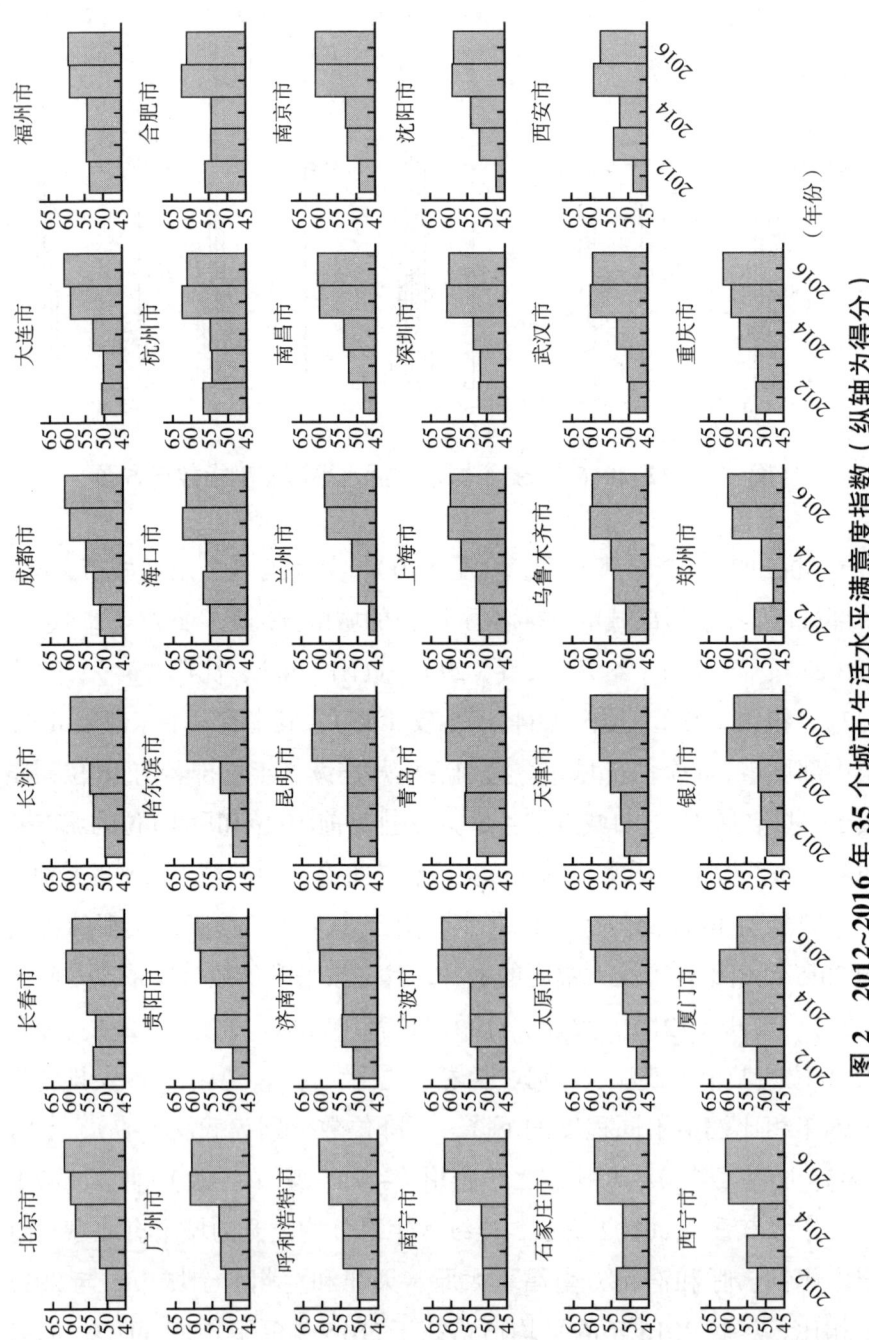

图 2 2012~2016 年 35 个城市生活水平满意度指数（纵轴为得分）

有16个城市的满意度高于2015年,其中,满意度提升幅度最大的是南宁市,生活水平满意度指数得分由58.58上升至61.62,位次由第30位升至第3位;19个城市的满意度低于2015年,降幅最大的是厦门市,生活水平满意度指数得分由62.26下降至57.66,位次由第5位落至第34位。

生活水平满意度指数由收入现状满意度指数和收入预期满意度指数加权平均获得。从收入现状满意度调查结果来看,如表2所示,2012~2016年,全国35个城市收入现状满意度指数加权平均值分别为51.52、52.54、52.92、59.65和60.66,连续5年都处在满意区间内,且满意度总体上呈上升趋势;增长幅度分别为1.98%、0.72%、12.72%和1.69%,增长速度波动性较大。

表2 2012~2016年中国35个城市收入现状满意度指数

城市	2016年			2015年		2014年		2013年		2012年	
	得分	排序	上升位次	得分	排序	得分	排序	得分	排序	得分	排序
济南市	63.01	1	10	60.72	11	52.52	19	54.15	11	52.11	14
昆明市	62.41	2	6	61.05	8	52.05	22	53.17	16	51.76	16
广州市	62.19	3	9	60.65	12	51.20	25	52.94	17	50.57	21
北京市	62.11	4	12	59.80	16	56.56	2	51.65	24	50.10	22
重庆市	62.00	5	23	58.57	28	55.58	5	51.38	25	53.45	7
宁波市	61.91	6	−4	63.28	2	54.58	10	55.21	6	53.65	6
海口市	61.73	7	−4	62.86	3	56.83	1	56.87	1	57.50	2
南宁市	61.49	8	21	58.45	29	50.05	31	51.20	27	50.00	23
成都市	61.43	9	17	58.99	26	53.39	14	53.82	12	50.88	19
大连市	61.31	10	8	59.68	18	51.86	23	50.46	30	49.69	24
西宁市	61.29	11	2	60.57	13	52.72	18	54.44	8	52.78	13
青岛市	61.28	12	−2	60.77	10	54.85	8	56.58	2	53.18	10
郑州市	61.18	13	10	59.08	23	49.44	33	48.42	34	53.10	12
合肥市	61.14	14	−10	62.09	4	54.15	11	54.42	9	55.04	3
杭州市	61.04	15	−14	63.38	1	55.67	4	56.25	5	58.25	1
长春市	60.86	16	−9	61.49	7	54.12	12	54.52	7	54.01	5
长沙市	60.74	17	5	59.37	22	52.83	17	52.62	18	48.10	30

续表

城市	2016年			2015年		2014年		2013年		2012年	
	得分	排序	上升位次	得分	排序	得分	排序	得分	排序	得分	排序
呼和浩特市	60.53	18	15	56.89	33	53.13	15	53.80	13	48.21	29
兰州市	60.46	19	16	56.12	35	49.03	35	48.87	33	44.60	35
石家庄市	60.42	20	12	57.22	32	49.95	32	51.85	22	53.43	8
南昌市	60.33	21	-4	59.68	17	51.49	24	51.18	28	48.58	26
哈尔滨市	60.17	22	-17	62.09	5	50.52	30	49.33	32	47.78	33
乌鲁木齐市	60.08	23	1	59.08	24	55.92	3	54.38	10	53.29	9
福州市	60.04	24	3	58.90	27	53.00	16	56.39	4	54.19	4
银川市	59.94	25	-19	61.65	6	49.28	34	51.37	26	53.13	11
上海市	59.94	26	-6	59.54	20	55.33	6	52.60	19	51.43	17
贵阳市	59.70	27	7	56.33	34	51.17	26	51.98	21	47.86	32
武汉市	59.62	28	-13	59.80	15	52.17	21	50.39	31	49.68	25
天津市	59.39	29	2	57.34	31	54.67	9	52.15	20	50.79	20
深圳市	59.06	30	-9	59.37	21	50.98	27	51.12	29	51.39	18
太原市	58.76	31	-12	59.55	19	50.78	28	48.32	35	48.51	27
南京市	58.54	32	-7	59.01	25	52.46	20	53.42	14	48.08	31
沈阳市	57.90	33	-3	58.12	30	53.40	13	51.75	23	46.57	34
西安市	57.83	34	-20	60.07	14	50.73	29	53.25	15	48.30	28
厦门市	56.81	35	-26	60.83	9	54.92	7	56.39	3	52.03	15
平均值	60.66			59.65		52.92		52.54		51.52	

从2012~2016年35个城市的收入现状满意度指数得分的分布看，如图3所示，满意度的最低分和最高分均有较大幅度提升，最低分的分布区间由2012年的40~45逐年上升到45~50、50~55、55~60的区间，最高分的分布区间也由55~60上升至60~65，最低分和最高分的区间差距也由2012年约20分的跨度缩小至2016年的10分以内。具体来说，2012年，城市收入现状满意度指数得分最高的城市是杭州（58.25），得分最低的城市是兰州（44.60），两者相差13.65，35个城市收入现状满意度指数得分的标准差为2.90；2013年，城市收入现状满意度指数得分最高的城市是海口（56.87），得分最低的城市是太原（48.32），两者相差8.55，35个城市得分的

标准差为2.26；2014年，城市收入现状满意度指数得分最高的城市是海口（56.83），得分最低的城市是兰州（49.03），两者相差7.80，35个城市得分的标准差为2.12；2015年，城市收入现状满意度指数得分最高的城市是杭州（63.38），得分最低的城市是兰州（56.12），两者相差7.26,35个城市得分的标准差为1.78；2016年，城市收入现状满意度指数得分最高的城市是济南（63.01），得分最低的城市是厦门（56.81），两者相差6.20,35个城市得分的标准差为1.36。

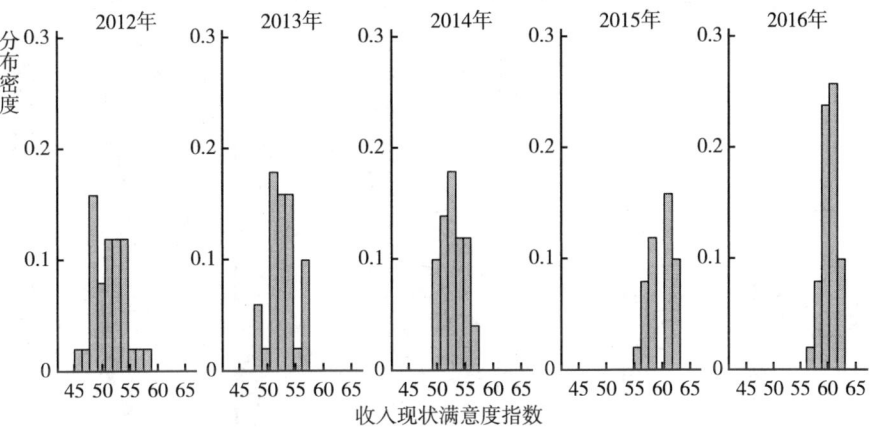

图3 2012~2016年35个城市收入现状满意度指数直方图

分城市看，如图4所示，得分连续4年均处于上升状态的城市有北京、长沙、成都、大连、兰州、南昌、上海、天津、乌鲁木齐，占全部调查城市的26%。收入现状满意指数波动上升的有福州、广州、贵阳、呼和浩特、济南、昆明、南宁、青岛、石家庄、西宁、郑州、重庆。2016年与2015年相比略有下降的有长春、哈尔滨、海口、杭州、合肥、南京、宁波、深圳、沈阳、太原、武汉、西安、厦门、银川。

2016年城市收入现状满意指数排名前10位的城市分别为济南

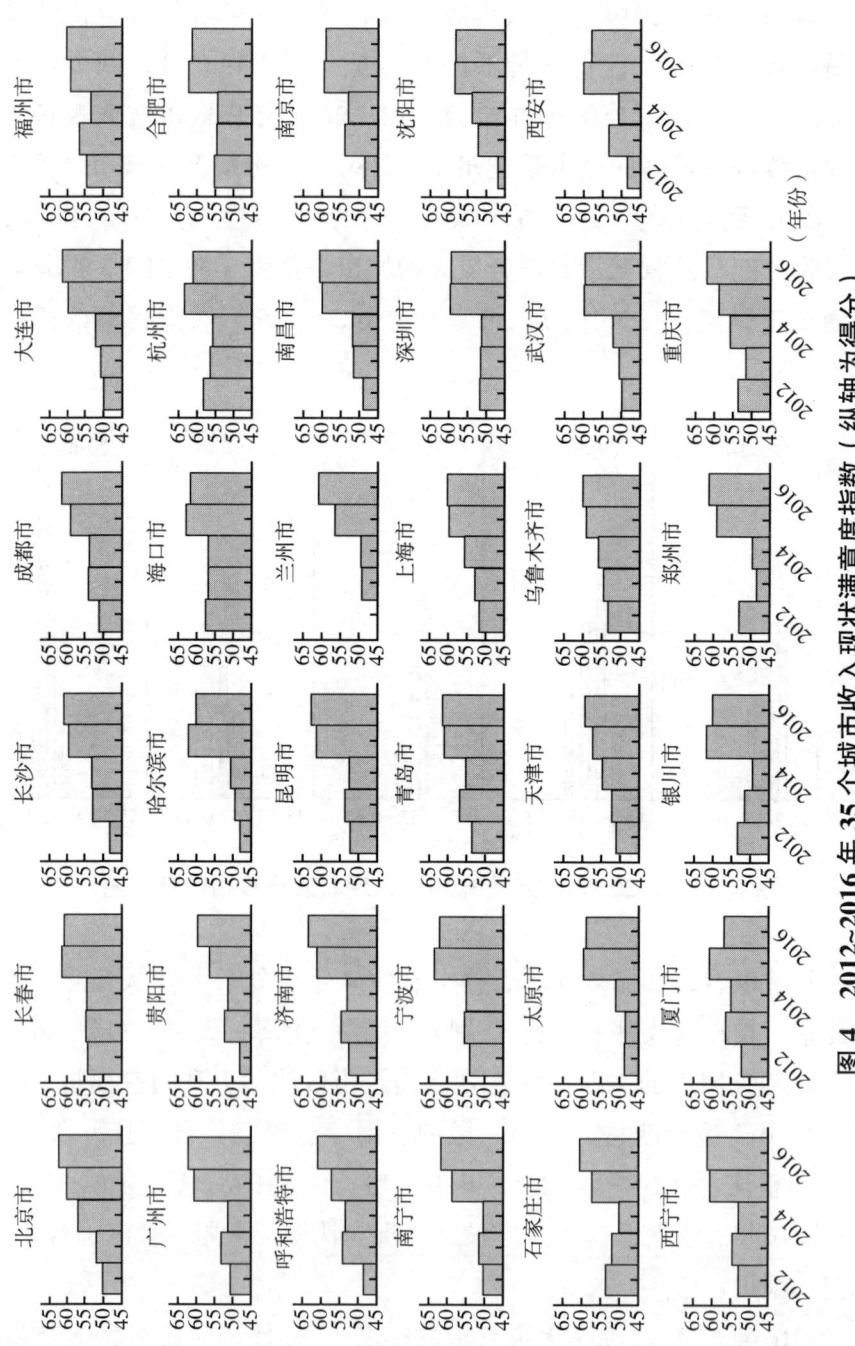

图 4 2012~2016 年 35 个城市收入现状满意度指数（纵轴为得分）

(1)、昆明(2)、广州(3)、北京(4)、重庆(5)、宁波(6)、海口(7)、南宁(8)、成都(9)和大连(10),排名后10位的城市分别为上海(26)、贵阳(27)、武汉(28)、天津(29)、深圳(30)、太原(31)、南京(32)、沈阳(33)、西安(34)、厦门(35)。与2015年相比,排名前10位的城市位次上升幅度较大的依次是重庆(+23)、南宁(+21)、成都(+17)、北京(+12)、济南(+10)、广州(+9)、大连(+8)和昆明(+6),排名下降的是宁波(-4)和海口(-4);与2015年相比,排名后10位的城市位次有所上升的是贵阳(+7)和天津(+2),位次下降的有厦门(-26)、西安(-20)、武汉(-13)、太原(-12)、深圳(-9)、南京(-7)、上海(-6)和沈阳(-3)。排名前10位的城市中变化最大的是重庆,排名后10位的城市中变化最大的是厦门。按地区分布看,排名前10位的城市中有6个东部城市、4个西部城市;排名后10位的城市中有6个东部城市、2个中部城市、2个西部城市。

从收入预期满意度调查结果来看,如表3所示,2012~2016年,全国35个城市收入预期满意度指数加权平均值分别为51.36、52.48、55.50、60.50、60.23,增长率分别为2.18%、5.75%、9.01%、-0.45%,可见,2012~2016年全国35个城市收入预期满意度指数在2015年之前是不断加速上升的,而在2016年出现了下降。

表3 2012~2016年中国35个城市收入预期满意度指数

城市	2016年			2015年		2014年		2013年		2012年	
	得分	排序	上升位次	得分	排序	得分	排序	得分	排序	得分	排序
南京市	62.66	1	5	62.28	6	52.91	32	51.26	29	50.38	26
宁波市	62.22	2	1	63.03	3	54.58	18	54.03	10	51.89	16
北京市	61.88	3	10	61.05	13	60.79	1	52.74	17	50.63	25
太原市	61.86	4	26	58.95	30	52.90	33	52.51	19	48.02	32

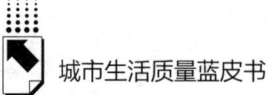

续表

城市	2016年			2015年		2014年		2013年		2012年	
	得分	排序	上升位次	得分	排序	得分	排序	得分	排序	得分	排序
南宁市	61.76	5	28	58.70	33	53.72	30	51.76	24	52.93	6
哈尔滨市	61.45	6	12	60.53	18	54.03	22	50.39	32	50.00	28
大连市	61.35	7	16	59.80	23	53.81	26	50.09	34	51.69	21
杭州市	61.18	8	8	60.69	16	54.27	21	51.94	23	54.72	2
天津市	61.14	9	25	58.45	34	55.29	15	52.34	21	51.75	20
呼和浩特市	61.10	10	18	59.40	28	55.73	13	54.82	6	52.50	10
深圳市	60.90	11	−1	61.46	10	55.99	10	52.18	22	52.78	8
成都市	60.79	12	2	60.84	14	56.65	4	52.78	16	51.90	15
海口市	60.69	13	−9	62.70	4	55.22	16	56.04	1	52.00	14
昆明市	60.68	14	−12	63.52	2	53.77	29	52.50	20	52.88	7
南昌市	60.66	15	5	60.31	20	55.46	14	53.18	13	47.97	33
合肥市	60.63	16	−11	62.45	5	53.83	25	53.85	11	56.47	1
重庆市	60.52	17	10	59.43	27	57.67	3	52.84	15	51.82	19
西宁市	60.22	18	8	59.51	26	51.27	35	55.56	2	51.85	18
乌鲁木齐市	59.95	19	−10	61.51	9	53.87	24	53.81	12	48.68	31
武汉市	59.89	20	−1	60.34	19	54.33	20	50.39	33	50.21	27
福州市	59.85	21	−4	60.61	17	55.80	12	52.90	14	53.32	5
沈阳市	59.80	22	3	59.67	25	53.90	23	51.33	28	47.34	34
青岛市	59.71	23	−11	61.17	12	55.89	11	55.04	4	52.00	13
上海市	59.56	24	−9	60.79	15	57.87	2	52.57	18	51.88	17
长沙市	59.46	25	−14	61.25	11	56.23	7	54.26	9	52.49	11
郑州市	59.11	26	3	59.08	29	52.51	34	47.58	35	52.62	9
广州市	58.99	27	−19	61.53	8	54.34	19	51.71	26	51.38	22
石家庄市	58.83	28	−4	59.70	24	53.43	31	51.74	25	53.33	4
济南市	58.68	29	−7	59.82	22	56.04	9	54.43	8	50.75	24
贵阳市	58.58	30	2	58.83	32	56.05	8	55.51	3	50.95	23
厦门市	58.51	31	−30	63.69	1	56.63	5	55.00	5	52.33	12
长春市	57.89	32	−25	61.80	7	56.52	6	51.62	27	53.48	3
西安市	57.33	33	2	57.81	35	53.79	28	54.50	7	49.27	29
兰州市	57.02	34	−13	59.97	21	53.80	27	50.56	31	49.15	30
银川市	56.49	35	−4	58.93	31	55.05	17	50.82	30	46.35	35
平均值	60.23			60.50		55.50		52.48		51.36	

从35个城市收入预期满意度指数的分布看，2012年，收入预期满意度指数得分最高的城市是合肥（56.47），最低的城市是银川（46.35）；2013年，收入预期满意度指数得分最高的城市是海口（56.04），最低的城市是郑州（47.58）；2014年，收入预期满意度指数得分最高的城市是北京（60.79），最低的城市是西宁（51.27）；2015年，收入预期满意度指数得分最高的城市是厦门（63.69），最低的城市是西安（57.81）；2016年，收入预期满意度指数得分最高的城市是南京（62.66），最低的城市是银川（56.49）。2012~2016年，35个城市收入预期满意度指数最高分和最低分的差距依次为10.12、8.46、9.52、5.88、6.17，标准差为2.04、1.80、1.74、1.43和1.45。可见，城市间收入预期满意度的差距总体呈缩小趋势。

如图5所示，2012~2016年，35个城市收入预期满意度指数最低分的分布区间由45~50提高到55~60，最高分的分布区间由55~60提高到60~65。

2016年收入预期满意度指数排名前10位的城市分别是南京（1）、宁波（2）、北京（3）、太原（4）、南宁（5）、哈尔滨（6）、

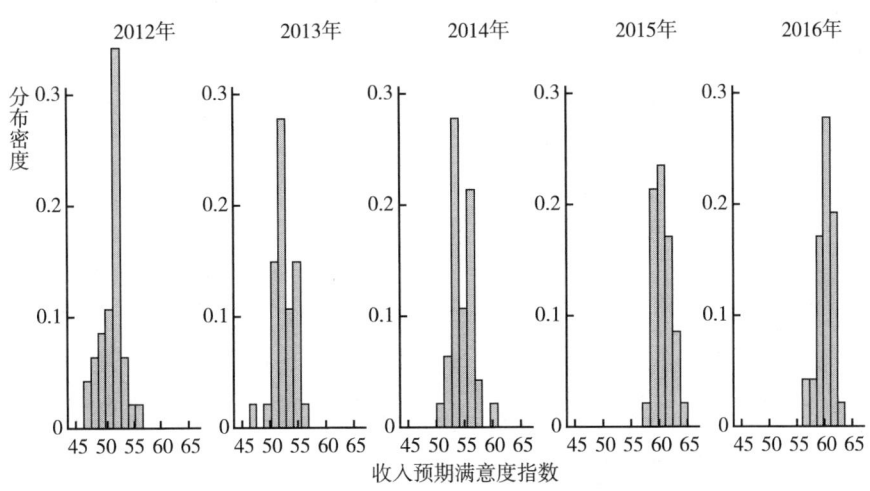

图5 2012~2016年35个城市收入预期满意度指数直方图

大连（7）、杭州（8）、天津（9）和呼和浩特（10），排名后10位的城市分别是郑州（26）、广州（27）、石家庄（28）、济南（29）、贵阳（30）、厦门（31）、长春（32）、西安（33）、兰州（34）、银川（35）。与2015年相比，排名前10位的城市排名均有不同程度的提升，其中，南京（+5）、宁波（+1）、北京（+10）、太原（+26）、南宁（+28）、哈尔滨（+12）、大连（+16）、杭州（+8）、天津（+25）和呼和浩特（+18）；排名后10位城市的位次变化情况分别为郑州（+3）、广州（-19）、石家庄（-4）、济南（-7）、贵阳（+2）、厦门（-30）、长春（-25）、西安（+2）、兰州（-13）、银川（-4）。从地区分布看，排名前10位的城市中有6个东部城市、2个中部城市、2个西部城市；排名后10位的城市中有4个东部城市、2个中部城市、4个西部城市。

2012~2016年35个城市的收入预期满意度指数得分整体呈现上升态势。分城市看，如图6所示，连续4年均保持上升的城市有北京、哈尔滨、呼和浩特、南昌、南京、沈阳、太原、天津和重庆，占所调查城市的26%；收入预期波动性上升的城市有大连、杭州、南宁、西宁和郑州，占所调查城市的14%；大多数城市的收入预期满意度在2016年略有下降，其中包括长春、长沙、成都、福州、广州、贵阳、海口、合肥、济南、昆明、兰州、宁波、青岛、上海、深圳、石家庄、乌鲁木齐、武汉、西安、厦门和银川，占被调查城市的60%。

（二）生活水平客观指数

根据QLICC体系，生活水平客观指数就是通过计算35个城市的收入水平、生活改善指数两个一级指标所属的消费率、人均财富、人均可支配收入以及人均消费增长、人均财富增长、人均可支配收入增长6个二级指标得出的。

35个城市生活水平客观指数的计算结果如表4所示，2012~2016

中国35个城市生活质量的细分指数

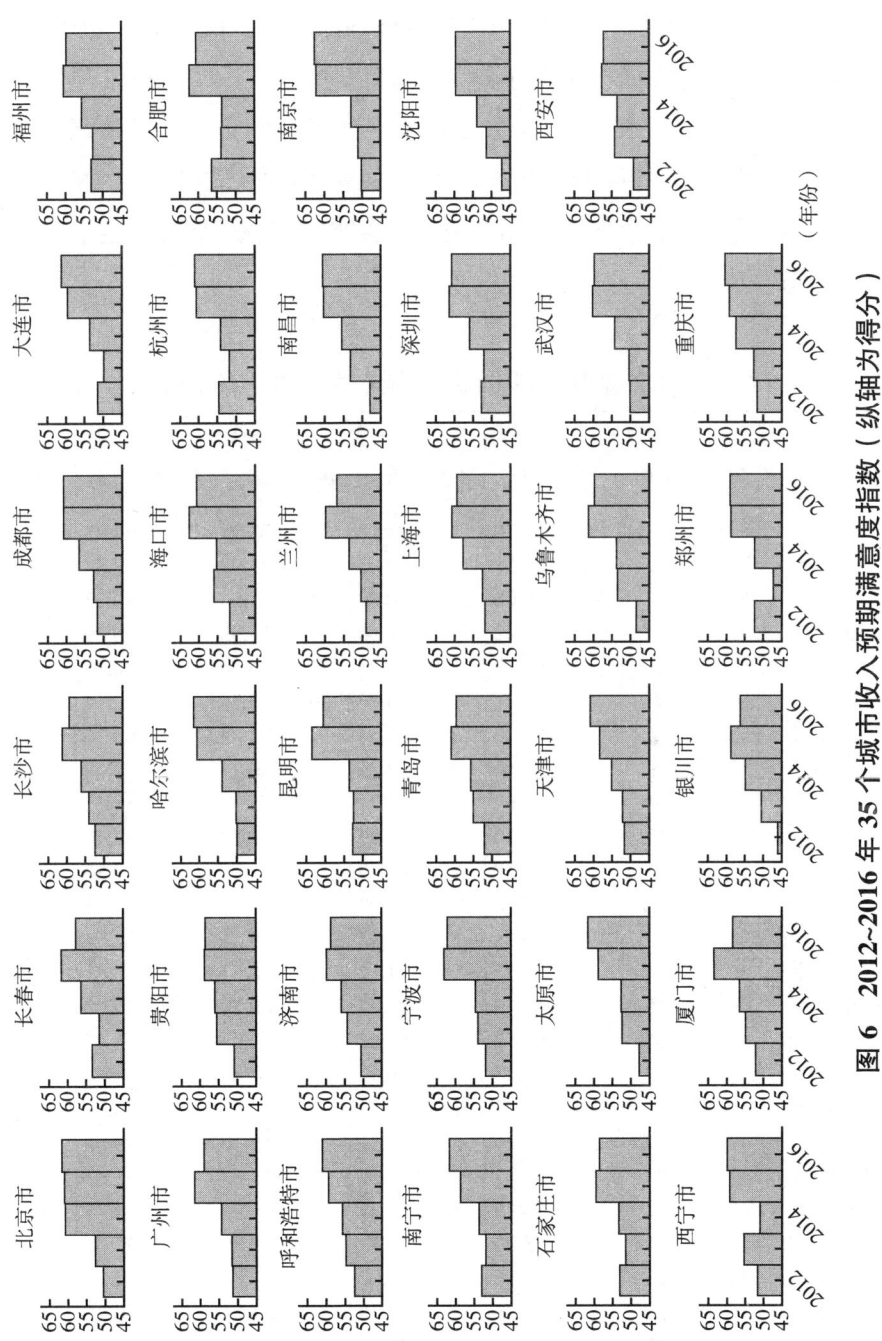

图6 2012~2016年35个城市收入预期满意度指数（纵轴为得分）

年加权平均值分别为 56.28、63.39、68.06、59.83 和 50.07。2014 年生活水平客观指数加权平均值达到最高值后趋于下降，2016 年达到 2012 年来的最低值 50.07，这主要是由于该指标的大小与经济增长情况有密切的联系，伴随着经济发展进入中高速阶段，2016 年的指数加权平均值勉强高于荣枯线。图 7 为 2012~2016 年 35 个城市生活水平客观指数直方图。

表 4 2012~2016 年中国 35 个城市生活水平客观指数

城市	2016 年			2015 年		2014 年		2013 年		2012 年	
	得分	排序	上升位次	得分	排序	得分	排序	得分	排序	得分	排序
深圳市	80.00	1	13	59.30	14	75.18	8	78.91	3	64.78	7
上海市	70.73	2	0	79.02	2	79.45	2	73.93	6	77.84	2
北京市	61.55	3	-2	80.00	1	80.00	1	77.84	5	80.03	1
杭州市	60.55	4	-1	76.42	3	72.60	10	73.83	7	76.79	3
南京市	59.44	5	0	69.77	5	77.90	4	80.00	1	66.33	6
广州市	56.76	6	4	60.71	10	75.76	6	70.24	11	72.14	4
宁波市	53.77	7	1	62.08	8	75.54	7	72.47	8	68.70	5
天津市	52.58	8	15	55.56	23	68.39	14	60.42	23	57.02	13
成都市	52.22	9	-3	62.62	6	71.21	13	72.13	10	58.80	11
厦门市	52.12	10	2	60.56	12	79.43	3	79.22	2	52.40	23
贵阳市	51.37	11	0	60.58	11	62.79	26	49.09	32	47.86	27
济南市	51.14	12	13	55.16	25	71.92	11	72.27	9	57.43	12
乌鲁木齐市	50.72	13	2	59.11	15	63.78	24	58.61	26	47.54	28
武汉市	49.53	14	-1	59.72	13	71.82	12	60.51	22	50.81	25
南昌市	49.07	15	1	58.46	16	52.77	34	60.59	21	46.60	31
哈尔滨市	48.15	16	15	50.58	31	63.60	25	49.04	33	55.47	18
沈阳市	47.68	17	13	52.73	30	66.32	17	57.82	27	48.84	26
长春市	47.64	18	0	57.86	18	66.77	16	63.27	16	53.67	20
海口市	47.41	19	5	55.30	24	64.21	23	69.40	12	59.80	10
呼和浩特市	47.27	20	9	52.83	29	65.87	18	68.67	13	55.87	16
青岛市	47.21	21	-12	61.36	9	65.47	19	56.06	28	64.76	8
石家庄市	46.97	22	4	53.79	26	60.53	27	58.80	25	53.09	21
合肥市	46.72	23	-1	55.80	22	74.09	9	67.04	14	55.75	17
福州市	46.20	24	-7	57.98	17	67.16	15	61.51	17	60.75	9
重庆市	45.96	25	9	44.60	34	58.86	30	40.00	35	53.90	19

续表

城市	2016年			2015年		2014年		2013年		2012年	
	得分	排序	上升位次	得分	排序	得分	排序	得分	排序	得分	排序
郑州市	45.14	26	-5	56.44	21	57.00	32	61.40	18	56.11	14
长沙市	44.69	27	-23	70.09	4	76.15	5	60.91	20	50.97	24
兰州市	43.67	28	4	50.15	32	64.84	21	65.59	15	46.30	32
银川市	43.62	29	-10	57.45	19	54.12	33	60.00	24	45.55	33
昆明市	43.45	30	-2	53.32	28	57.07	31	55.27	29	40.76	34
大连市	42.95	31	-11	57.17	20	64.56	22	61.23	19	47.14	29
西安市	42.78	32	-25	62.55	7	64.90	20	78.59	4	56.07	15
西宁市	41.95	33	-6	53.61	27	59.10	28	54.92	30	40.00	35
南宁市	41.55	34	-1	45.35	33	59.04	29	41.04	34	52.98	22
太原市	40.00	35	0	40.00	35	40.00	35	52.32	31	46.87	30
平均值		50.07			59.83		68.06		63.39		56.28

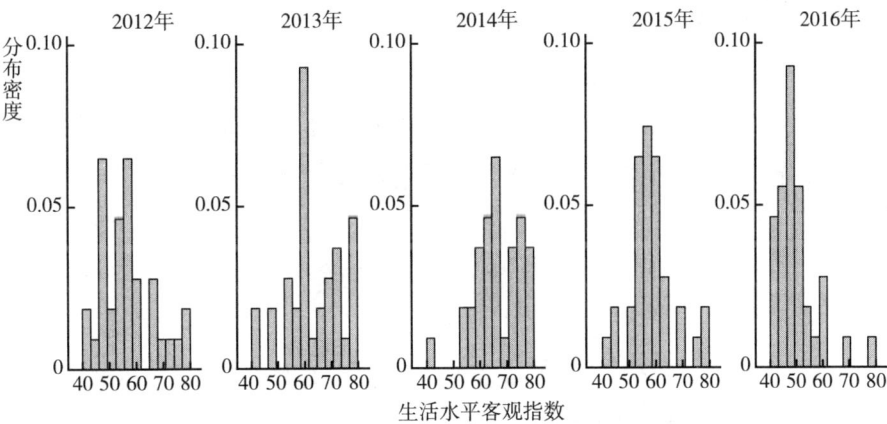

图7 2012~2016年35个城市生活水平客观指数直方图

2016年城市生活水平客观指数排名前10位的城市有深圳（1）、上海（2）、北京（3）、杭州（4）、南京（5）、广州（6）、宁波（7）、天津（8）、成都（9）和厦门（10），排名后10位的城市为郑州（26）、长沙（27）、兰州（28）、银川（29）、昆明（30）、大连（31）、西安（32）、西宁（33）、南宁（34）、太原（35）。35个城市中，2016年只有13个城市的得分超过50，而2015年为32个城市。2012年以

来、北京、上海、杭州、南京、宁波5个城市已经连续5年排在前10位城市的行列中；太原、昆明、西宁已经连续5年排在后10位城市的行列中。2016年排名前10位的城市中，位次上升幅度较大的城市是天津（+15）、深圳（+13）。排名后10位的城市中，位次下降幅度较大的城市是西安（-25）、长沙（-23）、大连（-11）、银川（-10）。从地区来看，城市生活水平客观指数排名前10位的城市中，有9个东部城市、1个西部城市；排名后10位的城市中，有1个东部城市、3个中部城市、6个西部城市。过去几年，在生活水平客观指数排名方面，北京一直位列榜首，2016年深圳取代北京位居第一，得分由2015年的59.30上升至80.00，而第35位太原市分值仅为40。由此看出，生活水平客观指数存在显著的地区差异。从描述客观生活水平的6个二级指标看，与2014年相比，2015年人均消费增长、人均财富增长下降显著，是导致生活水平客观指数下降的直接原因。

分城市看，从2015年开始，除深圳外的其他34个城市生活水平客观指数均呈现总体下降趋势，且下降幅度较大（见图8）。

二 生活成本指数

生活成本指数包括主观满意度指数和客观指数（社会经济数据指数），主观满意度指数是根据电话调查并结合答案赋值得到的，客观指数是通过社会经济指标计算出来的。

（一）生活成本满意度指数

生活成本满意度指数以及排序情况如表5所示。2016年，全国35个城市生活成本满意度指数加权平均值为39.74，没有一个城市的得分超过50，说明所有城市的居民对生活成本均不满意。尽管生活成本满意度指数处于不满意区间，但从动态变化看，2012~2016

中国 35 个城市生活质量的细分指数

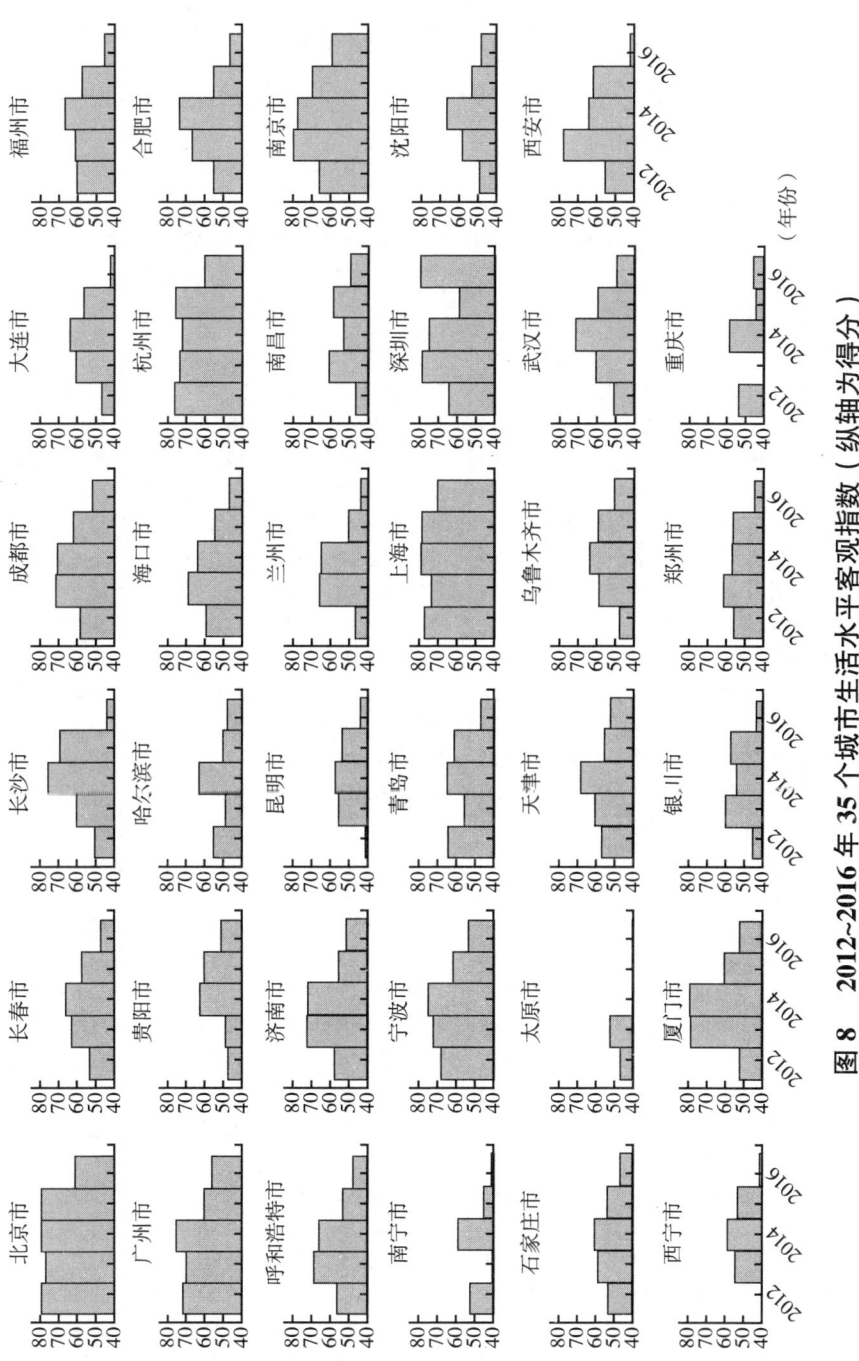

图 8 2012~2016 年 35 个城市生活水平客观指数（纵轴为得分）

年，35 个城市生活成本满意度指数加权平均值分别为 28.91、31.22、31.81、38.94 和 39.74，连续 5 年上升，表明人们对城市生活成本不满意的程度在不断降低。

表 5 2012~2016 年中国 35 个城市生活成本满意度指数

城市	2016 年			2015 年		2014 年		2013 年		2012 年	
	得分	排序	上升位次	得分	排序	得分	排序	得分	排序	得分	排序
银川市	45.30	1	28	36.56	29	30.29	28	27.47	31	27.60	22
济南市	43.45	2	8	41.33	10	35.72	2	36.16	3	35.39	2
呼和浩特	43.40	3	27	36.15	30	30.99	23	30.85	20	26.43	28
南昌市	41.97	4	11	39.68	15	33.87	7	33.18	12	28.66	14
昆明市	41.93	5	−1	42.97	4	31.82	16	30.00	22	28.04	18
宁波市	41.83	6	3	41.49	9	32.21	13	29.03	25	26.62	27
石家庄市	41.63	7	5	40.26	12	34.92	4	39.13	1	34.27	4
哈尔滨市	41.26	8	−1	42.21	7	32.33	11	32.06	17	28.38	17
成都市	41.26	9	13	37.93	22	32.12	14	32.41	15	30.92	12
海口市	41.23	10	−4	42.28	6	28.25	35	33.96	8	26.00	29
贵阳市	41.17	11	20	35.71	31	30.19	29	29.38	23	25.71	30
南宁市	41.15	12	1	40.15	13	31.72	18	33.45	10	27.16	24
合肥市	40.90	13	−11	43.82	2	35.02	3	34.40	6	35.43	1
大连市	40.84	14	0	40.06	14	29.70	30	27.04	32	25.15	33
重庆市	40.66	15	4	38.76	19	32.27	12	32.94	14	30.98	10
西安市	40.48	16	4	38.19	20	32.98	9	33.03	13	31.92	6
杭州市	40.41	17	−9	42.19	8	31.58	20	29.10	24	28.42	16
乌鲁木齐	40.05	18	7	37.10	25	29.23	31	28.53	28	24.67	34
长沙市	39.90	19	−2	38.93	17	30.49	26	31.08	19	27.63	21
沈阳市	39.89	20	−9	40.45	11	37.48	1	36.31	2	31.73	7
福州市	39.78	21	−3	38.87	18	31.70	19	33.65	9	31.21	9
太原市	39.69	22	12	35.32	34	33.04	8	34.22	7	30.94	11
郑州市	39.41	23	−7	39.66	16	31.75	17	35.03	5	31.67	8
武汉市	39.22	24	−1	37.81	23	32.44	10	31.96	18	30.57	13
青岛市	39.13	25	2	36.80	27	30.75	24	28.78	27	27.12	25
广州市	38.98	26	6	35.58	32	30.39	27	28.46	29	27.79	20
南京市	38.80	27	−22	42.50	5	31.55	21	30.10	21	27.95	19
西宁市	38.44	28	5	35.48	33	30.62	25	28.89	26	27.31	23
上海市	37.81	29	−8	37.96	21	28.58	32	25.59	35	25.45	31
厦门市	37.70	30	−27	43.34	3	31.25	22	32.36	16	28.49	15

续表

城市	2016年			2015年		2014年		2013年		2012年	
	得分	排序	上升位次	得分	排序	得分	排序	得分	排序	得分	排序
深圳市	37.58	31	−5	37.03	26	28.42	34	26.56	33	25.30	32
天津市	37.28	32	−8	37.77	24	34.82	6	33.32	11	32.62	5
长春市	37.24	33	−32	43.86	1	34.89	5	36.02	4	34.36	3
兰州市	35.97	34	−6	36.79	28	31.84	15	27.82	30	26.70	26
北京市	35.50	35	0	33.76	35	28.53	33	26.13	34	23.06	35
平均值	39.74			38.94		31.81		31.22		28.91	

分城市看，2012年，35个城市中，生活成本满意度指数得分最高的是合肥（35.42），得分最低的是北京（23.06），两者相差12.36；2013年，得分最高的是石家庄（39.13），得分最低的是上海（25.59），两者相差13.54；2014年，得分最高的是沈阳（37.48），得分最低的是海口（28.25），两者相差9.23；2015年，得分最高的是长春（43.86），得分最低的是北京（33.76），两者相差10.10；2016年，得分最高的是银川（45.30），得分最低的是北京（35.50），两者相差9.80。可见，2012-2016年35个城市生活成本满意度指数的分布区间不断增高且有集中趋势。如图9所示，生活成本满意度指数的最低分分布区间由20~30提高到30~40，最高分分布区间也由30~40上升至40~50。2012-2016年，35个城市间生活成本满意度指数得分标准差分别为3.14、13.54、9.23、10.1和9.8。

2016年城市生活成本满意度指数排名前10位的城市为银川（1）、济南（2）、呼和浩特（3）、南昌（4）、昆明（5）、宁波（6）、石家庄（7）、哈尔滨（8）、成都（9）、海口（10），排名后10位的城市为广州（26）、南京（27）、西宁（28）、上海（29）、厦门（30）、深圳（31）、天津（32）、长春（33）、兰州（34）、北京（35）。排名前10位的城市中排名上升幅度最大的是银川（+28），此后依次是呼和浩特（+27）、成都（+13）、南昌（+11）、济南（+8）、石家

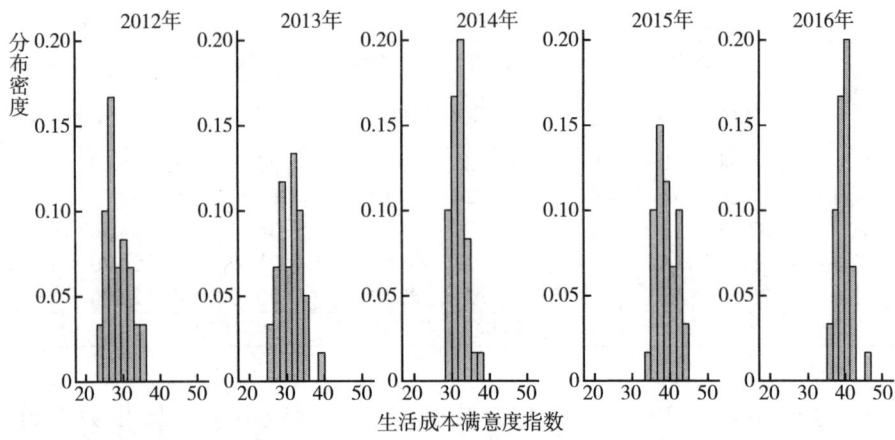

图9 2012~2016年35个城市生活成本满意度指数直方图

庄（+5）和宁波（+3）；排名后10位的城市中排名下降幅度最大的是长春（-32），其次是厦门（-27）和南京（-22）。也就是说，2016年银川和呼和浩特的生活成本满意度排名由2015年的第29位和第30位分别上升至2016年的第1位和第3位；而长春和厦门则分别由2015年的第1位和第3位下降至第33位和第30位。北京的排名没有变化，对生活成本最不满意的就是北京市居民。北京已经连续5年排在后3位，深圳连续5年排在后10位，广州连续4年排在后10位，上海也总体处于第20位以后。由此说明，一线城市居民总体对生活成本不满意程度最高。济南连续5年排名前10位，其居民对生活成本的不满意程度较低且稳定。

从整体上看，2012~2016年35个城市的生活成本满意度指数是不断上升的，表明满意度是不断提高的。连续上升的城市为北京、大连、广州、贵阳、呼和浩特、南昌、宁波、青岛、深圳、乌鲁木齐、武汉、西安、西宁，波动上升的城市是长沙、成都、福州、济南、南宁、石家庄、太原、重庆和银川，2016年略有下降的是长春、哈尔滨、海口、杭州、合肥、昆明、兰州、南京、上海、沈阳、天津、厦门和郑州。

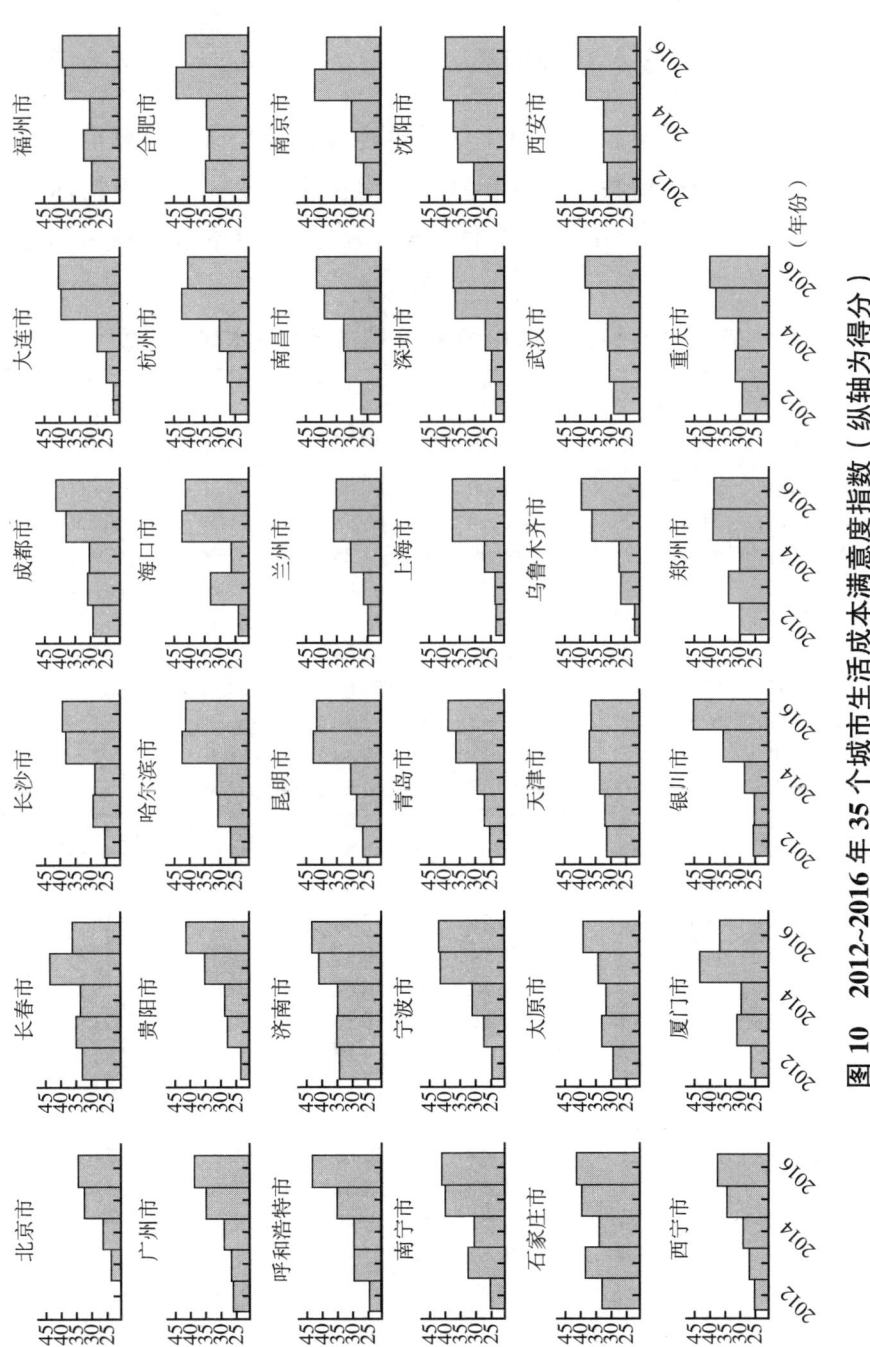

图10 2012~2016年35个城市生活成本满意度指数（纵轴为得分）

（二）生活成本客观指数

根据QLICC体系，城市生活成本客观指数是通过计算每个城市的房屋销售价格指数、通货膨胀率、房价收入比3个二级指标得出的。2016年35个城市生活成本客观指数及其排序情况如表6所示。

表6　2012~2016年中国35个城市生活成本客观指数

城市	2016年			2015年		2014年		2013年		2012年	
	得分	排序	上升位次	得分	排序	得分	排序	得分	排序	得分	排序
昆明市	80.00	1	0	80.00	1	80.00	1	80.00	1	74.00	2
长沙市	71.45	2	0	72.10	2	68.58	3	71.79	3	69.57	3
呼和浩特市	70.39	3	1	69.49	4	72.25	2	77.96	2	79.97	1
西安市	66.37	4	−1	71.13	3	63.89	4	65.27	6	61.38	9
银川市	65.40	5	0	61.74	5	60.96	7	65.18	7	59.38	14
西宁市	65.19	6	2	60.30	8	61.08	6	66.05	5	60.51	10
南昌市	63.26	7	0	61.35	7	59.61	8	64.81	8	63.36	5
石家庄市	62.99	8	−2	61.45	6	62.30	5	66.75	4	64.74	4
青岛市	62.54	9	0	60.11	9	58.38	11	63.40	10	62.34	8
沈阳市	62.07	10	1	59.19	11	56.66	15	62.89	12	60.11	11
重庆市	61.46	11	2	58.35	13	58.89	10	63.36	11	63.34	6
武汉市	60.94	12	−2	59.73	10	57.75	12	62.61	13	59.68	13
成都市	60.71	13	1	57.21	14	55.97	16	61.68	15	60.06	12
乌鲁木齐	60.67	14	5	54.76	19	52.94	23	58.33	22	46.58	29
济南市	60.40	15	−3	58.94	12	59.29	9	64.59	9	59.19	16
贵阳市	60.38	16	−1	56.32	15	56.67	14	61.67	16	58.21	17
兰州市	60.35	17	1	55.20	18	55.50	17	59.93	19	52.63	22
长春市	59.24	18	3	53.84	21	54.10	19	59.57	20	53.58	20
郑州市	59.16	19	−3	55.75	16	56.88	13	62.3	14	63.02	7
大连市	59.05	20	−3	55.35	17	52.44	24	57.15	24	56.00	18
南宁市	58.38	21	−1	54.44	20	54.83	18	60.61	18	54.24	19
哈尔滨市	58.05	22	0	53.71	22	53.87	21	58.67	21	52.46	23
合肥市	56.91	23	0	52.21	23	53.89	20	58.17	23	51.49	26
厦门市	53.93	24	2	49.57	26	53.86	22	60.70	17	59.22	15
南京市	53.80	25	−1	50.60	24	50.28	26	55.70	25	52.18	24
福州市	53.62	26	−1	50.26	25	49.00	28	55.43	26	51.01	27
天津市	53.26	27	1	48.50	28	51.02	25	54.63	28	51.83	25

续表

城市	2016年			2015年		2014年		2013年		2012年	
	得分	排序	上升位次	得分	排序	得分	排序	得分	排序	得分	排序
宁波市	52.77	28	2	47.78	30	49.75	27	55.19	27	46.16	30
太原市	52.70	29	2	47.17	31	46.66	30	53.84	29	46.09	31
海口市	52.57	30	2	46.31	32	47.74	29	40.00	35	39.97	35
杭州市	51.12	31	−4	48.89	27	44.41	32	48.73	32	42.50	33
广州市	51.10	32	−3	48.16	29	46.32	31	53.15	30	53.24	21
上海市	48.30	33	0	45.57	33	43.59	33	50.00	31	44.50	32
北京市	47.49	34	0	42.99	34	40.00	35	45.17	34	40.80	34
深圳市	40.00	35	0	40.00	35	40.87	34	45.82	33	50.14	28
平均值	58.74			54.58		53.84		58.67		56.10	

2012~2016年，生活成本客观指数加权平均值分别为56.10、58.67、53.84、54.58、58.74，平均值连续两年提高，表明生活成本客观上继续下降，与生活成本满意度指数连续上升形成呼应。尽管如此，但生活成本满意度指数得分没有超过50，这表明居民对生活成本的满意度仍处于不满意区间。

图11为2012~2016年35个城市生活成本客观指数直方图。

分城市看，2016年生活成本客观指数得分排名前10位的城市有

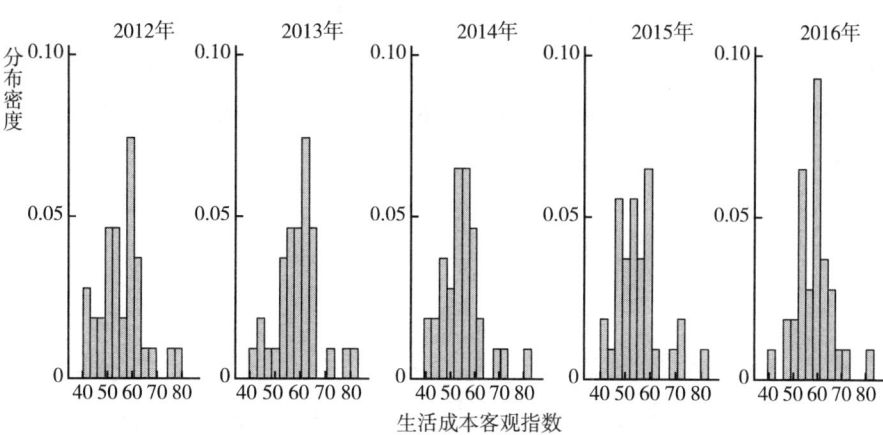

图11　2012~2016年35个城市生活成本客观指数直方图

昆明（1）、长沙（2）、呼和浩特（3）、西安（4）、银川（5）、西宁（6）、南昌（7）、石家庄（8）、青岛（9）、沈阳（10），排名后10位的城市有福州（26）、天津（27）、宁波（28）、太原（29）、海口（30）、杭州（31）、广州（32）、上海（33）、北京（34）、深圳（35）。从地区分布看，排名前10位的城市中有3个东部城市、2个中部城市、5个西部城市；排名后10位的城市中有9个是东部城市，只有1个是中部城市，没有西部城市。同时，昆明、长沙、西安、呼和浩特、石家庄、南昌、西宁7个城市已经连续5年排名在前10位的行列，说明这些城市生活成本相对较低，而深圳、北京、上海、海口、太原、宁波、杭州均已连续5年排名在后10位，说明这些城市居民的生活成本一直是相对较高的。但值得一提的是，2016年只有深圳、北京、上海的这一得分低于50。35个城市生活成本满意度指数得分平均值上升说明城市居民的生活成本有所降低，人们的满意度有所提高，这与生活成本客观指数的提高是一致的。最近一年来，全国居民消费价格指数（CPI）总体处于2%左右的低通胀区间，在一定程度上降低了生活成本。

如图12所示，35个城市中的生活成本客观指数得分连续5年不足50的只有北京、深圳、上海，2016年广州得分仅为51.10。可见，一线城市生活成本客观上较高，满意度较低。35个城市中，所有东部城市的生活成本客观指数平均值为52.47，中部城市的平均值为58.80，西部城市的平均值为62.76。

三 人力资本指数

人力资本指数由主观满意度指数和客观指数（社会经济数据指数）构成，前者是根据电话调查并结合答案赋值得到的，后者是通过对35个城市的社会经济指标计算得出的。

中国35个城市生活质量的细分指数

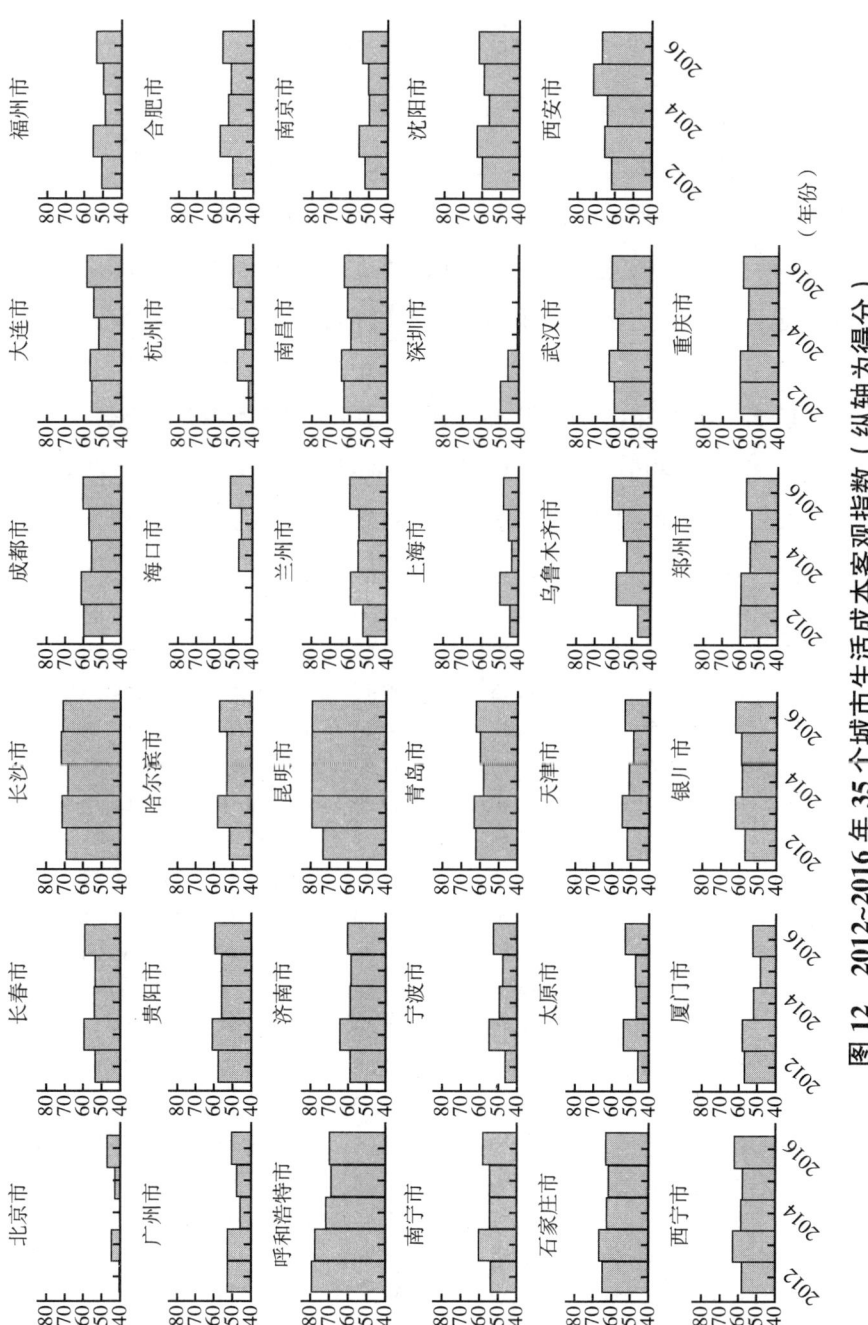

图12　2012~2016年35个城市生活成本客观指数（纵轴为得分）

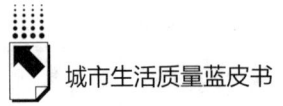

（一）人力资本满意度指数

人力资本满意度指数是通过询问受访者本人及其子女受教育的满意程度并通过答案赋值得出的。2016年35个城市人力资本满意度指数的调查结果如表7所示。2016年全国35个城市的人力资本满意度指数加权平均值为62.20，连续4年上升，35个城市中有33个城市得分超过60。总体上看，大多数城市居民人力资本满意度指数在稳步上升。

表7 2012~2016年中国35个城市居民人力资本满意度指数

城市	2016 得分	2016 排序	上升位次	2015年 得分	2015年 排序	2014年 得分	2014年 排序	2013年 得分	2013年 排序	2012年 得分	2012年 排序
武汉市	64.22	1	8	62.43	9	57.67	26	57.09	31	58.09	26
西宁市	63.98	2	5	62.48	7	61.59	4	60.09	10	58.80	21
杭州市	63.89	3	0	63.43	3	60.57	6	59.24	16	62.38	6
北京市	63.60	4	6	62.36	10	60.47	7	59.68	11	59.33	16
宁波市	63.40	5	-3	64.32	2	60.24	8	60.14	9	64.19	1
重庆市	63.25	6	10	61.70	16	59.56	13	57.74	27	58.83	20
天津市	63.16	7	17	61.10	24	60.20	9	59.30	14	61.27	9
沈阳市	63.15	8	3	62.36	11	59.78	11	57.79	26	57.61	28
广州市	62.95	9	-4	63.03	5	57.71	23	57.59	28	59.43	14
合肥市	62.84	10	-4	62.90	6	58.50	20	61.37	6	59.71	13
太原市	62.76	11	24	58.34	35	57.70	24	53.49	35	55.20	35
长沙市	62.72	12	19	59.76	31	57.26	32	58.20	24	60.38	12
南宁市	62.70	13	5	61.52	18	57.69	25	58.73	21	58.18	25
成都市	62.57	14	1	61.86	15	57.66	27	58.17	25	59.14	18
海口市	62.28	15	-11	63.37	4	61.69	3	59.11	17	58.00	27
哈尔滨市	62.12	16	-3	62.10	13	58.01	22	57.23	29	56.76	30
乌鲁木齐市	62.10	17	10	60.80	27	58.54	18	61.86	3	61.18	10
大连市	62.07	18	4	61.20	22	57.45	29	61.67	4	59.20	17
上海市	62.00	19	-11	62.44	8	61.26	5	60.35	8	58.79	22
郑州市	61.82	20	1	61.29	21	57.51	28	61.54	5	58.45	24
贵阳市	61.69	21	11	59.50	32	56.98	33	59.60	12	55.48	33

续表

城市	2016 得分	2016 排序	上升位次	2015年 得分	2015年 排序	2014年 得分	2014年 排序	2013年 得分	2013年 排序	2012年 得分	2012年 排序
济南市	61.67	22	−2	61.39	20	58.98	16	61.99	2	62.20	7
福州市	61.64	23	2	61.02	25	60.13	10	59.60	13	62.72	4
深圳市	61.56	24	6	60.54	30	56.75	34	57.03	32	57.34	29
昆明市	61.46	25	−2	61.19	23	56.15	35	54.33	34	55.45	34
南京市	61.33	26	−14	62.27	12	58.10	21	59.29	15	59.36	15
兰州市	61.10	27	6	59.09	33	61.74	2	57.20	30	58.52	23
青岛市	61.07	28	−14	61.91	14	61.84	1	62.61	1	62.62	5
呼和浩特市	60.96	29	0	60.63	29	57.29	30	60.96	7	61.07	11
长春市	60.86	30	−13	61.58	17	59.48	14	58.90	19	63.37	2
石家庄市	60.73	31	−5	60.99	26	58.67	17	58.86	20	63.31	3
南昌市	60.57	32	−4	60.78	28	58.51	19	58.45	23	56.10	32
银川市	60.08	33	1	58.63	34	59.13	15	58.52	22	61.98	8
西安市	59.65	34	−15	61.46	19	57.29	31	56.65	33	56.19	31
厦门市	58.38	35	−34	65.60	1	59.75	12	59.03	18	59.01	19
平均值	62.20			61.73		58.98		58.89		59.42	

由图13也可以看出人力资本满意度指数呈不断升高的趋势。其中，人力资本满意度指数最低分分布区间由2012年的50~55上升到55~60，最高分则除了2015年之外，都稳定在60~65的区间内。2012年人力资本满意度指数得分最高的城市是宁波（64.19），得分最低的是太原（55.20）；2013年得分最高的城市是青岛（62.61），得分最低的是太原（53.49）；2014年得分最高的城市是青岛（61.84），得分最低的是昆明（56.15）；2015年得分最高的城市是厦门（65.60），得分最低的是太原（58.34）；2016年得分最高的城市是武汉（64.22），得分最低的是厦门（58.38）。最高分与最低分的差值分别为8.99、9.12、5.69、7.26、5.84。这表明35个城市的人力资本满意度整体上升且差距缩小了。

分城市看，2016年人力资本满意度指数排名前10位的城市是武汉（1）、西宁（2）、杭州（3）、北京（4）、宁波（5）、重庆（6）、天

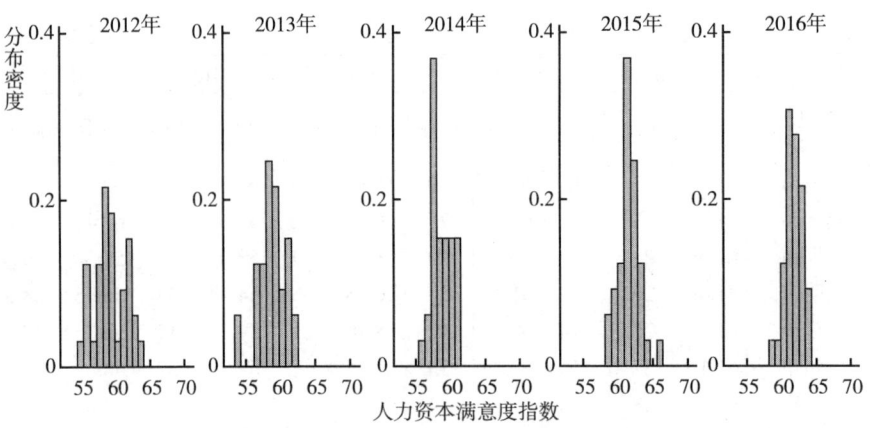

图13 2012~2016年35个城市人力资本满意度指数直方图

津（7）、沈阳（8）、广州（9）、合肥（10），排名后10位的城市为南京（26）、兰州（27）、青岛（28）、呼和浩特（29）、长春（30）、石家庄（31）、南昌（32）、银川（33）、西安（34）、厦门（35）。综合比较而言，西宁、杭州、北京、宁波4个城市连续3年位列前10位，其中宁波连续5年位列前10位，而深圳、呼和浩特、南昌等市则连续3年排名比较靠后，显示出当地居民对自己及子女受教育程度较为不满。值得一提的是，2015年厦门市人力资本满意度指数居第1位，而2016年则直线下落至最后一位，分值从65.60骤降至58.38，这一得分是2012年以来的最低值。从地区分布来看，城市居民人力资本满意度指数排名前10位的城市中，东、中、西部城市的比例为6:2:2；城市居民人力资本满意度指数排名后10位的城市中，东、中、西部城市的比例为3:3:4。

如图14所示，2012~2016年人力资本满意度指数连续4年保持上升的城市有北京、哈尔滨、沈阳、太原和西宁，波动上升的城市有长沙、成都、大连、福州、贵阳、杭州、呼和浩特、济南、昆明、兰州、南宁、深圳、天津、乌鲁木齐、武汉、银川、郑州和重庆，2016年略有下降的是长春、广州、海口、合肥、南昌、南京、宁波、青

中国35个城市生活质量的细分指数

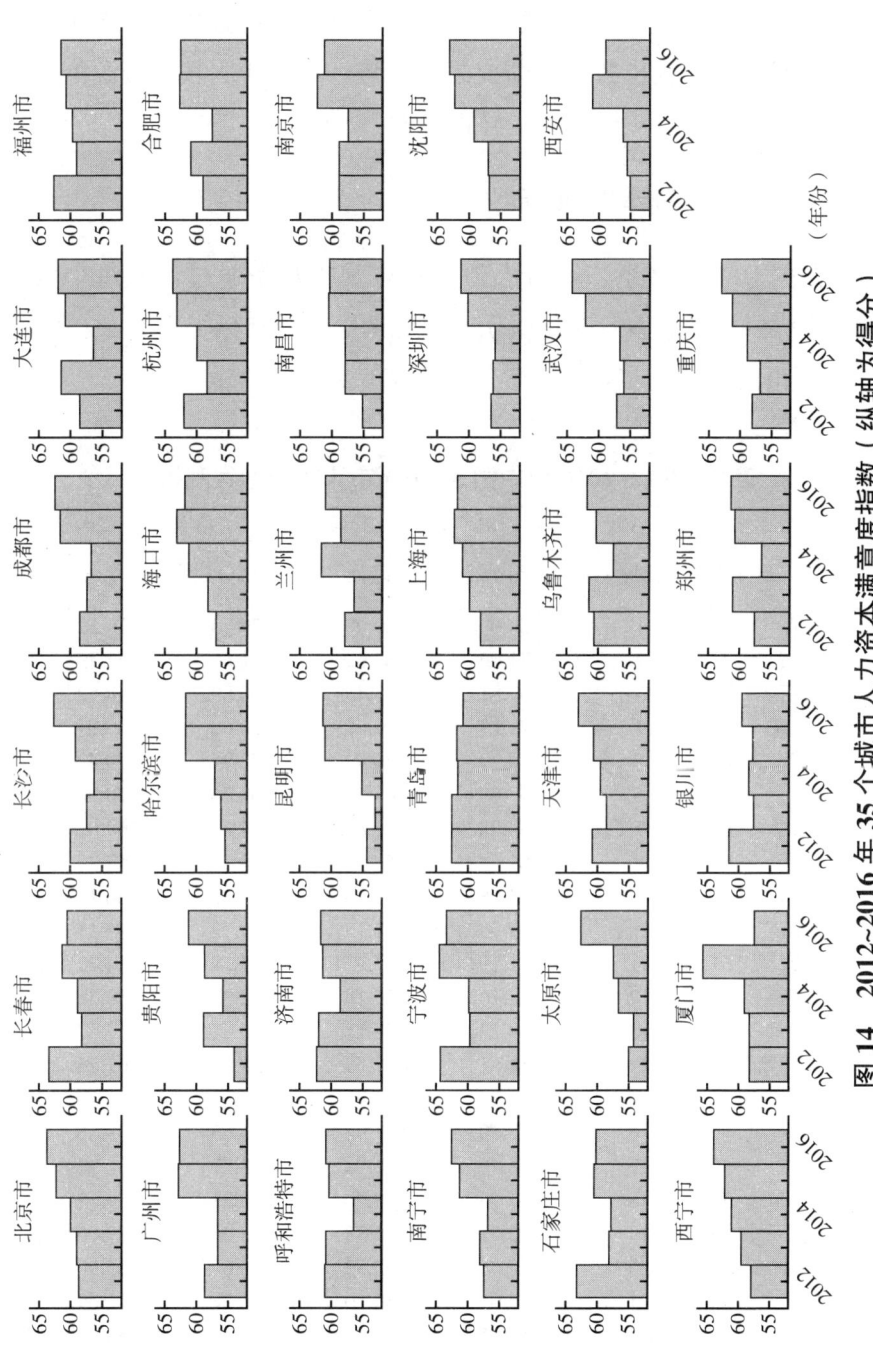

图14 2012~2016年35个城市人力资本满意度指数(纵轴为得分)

岛、上海、石家庄、西安和厦门。纵向比较的结果也表明，35个城市的人力资本满意度指数呈不断提高的趋势。尽管我国教育资源配置的地区差异仍然较大，但这一差异正在缩小。

（二）人力资本客观指数

根据QLICC体系，城市人力资本客观指数是通过计算每个城市的教育提供指数、教育文化娱乐支出比两个二级指标得出的。2016年35个城市的人力资本客观指数的计算结果如表8所示。

表8　2012~2016年中国35个城市人力资本客观指数

城市	2016年			2015年		2014年		2013年		2012年	
	得分	排序	上升位次	得分	排序	得分	排序	得分	排序	得分	排序
南京市	80.00	1	0	80.00	1	80.00	1	79.73	2	79.52	2
贵阳市	74.65	2	0	71.66	2	67.62	4	61.65	9	62.79	7
武汉市	70.87	3	3	67.81	6	63.45	7	60.89	10	58.52	13
广州市	69.28	4	-1	71.29	3	78.68	2	80.00	1	80.01	1
西安市	69.27	5	-1	70.29	4	70.94	3	72.94	3	79.42	3
北京市	67.66	6	-1	67.89	5	67.51	5	68.76	4	70.96	4
太原市	64.01	7	0	64.28	7	63.84	6	64.68	6	69.05	5
昆明市	63.53	8	1	61.64	9	59.92	10	56.19	17	57.20	17
上海市	62.59	9	-1	62.68	8	62.25	8	63.03	7	66.15	6
石家庄市	61.62	10	1	59.99	11	57.15	15	55.22	19	47.11	33
长春市	61.51	11	-1	61.19	10	61.22	9	61.79	8	54.72	21
杭州市	59.95	12	2	58.16	14	55.18	21	52.89	23	53.38	24
银川市	58.67	13	0	58.23	13	57.17	14	56.57	15	57.57	16
呼和浩特市	58.51	14	-2	58.65	12	57.59	13	58.83	13	61.75	8
大连市	56.95	15	3	55.84	18	53.98	22	52.62	24	52.09	27
长沙市	56.38	16	-1	57.50	15	57.92	12	66.65	5	58.80	11
南宁市	56.01	17	0	56.49	17	56.98	16	58.27	14	60.93	9
合肥市	55.97	18	-2	57.15	16	58.70	11	60.28	11	59.72	10
济南市	55.46	19	0	55.51	19	55.33	19	55.28	18	57.66	15
沈阳市	55.02	20	1	54.56	21	55.32	20	54.67	20	55.90	20
福州市	54.84	21	-1	55.01	20	56.40	18	56.38	16	51.09	28
宁波市	52.92	22	0	54.15	22	56.55	17	59.09	12	58.62	12

续表

城市	2016年			2015年		2014年		2013年		2012年	
	得分	排序	上升位次	得分	排序	得分	排序	得分	排序	得分	排序
深圳市	52.73	23	2	52.08	25	50.48	28	49.79	28	54.43	22
天津市	52.47	24	0	52.24	24	51.76	24	51.63	27	56.58	18
哈尔滨市	52.23	25	-2	52.53	23	52.17	23	52.90	22	52.83	25
南昌市	52.00	26	0	52.06	26	51.40	26	51.88	25	48.30	30
成都市	50.08	27	1	49.95	28	50.77	27	51.79	26	50.62	29
兰州市	49.63	28	-1	50.44	27	51.73	25	53.68	21	54.33	23
乌鲁木齐市	49.40	29	0	49.26	29	49.40	29	49.17	29	56.49	19
青岛市	48.60	30	0	48.10	30	47.37	31	46.32	33	45.56	34
郑州市	48.17	31	0	48.03	31	47.47	30	48.02	31	47.50	32
海口市	47.33	32	0	47.14	32	46.59	32	46.39	32	58.08	14
重庆市	44.59	33	0	45.26	33	46.15	33	48.03	30	48.28	31
厦门市	41.30	34	0	41.32	34	42.54	34	43.09	34	52.32	26
西宁市	40.00	35	0	40.00	35	40.00	35	40.00	35	39.99	35
平均值	56.98			57.34		57.33		57.78		57.66	

2012~2015年，35个城市人力资本客观指数得分加权平均值分别为57.66、57.78、57.33、57.34，不同年份间差异较小，处于基本持平的状态。相比往年，2016年该数值有所下降，为56.98。但总体而言，人力资本客观指数是一个相对稳定的指标。如图15所示，从人力资本客观指数得分在各年度的分布情况看，其大致分布在40~80的区间内。2012年、2013年人力资本客观指数得分最高的城市均是广州，2014~2016年得分最高的均是南京，连续5年得分最低的都是西宁，最高分和最低分的差异基本在40分以内，5年的标准差分别为9.21、9.02、8.84、8.77和8.99，西宁连续5年人力资本客观指数得分最低的主要原因是人力资本的积累是一项长期工作，无论是教育还是培训都需要一定的周期才能完成，不可能在短期内获得较大的改变。

横向比较而言，城市间排序变化不是很大。2016年排名前10位的城市分别是南京（1）、贵阳（2）、武汉（3）、广州（4）、西安（5）、北京（6）、太原（7）、昆明（8）、上海（9）、石家庄（10），排名

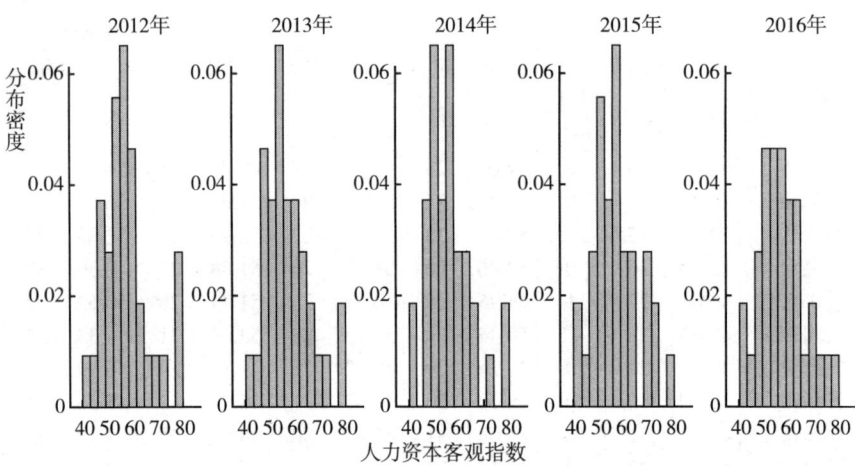

图15　2012~2016年35个城市人力资本客观指数直方图

后10位的城市分别是南昌（26）、成都（27）、兰州（28）、乌鲁木齐（29）、青岛（30）、郑州（31）、海口（32）、重庆（33）、厦门（34）、西宁（35）。在排名前10位的城市中，南京、贵阳、广州、西安、北京、太原、上海7个城市已经连续5年位列其中，武汉连续4年位列其中。在排名后10位的城市中，西宁、厦门、重庆、郑州、青岛、成都6个城市已经连续5年位列其中，海口和乌鲁木齐连续4年位列其中。

从动态角度看，如图16所示，大连、青岛、石家庄、武汉4个城市在这一个指标上保持了4年的连续增长；兰州、南宁、厦门、西安、重庆5个城市在这个指标上连续4年下降；其余城市得分在这4年间上下波动。

分地区看，东部、中部和西部地区的人力资本差距并不大，但同一区域内部差距较大。从2012~2016年三个地区的人力资本客观指数得分的平均值看，东部（57.58）和中部（57.36）基本相同，西部（54.35）略低，但差距并不大。但同一区域内的差距则较为显著。如仍以人力资本客观指数得分平均值计算，东部地区的南京（79.85）和厦门（44.11）得分相差35.74，西部地区的贵阳（67.67）和西宁（40.00）得分相差27.67。

中国35个城市生活质量的细分指数

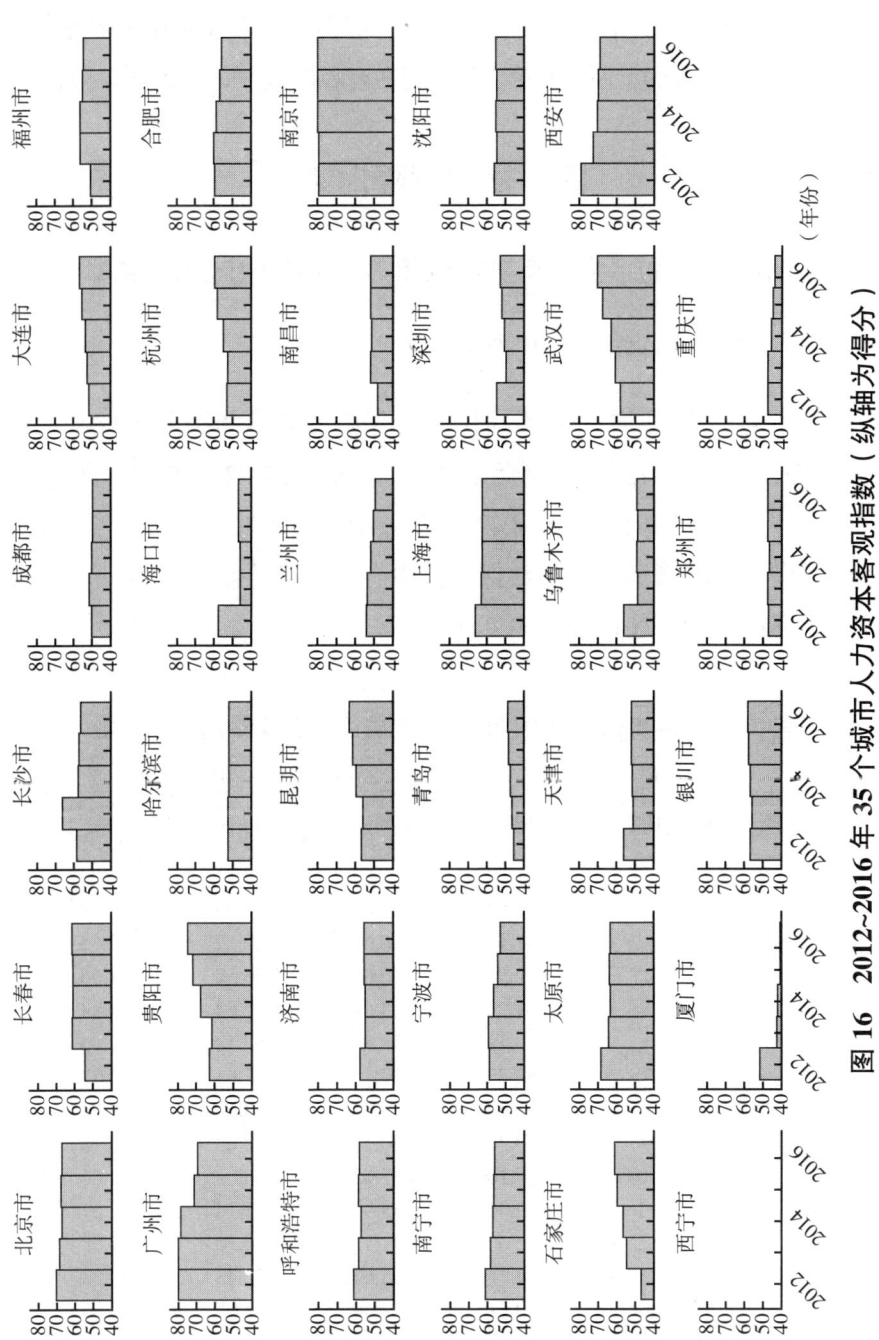

图16 2012~2016年35个城市人力资本客观指数（纵轴为得分）

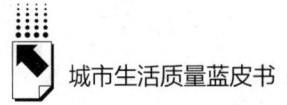

另外，就人力资本指数而言，西宁的主客观指数反差较为明显，在主观满意度指数方面，西宁居第2位，但在客观指数方面，则居第35位。

四 社会保障指数

社会保障指数包括主观满意度指数和客观指数（社会经济数据指数）。

（一）社会保障满意度指数

2016年，全国35个城市居民社会保障满意度指数的加权平均值为60.66，2012~2015年分别为59.19、56.64、57.87、60.47，年增长率分别为-4.31%、2.17%、4.49%和0.31%，除2013年外，35个城市的居民社会保障满意度指数保持稳中有升的态势。35个城市社会保障满意度指数和排序情况如表9所示。

表9 2012~2016年中国35个城市居民社会保障满意度指数

城市	2016年			2015年		2014年		2013年		2012年	
	得分	排序	上升位次	得分	排序	得分	排序	得分	排序	得分	排序
西宁市	63.04	1	4	61.38	5	57.97	16	59.31	7	62.04	9
北京市	62.32	2	1	61.57	3	58.85	14	58.94	9	61.27	12
宁波市	62.31	3	1	61.44	4	60.61	4	60.52	4	63.65	2
乌鲁木齐市	62.10	4	23	59.50	27	56.00	28	56.57	17	58.06	22
武汉市	62.02	5	2	61.28	7	55.39	32	52.64	32	56.83	26
大连市	61.57	6	12	60.49	18	58.91	13	57.18	13	61.73	10
重庆市	61.37	7	9	60.73	16	59.14	8	55.61	24	62.78	5
上海市	61.33	8	-6	61.94	2	59.44	7	58.04	10	58.71	18
呼和浩特市	61.31	9	12	60.28	21	56.55	24	52.63	33	60.18	14
太原市	61.15	10	21	59.16	31	57.03	23	56.63	16	58.66	19
天津市	61.05	11	18	59.36	29	58.92	12	55.14	25	58.57	21
杭州市	60.88	12	-11	62.60	1	61.17	1	60.76	3	64.68	1
南宁市	60.88	13	9	59.84	22	55.61	31	52.43	34	56.33	29
成都市	60.79	14	-1	60.81	13	57.90	17	57.05	14	61.33	11
昆明市	60.76	15	-7	61.06	8	51.88	35	54.09	30	54.65	34

续表

城市	2016年			2015年		2014年		2013年		2012年	
	得分	排序	上升位次	得分	排序	得分	排序	得分	排序	得分	排序
贵阳市	60.76	16	-1	60.76	15	55.83	30	51.98	35	52.26	35
济南市	60.57	17	-11	61.34	6	59.13	9	59.82	6	62.65	6
广州市	60.52	18	-1	60.54	17	55.03	33	54.70	27	56.81	27
银川市	60.50	19	16	58.89	35	59.74	6	60.03	5	62.24	8
青岛市	60.46	20	-11	61.04	9	60.80	3	61.87	1	62.26	7
沈阳市	60.45	21	4	59.60	25	57.26	21	56.40	18	57.04	25
合肥市	60.29	22	10	59.11	32	57.48	19	57.71	11	59.80	15
海口市	60.25	23	-12	60.95	11	59.06	11	53.86	31	55.75	32
郑州市	60.24	24	2	59.55	26	56.47	26	55.74	22	56.67	28
厦门市	60.01	25	-15	60.95	10	61.03	2	61.25	2	62.79	4
长春市	59.74	26	-3	59.64	23	60.47	5	57.59	12	62.83	3
石家庄市	59.68	27	1	59.38	28	57.05	22	56.64	15	61.24	13
长沙市	59.65	28	-14	60.77	14	54.23	34	54.09	29	56.14	31
哈尔滨市	59.51	29	-9	60.29	20	57.83	18	55.86	21	56.27	30
深圳市	59.47	30	3	59.06	33	56.48	25	55.11	26	57.04	24
南昌市	59.43	31	-19	60.94	12	56.08	27	54.09	28	55.18	33
南京市	59.30	32	-13	60.47	19	59.07	10	59.22	8	59.17	17
福州市	59.30	33	-9	59.60	24	58.45	15	56.23	20	58.60	20
兰州市	59.25	34	0	59.01	34	57.26	20	55.65	23	57.67	23
西安市	58.68	35	-5	59.16	30	55.84	29	56.27	19	59.65	16
平均值	60.66			60.47		57.87		56.64		59.19	

2016年，35个城市中有25个城市居民社会保障满意度得分超过60，略高于2015年（21个），但远高于2014年的5个城市。2016年，社会保障满意度指数排名前10位的城市是西宁（1）、北京（2）、宁波（3）、乌鲁木齐（4）、武汉（5）、大连（6）、重庆（7）、上海（8）、呼和浩特（9）、太原（10），排名后10位的城市有长春（26）、石家庄（27）、长沙（28）、哈尔滨（29）、深圳（30）、南昌（31）、南京（32）、福州（33）、兰州（34）、西安（35）。宁波、上海已经连续4年排名在前10位城市的行列。在排名前10位的城市中，东、中、西部城市的比例为4∶2∶4；在排名后10位的城市中，东、中、西部城市的比例为4∶4∶2。

相比以往，2016年，社会保障主观感受的地区差距在缩小。如图17所示，2012~2016年35个城市的社会保障满意度指数分布不断集中，由2012年的50~70区间缩小到2016年的55~65区间。最高值的分布区间保持在60~70的区间内，最低值的分布区间由50~55提高到55~60。2012~2016年城市社会保障满意度指数的标准差依次是2.94、2.60、2.07、0.94和1.01。

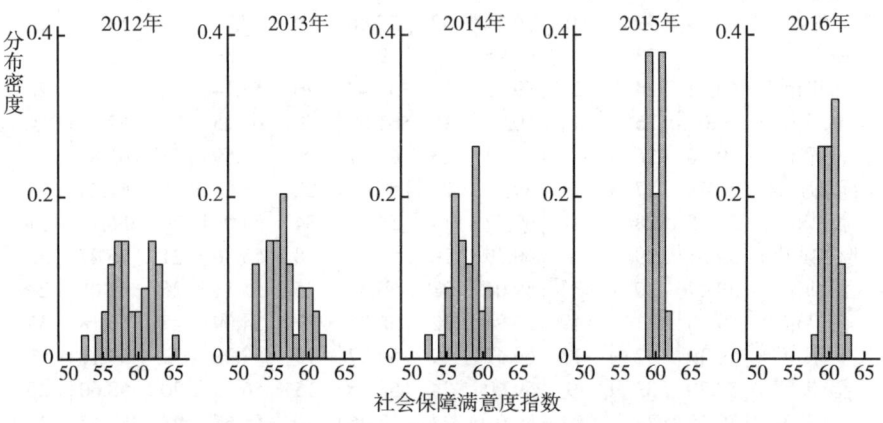

图17　2012~2016年35个城市社会保障满意度指数直方图

如图18所示，2012~2016年，除厦门连续4年保持下降外，大多数城市的社会保障满意度指数都是先降后升的。这主要是由于自2012年以来，国家在基本社会保障体系已经建立起来的基础上，进一步加快了社保领域的改革。社保问题与每个社会成员的利益息息相关，受社会关注度较高，而改革措施的落实和新问题的出现，以及地区、行业差距的存在，都会影响社会成员对社保满意度的评价，这是正常的。但是随着改革措施的到位和平等程度的提高，满意度是在不断提高的。

根据QLICC体系，社会保障满意度指数是医疗和养老保障满意度指数、城市安全状况满意度指数的加权平均值，和往年一样，也是通

中国35个城市生活质量的细分指数

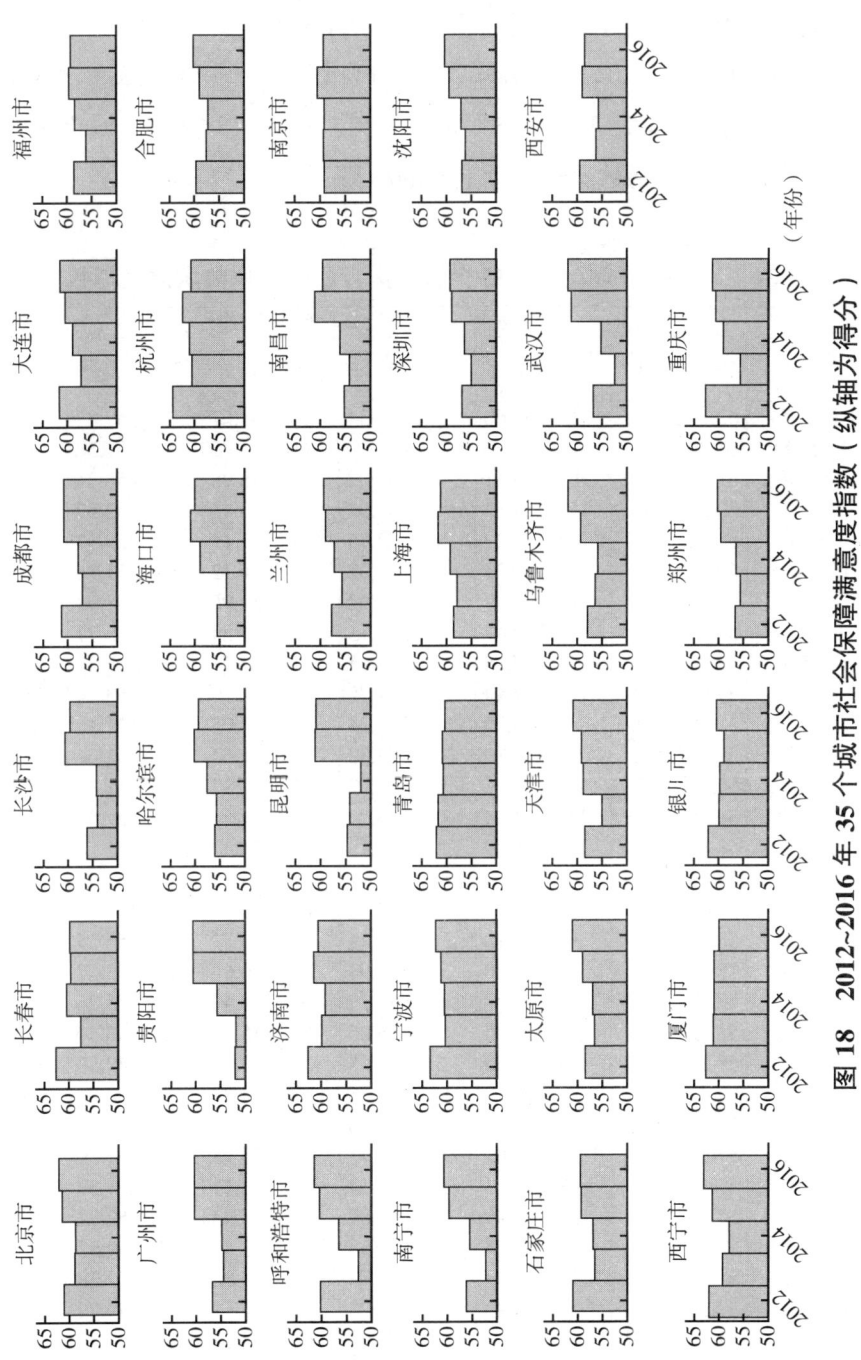

图18 2012~2016年35个城市社会保障满意度指数（纵轴为得分）

过问卷调查并对调查结果进行答案赋值得到的。

如表 10 所示，2012~2016 年，全国城市医疗和养老保障满意度指数加权平均值分别为 53.61、54.34、54.80、58.04 和 58.68，城市医疗和养老保障满意度指数呈现持续上升的趋势。

表 10　2012~2016 年中国 35 个城市医疗和养老保障满意度指数

城市	2016 年			2015 年		2014 年		2013 年		2012 年	
	得分	排序	上升位次	得分	排序	得分	排序	得分	排序	得分	排序
西宁市	62.10	1	2	59.60	3	56.34	7	61.67	1	57.87	3
乌鲁木齐市	61.29	2	9	58.76	11	56.37	6	56.36	9	57.57	4
宁波市	61.16	3	1	59.31	4	58.02	1	58.96	2	58.24	2
武汉市	60.30	4	12	58.33	16	53.01	27	50.45	35	52.52	20
大连市	60.21	5	21	57.22	26	52.75	30	52.13	30	53.37	18
昆明市	60.07	6	0	59.21	6	52.62	32	54.42	18	51.76	27
上海市	59.88	7	-6	59.79	1	55.62	14	51.96	32	48.93	35
北京市	59.88	8	-1	59.17	7	56.15	9	57.29	5	55.71	12
南宁市	59.80	9	10	57.85	19	52.85	29	52.11	31	52.47	21
重庆市	59.67	10	10	57.84	20	57.75	2	54.79	15	53.74	15
太原市	59.28	11	24	55.72	35	53.74	22	54.05	23	57.18	7
天津市	59.21	12	20	56.19	32	54.33	20	51.64	33	52.06	24
广州市	59.08	13	-4	59.01	9	53.32	25	52.37	29	51.38	29
呼和浩特市	58.85	14	11	57.34	25	55.73	12	54.53	17	57.50	5
合肥市	58.50	15	15	56.89	30	53.79	21	54.42	19	55.58	13
济南市	58.44	16	1	58.09	17	53.44	24	54.24	22	51.96	26
银川市	58.43	17	5	57.75	22	55.53	15	56.59	7	55.73	11
石家庄市	58.26	18	3	57.78	21	54.79	19	56.39	8	56.55	9
贵阳市	58.21	19	4	57.60	23	54.94	17	56.64	6	53.57	16
成都市	58.20	20	-8	58.70	12	56.23	8	54.40	20	55.26	14
厦门市	58.12	21	-13	59.05	8	56.06	11	55.83	12	56.40	10
海口市	58.11	22	-20	59.65	2	57.68	3	53.11	25	49.50	34
沈阳市	58.05	23	-5	57.88	18	52.15	35	54.37	21	50.00	31
南昌市	58.03	24	-11	58.61	13	55.36	16	55.64	13	51.63	28
福州市	57.82	25	3	57.07	28	55.73	13	53.75	24	51.30	30
杭州市	57.47	26	-21	59.23	5	57.14	4	56.11	10	58.37	1
兰州市	57.40	27	2	56.98	29	54.89	18	58.33	3	52.27	23
哈尔滨市	57.31	28	3	56.85	31	52.58	33	52.47	27	49.52	33
郑州市	57.30	29	5	56.13	34	52.73	31	54.82	14	52.38	22
南京市	57.22	30	-20	58.83	10	53.73	23	54.61	16	49.74	32
青岛市	57.20	31	-16	58.51	15	56.09	10	58.19	4	53.42	17

续表

城市	2016年			2015年		2014年		2013年		2012年	
	得分	排序	上升位次	得分	排序	得分	排序	得分	排序	得分	排序
长沙市	57.10	32	-18	58.51	14	53.05	26	52.45	28	52.05	25
长春市	56.84	33	-9	57.44	24	56.73	5	52.90	26	57.22	6
深圳市	56.77	34	-7	57.13	27	52.58	34	51.23	34	52.98	19
西安市	56.70	35	-2	56.15	33	52.90	28	55.96	11	57.04	8
平均值	58.68			58.04		54.80		54.34		53.61	

2016年医疗和养老保障满意度指数排名前10位的城市分别是西宁（1）、乌鲁木齐（2）、宁波（3）、武汉（4）、大连（5）、昆明（6）、上海（7）、北京（8）、南宁（9）、重庆（10），排名后10位的城市有杭州（26）、兰州（27）、哈尔滨（28）、郑州（29）、南京（30）、青岛（31）、长沙（32）、长春（33）、深圳（34）、西安（35）。从地区分布来看，排名前10位的城市中，有4个东部城市、1个中部城市、5个西部城市；排名后10位的城市中，有4个东部城市、4个中部城市、2个西部城市。相比2015年，排名后10位城市的地区分布没有改变，但排名前10位的城市中，东部城市由8个减至4个，西部城市由2个增至5个，地区差异显著减小。其中，排名前10位的城市中位次上升的是大连（+21）、武汉（+12）、南宁（+10）、重庆（+10）、乌鲁木齐（+9）、西宁（+2）、宁波（+1），昆明的位次没有变化，排名下降的城市是上海（-6）、北京（-1）；排名后10位的城市中位次上升的有兰州（+2）、哈尔滨（+3）、郑州（+5），排名下降的城市有杭州（-21）、南京（-20）、青岛（-16）、长沙（-18）、长春（-9）、深圳（-7）、西安（-2）。西宁和宁波是连续5年均排在前10名的城市，没有任何一个城市连续5年排在后10名。

如图19所示，从指数直方图看，城市间医疗和养老保障满意度在整体提高的同时差距也在缩小。2012年35个城市医疗和社会保障满意度指数分值最低值分布在50以下，最高值分布在55~60区

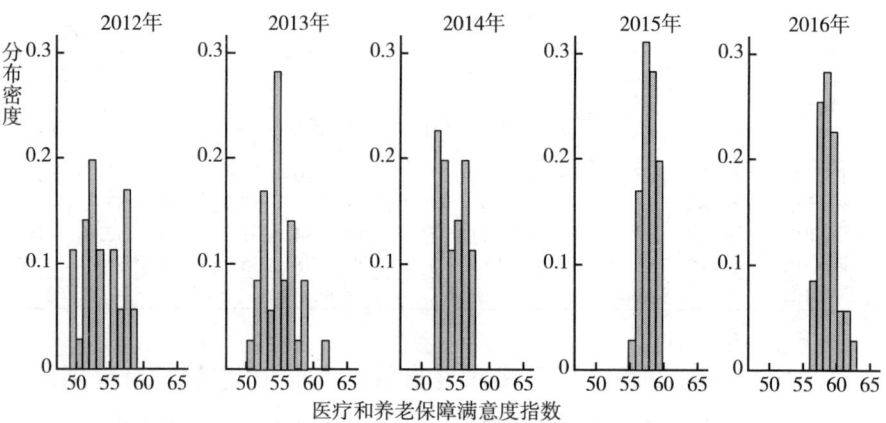

图 19　2012~2016 年 35 个城市医疗和养老保障满意度指数直方图

间，至 2016 年，最低值分布已经提升至 55~60 的区间，最高值也分布在 60~65 的区间内，而且多数城市的得分更加集中于 60 左右的区间内。2012 年对医疗和养老保障状况满意度最高的城市是杭州（58.37），满意度最低的城市是上海（48.93），两者得分相差 9.44；2013 年满意度最高的城市是西宁（61.67），最低的是武汉（50.45），两者得分相差 11.22；2014 年满意度最高的城市是宁波（58.02），最低的是沈阳（52.15），两者得分相差 5.87；2015 年满意度最高的城市是上海（59.79），最低的是太原（55.72），两者得分相差 4.07；2016 年满意度最高的城市是西宁（62.10），最低的是西安（56.70），两者得分相差 5.40。

2012~2016 年 35 个城市医疗和养老保障满意度指数整体呈现上升趋势。如图 20 所示，连续 4 年保持增长的城市有福州、广州、哈尔滨、上海、重庆，2016 年与 2012 年相比满意度下降的城市有 3 个，分别是杭州、长春和西安。

总体而言，调查涉及的 35 个城市的医疗保障和养老保障状况都在不断改善，居民的满意度不断提高。但是由于各地保障制度侧重点不同、劳动力的流动程度以及各地筹资模式存在较大差异，所以不同城市间医疗和养老保障满意度指数的排名不稳定，变化较大且不能持续。

中国 35 个城市生活质量的细分指数

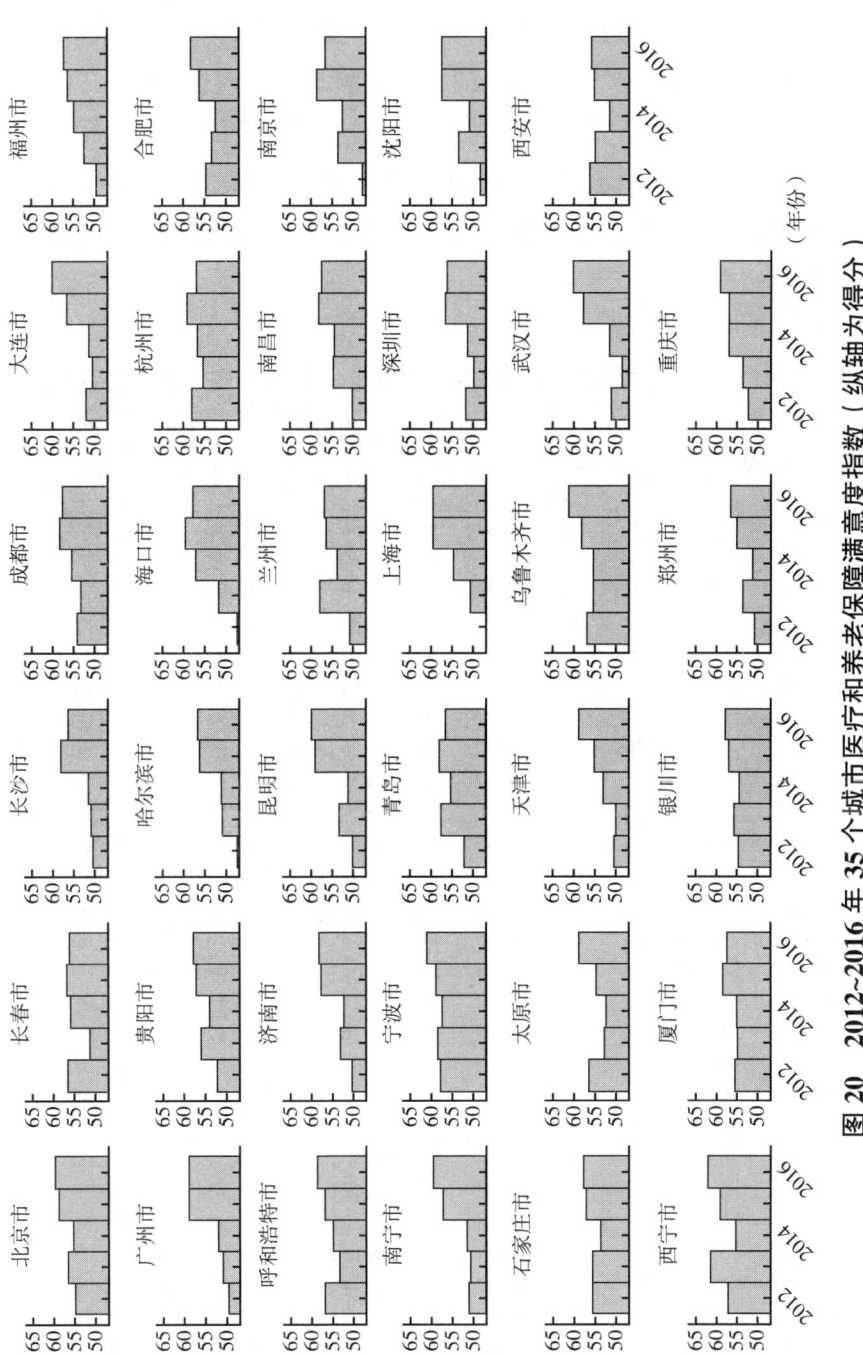

图 20　2012~2016 年 35 个城市医疗和养老保障满意度指数（纵轴为得分）

如表11所示，2016年全国35个城市的城市安全（社会治安）状况满意度指数加权平均值为62.63，处在满意区间内，但相比2015年稍微有所下降，城市安全状况满意度指数不断上升的态势中断。从地区分布来看，排名前10位的城市中，有4个东部城市、2个中部城市、4个西部城市。排名后10位的城市中，有4个东部城市、2个中部城市、4个西部城市。

表11 2012~2016年中国35个城市的城市安全（社会治安）状况满意度指数

城市	2016年			2015年		2014年		2013年		2012年	
	得分	排序	上升位次	得分	排序	得分	排序	得分	排序	得分	排序
北京市	64.75	1	4	63.97	5	61.56	14	60.58	12	66.82	13
杭州市	64.29	2	-1	65.98	1	65.20	3	65.42	3	70.99	4
西宁市	63.98	3	11	63.16	14	59.60	23	56.94	21	66.20	14
呼和浩特市	63.76	4	9	63.21	13	57.38	29	50.73	34	62.86	22
武汉市	63.74	5	-2	64.23	3	57.77	28	54.83	28	61.13	26
青岛市	63.72	6	4	63.57	10	65.51	2	65.55	2	71.11	3
宁波市	63.47	7	4	63.57	11	63.21	11	62.08	10	69.05	7
成都市	63.39	8	9	62.92	17	59.56	24	59.69	13	67.40	12
贵阳市	63.31	9	-3	63.92	6	56.73	32	47.32	35	50.95	35
郑州市	63.18	10	6	62.96	16	60.20	21	56.66	24	60.95	28
重庆市	63.07	11	-2	63.62	9	60.53	17	56.43	26	71.83	2
太原市	63.02	12	8	62.60	20	60.32	20	59.22	15	60.15	31
大连市	62.93	13	-6	63.75	7	65.07	4	62.22	9	70.09	5
乌鲁木齐市	62.90	14	20	60.25	34	55.63	33	56.78	23	58.55	33
天津市	62.89	15	6	62.54	21	63.51	9	58.64	18	65.08	17
沈阳市	62.84	16	14	61.32	30	62.37	13	58.43	19	64.09	18
上海市	62.78	17	-13	64.08	4	63.26	10	64.12	5	68.48	10
济南市	62.70	18	-16	64.60	2	64.82	5	65.41	4	73.34	1
长春市	62.63	19	8	61.84	27	64.22	7	62.29	8	68.45	11
银川市	62.57	20	15	60.04	35	63.94	8	63.46	7	68.75	8
海口市	62.39	21	1	62.24	22	60.44	18	54.61	29	62.00	25
长沙市	62.21	22	-7	63.02	15	55.42	34	55.73	27	60.23	29
深圳市	62.17	23	9	60.98	32	60.39	19	58.98	16	61.11	27
合肥市	62.07	24	5	61.33	29	61.18	15	61.00	11	64.03	19
广州市	61.96	25	1	62.08	26	56.74	31	57.02	20	62.25	24
南宁市	61.96	26	2	61.83	28	58.37	27	52.75	32	60.19	30
厦门市	61.91	27	-8	62.85	19	66.00	1	66.67	1	69.19	6

续表

城市	2016年			2015年		2014年		2013年		2012年	
	得分	排序	上升位次	得分	排序	得分	排序	得分	排序	得分	排序
哈尔滨市	61.71	28	−20	63.73	8	63.07	12	59.25	14	63.03	21
昆明市	61.46	29	−11	62.92	18	51.15	35	53.75	30	57.53	34
南京市	61.39	30	−5	62.11	25	64.41	6	63.83	6	68.59	9
兰州市	61.10	31	0	61.03	31	59.63	22	52.97	31	63.07	20
石家庄市	61.09	32	1	60.97	33	59.32	25	56.89	22	65.93	15
南昌市	60.82	33	−21	63.28	12	56.80	30	52.55	33	58.74	32
福州市	60.78	34	−10	62.13	24	61.17	16	58.71	17	65.90	16
西安市	60.65	35	−12	62.18	23	58.78	26	56.58	25	62.26	23
平均值	62.63			62.90		60.45		58.93		64.58	

如图21所示，2012~2016年35个城市的城市安全（社会治安）状况满意度在下降的同时，还呈现出高度的一致性。2012年城市安全状况满意度指数分值分散在50~75的区间内，到2015年和2016年这种分布则收缩至60~70区间。2012年城市安全状况满意度最高的城市是济南（73.34），最低的是贵阳（50.95）；2013年城市安全状况满意度最高的是厦门（66.67），最低的是贵阳（47.32）；2014年城市安全

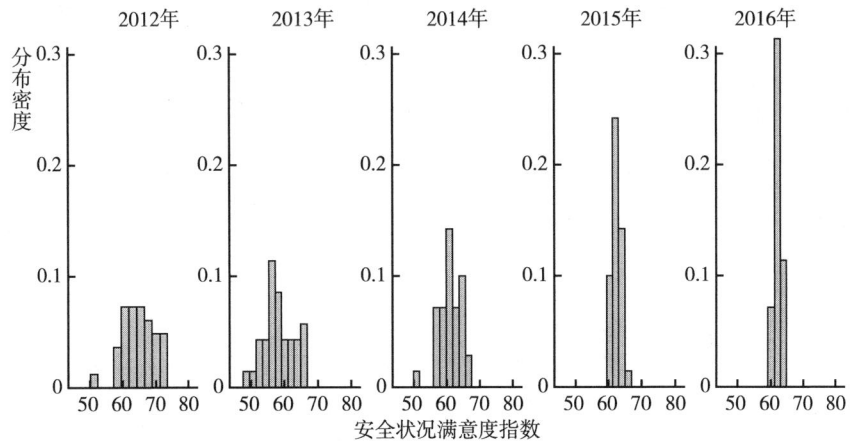

图21 2012~2016年35个城市的城市安全（社会治安）状况满意度指数直方图

状况满意度最高的是厦门（66.00），最低的是昆明（51.15）；2015年城市安全状况满意度最高的是杭州（65.98），最低的是银川（60.04）；2016年城市安全状况满意度最高的是北京（64.75），最低的是西安（60.65），两者得分的差值依次是22.39、19.35、14.85、5.94、4.10。

如图22所示，2012~2016年35个城市的城市安全状况满意度总体上呈现下降趋势。从地区整体情况看，东部、中部和西部地区的城市安全状况满意度指数平均值分别为63.31、60.99和60.21，这表明东部地区城市安全状况满意度最高、西部最低，且连续5年城市安全状况满意度得分不足60的城市基本分布在西部地区。但是从指数的变化看，2012~2016年城市安全状况满意度得分提高较多的3个城市全部为西部城市，分别是贵阳（+12.36）、乌鲁木齐（+4.35）、昆明（+3.93），得分下降较多的3个城市分别是济南（-10.64）、重庆（-8.76）、青岛（-7.39），其中有2个来自东部地区，安全状况满意度指数连续4年下降的城市只有济南和厦门，也均为东部城市。

城市安全状况满意度本身是一种主观心理感受，并不代表实际治安状况的恶化。这种心理感受除了受身边发生的真实事件的影响外，更多地受到媒体传播方式和导向的影响。由此，一个城市经济发展水平越高，居民获取信息的渠道越多、越快，小众传播性越高，因此经济发达地区得到相关信息的速度也就快于经济落后地区。从这个角度上讲，经济发达地区，即使客观上安全程度提高了，但是由于居民对治安的敏感度提高了，加之一些媒体传播的悲观导向，居民的安全感也就降低了。

（二）社会保障客观指数

根据QLICC体系，社会保障客观指数的分值是根据每个城市的社保覆盖率、基本医疗保险覆盖率、失业保险覆盖率3个二级指标计算得出的。35个城市社会保障客观指数如表12所示。

中国35个城市生活质量的细分指数

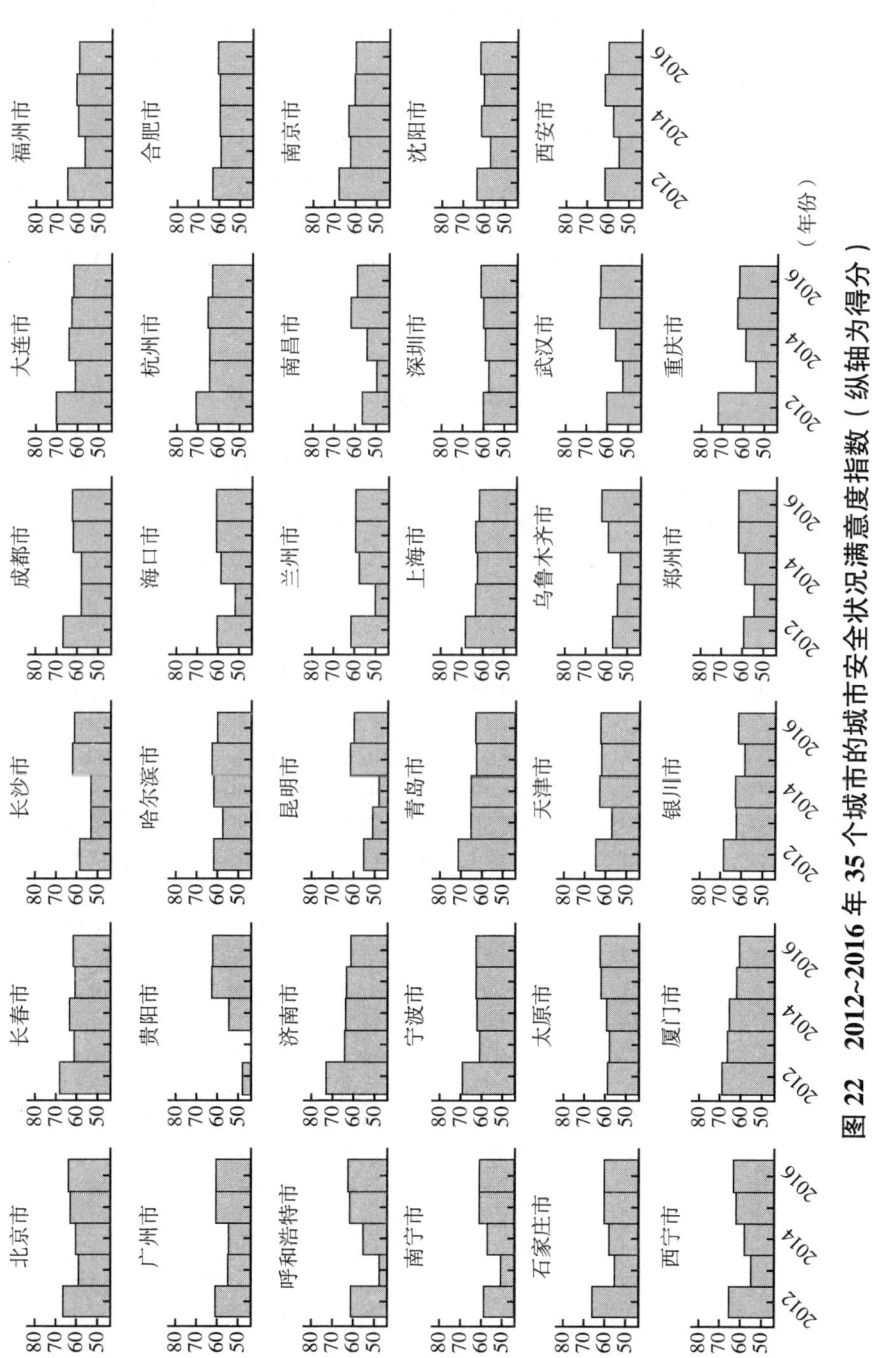

图22 2012~2016年35个城市的城市安全状况满意度指数（纵轴为得分）

表12　2012~2016年中国35个城市社会保障客观指数

城市	2016年		上升位次	2015年		2014年		2013年		2012年	
	得分	排序		得分	排序	得分	排序	得分	排序	得分	排序
深圳市	80.00	1	0	80.00	1	80.00	1	80.00	1	80.01	1
杭州市	65.76	2	1	64.23	3	65.70	5	63.84	7	58.36	7
北京市	65.41	3	−1	66.18	2	76.39	2	77.24	2	71.82	2
厦门市	63.87	4	0	63.40	4	73.85	3	74.37	3	71.43	3
宁波市	60.30	5	0	61.39	5	71.22	4	72.36	4	56.19	8
广州市	58.25	6	0	57.36	6	64.52	7	66.71	6	60.11	5
上海市	58.05	7	0	56.82	7	65.66	6	67.23	5	68.68	4
沈阳市	56.12	8	0	55.30	8	60.46	8	62.01	9	55.20	12
南京市	55.78	9	0	54.14	9	58.56	11	58.11	12	55.65	10
天津市	53.41	10	1	52.06	11	58.90	9	63.13	8	59.89	6
大连市	53.17	11	−1	53.26	10	58.85	10	59.82	11	55.67	9
银川市	51.86	12	0	50.42	12	53.28	12	51.93	16	47.15	18
太原市	51.31	13	0	50.23	13	49.40	19	49.08	19	50.61	14
西安市	50.44	14	0	49.57	14	52.48	13	52.15	15	55.62	11
成都市	49.58	15	0	48.60	15	51.14	15	50.84	17	45.00	22
乌鲁木齐市	49.13	16	0	48.14	16	51.79	14	52.63	13	51.44	13
青岛市	47.62	17	0	47.16	17	50.50	17	52.34	14	48.63	16
济南市	47.61	18	2	46.94	20	46.71	21	47.36	20	46.08	20
武汉市	47.44	19	2	46.69	21	50.71	16	50.48	18	49.51	15
长春市	46.93	20	−1	46.95	19	50.17	18	59.84	10	48.23	17
贵阳市	46.52	21	1	45.70	22	45.22	24	44.95	25	44.14	24
呼和浩特市	46.50	22	−4	47.01	18	46.75	20	46.91	21	45.68	21
长沙市	45.33	23	0	45.20	23	45.92	23	45.97	23	43.07	27
重庆市	44.63	24	0	44.82	24	44.97	25	44.57	26	41.48	32
南宁市	44.56	25	0	44.61	25	46.04	22	46.09	22	40.85	34
合肥市	44.13	26	2	43.49	28	44.14	30	43.72	29	44.71	23
福州市	43.90	27	−1	43.76	26	44.79	27	44.06	27	42.17	31
海口市	43.27	28	4	42.55	32	44.72	28	43.91	28	42.54	30
兰州市	43.17	29	−2	43.54	27	44.91	26	45.14	24	46.35	19
昆明市	42.92	30	1	42.77	31	44.52	29	41.21	33	42.85	29
石家庄市	42.76	31	−1	42.89	30	41.80	32	41.77	31	40.86	33
郑州市	42.17	32	−3	43.19	29	40.61	34	40.98	34	42.99	28
南昌市	41.63	33	0	41.59	33	42.87	31	43.05	30	43.46	25
哈尔滨市	41.37	34	0	41.04	34	41.58	33	41.73	32	43.21	26
西宁市	40.00	35	0	40.00	35	40.00	35	40.00	35	39.98	35
平均值	50.43			51.26		54.66		55.26		50.85	

2016年全国35个城市社会保障客观指数加权平均值为50.43，从动态变化的角度看，在2015年大幅降低的基础上继续下降。35个城市中有21个城市的社会保障客观指数的分值低于50，与2015年大致持平，但2014年只有17个城市的社会保障客观指数得分低于50。我们认为，社会保障客观指数得分下降的主要原因在于，受经济下行的影响，失业率上升，但我国失业保险参保人数和比例相对较低，失业保险覆盖面窄。此外，值得注意的是，社会保障客观指数存在较大的地区差异。

分城市看，2016年社会保障客观指数排名前10位的城市有深圳（1）、杭州（2）、北京（3）、厦门（4）、宁波（5）、广州（6）、上海（7）、沈阳（8）、南京（9）、天津（10），排名后10位的城市有合肥（26）、福州（27）、海口（28）、兰州（29）、昆明（30）、石家庄（31）、郑州（32）、南昌（33）、哈尔滨（34）、西宁（35）。其中，深圳、北京、杭州、厦门、宁波、广州、上海7个城市已经连续5年排在前10位城市的行列中，沈阳和天津在过去5年中有4年位于前10位。福州、郑州、石家庄、昆明、海口、南昌、哈尔滨、西宁8个城市已经连续5年排在后10位城市的行列中。深圳一直保持在第一的位置上，西宁则连续5年垫底，但2016年西宁的社会保障满意度指数位居第一。此外，值得注意的是，社会保障客观指数存在较大的地区差异。

如图23所示，2012~2016年35个城市社会保障客观指数分布在低分区间的城市数目多于分布在高分区间的城市数目。35个城市中，社会保障客观指数得分连续5年在50以上的11个城市全部来自东部地区，这表明社会保障的主要影响因素是经济发展水平。

图24能更好地说明35个城市的社会保障客观指数差别较大，而且相对比较稳定。这主要是由于社会成员所处的地区和行业不同，社

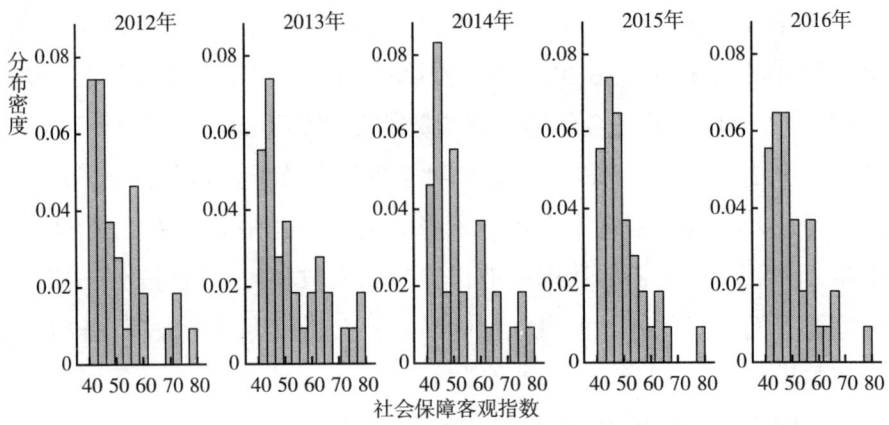

图 23　2012~2016 年 35 个城市社会保障客观指数直方图

会保障、基本医疗保险的统筹层次不同，不同层次的缴费办法不尽相同，在国家层面统一的难度较大，这使得地区差距长期存在。同时，保障范围和力度与收入紧密相关，因此东部地区的保障程度高于中部和西部地区。

五　生活感受指数

生活感受指数同样由主观满意度指数和客观指数（社会经济数据指数）构成。

（一）生活感受满意度指数

根据 QLICC 体系，生活感受满意度指数是通过问卷调查得出的，由生活节奏满意度指数和生活便利满意度指数加权平均得到。2016 年 35 个城市生活感受满意度指数的调查结果如表 13 所示。

中国35个城市生活质量的细分指数

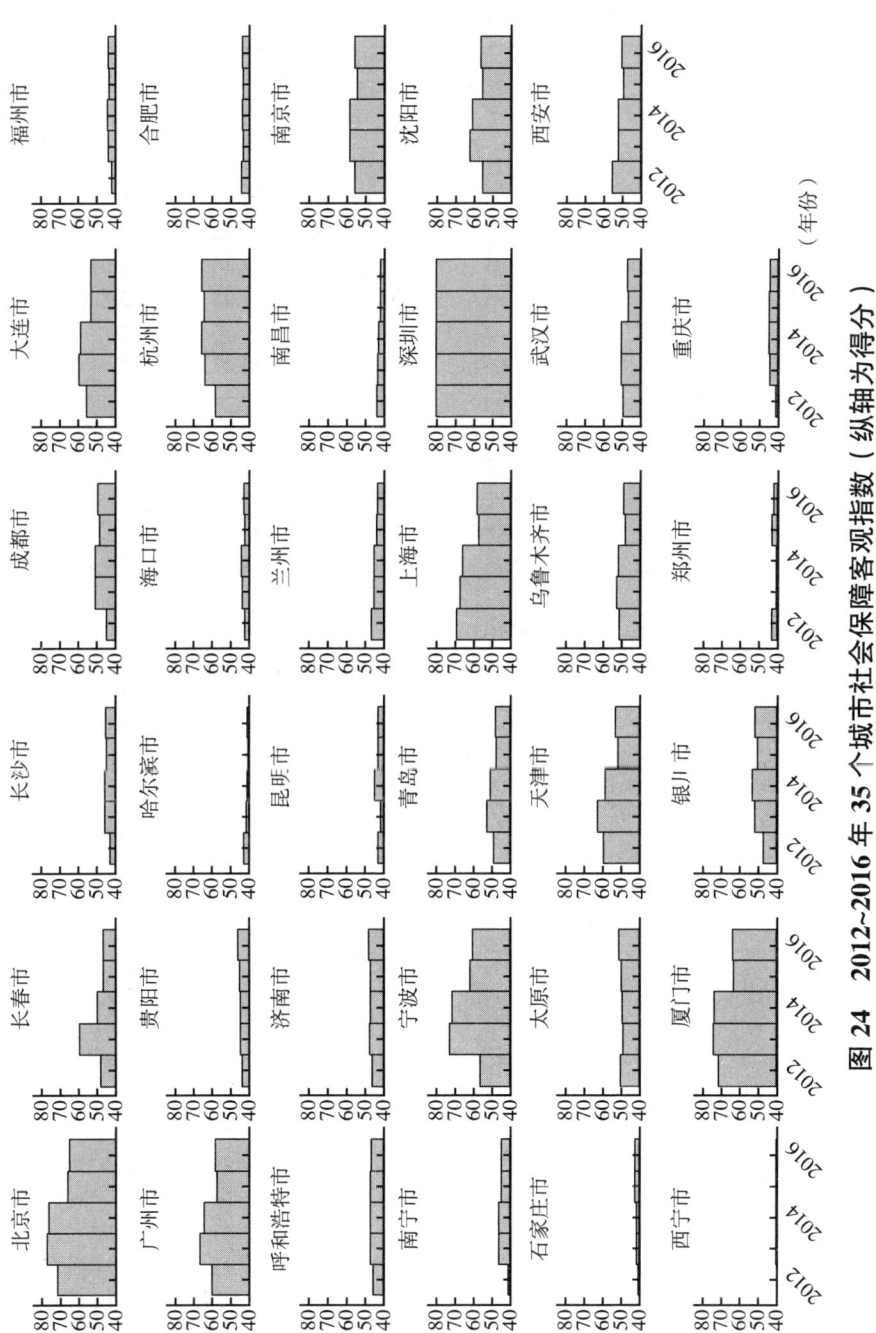

图24 2012~2016年35个城市社会保障客观指数（纵轴为得分）

077

表13　2012~2016年中国35个城市生活感受满意度指数

城市	2016年 得分	2016年 排序	2016年 上升位次	2015年 得分	2015年 排序	2014年 得分	2014年 排序	2013年 得分	2013年 排序	2012年 得分	2012年 排序
太原市	57.60	1	29	54.52	30	54.91	17	54.75	18	53.84	28
南昌市	57.54	2	16	55.66	18	54.61	22	53.84	26	53.86	27
青岛市	57.47	3	20	55.17	23	56.54	4	56.20	9	56.96	11
昆明市	57.47	4	−1	57.63	3	55.37	12	52.40	34	53.13	33
杭州市	57.44	5	−3	57.65	2	55.85	9	57.05	4	58.25	3
宁波市	57.17	6	8	55.79	14	55.49	11	56.56	8	55.34	19
石家庄市	57.03	7	10	55.66	17	56.43	5	54.43	19	57.11	9
南京市	56.90	8	−4	57.60	4	55.75	10	57.54	3	58.08	5
成都市	56.81	9	−3	56.78	6	58.01	2	56.06	15	57.86	6
沈阳市	56.65	10	6	55.72	16	56.08	7	54.21	21	55.33	20
南宁市	56.59	11	−1	56.11	10	53.09	33	52.96	32	54.86	23
广州市	56.52	12	14	54.76	26	54.36	25	52.99	31	53.67	30
天津市	56.32	13	12	54.95	25	55.13	16	56.75	5	56.63	13
大连市	56.30	14	−1	55.97	13	54.17	27	54.35	20	55.06	22
重庆市	56.26	15	−4	56.10	11	55.85	8	56.66	7	56.18	16
厦门市	56.15	16	−1	55.74	15	56.30	6	56.67	6	59.01	2
合肥市	56.04	17	−8	56.17	9	54.70	21	54.09	22	55.31	21
哈尔滨市	56.03	18	−13	57.04	5	54.83	18	53.95	23	53.62	31
西安市	55.95	19	1	55.48	20	54.51	24	55.96	16	55.46	18
武汉市	55.94	20	4	55.11	24	53.48	31	53.29	27	54.31	24
银川市	55.87	21	8	54.65	29	58.17	1	58.24	1	59.90	1
西宁市	55.78	22	11	54.20	33	57.52	3	57.76	2	57.41	7
长沙市	55.75	23	4	54.69	27	55.33	13	53.94	24	57.02	10
济南市	55.52	24	8	54.32	32	54.76	20	56.13	12	57.23	8
海口市	55.48	25	−13	56.09	12	54.14	28	55.63	17	55.75	17
呼和浩特市	55.41	26	−25	57.98	1	53.82	30	53.07	29	52.68	34
福州市	55.36	27	−6	55.36	21	54.82	19	56.2	10	56.72	12
兰州市	55.29	28	6	53.59	34	55.27	14	52.47	33	50.00	35
贵阳市	55.29	29	−7	55.28	22	53.12	32	53.18	28	53.81	29
长春市	55.20	30	−23	56.25	7	54.26	26	56.14	11	58.22	4
乌鲁木齐市	55.17	31	−3	54.69	28	55.14	15	50.85	35	56.25	15
上海市	55.09	32	−24	56.22	8	53.84	29	56.10	13	56.58	14
北京市	54.80	33	−2	54.35	31	52.39	35	53.87	25	53.30	32
深圳市	54.76	34	1	53.26	35	52.40	34	53.07	30	54.02	26
郑州市	54.65	35	−16	55.59	19	54.55	23	56.09	14	54.17	25
平均值	56.05			55.66		54.88		55.07		55.63	

2012~2016年，35个城市生活感受满意度指数平均值分别为55.63、55.07、54.88、55.66、56.05，连续两年呈现上升态势，总体变化很小，均处于满意区间，并且城市间的差距相对较小。

2016年城市生活感受满意度指数排名前10位的城市包括太原（1）、南昌（2）、青岛（3）、昆明（4）、杭州（5）、宁波（6）、石家庄（7）、南京（8）、成都（9）、沈阳（10），排名后10位的城市包括呼和浩特（26）、福州（27）、兰州（28）、贵阳（29）、长春（30）、乌鲁木齐（31）、上海（32）、北京（33）、深圳（34）、郑州（35）。其中，杭州和南京已经连续5年排在前10名城市的行列，深圳已经连续5年排在后10名的城市行列。与2015年相比，排在前10名的城市位次上升的是太原（+29）、青岛（+20）、南昌（+16）、石家庄（+10）、宁波（+8）、沈阳（+6），位次下降的是昆明（-1）、杭州（-3）、南京（-4）、成都（-3）；排在后10名的城市位次上升的只有兰州（+6）和深圳（+1），位次下降的城市依次是呼和浩特（-25）、上海（-24）、长春（-23）、郑州（-16）、贵阳（-7）、福州（-6）、乌鲁木齐（-3）、北京（-2）。在2012年到2016年的5年中，杭州和南京都排名前10位，深圳和贵阳都排名后10位，北京有4年处在排名后10位城市的行列中，另有1年处在排名后11位城市的行列中。排名前10位的城市中有5个东部城市、3个中部城市、2个西部城市；排名后10位的城市中有4个东部城市、2个中部城市和4个西部城市。

从指数的分布情况看，城市的生活感受满意度基本稳定，但差距是不断缩小的。如图25所示，2012~2016年35个城市生活感受满意度指数整体分布在50~60的区间内，但相对越来越集中。2012~2014年对生活感受满意度最高的城市都是银川（得分分别为59.90、58.24、58.17），相应年份满意度最低的城市分别是兰州（50.00）、乌鲁木齐（50.85）、北京（52.39）；2015~2016年

生活感受满意度指数得分最高的城市分别是呼和浩特（57.98）和太原（57.60），得分最低的分别是深圳（53.26）和郑州（54.65）。2012~2016年最高得分与最低得分的差值依次是9.90、7.39、5.78、4.72和2.95。差值变小，恰恰说明了不同城市间的生活感受满意度差距变小了。

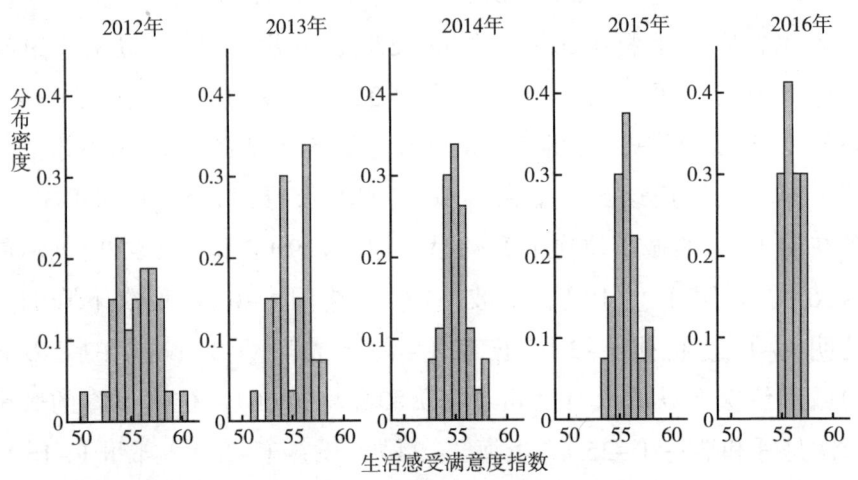

图25　2012~2016年35个城市生活感受满意度指数直方图

如图26所示，35个城市的生活感受满意度虽然变化趋势不尽相同，但得分都是相对较高的。从动态角度看，南昌在这一个指标上保持连续4年增长；济南、厦门和银川在这个指标上连续4年得分下降后，于2016年由降转升。

生活感受满意度指数是由生活节奏满意度指数和生活便利满意度指数两个细分指数构成的。

如表14所示，2012~2016年，35个城市生活节奏满意度指数平均值分别为42.87、42.97、41.90、43.12、44.07，总体变化较小。从得分情况来看，35个城市对生活节奏的满意度一直未越过满意与不满意的临界点（50），说明过快的生活节奏给人们带来了不小的生活压力。

中国 35 个城市生活质量的细分指数

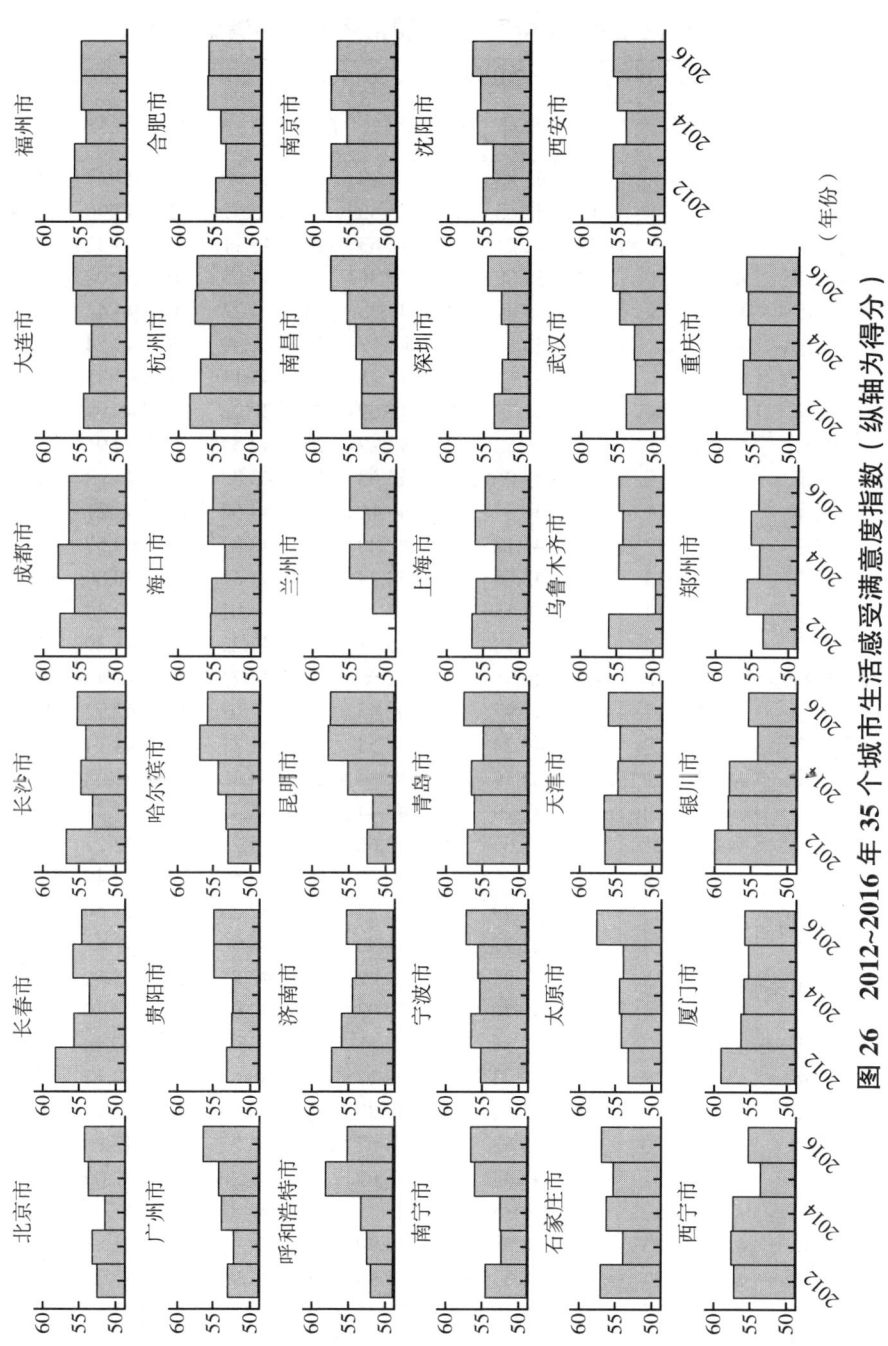

图 26　2012~2016 年 35 个城市生活感受满意度指数（纵轴为得分）

表 14　2012~2016 年中国 35 个城市生活节奏满意度指数

城市	2016 年			2015 年		2014 年		2013 年		2012 年	
	得分	排序	上升位次	得分	排序	得分	排序	得分	排序	得分	排序
昆明市	48.26	1	6	45.83	7	45.32	6	44.90	13	43.27	16
南昌市	47.21	2	17	42.63	19	43.66	9	43.62	22	43.90	13
太原市	47.04	3	27	41.21	30	42.63	22	45.11	9	43.32	15
银川市	46.69	4	28	39.88	32	47.36	1	45.05	10	50.00	1
南宁市	46.49	5	4	45.40	9	43.38	12	44.23	19	44.44	11
宁波市	46.13	6	8	43.61	14	41.17	30	42.99	25	40.54	28
石家庄市	46.00	7	9	43.52	16	45.48	4	43.11	23	44.35	12
青岛市	45.99	8	21	41.25	29	41.69	29	39.22	32	40.09	29
哈尔滨市	45.86	9	−6	46.88	3	43.29	14	42.54	28	39.96	30
杭州市	45.77	10	−9	47.06	1	43.63	10	45.83	8	44.93	8
南京市	45.57	11	−6	46.07	5	43.11	16	44.62	16	43.21	17
大连市	45.42	12	0	44.12	12	42.20	25	42.87	26	39.57	31
沈阳市	45.36	13	2	43.56	15	43.29	13	41.81	29	40.86	27
重庆市	45.17	14	−3	44.15	11	42.19	26	44.01	20	42.34	22
成都市	45.13	15	−5	45.10	10	45.98	2	47.22	4	48.39	2
呼和浩特市	45.08	16	−14	46.96	2	42.45	24	44.74	15	41.43	26
济南市	44.72	17	9	41.97	26	42.45	23	45.02	11	42.92	19
乌鲁木齐市	44.35	18	−1	43.23	17	44.54	7	41.81	30	44.74	10
西安市	44.17	19	−1	42.79	18	42.84	17	44.32	17	42.23	24
兰州市	44.13	20	5	41.99	25	45.44	5	46.47	5	41.48	25
合肥市	44.05	21	−13	45.67	8	42.66	20	44.27	18	42.27	23
武汉市	43.82	22	2	42.09	24	42.80	19	43.69	21	43.49	14
海口市	43.75	23	−17	45.89	6	43.24	15	47.25	3	47.50	3
福州市	43.60	24	−1	42.27	23	41.90	28	44.90	14	42.49	21
长沙市	43.48	25	2	41.85	27	44.02	8	42.81	27	45.61	6
天津市	43.42	26	2	41.70	28	39.93	31	44.95	12	42.70	20
贵阳市	43.41	27	−5	42.31	22	42.65	21	45.90	7	45.48	7
广州市	43.26	28	3	40.83	31	39.07	32	36.67	34	38.12	32
厦门市	43.06	29	−8	42.42	21	42.80	18	43.06	24	44.77	9
郑州市	41.73	30	−17	43.63	13	43.57	11	46.27	6	42.98	18
上海市	41.68	31	−11	42.43	20	35.69	33	38.20	33	37.05	34
长春市	41.38	32	−28	46.35	4	42.17	27	49.88	1	45.72	5
深圳市	41.14	33	0	38.84	33	34.90	35	34.93	35	35.81	35
西宁市	40.32	34	0	38.83	34	45.83	3	47.95	2	47.22	4
北京市	39.25	35	0	38.72	35	35.41	34	39.32	31	37.11	33
平均值	44.07			43.12		41.90		42.97		42.87	

2016年，生活节奏满意度指数排名前10位的城市是昆明（1）、南昌（2）、太原（3）、银川（4）、南宁（5）、宁波（6）、石家庄（7）、青岛（8）、哈尔滨（9）、杭州（10），其中包括4个东部城市、3个中部城市和3个西部城市；排名后10位的城市是天津（26）、贵阳（27）、广州（28）、厦门（29）、郑州（30）、上海（31）、长春（32）、深圳（33）、西宁（34）、北京（35），其中包括6个东部城市、2个中部城市和2个西部城市。排名前10位城市中位次上升的依次是：银川（+28）、太原（+27）、青岛（+21）、南昌（+17）、石家庄（+9）、宁波（+8）、昆明（+6）、南宁（+4），排名下降的城市是：杭州（-9）、哈尔滨（-6）；排名后10位的城市位次上升的是：广州（+3）和天津（+2），位次下降的城市依次是：长春（-28）、郑州（-17）、上海（-11）、厦门（-8）、贵阳（-5），位次没有变化的是深圳、西宁和北京。北京、深圳、广州连续5年排名后10位，而上海除在2015年排名第20位以外，均排名后10位，可见，一线城市的生活节奏普遍较快。

如图27所示，2012~2016年35个城市生活节奏满意度指数的分布区间变化不大，但集中度提高了。2012年生活节奏满意度指数分布于35~50的区间内，2016年则主要分布在40~45的区间内。2012~2016年35个城市中生活节奏满意度指数最高分值与最低分值的差额分别是14.19、14.95、12.46、8.34和9.01。生活节奏满意度指数的最高分值没有显著变化，但最低分值有所提高，这表明城市间的差距缩小了。

分城市看，2012~2015年生活节奏满意度指数连续3年保持上升的只有昆明和沈阳，连续下降的是成都。其余大多数城市的生活节奏满意度指数整体趋势是提高的，只是提高幅度很小（见图28）。将2012年与2016年35个城市的生活节奏满意度指数进行

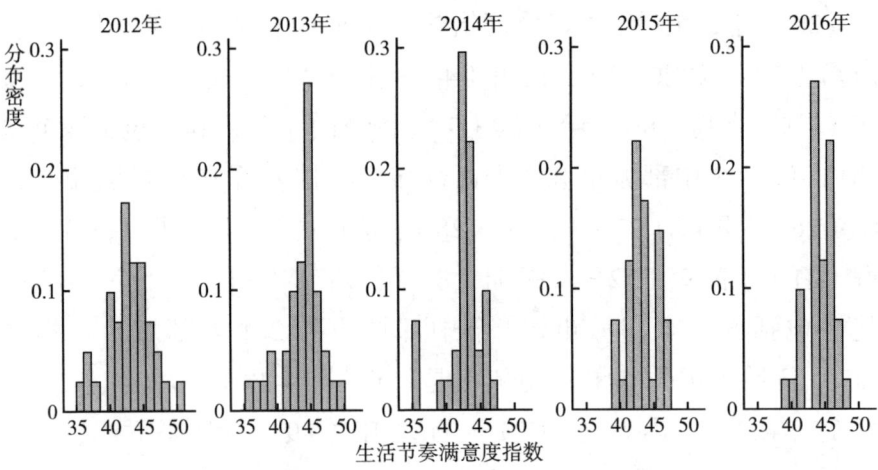

图 27 2012~2016 年 35 个城市生活节奏满意度指数直方图

比较，变化的平均值仅为 1.49。指数下降的城市有 10 个，余下 25 个城市都总体表现为上升，上升幅度最大是青岛和哈尔滨，均上升了 5.90，下降最多的是西宁，下降了 6.90。从地区间比较可见，西部地区的城市生活节奏满意度指数平均值最高，为 44.50；东部地区的城市生活节奏满意度指数平均值最低，为 42.26；中部地区的城市生活节奏满意度指数平均值为 43.88。可见，东部地区生活节奏最快，西部地区最慢，因此西部地区城市的生活节奏满意度最高，东部地区最低。

如表 15 所示，2016 年 35 个城市生活便利满意度指数平均值为 68.03，2012~2015 年，35 个城市生活便利满意度指数平均值分别为 68.39、67.18、67.66、68.20，与生活节奏满意度指数相比较高，说明中国 35 个城市的居民对生活便利普遍感到满意，且相对稳定。

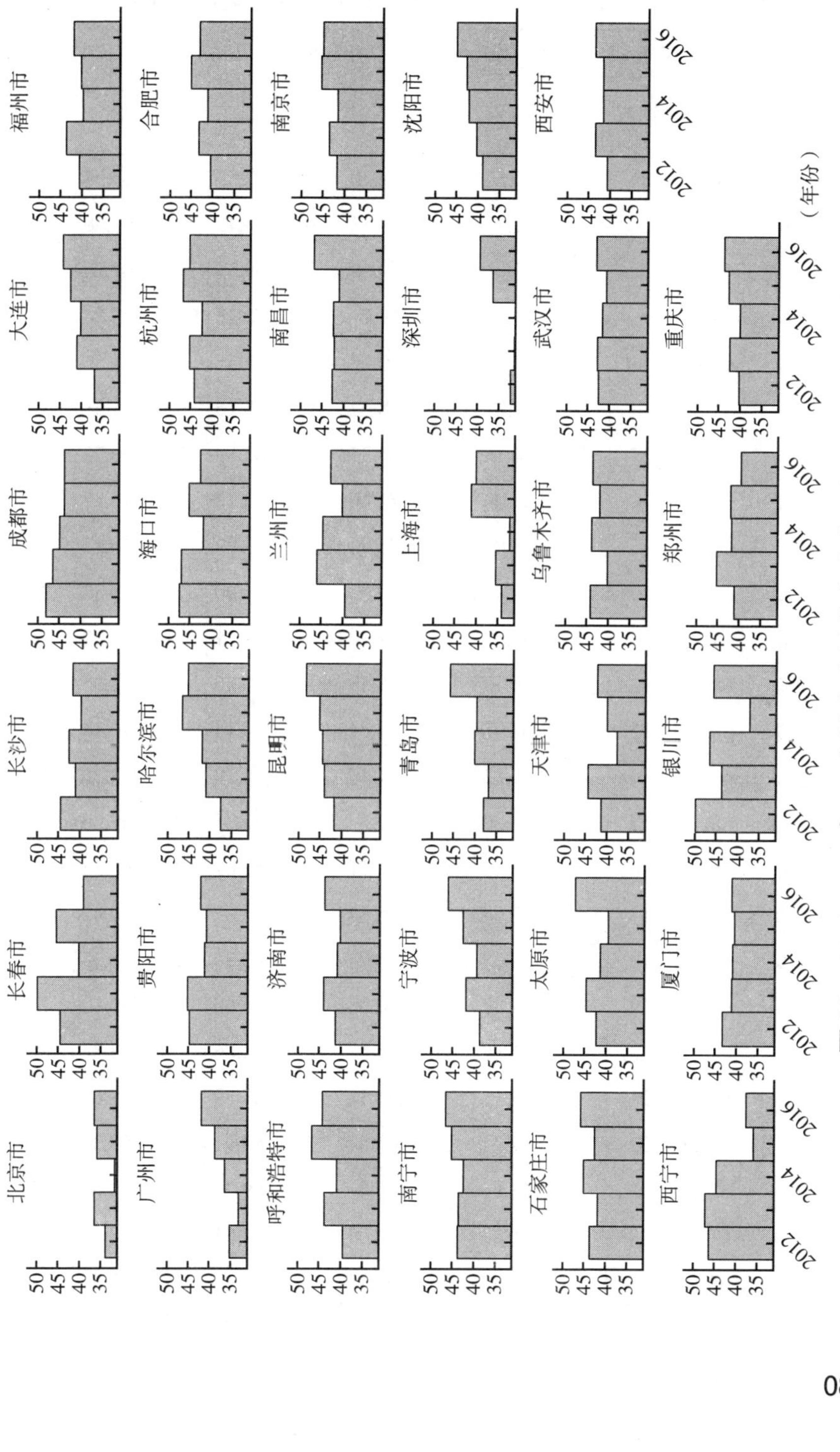

中国35个城市生活质量的细分指数

图 28 2012~2016 年 35 个城市生活节奏满意度指数（纵轴为得分）

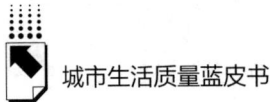

表15 2012~2016年中国35个城市生活便利满意度指数

城市	2016年			2015年		2014年		2013年		2012年	
	得分	排序	上升位次	得分	排序	得分	排序	得分	排序	得分	排序
西宁市	71.24	1	2	69.56	3	69.20	11	67.57	14	67.59	23
北京市	70.35	2	0	69.98	2	69.38	10	68.42	11	69.50	17
广州市	69.78	3	8	68.68	11	69.65	8	69.31	9	69.23	18
厦门市	69.24	4	4	69.05	8	69.79	7	70.28	6	73.26	3
天津市	69.21	5	11	68.21	16	70.33	3	68.55	10	70.56	10
杭州市	69.11	6	8	68.25	14	68.07	15	68.26	12	71.58	6
长春市	69.01	7	26	66.16	33	66.35	23	62.39	29	70.72	9
青岛市	68.95	8	−1	69.09	7	71.40	2	73.18	2	73.82	2
上海市	68.50	9	−8	70.02	1	71.98	1	73.99	1	76.12	1
成都市	68.49	10	2	68.46	12	70.03	4	64.90	23	67.32	24
深圳市	68.38	11	14	67.68	25	69.89	5	71.21	4	72.22	5
南京市	68.23	12	−6	69.13	6	68.39	14	70.46	5	72.95	4
宁波市	68.20	13	7	67.97	20	69.81	6	70.14	7	70.14	12
太原市	68.17	14	8	67.83	22	67.19	18	64.39	24	64.36	29
石家庄市	68.07	15	9	67.80	24	67.37	17	65.75	20	69.86	14
武汉市	68.06	16	2	68.14	18	64.17	33	62.89	28	65.13	28
长沙市	68.03	17	10	67.54	27	66.64	21	65.07	22	68.42	20
合肥市	68.03	18	12	66.68	30	66.74	20	63.91	27	68.35	21
沈阳市	67.93	19	2	67.87	21	68.86	13	66.60	17	69.80	15
南昌市	67.87	20	−10	68.69	10	65.57	27	64.06	25	63.82	32
西安市	67.73	21	−4	68.18	17	66.18	24	67.59	13	68.69	19
郑州市	67.57	22	4	67.54	26	65.54	28	65.91	18	65.36	26
重庆市	67.36	23	−4	68.06	19	69.51	9	69.31	8	70.01	13
海口市	67.21	24	8	66.29	32	65.04	32	64.01	26	64.00	30
大连市	67.18	25	−2	67.83	23	66.13	25	65.83	19	70.55	11

续表

城市	2016年			2015年		2014年		2013年		2012年	
	得分	排序	上升位次	得分	排序	得分	排序	得分	排序	得分	排序
贵阳市	67.16	26	−11	68.24	15	63.58	34	60.45	32	62.14	34
福州市	67.12	27	−14	68.44	13	67.74	16	67.49	15	70.95	8
南宁市	66.69	28	1	66.82	29	62.81	35	61.69	30	65.28	27
昆明市	66.67	29	−25	69.44	4	65.41	29	59.90	33	62.98	33
兰州市	66.45	30	5	65.18	35	65.09	31	58.48	35	58.52	35
济南市	66.32	31	0	66.67	31	67.07	19	67.25	16	71.54	7
哈尔滨市	66.21	32	−4	67.20	28	66.37	22	65.36	21	67.28	25
乌鲁木齐市	65.99	33	1	66.16	34	65.74	26	59.89	34	67.76	22
呼和浩特市	65.73	34	−25	68.99	9	65.19	30	61.40	31	63.93	31
银川市	65.06	35	−30	69.42	5	68.99	12	71.43	3	69.79	16
平均值	68.03			68.20		67.66		67.18		68.39	

2016年，城市生活便利满意度指数满意度排名前10位的城市是：西宁（1）、北京（2）、广州（3）、厦门（4）、天津（5）、杭州（6）、长春（7）、青岛（8）、上海（9）、成都（10），其中包括7个东部城市、1个中部城市和2个西部城市；排名后10位的城市是：贵阳（26）、福州（27）、南宁（28）、昆明（29）、兰州（30）、济南（31）、哈尔滨（32）、乌鲁木齐（33）、呼和浩特（34）、银川（35），其中包括2个东部城市、1个中部城市和7个西部城市。总体上看，生活便利化程度高的城市主要分布在东部地区，而生活便利化程度低的城市主要分布在西部地区。与2015年相比，2016年排名前10位的城市中有7个的位次有不同程度的上升，分别是长春（26）、天津（11）、杭州（8）、广州（8）、厦门（4）、西宁（2）、成都（2），有两个城市位次下降，分别是青岛（−1）、上海（−8），北京的位次没有发生变化。排名后10位的城市中位

次上升的有兰州（+5）、南宁（+1）和乌鲁木齐（+1），济南的位次没有变化，位次下降的依次是银川（-30）、昆明（-25）、呼和浩特（-25）、福州（-14）、贵阳（-11）和哈尔滨（-4）。厦门、青岛、上海连续5年均排在前10位，而兰州和南宁是连续5年排在后10位的城市。

如图29所示，2012~2016年35个城市的生活便利满意度指数分布由55~75的区间收窄到60~75的区间内，可见最高值变化不大，但最低值提高了。这说明调查的35个城市间的生活便利满意度差距缩小了。

分城市看，2012~2016年对生活便利满意度连续提高的城市有海口、西宁、太原，而济南、宁波、青岛、上海、深圳、厦门则呈现连续的小幅下降趋势（见图30）。

（二）生活感受客观指数

根据QLICC体系，生活感受客观指数是通过计算每个城市的3个一级指标即生活便利指数、生态环境指数、收入差距感受指数及其所属的6个二级指标的数值得到的。2016年35个城市生活感受客观指数的计算结果如表16所示。

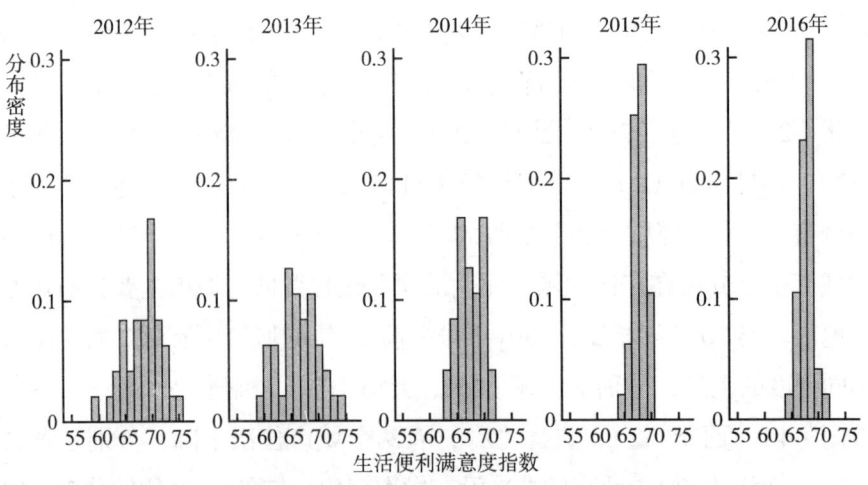

图29　2012~2016年35个城市生活便利满意度指数直方图

中国35个城市生活质量的细分指数

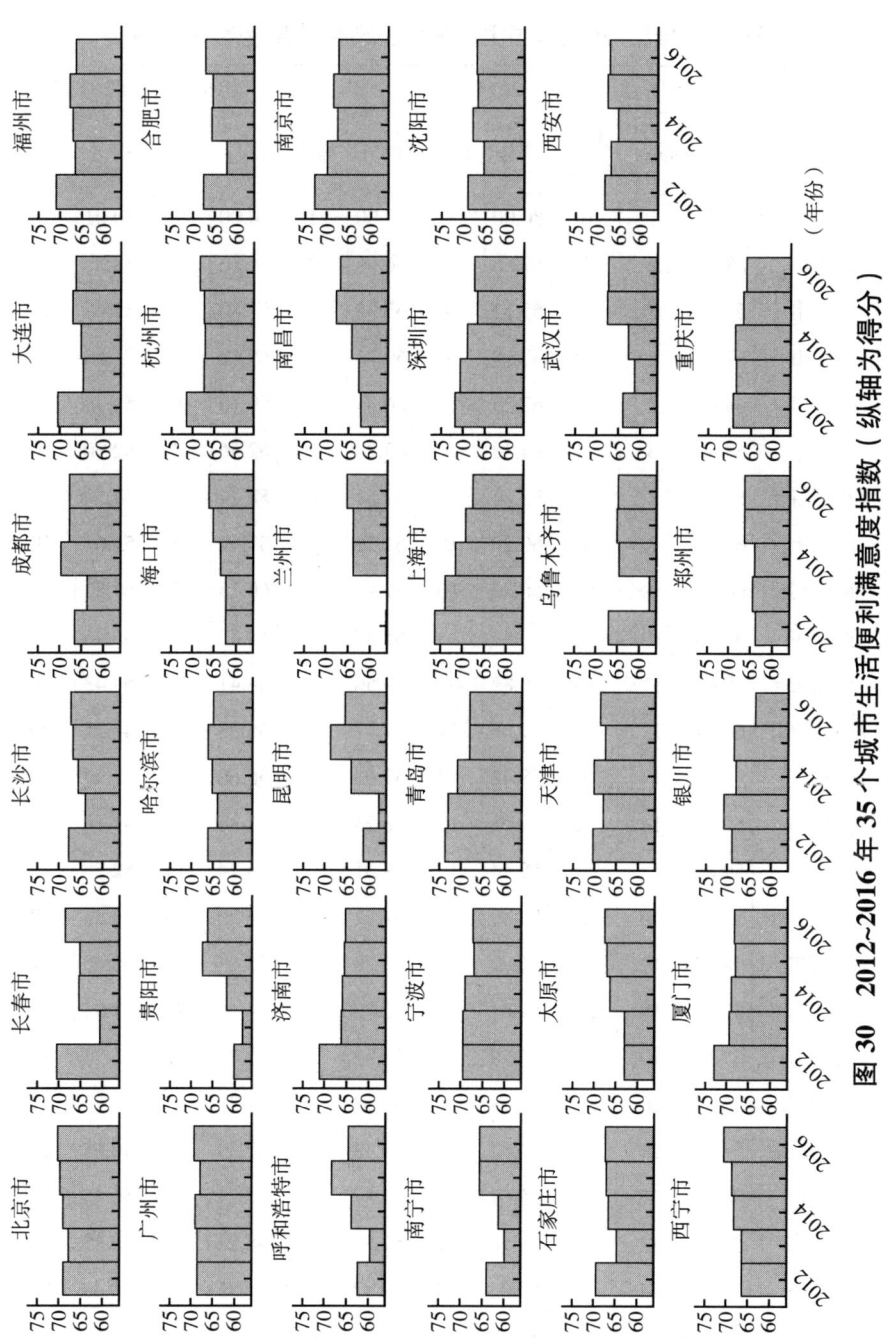

图30 2012~2016年35个城市生活便利满意度指数(纵轴为得分)

表16 2012~2016年中国35个城市生活感受客观指数

城市	2016年			2015年		2014年		2013年		2012年	
	得分	排序	上升位次	得分	排序	得分	排序	得分	排序	得分	排序
北京市	80.00	1	0	80.00	1	80.00	1	80.00	1	80.01	1
广州市	68.40	2	1	67.86	3	66.66	3	64.16	3	58.88	7
海口市	67.63	3	1	65.12	4	65.35	4	57.80	9	55.45	12
深圳市	67.30	4	−2	67.95	2	69.71	2	65.12	2	71.86	2
南京市	64.92	5	2	62.35	7	60.84	8	59.70	6	58.24	8
沈阳市	64.32	6	−1	64.32	5	63.28	5	62.56	4	62.90	5
呼和浩特市	63.16	7	−1	62.84	6	62.51	6	58.74	7	54.50	13
昆明市	61.27	8	1	60.70	9	61.54	7	57.57	10	55.61	10
武汉市	60.95	9	1	60.39	10	57.93	13	60.15	5	64.52	3
西安市	60.78	10	3	58.43	13	55.87	18	54.32	17	55.46	11
杭州市	60.62	11	−3	60.82	8	59.56	9	58.41	8	64.43	4
哈尔滨市	60.34	12	−1	59.39	11	57.77	14	56.98	12	48.25	20
青岛市	59.85	13	1	58.42	14	57.63	15	55.68	13	48.97	19
太原市	59.64	14	−2	59.08	12	58.23	11	57.34	11	48.10	21
银川市	59.08	15	0	58.14	15	58.31	10	54.74	14	52.58	14
乌鲁木齐市	58.76	16	2	56.39	18	54.22	20	54.20	18	46.58	23
厦门市	58.33	17	0	56.77	17	58.20	12	52.07	20	58.95	6
合肥市	57.40	18	3	54.81	21	53.30	21	54.46	16	42.91	31
长春市	57.16	19	0	56.28	19	55.92	17	53.70	19	51.25	16
兰州市	56.85	20	−4	56.78	16	56.98	16	51.76	21	50.77	17
石家庄市	55.81	21	2	51.87	23	50.43	26	51.39	22	46.63	22
上海市	54.99	22	−2	55.67	20	55.57	19	54.71	15	56.45	9
宁波市	54.65	23	−1	53.10	22	52.51	22	48.24	23	46.35	24
南昌市	53.99	24	1	50.93	25	49.82	28	44.81	30	43.40	30
西宁市	53.80	25	−1	51.52	24	50.56	25	45.51	28	45.60	27

续表

城市	2016年 得分	2016年 排序	上升位次	2015年 得分	2015年 排序	2014年 得分	2014年 排序	2013年 得分	2013年 排序	2012年 得分	2012年 排序
贵阳市	53.08	26	1	50.34	27	49.98	27	44.89	29	41.91	32
福州市	52.02	27	−1	50.76	26	52.46	23	45.93	27	51.84	15
大连市	51.33	28	0	50.29	28	50.90	24	47.37	24	49.07	18
南宁市	50.76	29	1	48.05	30	47.77	29	43.97	32	44.47	29
天津市	50.04	30	1	47.91	31	47.34	30	47.28	25	46.20	25
长沙市	49.94	31	1	47.48	32	47.20	32	46.47	26	45.23	28
成都市	49.79	32	−3	48.35	29	45.34	34	43.35	33	41.30	34
重庆市	49.19	33	1	46.61	34	46.34	33	43.18	34	40.02	35
济南市	47.87	34	−1	47.07	33	47.26	31	44.71	31	45.72	26
郑州市	40.00	35	0	40.00	35	40.00	35	40.00	35	41.65	33
平均值	57.54			56.17		55.57		53.67		51.89	

2016年35个城市生活感受客观指数的均值为57.54，处于满意区间。整体来看，35个城市间最高分值和最低分值悬殊；从二级指标来看，城市间交通提供能力、万人影剧院数、医疗提供能力、人均绿地面积、空气质量、基尼系数等方面存在较大差距。

2012~2016年，35个城市生活感受客观指数平均值总体呈现小幅上升的态势。分城市看，大多数城市相比上年都有所增长，其中有15个城市的得分连续5年增长，广州市、贵阳市、南昌市、乌鲁木齐市和宁波市的这一变化趋势尤为突出。

分区域来看，北京、深圳、广州、沈阳、南京、昆明6个城市已经连续5年保持在前10名城市的行列，杭州、海口、呼和浩特和武汉4个城市有4年保持在前10名城市的行列。北京已经连续5年排名第1，并且得分均在80或80以上。贵阳、成都、南宁、长沙、济

南、重庆、郑州7个城市已经连续5年排名后10位城市的行列，其中郑州已经连续4年垫底，即排在第35位。总体来讲，就这一指标而言，东、中、西部发展较为均衡。

如图31所示，2012~2016年35个城市生活感受客观指数分布基本保持稳定，分布在40~80的区间内，且相对比较分散。分城市看，35个城市的生活感受客观指数的差异较大。连续5年均排名第1位的北京和排名最后的郑州生活感受客观指数基本没有变化，其余的城市，除了杭州、上海、深圳、武汉、厦门外，都保持了一定程度的上升态势（见图32）。

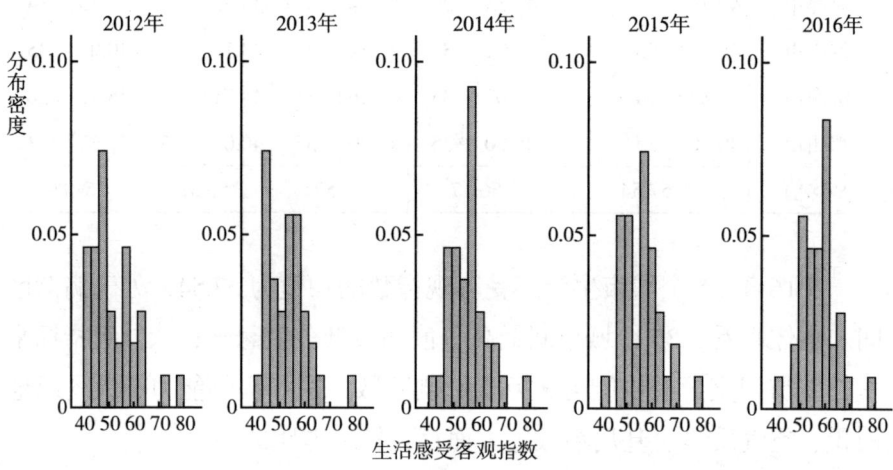

图31　2012~2016年35个城市生活感受客观指数直方图

从以上调查结果可以看出，中国经济发展步入新常态以来，尽管城市居民对生活质量的满意度在稳定上升，生活质量的客观指数却在2015年由升转降之后继续下跌。究其原因，这主要是由城市生活水平客观指数大幅下滑所致。具体而言，在经济增速下滑的背景下，我国政府以"调整经济发展方式、共享经济与社会发展成果"为基本政策理念，出台了一系列调整政策。35个城市生活质量主观满意度继续

中国35个城市生活质量的细分指数

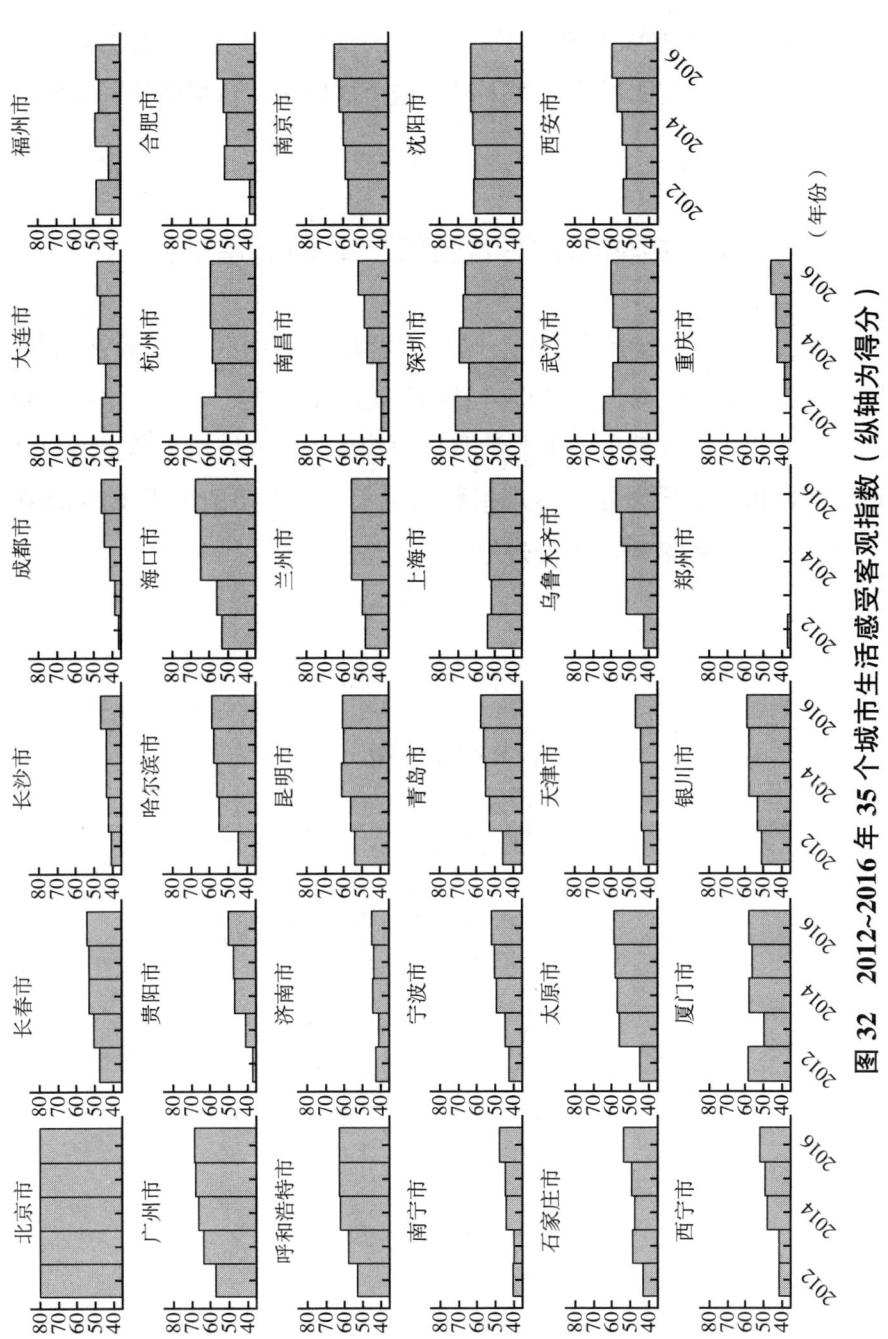

图32 2012~2016年35个城市生活感受客观指数（纵轴为得分）

提升，说明这些政策得到了广大群众的支持。但生活质量客观指数连续两年下降，说明经济增速下滑对城市居民生活造成的实际影响不容忽视。

六 中国城市生活质量一级指标雷达图

图33给出了2016年35个城市主客观指数的一级指标雷达图。根据雷达图，可以对比各城市自身和其他城市的主、客观一级指标情况。从雷达图可以看出一个非常明显的特征，即大城市生活成本仍然是拉低城市生活质量主、客观指数的一个非常重要的因素（图33按35个城市客观指数排名顺序排列）。

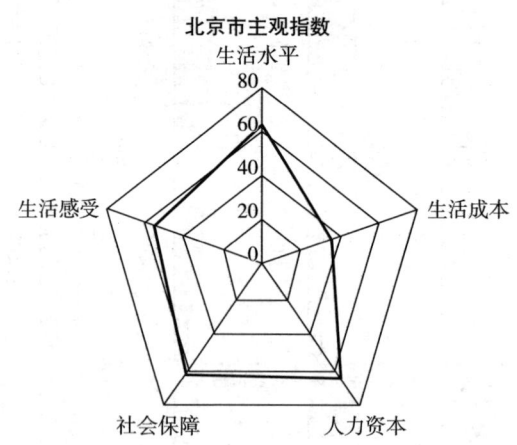

中国 35 个城市生活质量的细分指数

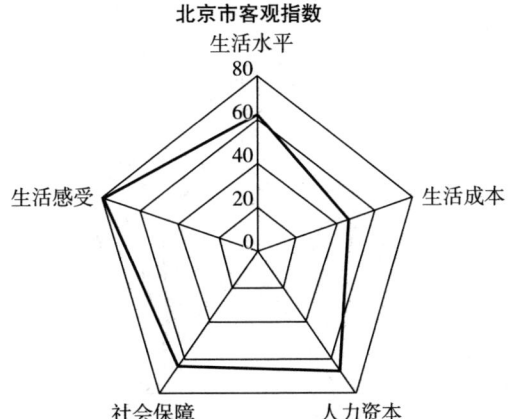

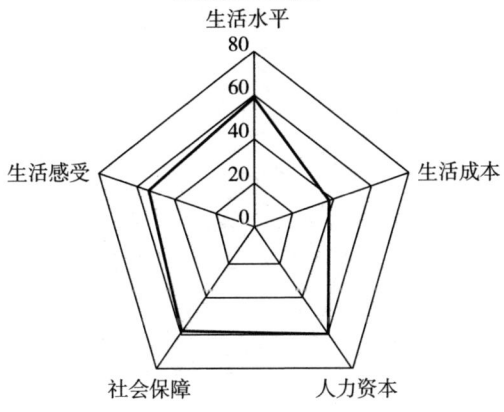

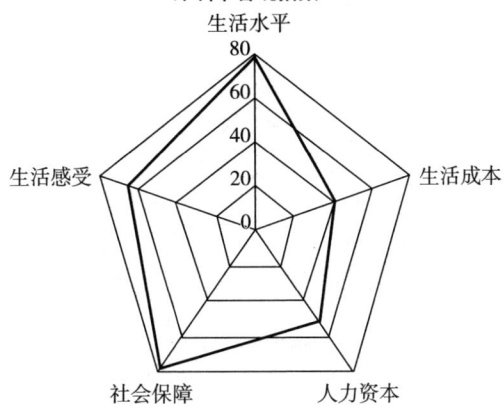

095

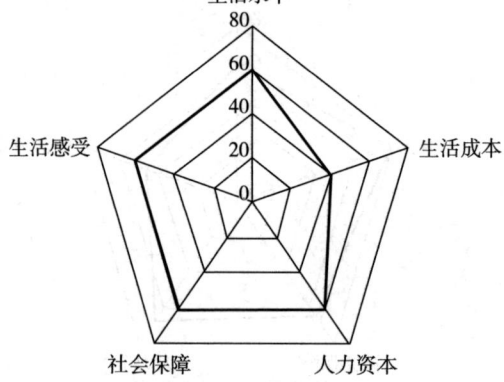

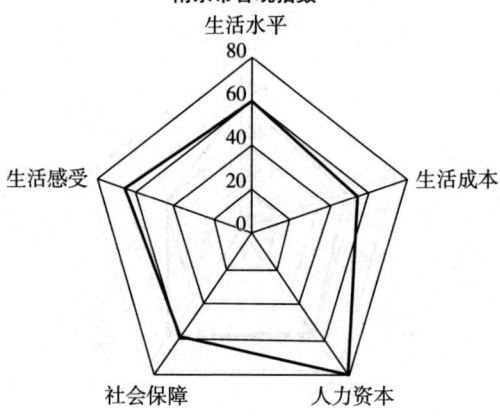

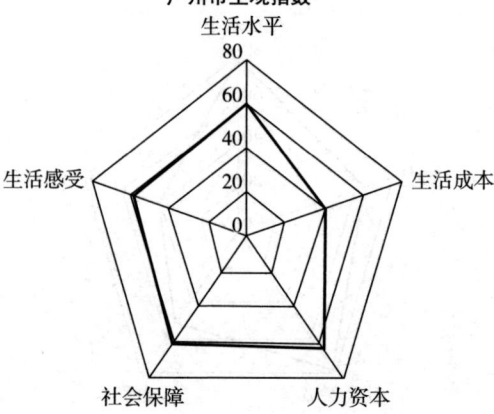

中国35个城市生活质量的细分指数

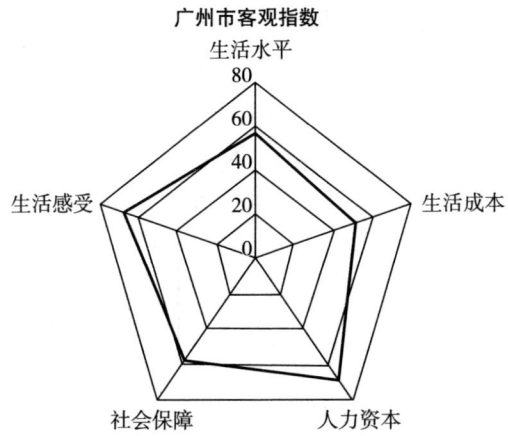

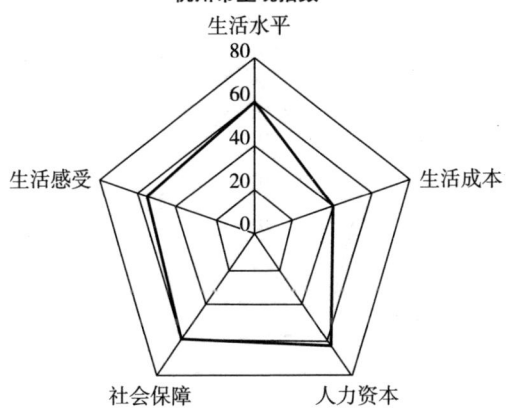

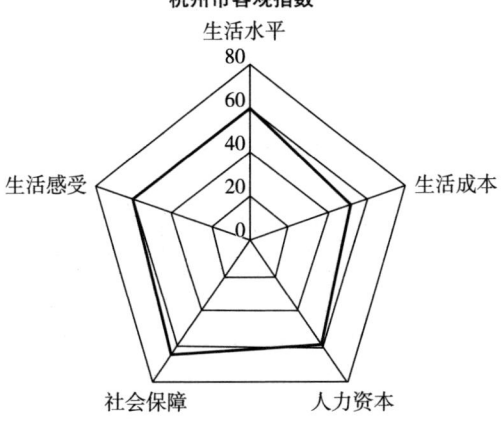

097

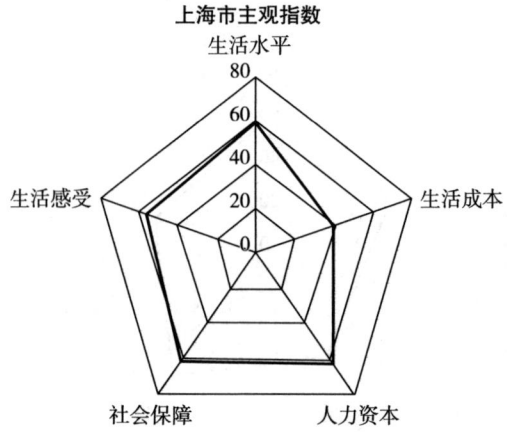

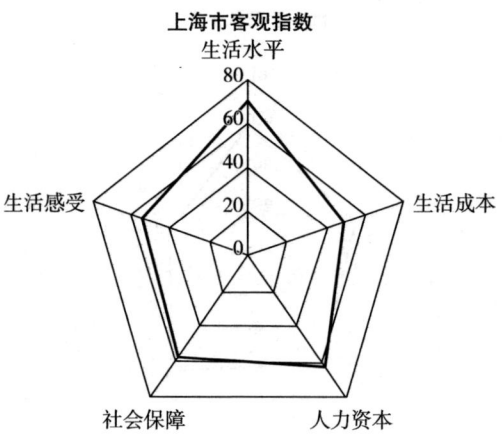

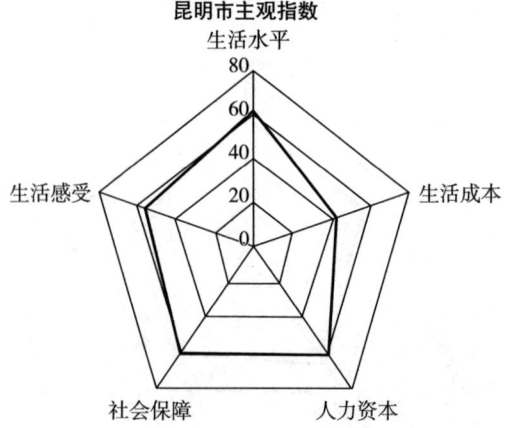

中国35个城市生活质量的细分指数

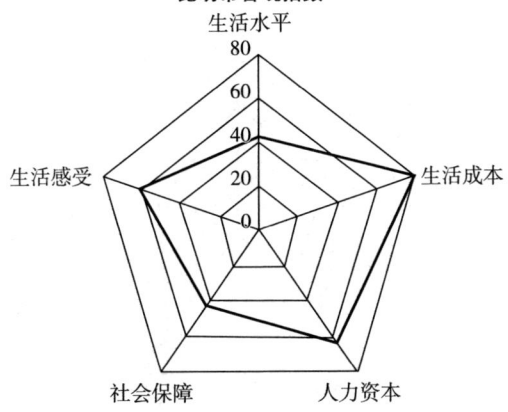

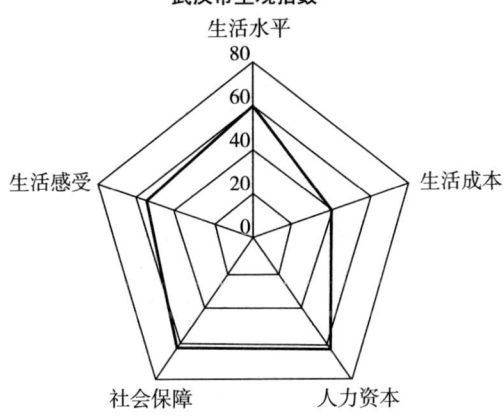

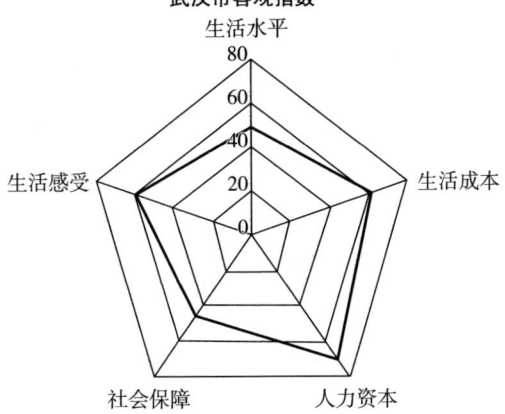

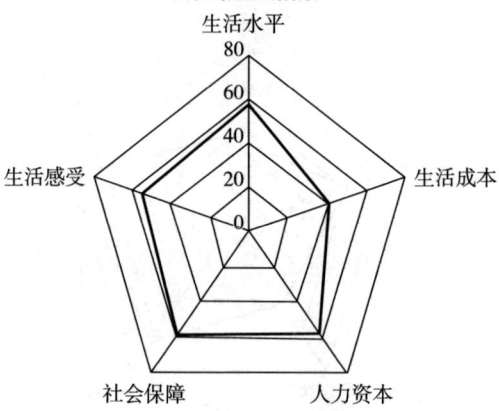

西安市主观指数

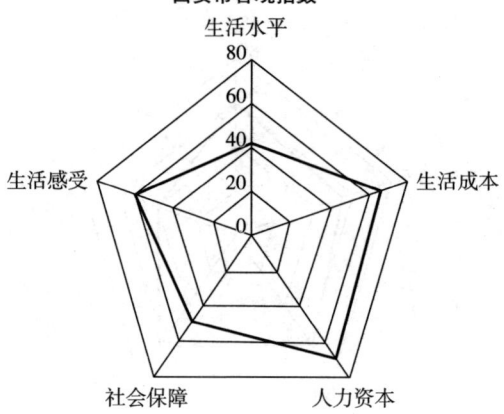

西安市客观指数

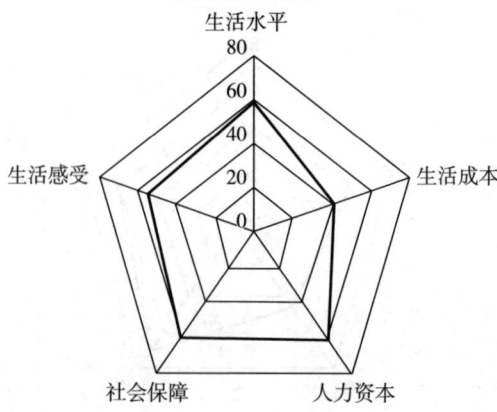

贵阳市主观指数

中国35个城市生活质量的细分指数

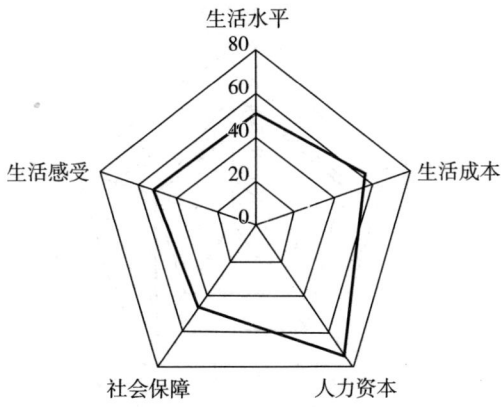

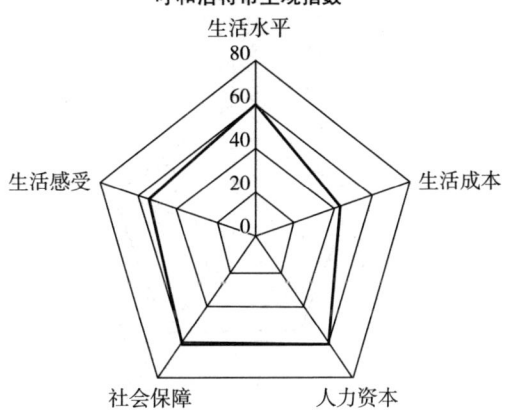

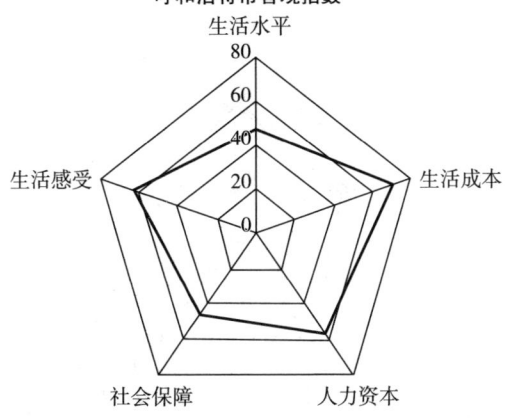

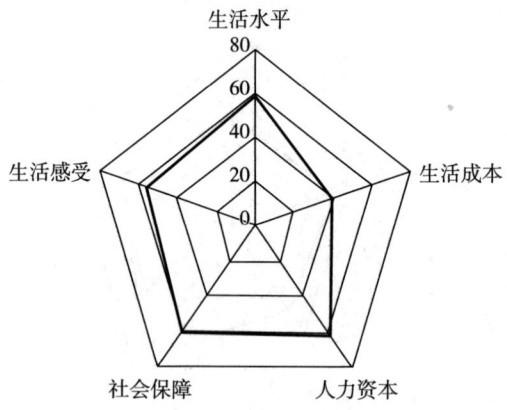

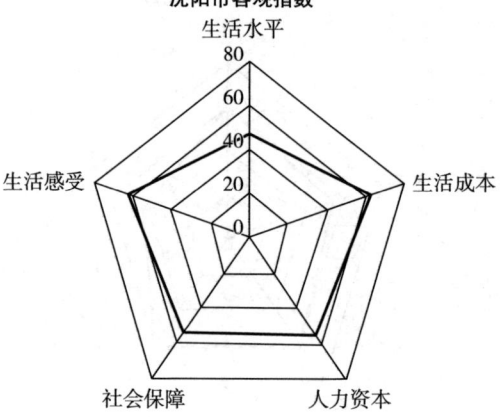

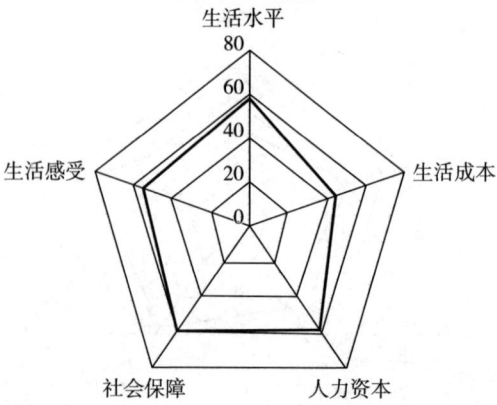

中国35个城市生活质量的细分指数

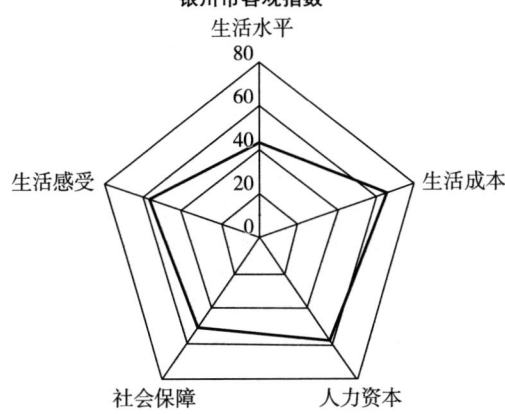

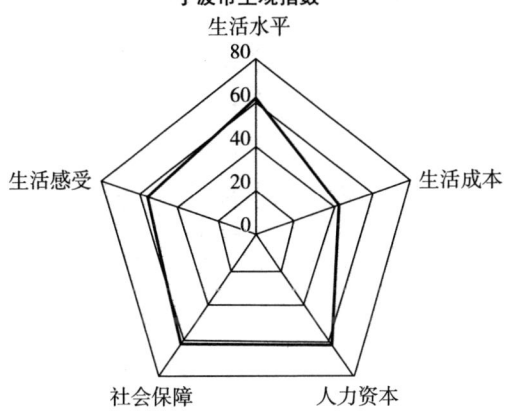

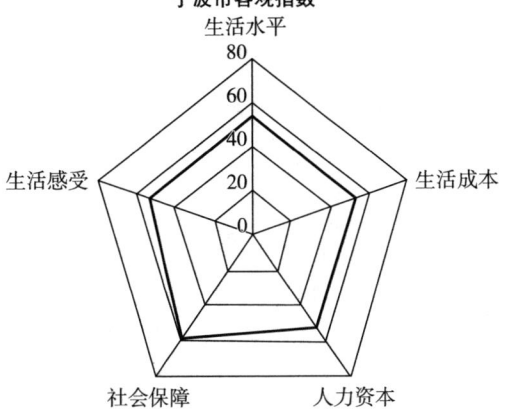

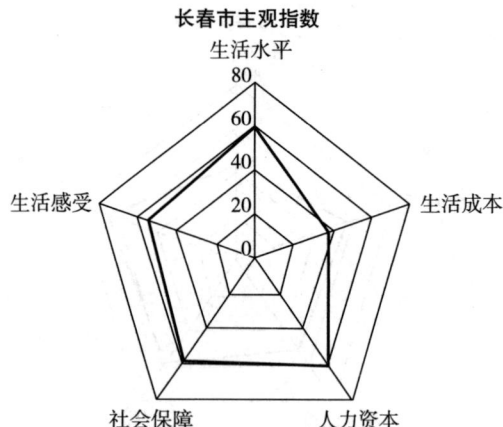

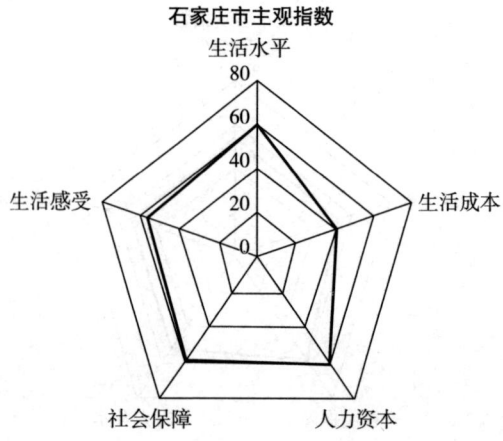

中国 35 个城市生活质量的细分指数

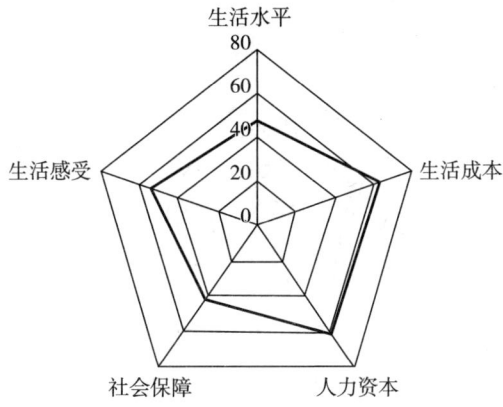

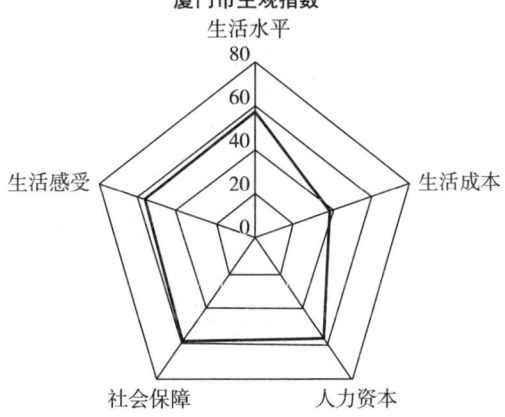

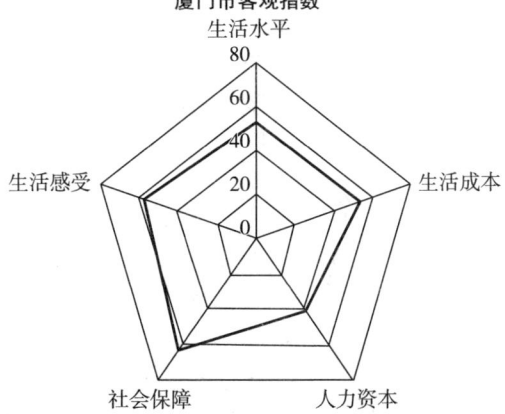

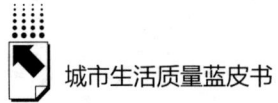

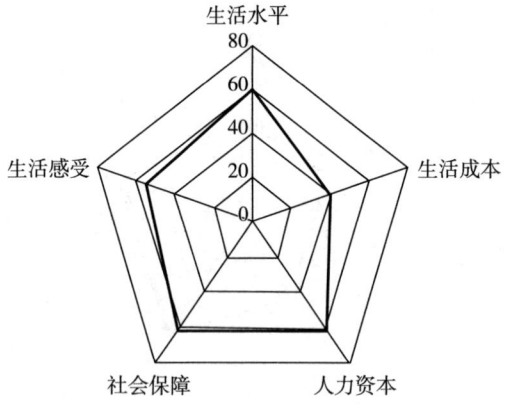

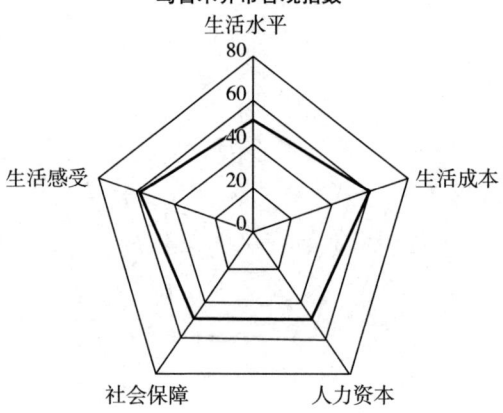

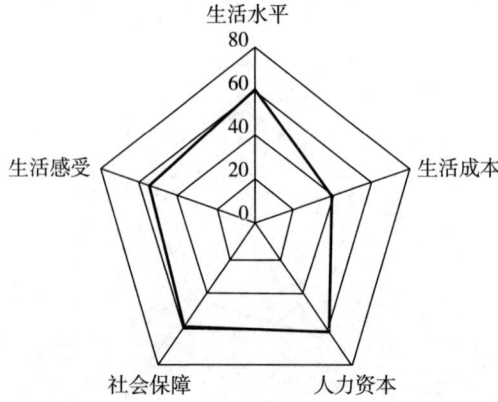

中国 35 个城市生活质量的细分指数

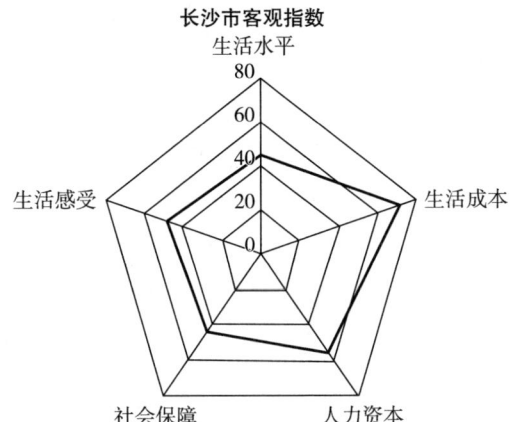

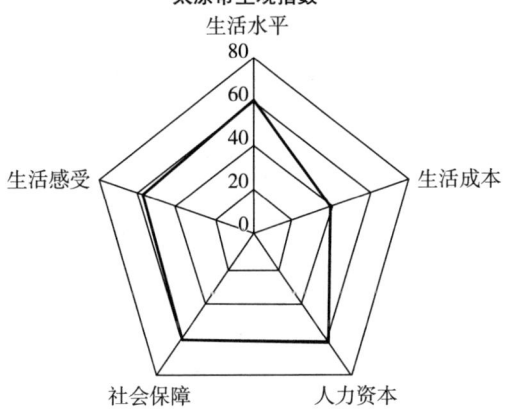

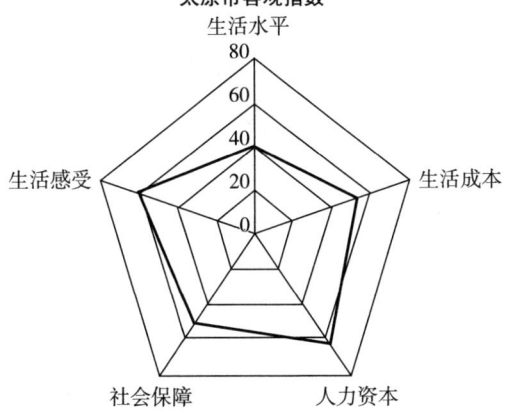

107

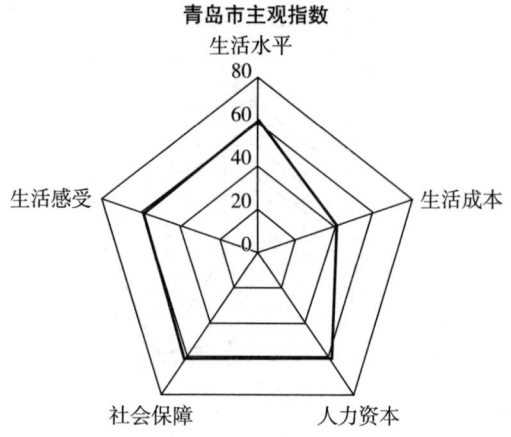

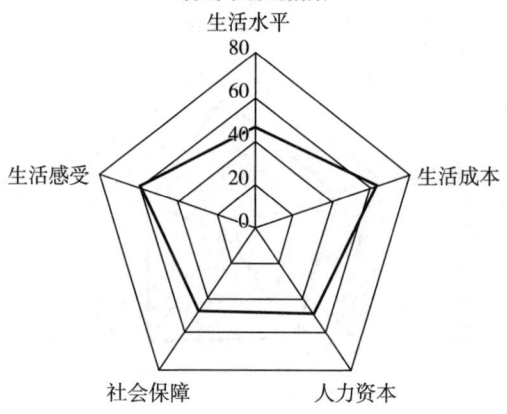

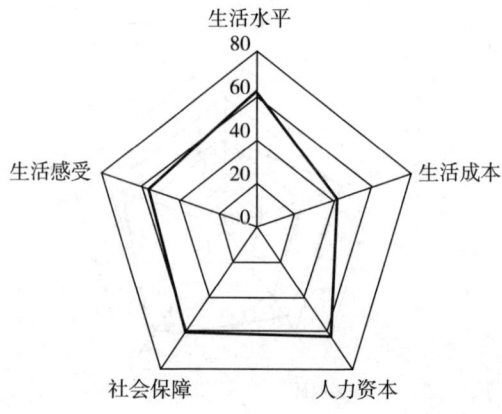

中国 35 个城市生活质量的细分指数

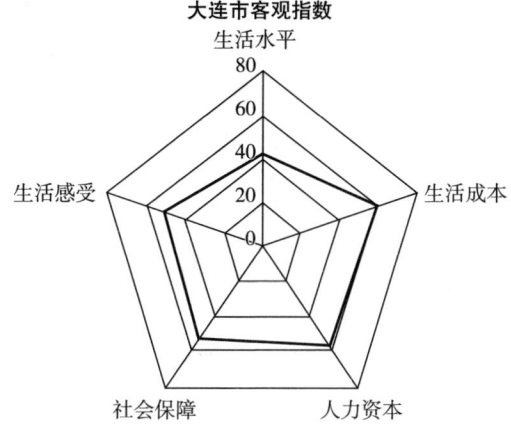

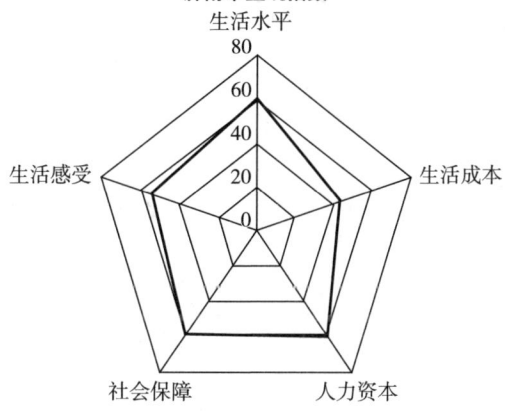

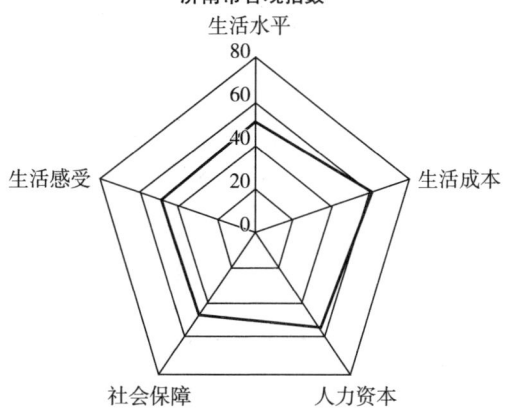

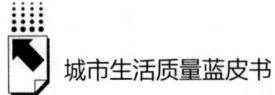

成都市主观指数

成都市客观指数

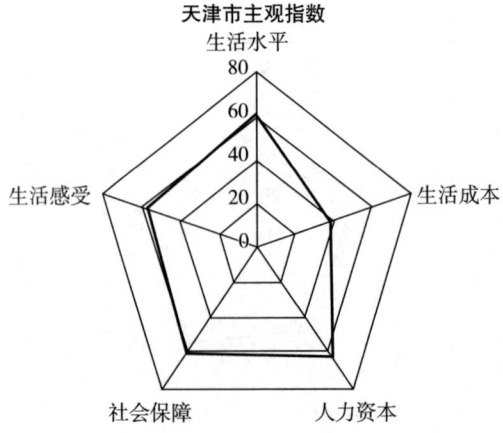

天津市主观指数

中国 35 个城市生活质量的细分指数

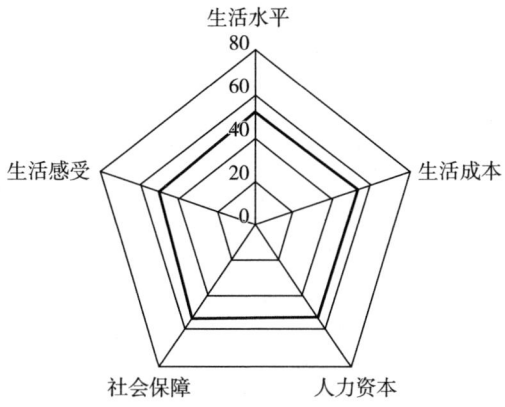

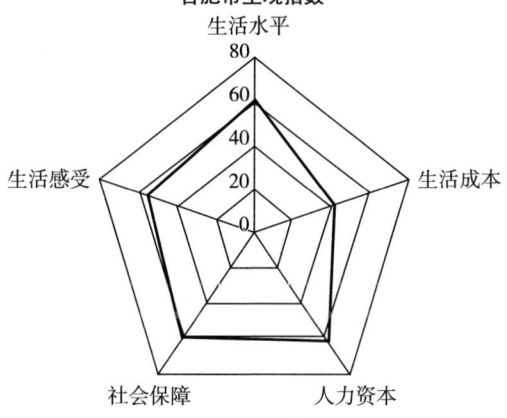

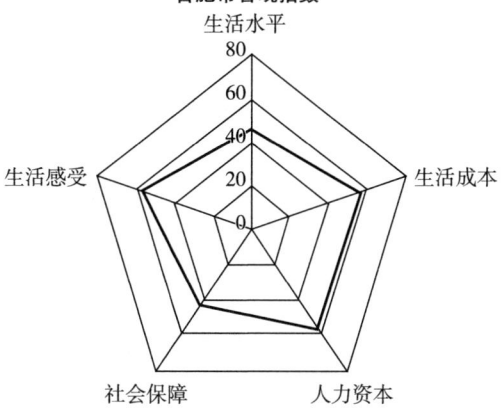

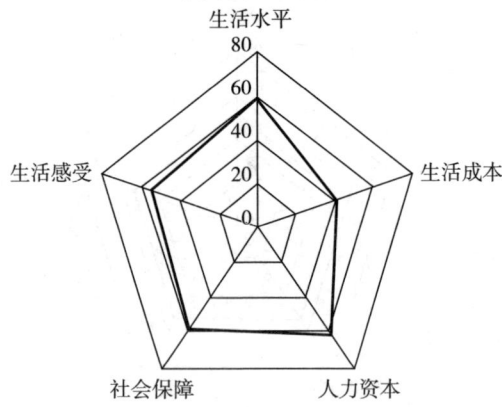

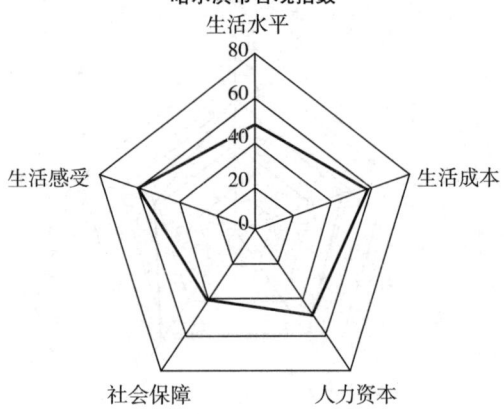

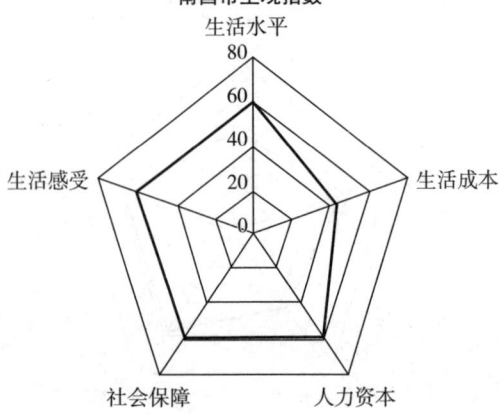

中国35个城市生活质量的细分指数

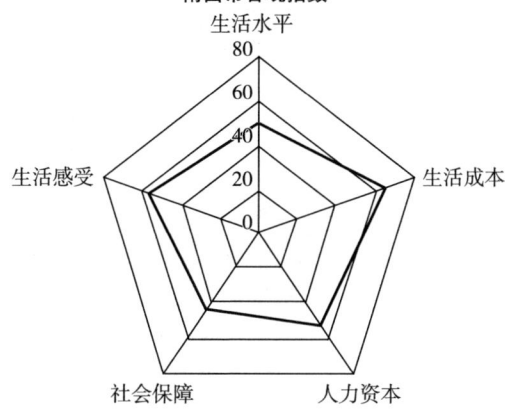

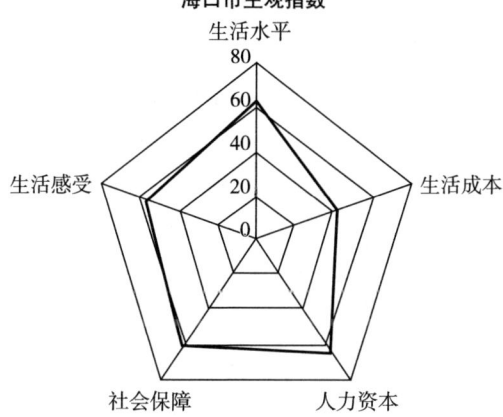

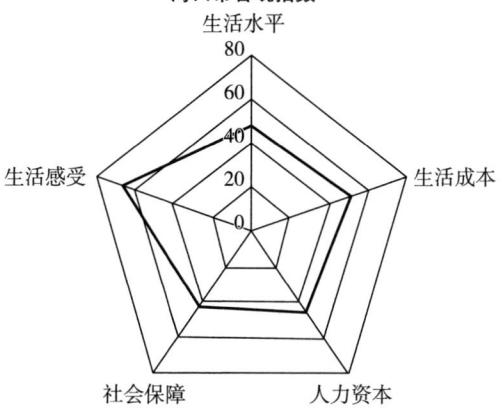

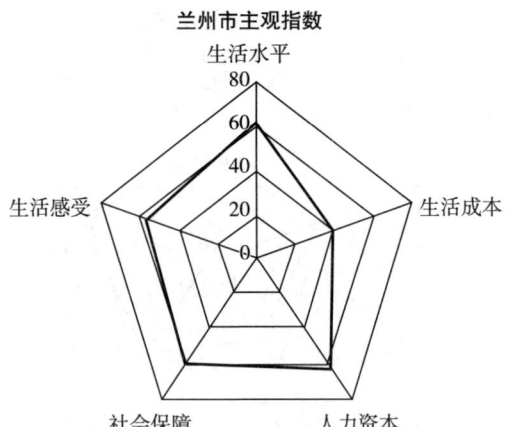

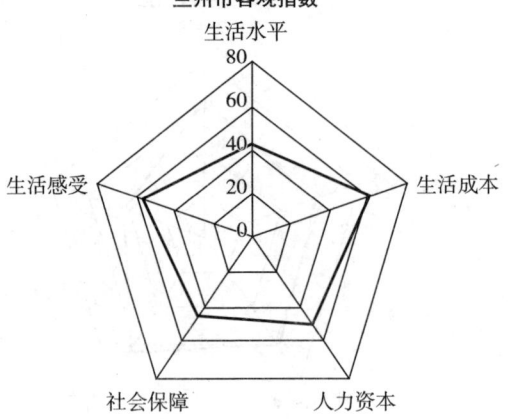

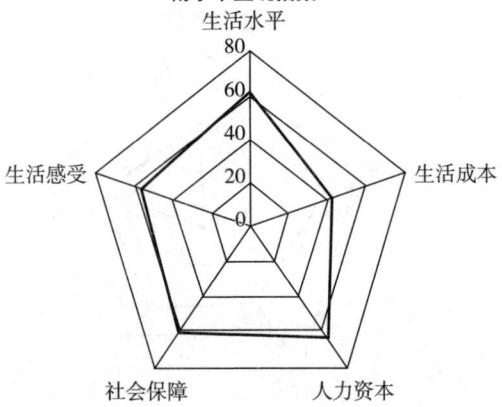

中国 35 个城市生活质量的细分指数

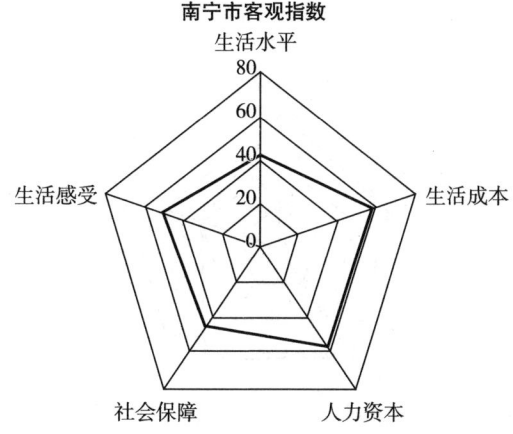

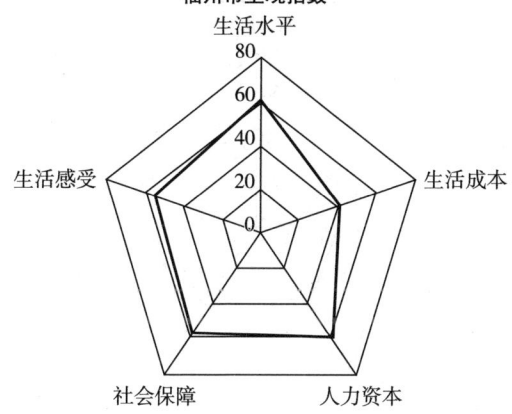

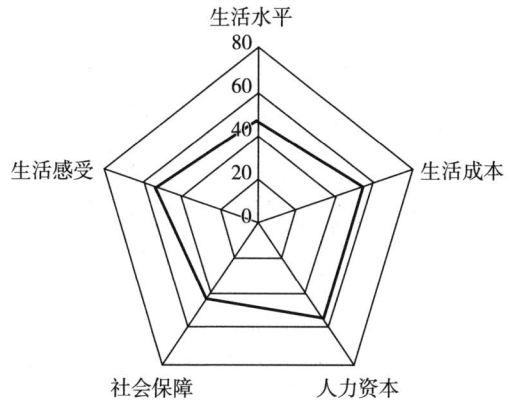

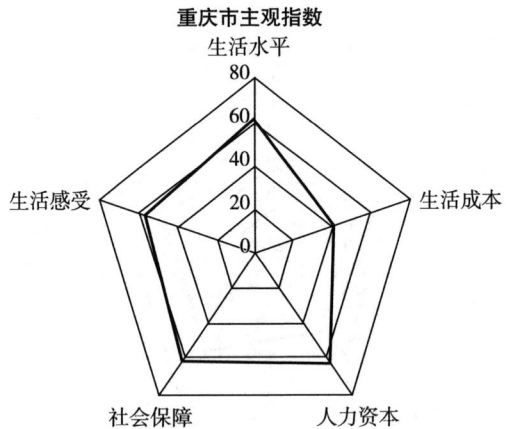

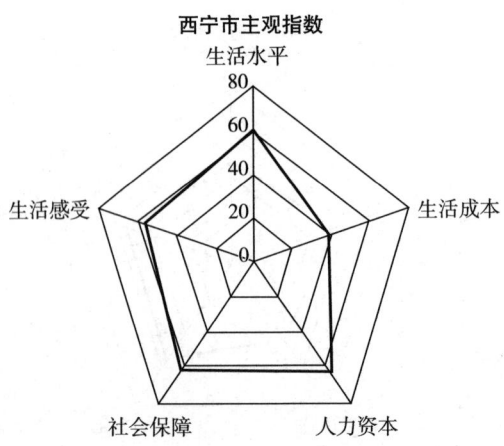

中国 35 个城市生活质量的细分指数

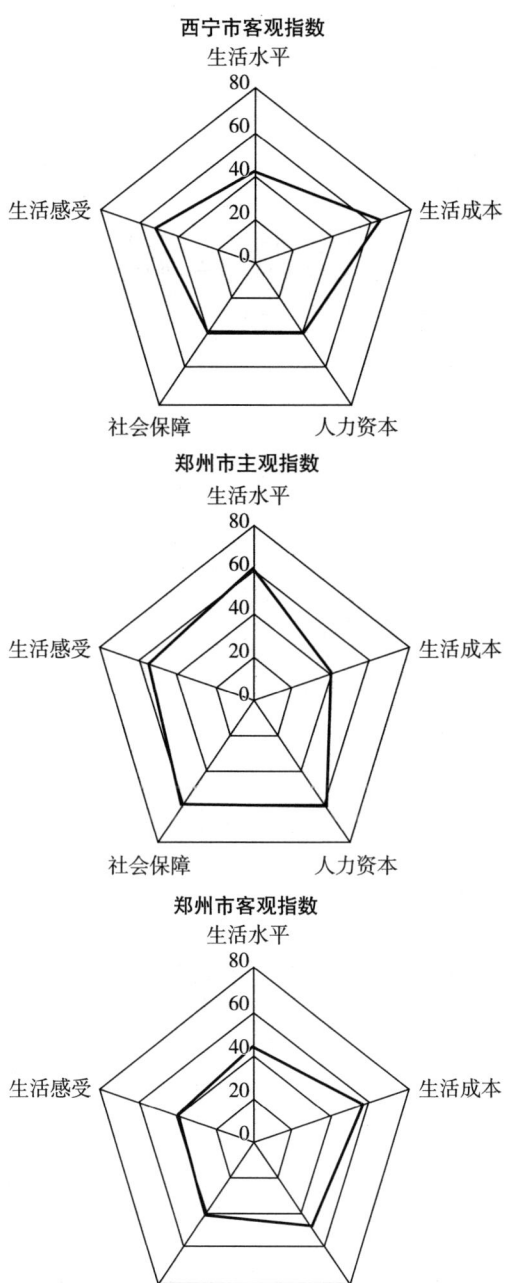

图 33 中国城市生活质量一级指标雷达图

专项调查篇

B.6 房价预期专项调查

2016年,课题组继续对房价预期进行专项调查。[①] 35个城市房价预期指数如表1所示。

表1　2012~2016年中国35个城市房价预期指数[②]

城市	2016年			2015年		2014年		2013年		2012年	
	得分	排名	上升位次	得分	排名	得分	排名	得分	排名	得分	排名
银川市	43.65	1	6	45.24	7	61.54	16	65.93	9	55.21	17

① 我们对该问题的设计如下:您认为您所居住城市的房价今后(1~2年)是涨还是跌?①大涨;②涨;③一般;④跌;⑤大跌。答案和赋值分别是:①大涨(100);②涨(75);③一般(50);④跌(25);⑤大跌(0)。
② 该指数越高,说明该城市居民预期房价上涨的幅度越大;越低,说明该城市居民预期房价下降的幅度越大。

续表

城市	2016 年			2015 年		2014 年		2013 年		2012 年	
	得分	排名	上升位次	得分	排名	得分	排名	得分	排名	得分	排名
呼和浩特市	43.12	2	20	43.64	22	57.81	32	61.26	34	56.07	11
济南市	42.90	3	28	41.97	31	61.46	18	65.68	12	50.00	33
沈阳市	42.71	4	16	43.89	20	59.33	26	62.43	30	56.35	10
昆明市	42.62	5	14	43.98	19	60.02	24	65.38	14	55.77	13
大连市	42.51	6	2	45.18	8	56.83	34	62.13	32	54.91	19
贵阳市	42.41	7	10	44.05	17	61.73	14	62.99	28	60.48	3
宁波市	42.27	8	−4	45.76	4	56.74	35	62.15	31	50.68	31
重庆市	42.24	9	3	44.41	12	59.22	27	64.46	19	55.84	12
成都市	42.21	10	6	44.24	16	61.80	10	63.06	27	54.53	20
西宁市	41.40	11	3	44.31	14	61.05	20	68.33	2	63.89	2
石家庄市	41.27	12	−2	44.62	10	61.49	17	65.19	15	54.13	23
哈尔滨市	41.26	13	−7	45.33	6	58.63	30	60.99	35	50.39	32
西安市	41.23	14	9	43.61	23	60.36	22	63.64	24	55.10	18
海口市	41.12	15	15	42.55	30	61.75	13	61.26	33	64.00	1
乌鲁木齐市	40.73	16	12	42.71	28	57.04	33	67.37	3	55.26	15
长沙市	40.28	17	−8	44.97	9	60.16	23	63.39	25	51.90	29
合肥市	40.22	18	−17	46.70	1	64.68	1	66.07	6	53.42	25
南宁市	40.20	19	−4	44.24	15	64.02	2	63.66	23	58.80	6
青岛市	39.95	20	−7	44.39	13	61.63	15	64.57	17	46.82	35
南昌市	39.84	21	3	43.45	24	61.13	19	66.73	4	55.28	14
武汉市	39.84	22	10	41.74	32	61.77	11	65.40	13	54.41	21

续表

城市	2016年			2015年		2014年		2013年		2012年	
	得分	排名	上升位次	得分	排名	得分	排名	得分	排名	得分	排名
南京市	39.75	23	-20	45.83	3	61.98	9	65.92	10	54.36	22
广州市	39.57	24	3	43.04	27	62.28	6	68.64	1	58.55	7
福州市	39.53	25	-14	44.44	11	60.61	21	64.45	20	52.75	27
太原市	39.30	26	8	41.03	34	62.22	7	64.53	18	57.18	8
长春市	39.14	27	-22	45.43	5	59.07	28	63.7	22	51.20	30
天津市	38.95	28	-2	43.42	26	59.49	25	63.18	26	53.65	24
郑州市	38.37	29	0	42.67	29	61.77	12	66.60	5	55.24	16
深圳市	38.34	30	5	40.15	35	62.92	4	65.96	8	56.55	9
上海市	37.97	31	-10	43.66	21	62.53	5	65.97	7	53.35	26
杭州市	37.90	32	-30	46.40	2	58.05	31	62.85	29	47.17	34
兰州市	37.12	33	-8	43.45	25	58.85	29	63.98	21	59.94	4
厦门市	37.04	34	-16	43.98	18	64.02	3	65.14	16	59.59	5
北京市	35.98	35	-2	41.43	33	62.08	8	65.71	11	52.04	28
平均值	40.16			43.86		60.78		64.65		54.99	

根据调查结果，2016年房价预期指数的加权平均值为40.16，低于2015年的43.86，连续三年处于下跌区间，说明居民普遍认为当前城市房价过高，未来应该回调。35个城市房价预期指数全部低于50，这意味着与2015年类似，所有城市居民对未来房价的预期都是下跌。图1描述了2012~2016年35个城市房价预期指数的变动情况。

本次调查的35个城市中，排名前10位的城市是：银川（1）、呼

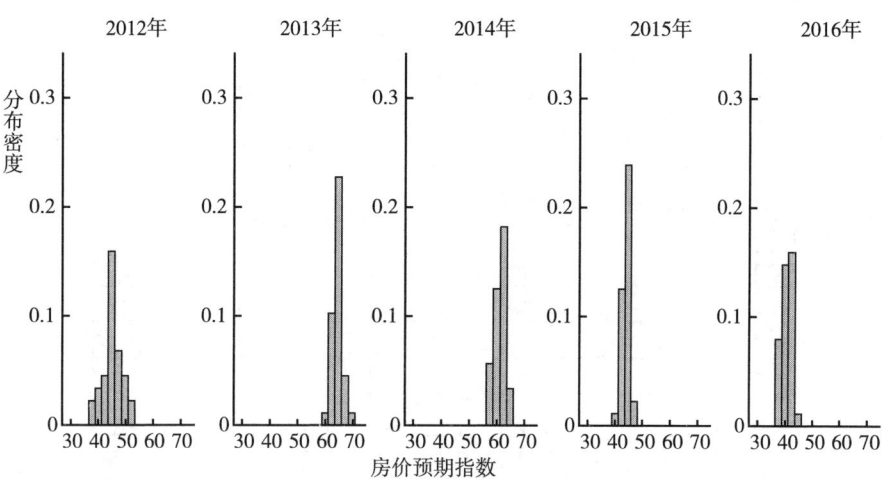

图1 2012~2016年房价预期指数直方图

和浩特（2）、济南（3）、沈阳（4）、昆明（5）、大连（6）、贵阳（7）、宁波（8）、重庆（9）、成都（10）。这意味着上述10个城市虽然都预期房价将会下跌，但下跌的幅度相对较小或下跌预期趋弱。2014年、2015年连续两年排名第一的合肥市在2016年被银川所取代。排名前10位的城市中，上升位次较多的城市有：济南（+28）、呼和浩特（+20）、沈阳（+16）、昆明（+14）。排名前10位的城市中，只有宁波较上年位次有所下降。排名后10位的城市是：太原（26）、长春（27）、天津（28）、郑州（29）、深圳（30）、上海（31）、杭州（32）、兰州（33）、厦门（34）、北京（35）。这意味着上述10个城市预期未来房价下跌的幅度相对较大或下跌预期趋强。排名后10位的城市中，下降位次较多的城市有：杭州（-30）、长春（-22）、厦门（-16）、上海（-10）。事实上，35个城市间的分值相差不大，最高为43.65，最低为35.98。这说明不同城市居民对房价下跌预期趋强或趋弱的差距不大。图2的柱状图展现了2012~2016年35个城市房价预期指数的变动情况。

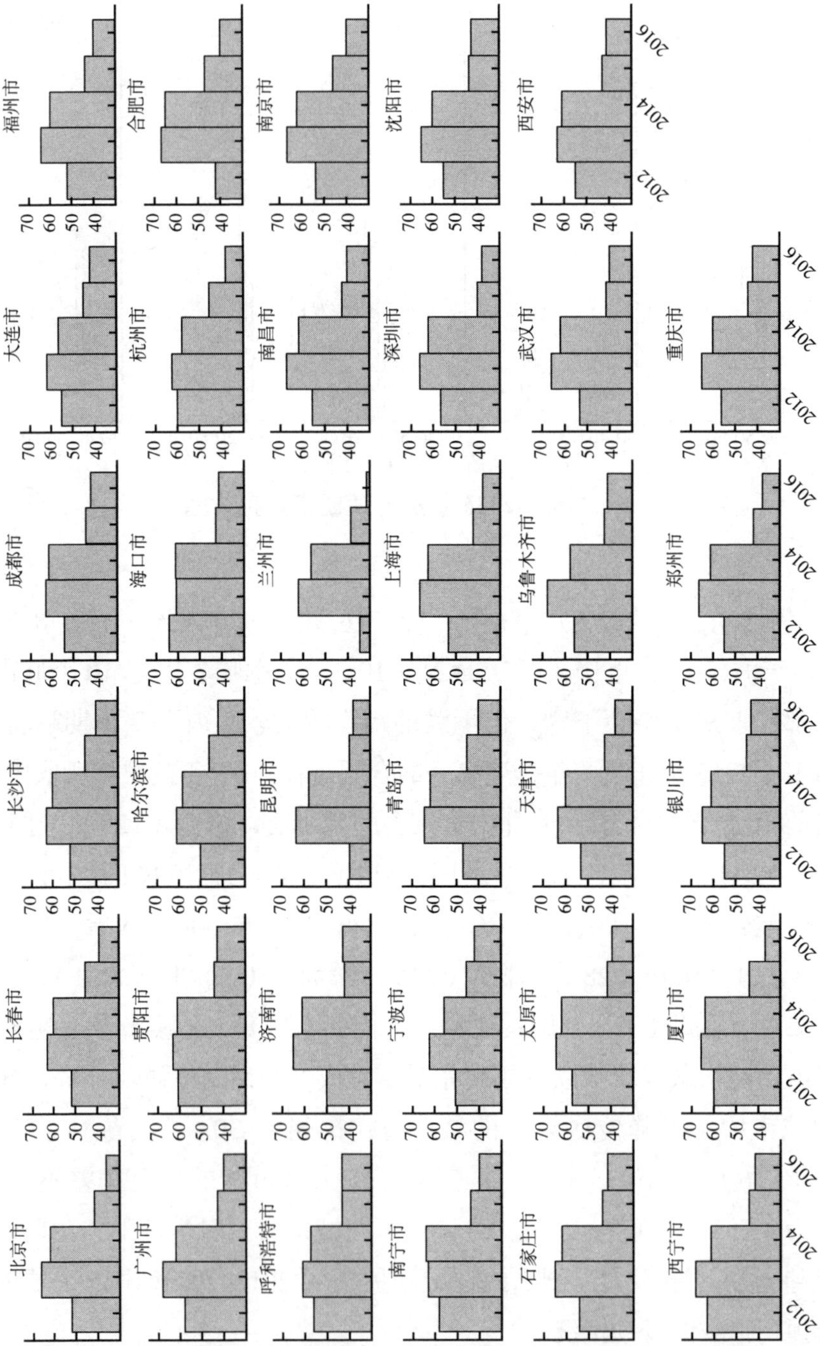

图 2 2012~2016 年 35 个城市房价预期指数

B.7
最关注因素调查：空气质量居首位，物价跃居第二

2016年我们继续对城市居民最关注因素进行调查。表1的调查结果显示，与往年不同，2016年35个城市均把空气质量视为影响生活质量的最重要因素，而2014年选择空气质量的为17个城市，2015年为32个城市。由此说明，我国主要城市居民越来越重视空气质量对生活质量的影响。就各项指标而言，35个城市居民认为对生活质量产生重要影响的因素依次为空气质量（46.33%）、物价（23.94%）、食品安全（20.87%）、交通状况（8.86%），而2015年依次为空气质量（39.12%）、食品安全（28.77%）、物价（21.17%）、交通状况（10.94%）。比较而言，空气质量仍然位居第一，而且居民对空气质量的关注度进一步明显提升；居民对物价的关注度提升，对食品安全的关注度下降，物价取代食品安全成为影响城市居民生活质量的第二因素。我们认为，这主要是因为经济增速下行，居民收入增长趋缓，而且在本次调查所进行的那段时间，农产品价格处于相对高位，因此城市居民对物价的关注度提升。

表1 2016年生活质量影响因素调查结果

城市	食品安全	空气质量	物价	交通状况
北京市	17.91%	52.82%	21.96%	7.32%
南宁市	20.54%	52.16%	20.54%	6.76%
合肥市	18.37%	52.04%	21.77%	7.82%
银川市	19.89%	51.38%	22.10%	6.63%

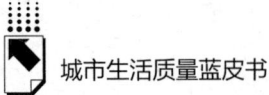

续表

城市	食品安全	空气质量	物价	交通状况
郑州市	20.93%	51.16%	20.93%	6.98%
宁波市	20.70%	50.12%	20.70%	8.48%
济南市	19.24%	49.53%	22.40%	8.83%
西安市	22.56%	49.37%	18.55%	9.52%
长沙市	18.16%	48.59%	26.85%	6.39%
乌鲁木齐市	17.74%	48.39%	22.04%	11.83%
石家庄市	20.53%	47.02%	23.82%	8.62%
天津市	19.82%	47.02%	23.68%	9.47%
上海市	19.76%	46.94%	23.74%	9.56%
长春市	24.74%	46.84%	20.79%	7.63%
青岛市	22.55%	46.74%	21.20%	9.51%
成都市	22.04%	46.63%	20.95%	10.38%
福州市	16.50%	46.55%	29.31%	7.64%
大连市	22.14%	46.37%	23.47%	8.02%
南京市	21.01%	45.57%	24.56%	8.86%
海口市	18.86%	45.18%	25.88%	10.09%
广州市	21.22%	45.14%	25.90%	7.73%
昆明市	20.83%	45.14%	24.65%	9.38%
重庆市	21.89%	44.25%	24.72%	9.15%
深圳市	22.00%	44.20%	25.66%	8.15%
呼和浩特市	17.98%	43.82%	28.09%	10.11%
哈尔滨市	18.81%	43.15%	27.40%	10.63%
武汉市	24.18%	43.13%	23.63%	9.07%
西宁市	27.96%	43.01%	19.35%	9.68%
沈阳市	27.05%	42.55%	22.80%	7.60%
南昌市	22.30%	42.30%	25.25%	10.16%
贵阳市	18.41%	41.79%	27.86%	11.94%
兰州市	21.43%	41.33%	28.06%	9.18%
厦门市	23.04%	38.74%	26.70%	11.52%
太原市	21.13%	38.14%	28.35%	12.37%
杭州市	24.87%	37.57%	28.31%	9.26%
平均值*	20.87%	46.33%	23.94%	8.86%

* 该平均值是由所有受访者中选择每个最关注因素的人数除以受访者总人数获得的。

分区域来看，不同城市对第二影响因素的认识存在分歧。南宁、郑州和宁波3个城市认为食品安全和物价同等重要；西安、长春、青岛、成都、武汉、沈阳、西宁7个城市认为食品安全是第二影响因素；其他25个城市均把物价作为第二影响因素。

进一步分析表明，受访者对空气质量、食品安全、物价和交通状况的关注程度因性别、学历、工作状态、年龄的不同而有所不同（见表2、表3）。

表2 不同性别、学历、工作状态的居民对四项因素的关注度

影响因素	性别		学历		工作状态	
	男	女	大专及以上	大专以下	有工作	没有工作
食品安全	20.42%	21.29%	20.92%	20.68%	21.65%	19.67%
空气质量	46.03%	46.62%	47.65%	41.39%	46.47%	46.12%
物价	24.14%	23.75%	22.48%	29.44%	23.31%	24.91%
交通状况	9.41%	8.34%	8.95%	8.49%	8.57%	9.30%
总计	100.00%	100.00%	100.00%	100.00%	100.00%	100.00%

根据表2，无论男性和女性、受教育程度以及工作状态如何，最关注的都是空气质量，其次是物价。相比较而言，男性对物价和交通状况的关注度高于女性，而女性对食品安全和空气质量的关注度高于男性；学历高的人群更为关注空气质量，学历低的人更关注物价水平，学历高低对食品安全和交通状况的评价没有影响；有工作的人似乎更为关注空气质量和食品安全，没有工作的人似乎更为关注物价和交通状况。

表3 不同年龄段居民对四项因素的关注度

年龄	20~30岁	31~40岁	41~50岁	51~60岁	60岁以上
食品安全	21.54%	19.80%	19.49%	24.39%	24.42%
空气质量	44.53%	50.29%	47.17%	39.51%	36.82%
物价	23.12%	23.14%	26.14%	29.11%	27.91%
交通状况	10.81%	6.78%	7.19%	6.99%	10.85%
总计	100.00%	100.00%	100.00%	100.00%	100.00%

表3给出了不同年龄段居民对四项因素的关注度,无论年龄大小,最关注的前两个因素都是空气质量和物价。所不同的是,在食品安全方面,50岁以上的人群对食品安全的关注程度较高,20~30岁的人群次之,31~50岁的人群对食品安全的关注程度较低;在空气质量方面,31~40岁的人群对空气质量的关注程度较高,41~50岁的人群次之,20~30岁的人群位列第三,51~60岁、60岁以上的人群对空气质量的关注程度依次降低;在物价方面,51~60岁的人群对物价的关注度最高,60岁以上的人群次之,41~50岁的人群位列第三,20~30岁和31~40岁的人群对物价的关注度区别不大;在交通状况方面,出乎我们的预料,60岁以上的人群和20~30岁的人群对交通状况的关注程度较高,41~50岁的人群次之,51~60岁的人群排第四位,31~40岁年龄段的人群对交通状况的关注度最低。

B.8
就业满意度调查

就业是民生之本，就业是民众生活收入来源的基本保障。在经济增长由高速转向中高速的新常态阶段，我国就业市场压力将有所加大，因此对就业前景的预期将是决定城市居民生活质量的最重要因素。本次调查我们新增加了城市居民对就业问题的满意度调查。我们对该问题的设计是：您对未来两三年内（您所居住的这个城市的）就业前景乐观吗？答案分别是：①很乐观；②乐观；③一般；④不乐观；⑤很不乐观。调查结果见表1。

表1 2016年中国35个城市居民就业满意度指数

城市	就业满意度	排名	城市	就业满意度	排名
太原市	61.47	1	深圳市	57.64	14
大连市	59.49	2	南京市	57.59	15
济南市	58.75	3	昆明市	57.55	16
南宁市	58.65	4	北京市	57.35	17
重庆市	58.54	5	青岛市	57.34	18
杭州市	58.33	6	上海市	57.28	19
合肥市	58.16	7	石家庄市	57.24	20
银川市	58.15	8	沈阳市	57.22	21
天津市	57.89	9	海口市	57.07	22
呼和浩特市	57.87	10	长春市	56.91	23
宁波市	57.86	11	郑州市	56.72	24
哈尔滨市	57.77	12	广州市	56.65	25
成都市	57.65	13	乌鲁木齐市	56.59	26

续表

城市	就业满意度	排名	城市	就业满意度	排名
厦门市	56.28	27	贵阳市	55.85	32
武汉市	56.25	28	西安市	55.08	33
长沙市	56.20	29	兰州市	54.97	34
南昌市	55.98	30	西宁市	54.30	35
福州市	55.97	31	平均值	57.41	

由调查结果可以看出，尽管近两年来中国经济增速下滑，但35个城市居民就业满意度指数平均值仍为57.41，处于满意与不满意的分界线之上，即广大居民对未来2~3年内的就业前景较为乐观。从区域比较来看，太原市居民乐观程度最高，就业满意度指数为61.47；西宁市居民乐观程度最低，就业满意度指数为54.30，但仍处于满意区间。

实际的经济数据或许能说明为何居民对就业前景保持较为乐观的态度。根据《2015年国民经济和社会发展统计公报》，2015年末全国就业人员77451万人，其中城镇就业人员40410万人。2015年，全年城镇新增就业1312万人；年末城镇登记失业率为4.05%；全国农民工总量为27747万人，比上年增长1.3%。其中，外出农民工16884万人，增长0.4%；本地农民工10863万人，增长2.7%。对于国家统计局公布的失业率，国内外社会各界有所质疑，认为城镇登记失业率无法表示真实的失业状况。为此，覆盖全国所有地市级城市的劳动力调查于2015年7月开始试运营，并于2016年1月开始正式实施。2016年2月，李克强总理在春节后首次国务院常务会议上指出，2016年1月全国的调查失业率为4.99%，相比经济增长而言，就业形势较为稳定。

从进一步的调查分析来看，不同的性别、年龄、学历以及在职状态对于未来就业前景的态度还有所不同（见表2）。

表2　不同性别、年龄、学历、工作状态对未来就业前景的态度

指标		很不乐观	不乐观	一般	乐观	很乐观
性别	男	1.43%	22.58%	23.61%	45.94%	6.43%
	女	1.06%	25.61%	24.12%	44.55%	4.66%
年龄	20~30岁	1.24%	28.10%	19.18%	45.18%	6.31%
	31~40岁	1.07%	17.34%	26.39%	49.71%	5.50%
	41~50岁	1.22%	24.11%	30.80%	40.57%	3.30%
	51~60岁	1.79%	30.24%	29.59%	33.98%	4.39%
	60岁以上	3.10%	18.99%	32.56%	38.37%	6.98%
学历	大专及以上	1.04%	24.08%	21.62%	47.29%	5.97%
	大专以下	1.98%	24.37%	32.33%	37.46%	3.86%
是否在职	是	1.17%	20.88%	24.25%	47.95%	5.75%
	否	1.35%	29.12%	23.29%	41.05%	5.19%

由上述表格可以看出，就不同性别而言，相对于女性，男性对未来就业的形势更为乐观，其具体表现为：男性中乐观和很乐观的比例为52.37%，女性的这一比例为49.21%；男性中很不乐观和不乐观的比例为24.01%，女性的这一比例为26.67%。由于在现实职场中，男性比女性更具有竞争力，因此这个调查结果基本符合社会现状。

就不同年龄段而言，31~40岁年龄段的人最为乐观，乐观和很乐观的比例为55.21%，很不乐观和不乐观的比例为18.41%；20~30岁年龄段的人次之，乐观和很乐观的比例为51.49%，很不乐观和不乐观的比例为29.34%；60岁以上年龄段人群位列第三，乐观和很乐观的比例为45.35%，很不乐观和不乐观的比例为22.09%；41~50岁的人位列第四，乐观和很乐观的比例为43.87%，很不乐观和不乐观的比例为25.33%；51~60岁的人最悲观，乐观和很乐观的比例仅为38.37%，很不乐观和不乐观的比例高达32.03%。值得一提的是，相比60岁以

上的人，20~30岁的人群中持乐观态度的人占比较高，但持悲观态度的人占比也较高，两极分化较为突出。

就不同学历而言，相对于大专以下学历，大专及以上的人在人力资本积累方面具有优势，因此对未来就业的形势更为乐观。具体表现为：在大专及以上学历的人群中，乐观和很乐观的比例为53.26%，不乐观和很不乐观的比例为25.12%；在大专以下学历人群中，乐观和很乐观的比例仅为41.32%，不乐观和很不乐观的比例为26.35%。

就在职与否而言，由于失业本身就是经济增长低迷以及产业结构调整的结果，而目前在职的人本身就说明其具有较强的市场竞争力，因此目前在职的人比没有工作的人对未来就业形势更为乐观。具体表现为：在职人群中，乐观和很乐观的比例为53.70%，不乐观和很不乐观的比例为22.05%；在目前没有工作的人群中，乐观和很乐观的比例为46.24%，不乐观和很不乐观的比例高达30.47%。

结合本次调查结果以及国家统计局的相关数据来看，与2015年底及2016年第一季度不同，当前居民的就业预期正在好转，处于相对乐观的区间。然而，反观现实，根据中国人民大学就业研究所等相关机构的研究，自2015年第一季度以来，中国就业市场景气指数（CIER指数）处于持续下行的状态。分行业来看，由于当前国内经济结构性问题较为突出，就业方面体现为不同行业的CIER指数差异比较明显，互联网/电子商务、基金/证券、交通/运输以及中介服务等行业的就业景气指数相对较高；会计、航空/航天、能源/矿产、跨领域经营和电气/电力/水利等传统服务业、重工业以及矿产业的就业形势相对较差。总的来说，由于中国经济处于发展的转型期，就业市场在很大程度上将面临转型期的阵痛。在调结构、去产能的大背景下，煤炭、钢铁、石油等传统行业用工明显减少，"互联网+"等新业态发展速度较快，但其带动就业的能力相对有限，不及传统行业，因此当前我国就业压力较大。对此我们认为，中央政府一方面要

积极出台措施加强再就业培训等扶持政策，另一方面要稳步推进产业结构转型。未来产业结构调整发展的重点在于制造业的转型升级与生产性服务业以及金融、信息等现代服务业的协调发展。

  2016年城市生活质量调查表明，在中国经济发展持续放缓的新常态背景下，经济与社会发展面临一系列的挑战与风险。在客观生活质量指数与上年相比有所下降的情况下，主观满意度指数保持了基本稳定。但是，当前我们仍面临着巨大的挑战：居高不下的生活成本、过快的生活节奏、不确定的房地产价格以及令人担忧的就业前景。在未来的经济与社会发展转型过程中，中央以及地方各级政府要继续致力于推进民生体系建设，稳定经济增长，实现居民生活质量的进一步提升。

结 论 篇

B.9 结论与启示

一 城市生活质量存在主客观反差，并具有明显的区域特征

表1给出了描述2012~2016年35个城市生活质量主观满意度指数和生活质量客观指数的5个细分指数，从中可以看出各项细分指数的变化情况。

表1 2012~2016年主客观细分指数

指数		2016年	2015年	2014年	2013年	2012年
主观满意度指数	生活水平满意度指数	60.44	60.07	54.32	52.51	51.28

续表

指数		2016年	2015年	2014年	2013年	2012年
主观满意度指数	生活成本满意度指数	39.74	38.94	31.81	31.22	28.91
	人力资本满意度指数	62.20	61.73	58.98	58.89	59.42
	社会保障满意度指数	60.66	60.47	57.87	56.64	59.19
	生活感受满意度指数	56.05	55.66	54.88	55.07	55.63
客观指数	生活水平客观指数	50.07	59.83	68.06	63.39	56.28
	生活成本客观指数	58.74	54.58	53.84	58.67	56.10
	人力资本客观指数	56.98	57.34	57.33	57.78	57.66
	社会保障客观指数	50.43	51.26	54.66	55.26	50.85
	生活感受客观指数	57.54	56.17	55.57	53.67	51.89

从表1可以看出，城市生活质量主客观指数存在明显反差。2012年特别是2013年以来，除个别年份外，主观满意度指数基本上处于稳中有升的态势。而在客观指数中，生活水平客观指数经过3年的持续上升后，近两年连续下跌，且下跌的幅度较大。人力资本客观指数和社会保障指数在2016年也有所下降，生活成本客观指数和生活感受指数则有所上升。这与近两年经济增速持续下降基本上是一致的。尽管出现上述情况，但生活水平主观满意度指数继2015年首次高于生活水平客观指数后，2016年更是高出了10.37。

2012~2016年，主客观指数及其细分指数呈现一定的区域特征。具体到主观满意度指数，其区域差异不是特别明显，西部地区主观满意度指数有所上升，以往东高西低的格局有所改变，呈现西高东低的局面。反观客观指数，东、中、西三个地区均有不同程度的下降，东部城市要高于中西部城市，中西部城市差异不是特别明显（见表2）。

表2　按区域分主观满意度指数及客观指数

指数	地区	2016年	2015年	2014年	2013年	2012年
主观满意度指数	东部	55.74	55.71	51.90	51.44	51.44
	中部	55.75	55.50	51.14	50.65	50.66
	西部	55.92	54.76	51.06	50.39	50.24
客观指数	东部	56.43	56.93	59.60	59.59	57.46
	中部	52.84	53.80	54.88	55.57	51.90
	西部	53.71	54.48	55.88	55.27	52.26

继续观察5个主观满意度细分指数。如表3所示，与上年相比，2016年东、中部城市生活水平满意度指数略有下降，西部城市略有上升，东、中、西三个区域基本持平，没有太大差别。与上年相比，东、中部城市生活成本满意度指数变化不大，西部地区有了一定程度的上升，并且超过了其他两个地区。中部和西部地区的人力资本满意度指数均略有上升，东部地区略有下降，2016年人力资本满意度指数中部最高，东部次之。社会保障满意度指数与上年相比基本没有发生太大的变化。三个地区的生活感受满意度指数均有所上升，其中东部城市最高，其次为中部城市。

表3　按区域分5个主观满意度细分指数

指数	地区	2016年	2015年	2014年	2013年	2012年
生活水平满意度指数	东部	60.39	60.56	54.55	53.28	51.91
	中部	60.23	60.49	53.21	51.44	51.00
	西部	60.07	59.37	53.38	52.87	50.57
生活成本满意度指数	东部	39.49	39.48	31.62	30.98	28.54
	中部	39.95	40.16	32.98	33.49	30.96
	西部	40.89	37.80	31.28	30.43	27.95
人力资本满意度指数	东部	62.05	62.33	59.60	59.58	60.42
	中部	62.24	61.15	58.08	58.28	58.51
	西部	61.78	60.81	58.51	58.53	58.62

续表

指数	地区	2016年	2015年	2014年	2013年	2012年
社会保障满意度指数	东部	60.59	60.65	58.83	57.86	60.12
	中部	60.25	60.09	56.87	55.54	57.80
	西部	60.86	60.13	56.70	55.60	58.84
生活感受满意度指数	东部	56.18	55.54	54.90	55.48	56.19
	中部	56.09	55.63	54.59	54.51	55.04
	西部	55.99	55.68	55.44	54.51	55.23

5个客观细分指数也呈现明显的区域特征。表4表明，生活水平客观指数呈现东、中、西部依次递减的局面。与上年相比，三个地区的生活水平客观指数下降明显。其中，中部城市下降最为明显，其次是西部地区。三个地区的生活成本客观指数均有不同程度的提高，仍旧呈现西高东低的布局。三个地区的人力资本客观指数差异不显著，与上年相比略有变化。社会保障客观指数的区域特征明显，东部最高，西部其次，中部最低。与上年相比，社会保障客观指数均略有提升，但幅度不大。三个地区的生活感受客观指数变化态势比较平稳，东部最高，其次为西部，中部得分最低。

表4 按区域分5个客观细分指数

指数	地区	2016年	2015年	2014年	2013年	2012年
生活水平客观指数	东部	54.82	62.31	71.53	69.00	62.99
	中部	46.37	56.12	62.77	59.39	52.03
	西部	45.87	54.74	61.96	58.54	49.60
生活成本客观指数	东部	54.06	50.85	50.37	54.96	52.12
	中部	60.21	56.98	56.42	61.47	57.41
	西部	64.48	61.72	61.18	65.46	60.94
人力资本客观指数	东部	57.42	57.25	57.32	57.18	58.72
	中部	57.64	57.57	57.02	58.39	56.18
	西部	55.85	55.62	55.30	55.19	57.22

续表

指数	地区	2016年	2015年	2014年	2013年	2012年
社会保障客观指数	东部	55.95	55.47	60.16	60.89	57.08
	中部	45.04	44.80	45.67	46.86	45.72
	西部	46.30	45.92	47.37	46.95	45.50
生活感受客观指数	东部	59.88	58.77	58.61	55.95	56.37
	中部	54.93	53.55	52.52	51.74	48.16
	西部	56.05	54.38	53.58	50.20	48.07

二 房价预期与走势显著分化，住房调控体系亟待完善

根据房价预期专项调查结果，一线城市总体排名靠后，北京和深圳连续两年处于后10位，上海和广州则连续两年处于第20位之后，说明城市居民认为一线城市房价过高，预期下跌较强烈；二线城市中，宁波和大连连续两年处于前10位，郑州连续两年处于后10位；三线城市中，银川连续两年居于前10位，太原连续两年居于后10位。根据经济学理论，价格预期是影响价格的重要因素。一旦消费者和投资者形成强烈的通胀预期，就会改变其消费和投资行为，从而加剧通胀，并可能造成通胀螺旋式地上升；反之亦然。然而，需要提出的是，中国房地产市场以及资本市场具有强烈的政策属性。由于人们无法对政策做出正确的预期，政策冲击可能会导致人们的预期出现系统性偏差，从而导致房价预期与实际房价变动出现偏离。

例如，2015年初课题组进行的调查研究表明，35个城市居民普遍认为房价会下跌。然而，根据易居研究院监测的35个城市房地产数据，2015年下半年开始，全国35个城市房地产成交量持续上升，

量价齐升的局面持续数月，库存规模已出现连续7个月环比下跌、连续9个月同比下跌的态势。根据国家统计局2016年5月发布的70个大中城市住宅销售价格指数，70个大中城市住宅平均销售价格连续12个月环比上涨。从区域的角度来看，过去一年房价分化趋势明显，一、二线城市房价走势强劲；三、四线城市房地产库存压力仍然很大，房价走势疲软。

关于房价重拾强劲涨势的原因，我们认为有以下几点。第一，房地产投资是中国经济发展的重要支柱之一，为应对房地产投资持续下滑、房产库存高企的局面，中央政府出台了一系列的金融信贷优惠政策，刺激房产需求。与此同时，各地方配套实施一系列宽松政策，以公积金政策调整为主，包括财政补贴和税费减免等政策，刺激了居民住房需求特别是改善性住房需求的释放。第二，为应对经济下滑，我国央行在过去实施了宽松的货币政策，在实体经济低迷的背景下，大量的资金流入资本市场。然而，2015年6月以来，中国股市大幅下挫，从而导致大量的信贷资金流出股市，流入房地产市场。第三，我国区域间发展差异总体较为显著，相比二、三线城市，一线城市的就业和发展机会、公共服务水平（尤其是教育和医疗）、基础设施便利程度都是吸引外来务工人员定居的关键因素。另外，二、三线城市乃至四线城市，由于房地产总体库存较大，前期房价上涨幅度过大，因此在本轮上涨中二、三线城市的房价涨幅不及一线城市。

然而，尽管房价连续数月上涨，但本次调查的结果表明，35个城市的居民仍然认为未来一两年内房价应该下调。这说明在经济增速下滑、居民收入增长放缓的背景下，在广大群众看来，房价上涨已经超出了人们可接受的范围，当前的房价涨势难以为继。对此，我们认为，房产的本质属性应是满足人们居住的需求，在我国继续推进城市化的背景下，政府应该优化房地产调控体系，稳定房地产政策，防止房价在短期内大幅震荡，以促进房地产业健康发展。

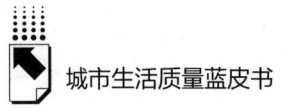

三 加大环境治理的财政支持，保障居民生活的环境质量

表5为2016年我们对中国35个城市居民对空气质量的关注程度以及受调查城市空气质量的调查结果。

表5 35个城市空气质量情况

城市	空气质量关注度	PM 2.5 浓度	关注度排名	PM 2.5 浓度排名	排名变化
南宁市	52.16%	49.00	2	26	−24
宁波市	50.12%	46.00	6	29	−23
银川市	51.38%	53.00	4	22	−18
福州市	46.55%	34.00	17	33	−16
海口市	45.18%	23.00	20	35	−15
上海市	46.94%	52.00	13	24	−11
深圳市	44.20%	34.00	24	34	−10
昆明市	45.14%	35.00	22	32	−10
乌鲁木齐市	48.39%	61.00	10	19	−9
广州市	45.14%	49.00	21	27	−6
青岛市	46.74%	58.00	15	21	−6
呼和浩特市	43.82%	46.00	25	30	−5
大连市	46.37%	53.00	18	23	−5
北京市	52.82%	86.00	1	4	−3
合肥市	52.04%	83.00	3	5	−2
长春市	46.84%	68.00	14	15	−1
长沙市	48.59%	74.00	9	10	−1
西安市	49.37%	77.00	8	8	0
厦门市	38.74%	37.00	33	31	2
贵阳市	41.79%	48.00	31	28	3
郑州市	51.16%	88.00	5	2	3
济南市	49.53%	87.00	7	3	4
南昌市	42.30%	52.00	30	25	5

续表

城市	空气质量关注度	PM 2.5 浓度	关注度排名	PM 2.5 浓度排名	排名变化
天津市	47.02%	83.00	12	6	6
重庆市	44.25%	65.00	23	16	7
成都市	46.63%	77.00	16	9	7
南京市	45.57%	74.00	19	11	8
西宁市	43.01%	63.00	28	18	10
石家庄市	47.02%	124.00	11	1	10
兰州市	41.33%	61.00	32	20	12
哈尔滨市	43.15%	72.00	26	13	13
沈阳市	42.55%	74.00	29	12	17
杭州市	37.57%	65.00	35	17	18
太原市	38.14%	72.00	34	14	20
武汉市	43.13%	82.00	27	7	20

注：排名按照由高至低的顺序，PM 2.5 的平均浓度越高，表示空气质量越差。
资料来源：《中国统计年鉴》。

比较本次调查的城市居民对空气质量的关注程度和这些城市的空气质量可以发现，PM 2.5 的浓度与城市居民对空气质量的关注度并不成正比，也就是说，空气质量的优劣与城市居民对空气质量的关注度并没有一致的相关关系。按照空气质量与居民关注度之间的关系，可以将城市大致划分为三类。

第一类为城市的空气质量为优或接近优的水平，但当地居民却十分关注空气质量，即城市居民对空气质量的关注度排名小于 PM 2.5 浓度排名 5 位以上。这些城市包括以南宁、宁波、银川为代表的 11 个城市，其中东、中、西部城市的比例为 8∶0∶3。这说明随着收入的增加，人们对环境质量的关注度在不断提高，环境安全已日渐成为人们关注的焦点。

第二类城市的空气质量相对较差甚至达到污染的程度，但相对来说当地居民对空气质量的关注度较低，即城市居民对空气质量的关注度排名大于 PM 2.5 浓度排名 5 位以上。这些城市包括以太原、沈阳、

石家庄为代表的12个城市,东、中、西部城市的比例为4∶4∶4。之所以出现这种结果,我们认为主要是由于这些地区的产业结构以传统工业为主,除杭州等少数城市外,其他城市一直以来环境质量都不太好。因此,当地居民对环境质量的诉求并不高。

第三类城市空气质量排名与居民环境关注度排名成反比,即空气质量好的城市的居民对环境质量关注度较低,空气质量差的城市的居民对环境质量关注度较高,城市居民对空气质量的关注度排名与PM 2.5浓度排名差异在5名以内(含5名)。这些城市包括以呼和浩特、南昌为代表的12个城市,东、中、西部城市比例为4∶6∶2。这类城市中既有环境质量较高、环境关注度较低的地区,如呼和浩特、大连、厦门、贵阳等城市;也有环境质量较差、环境关注度较高的地区,如北京、合肥、济南、郑州等。因此,并不是环境质量关注度越高越好,一些城市环境质量关注度较高,是因为其糟糕的空气质量,而一些城市环境质量关注度较低,则源于其良好的环境本底。①

综上所述,改革开放以来,我国经济发展取得了举世瞩目的成就,但随之而来的环境污染问题严重制约了我国国民经济发展。城市环境污染对人民群众的生活造成较大影响,对此,中央政府进行了一系列立法建设,彰显了党和国家治理污染的坚定决心。但居民对空气质量关注度的不断提高以及环境治理尚存的问题表明,我国在环境治理方面还存在很大的改善空间。国际经验表明,在经济发展过程中环保投入占GDP的比重达到1.5%才能阻止环境恶化,达到2%~3%才能真正改善环境。"十二五"期间,我国环保投资额在GDP中的占比约为1.5%,而早在20世纪80年代,德国、英国的环保投资占比就超过了2%,日本更是达到3.4%。因此在未

---

① 环境本底是指自然环境在未受污染的情况下,各种环境要素中化学元素或化学物质的基线含量。

来的环境治理中，在强化各项政策法规的同时，我国政府要加大对环保治理的投入，这不仅能够改善环境质量，而且有利于获得新的经济增长点。

四 健全统一权威的监管体制，继续提升食品安全满意度

根据2014~2015年连续两年的调查结果，空气质量和食品安全两个因素是排在前两位的影响居民生活质量的最重要因素。然而，2016年的调查结果表明，在35个调查城市中，只有10个城市的居民认为食品安全是影响生活质量的第二大因素。该调查结果也得到其他社会调查的佐证。在《小康》杂志与清华大学媒介调查实验室联合进行的"2015中国综合小康指数"调查中，食品安全问题连续第四年位居"最受关注的十大焦点问题"首位，关注度达到44.8%，但公众对于食品安全状况的满意度比往年提升了"一个档次"。①

综观世界各国食品安全的发展历程，中国食品安全发展总体上处于第二、第三阶段过渡期，即针对食品工业化和农业工业化粗放发展，监管措施在不断提升，但尚未达到食品产业规范化、法治化发展的阶段。在规范化与法治化的阶段，应严格限制食品添加剂、色素等各种化学原料在食品生产中的使用量，相关质量体系标准、法律法规制度应日渐完善。2015年4月24日，十二届全国人大常委会第十四次会议以160票赞成、1票反对、3票弃权表决通过了新修订的《食品安全法》，该法于2015年10月1日起开始实施。针对原《食品安全法》存在的缺陷与漏洞，新修订的《食品安全法》（以下简称新法）在总则中规定了食品安全工作要实行预防为主、风

---

① 腾讯财经：《2015最受关注十大焦点问题：食品安全仍热》，http://finance.qq.com/a/20151215/028601.htm。

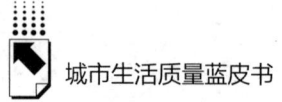

险管理、全程控制、社会共治的基本原则,要建立科学、严格的监管制度。

在监管方面,新法从8个方面的制度设计确保监管力度:一是完善统一权威的食品安全监管机构,由分段监管变成食药监部门统一监管;二是建立最严格的全过程监管制度,对食品生产的整个产业链以及网络食品交易等新兴业态等进行了细化和完善;三是更加突出预防为主、风险防范;四是建立最严格的标准,加强标准制定与标准执行的衔接;五是对特殊医学用途配方食品、婴幼儿配方乳粉的产品配方实行注册制度;六是加强对农药的管理;七是加强风险评估管理;八是建立最严格的法律责任制度,从民事和刑事等方面强化对食品安全违法行为的惩处力度。

针对原来法律中存在的惩罚力度不足的问题,新法从6个方面改进,以求"重典治乱"。一是强化刑事责任追究。二是增设了行政拘留。新法对用非食品原料生产食品、经营病死畜禽、违法使用剧毒高毒农药等严重行为增设拘留行政处罚。三是明显提高罚款额度。比如,对生产经营添加药品的食品、生产经营营养成分不符合国家标准的婴幼儿配方乳粉等性质恶劣的违法行为,原《食品安全法》规定最高可以处罚货值金额10倍的罚款,而新法规定最高可以处罚货值金额30倍的罚款。四是对重复违法行为加大处罚。新法规定,行为人在一年内累计3次因违法受到罚款、警告等行政处罚的,给予责令停产停业直至吊销许可证的处罚。五是对非法提供场所增设罚则。为了加强源头监管、全程监管,新法对明知从事无证生产经营或者从事非法添加非食用物质等违法行为,仍然为其提供生产经营场所的行为,规定最高处以10万元罚款。六是强化民事责任追究。

总的来讲,我国监管法规日臻完善,法律实施日益严格。这一系列政策措施的实行,促进了我国食品安全水平的提升。2016年2月,国家食品药品监管总局发布的报告指出,2015年,总局在全国范围内

组织抽检了172310批次食品样品,其中检验不合格样品5541批次,合格率为96.8%,比2014年提高2.1个百分点,当前食品安全整体形势稳中趋好。2016年6月,农业部发布了2016年1~5月对农产品的监测检查结果,结果显示,监测样品总体合格率为97.2%,合格率继续提升。

然而,当前我国食品安全监管体系还存在对占食品生产企业总数80%的小微企业缺乏监管的问题。对此,新修订的《食品安全法》要求各地方应当制定针对食品生产加工小作坊和食品摊贩的具体管理办法。而按照新修订完成的《立法法》,法律规定明确要求国家机关对专门事项做出配套规定的,有关国家机关应在法律实施一年内做出规定,即在2016年10月1日之前,各个省、自治区、直辖市都必须制定对小加工作坊和小摊贩具体的管理办法。

五 基础设施与区域布局并重,进一步缓解城市交通拥堵

本次对城市居民最关注的影响生活质量的四个相关因素的调查结果表明,交通状况虽然位列第四,但从35个调查城市样本的平均值来看,有8.86%的受访者认为交通状况是影响生活质量的最重要因素,低于2015年的10.69%。其中,该比例最低的为银川市(6.63%),最高的为太原市(12.37%),相比上年均明显降低。由此得出,从35个城市居民的感受来看,我国城市交通状况在逐渐改善。

从客观评价指标来看,结合我们所设计的生活质量体系,这里通过两个细分指标来衡量交通状况,一是交通安全指标,具体又可分为反映交通事故次数的相对指标——万车死亡人数和交通事故死亡总人数;二是交通拥堵情况。

从交通安全来看,根据国家统计局发布的《2015年国民经济和

社会发展统计公报》，2015年全国道路交通事故万车死亡人数为2.1人，同比下降5.4%；根据汽车保有量进行换算后，2015年交通事故死亡总人数约为37426人，增长率为9.1%，高于2014年0.6个百分点，交通安全形势依然严峻。针对交通事故居高不下的状态，我们认为：第一，应进一步加大对交通违法行为的处理执行力度；第二，应加大交通安全宣传，增强公民的交通安全意识；第三，应进一步完善机动车驾驶人的培训体系，提升考核要求。

从居民出行满意程度来说，堵车已经成为目前中国大中城市居民出行的最大困扰。2016年4月，高德地图联合清华大学戴姆勒可持续交通研究中心正式发布了《2016年第一季度中国主要城市交通分析报告》。该报告指出，同比上年一季度，在高德地图交通大数据监测的60个城市中，总体拥堵情况有所缓解，其中，近1/3的城市较上年拥堵有所缓解，这部分城市以东部沿海地区较为明显，而另外1/3的城市拥堵情况呈上升趋势，这些城市多集中在珠三角区域，另有部分城市拥堵情况较上年持平。一季度城市拥堵情况缓解榜中，天津、上海、福州、石家庄等城市位列其中，高峰拥堵延时指数分别下降9.2%、7.8%、4.0%、3.8%；与此同时，一季度城市拥堵情况加剧榜中，济南、长沙、合肥、长春、深圳、哈尔滨等城市位列其中，高峰拥堵延时指数分别上升9.6%、8.4%、7.8%、7.1%、4.9%、3.4%。由此说明，我国交通拥堵治理有所成效。

从国际经验来看，为进一步治理城市交通拥堵，我们认为应做好以下几点。第一，提升城市基础设施建设水平。作为经济发达城市的代表，香港的自由流车速之所以远远高于同级别的内地城市，是因为其高水平的基础设施建设。数据显示，香港的高速路（香港没有快速路而全是高速路）占比达到5.6%以上，而交通拥堵表现较为突出的城市——北京和济南的高速与快速路占比都小于2.5%，不及香港的一半。另外，内地多数城市排水系统较为落后，雨季很容易发生城市内

涝，恶化了城市的交通拥堵状况。第二，进一步推行混合用地模式，摒弃"雅典宪章"的功能分区观念，避免城市布局功能单一化，改变职住失衡的现象。第三，推进由中心城市与卫星城市相结合的城市圈建设，以抑制城市中心区人口密度的提高，引导人口、产业和城市功能分散至周边卫星城市。①

---

① 钱七虎：《城市交通拥堵和空气污染的治本之策》，《科技日报》2014年4月21日。

参考文献

[1] 张连城等:《经济发展中的两个反差——中国 30 个城市生活质量调查报告》,《经济学动态》2011 年第 7 期。

[2] 张连城等:《高生活成本拖累城市生活质量满意度提高——中国 35 个城市生活质量调查报告》,《经济学动态》2012 年第 7 期。

[3] 张连城等:《生活质量:态势平稳,挑战严峻》,《经济学动态》2013 年第 8 期。

[4] 张连城等:《生活质量指数趋升 空气质量食品安全堪忧》,《经济学动态》2014 年第 8 期。

[5] 张连城等:《预期稳定 调整犹存》,《经济学动态》2015 年第 8 期。

[6] 中国经济实验研究院:《中国城市生活质量报告》(2012),社会科学文献出版社,2013。

[7] 中国经济实验研究院:《中国城市生活质量报告》(2013),社会科学文献出版社,2014。

[8] 中国经济实验研究院:《中国城市生活质量报告》(2014),社会科学文献出版社,2014。

[9] 中国经济实验研究院:《中国城市生活质量报告》(2015),社会科学文献出版社,2015。

[10] 陈刚、李树:《政府如何能够让人幸福?——政府质量影响居民幸福感的实证研究》,《管理世界》2012 年第 8 期。

[11] 张克中、何凌云:《政府质量与国民幸福：文献回顾与评论》，《国外社会科学》2012年第4期。

[12] 陈刚、李树:《中国的腐败、收入分配和收入差距》，《经济科学》2010年第2期。

[13] 陈刚:《腐败与收入不平等——来自中国的经验证据》，《南开经济研究》2011年第5期。

[14] 何立新、潘春阳:《破解中国的"Easterlin"悖论：收入差距、机会不均与居民幸福感》，《管理世界》2011年第8期。

[15] 林南、卢汉龙:《社会指标与生活质量的结构模型探讨——关于上海城市居民生活的一项研究》，《中国社会科学》1987年第4期。

[16] 周长城等:《建立人民生活质量指标体系的理论依据》，《武汉大学学报》（社会科学版）2001年第3期。

[17] 罗萍等:《国内生活质量指标体系研究现状评析》，《武汉大学学报》（社会科学版）2000年第9期。

[18] 赵彦云、王作成:《我国生活质量的国际比较》，《统计与信息论坛》2003年第7期。

[19] 纪竹荪:《我国国民生活质量统计指标体系的构建》，《统计与信息论坛》2003年第7期。

[20] 张润清、谢艳辉:《中国农村居民生活质量评价指标体系研究》，《经济论坛》2004年第2期。

[21] 贾海薇:《高校教师工作生活质量的模糊综合评价模型》，《华南农业大学学报》（社会科学版）2005年第9期。

[22] 王予东等:《开封市老年人生活质量评价》，《河南大学学报》（医学科学版）2001年第3期。

[23] 廖湘岳、贺春临:《要素分析法在生活质量评价中的应用——美国生活质量状况研究》，《湘潭工学院学报》（社会科学版）2002年第12期。

[24] Alesina, A. et al., "Inequality and Happiness: Are Europeans and Americans Different?", *Journal of Public Economics* (88) 2004.

[25] Alesina, A. et al., "Segregation and the Quality of Government in a Cross-section of Countries", *American Economic Review*, 2005.

[26] Bjornskov, C. et al., "Formal Institutions and Subjective Well-being: Revisiting the Cross-country Evidence", *European Journal of Political Economy* (26) 2010 年.

[27] Dolan, P. et al., "Do We Really Know What Makes Us Happy? A Review of the Economic Literature on the Factors Associated with Subjective Well-being", *Journal of Economic Psychology* (29) 2008.

[28] Helliwell, J. F., H. Huang, "How's Your Government? International Evidence Linking Good Government and Well-being", *British Journal of Political Science* (4) 2008.

[29] Helliwell, J. F., R.D.Putnam, "The Social Context of Well-being", *Biological Sciences* (359) 2004.

[30] Holmberg, S. et al., "Quality of Government: What You Get", *Annual Review of Political Science* (12) 2009.

[31] Hudson, J., "Institutional Trust and Subjective Well-being across the EU", *Kyklos* (59) 2006.

[32] Kim, S., D. Kim, "Does Government Make People Happy? Exploring New Research Directions for Government's Roles in Happiness", *Journal of Happiness Studies* (34) 2011.

[33] La Porta, R. et al., "The Quality of Government", *Journal of Law, Economics and Organization* (15) 1999.

［34］Mauro, P., "Corruption and the Composition of Government Expenditure", *Journal of Public Economics* (69) 1998.

［35］Treisman, D., "Decentralization and the Quality of Government", working paper, 2002.

社长致辞

伴随着今冬的第一场雪，2017年很快就要到了。世界每天都在发生着让人眼花缭乱的变化，而唯一不变的，是面向未来无数的可能性。作为个体，如何获取专业信息以备不时之需？作为行政主体或企事业主体，如何提高决策的科学性让这个世界变得更好而不是更糟？原创、实证、专业、前沿、及时、持续，这是1997年"皮书系列"品牌创立的初衷。

1997～2017，从最初一个出版社的学术产品名称到媒体和公众使用频率极高的热点词语，从专业术语到大众话语，从官方文件到独特的出版型态，作为重要的智库成果，"皮书"始终致力于成为海量信息时代的信息过滤器，成为经济社会发展的记录仪，成为政策制定、评估、调整的智力源，社会科学研究的资料集成库。"皮书"的概念不断延展，"皮书"的种类更加丰富，"皮书"的功能日渐完善。

1997～2017，皮书及皮书数据库已成为中国新型智库建设不可或缺的抓手与平台，成为政府、企业和各类社会组织决策的利器，成为人文社科研究最基本的资料库，成为世界系统完整及时认知当代中国的窗口和通道！"皮书"所具有的凝聚力正在形成一种无形的力量，吸引着社会各界关注中国的发展，参与中国的发展。

二十年的"皮书"正值青春，愿每一位皮书人付出的年华与智慧不辜负这个时代！

社会科学文献出版社社长
中国社会学会秘书长

2016年11月

社会科学文献出版社简介

社会科学文献出版社成立于1985年,是直属于中国社会科学院的人文社会科学专业学术出版机构。

成立以来,社科文献依托于中国社会科学院丰厚的学术出版和专家学者资源,坚持"创社科经典,出传世文献"的出版理念和"权威、前沿、原创"的产品定位,逐步走上了智库产品与专业学术成果系列化、规模化、数字化、国际化、市场化发展的经营道路,取得了令人瞩目的成绩。

学术出版 社科文献先后策划出版了"皮书"系列、"列国志"、"社科文献精品译库"、"全球化译丛"、"全面深化改革研究书系"、"近世中国"、"甲骨文"、"中国史话"等一大批既有学术影响又有市场价值的图书品牌和学术品牌,形成了较强的学术出版能力和资源整合能力。2016年社科文献发稿5.5亿字,出版图书2000余种,承印发行中国社会科学院院属期刊72种。

数字出版 凭借着雄厚的出版资源整合能力,社科文献长期以来一直致力于从内容资源和数字平台两个方面实现传统出版的再造,并先后推出了皮书数据库、列国志数据库、中国田野调查数据库等一系列数字产品。2016年数字化加工图书近4000种,文字处理量达10亿字。数字出版已经初步形成了产品设计、内容开发、编辑标引、产品运营、技术支持、营销推广等全流程体系。

国际出版 社科文献通过学术交流和国际书展等方式积极参与国际学术和国际出版的交流合作,努力将中国优秀的人文社会科学研究成果推向世界,从构建国际话语体系的角度推动学术出版国际化。目前已与英、荷、法、德、美、日、韩等国及港澳台地区近40家出版和学术文化机构建立了长期稳定的合作关系。

融合发展 紧紧围绕融合发展战略,社科文献全面布局融合发展和数字化转型升级,成效显著。以核心资源和重点项目为主的社科文献数据库产品群和数字出版体系日臻成熟,"一带一路"系列研究成果与专题数据库、阿拉伯问题研究国别基础库及中阿文化交流数据库平台等项目开启了社科文献向专业知识服务商转型的新篇章,成为行业领先。

此外,社科文献充分利用网络媒体平台,积极与各类媒体合作,并联合大型书店、学术书店、机场书店、网络书店、图书馆,构建起强大的学术图书内容传播平台,学术图书的媒体曝光率居全国之首,图书馆藏率居于全国出版机构前十位。

有温度,有情怀,有视野,更有梦想。未来社科文献将继续坚持专业化学术出版之路不动摇,着力搭建最具影响力的智库产品整合及传播平台、学术资源共享平台,为实现"社科文献梦"奠定坚实基础。

经 济 类

经济类皮书涵盖宏观经济、城市经济、大区域经济，提供权威、前沿的分析与预测

经济蓝皮书
2017年中国经济形势分析与预测
李扬 / 主编　2016年12月出版　定价：89.00元

◆ 本书为总理基金项目，由著名经济学家李扬领衔，联合中国社会科学院等数十家科研机构、国家部委和高等院校的专家共同撰写，系统分析了2016年的中国经济形势并预测2017年我国经济运行情况。

中国省域竞争力蓝皮书
中国省域经济综合竞争力发展报告（2015～2016）
李建平　李闽榕　高燕京 / 主编　2017年2月出版　估价：198.00元

◆ 本书融多学科的理论为一体，深入追踪研究了省域经济发展与中国国家竞争力的内在关系，为提升中国省域经济综合竞争力提供有价值的决策依据。

城市蓝皮书
中国城市发展报告 No.10
潘家华　单菁菁 / 主编　2017年9月出版　估价：89.00元

◆ 本书是由中国社会科学院城市发展与环境研究中心编著的，多角度、全方位地立体展示了中国城市的发展状况，并对中国城市的未来发展提出了许多建议。该书有强烈的时代感，对中国城市发展实践有重要的参考价值。

皮书系列重点推荐

经济类

人口与劳动绿皮书

中国人口与劳动问题报告 No.18

蔡昉　张车伟/主编　2017年10月出版　估价：89.00元

◆ 本书为中国社科院人口与劳动经济研究所主编的年度报告，对当前中国人口与劳动形势做了比较全面和系统的深入讨论，为研究我国人口与劳动问题提供了一个专业性的视角。

世界经济黄皮书

2017年世界经济形势分析与预测

张宇燕/主编　2016年12月出版　定价：89.00元

◆ 本书由中国社会科学院世界经济与政治研究所的研究团队撰写，2016年世界经济增速进一步放缓，就业增长放慢。世界经济面临许多重大挑战同时，地缘政治风险、难民危机、大国政治周期、恐怖主义等问题也仍然在影响世界经济的稳定与发展。预计2017年按PPP计算的世界GDP增长率约为3.0%。

国际城市蓝皮书

国际城市发展报告（2017）

屠启宇/主编　2017年2月出版　估价：89.00元

◆ 本书作者以上海社会科学院从事国际城市研究的学者团队为核心，汇集同济大学、华东师范大学、复旦大学、上海交通大学、南京大学、浙江大学相关城市研究专业学者。立足动态跟踪介绍国际城市发展时间中，最新出现的重大战略、重大理念、重大项目、重大报告和最佳案例。

金融蓝皮书

中国金融发展报告（2017）

李扬　王国刚/主编　2017年1月出版　估价：89.00元

◆ 本书由中国社会科学院金融研究所组织编写，概括和分析了2016年中国金融发展和运行中的各方面情况，研讨和评论了2016年发生的主要金融事件，有利于读者了解掌握2016年中国的金融状况，把握2017年中国金融的走势。

经济类 — 皮书系列重点推荐

农村绿皮书
中国农村经济形势分析与预测（2016~2017）

魏后凯　杜志雄　黄秉信 / 著　2017年4月出版　估价：89.00元

◆ 本书描述了2016年中国农业农村经济发展的一些主要指标和变化，并对2017年中国农业农村经济形势的一些展望和预测，提出相应的政策建议。

西部蓝皮书
中国西部发展报告（2017）

姚慧琴　徐璋勇 / 主编　2017年9月出版　估价：89.00元

◆ 本书由西北大学中国西部经济发展研究中心主编，汇集了源自西部本土以及国内研究西部问题的权威专家的第一手资料，对国家实施西部大开发战略进行年度动态跟踪，并对2017年西部经济、社会发展态势进行预测和展望。

经济蓝皮书·夏季号
中国经济增长报告（2016~2017）

李扬 / 主编　2017年9月出版　估价：98.00元

◆ 中国经济增长报告主要探讨2016~2017年中国经济增长问题，以专业视角解读中国经济增长，力求将其打造成一个研究中国经济增长、服务宏微观各级决策的周期性、权威性读物。

就业蓝皮书
2017年中国本科生就业报告

麦可思研究院 / 编著　2017年6月出版　估价：98.00元

◆ 本书基于大量的数据和调研，内容翔实，调查独到，分析到位，用数据说话，对我国大学生教育与发展起到了很好的建言献策作用。

皮书系列重点推荐 社会政法类

社会政法类

社会政法类皮书聚焦社会发展领域的热点、难点问题，提供权威、原创的资讯与视点

社会蓝皮书
2017年中国社会形势分析与预测
李培林　陈光金　张翼 / 主编　2016年12月出版　定价：89.00元

◆ 本书由中国社会科学院社会学研究所组织研究机构专家、高校学者和政府研究人员撰写，聚焦当下社会热点，对2016年中国社会发展的各个方面内容进行了权威解读，同时对2017年社会形势发展趋势进行了预测。

法治蓝皮书
中国法治发展报告No.15（2017）
李林　田禾 / 主编　2017年3月出版　估价：118.00元

◆ 本年度法治蓝皮书回顾总结了2016年度中国法治发展取得的成就和存在的不足，并对2017年中国法治发展形势进行了预测和展望。

社会体制蓝皮书
中国社会体制改革报告No.5（2017）
龚维斌 / 主编　2017年4月出版　估价：89.00元

◆ 本书由国家行政学院社会治理研究中心和北京师范大学中国社会管理研究院共同组织编写，主要对2016年社会体制改革情况进行回顾和总结，对2017年的改革走向进行分析，提出相关政策建议。

社会政法类　　皮书系列 重点推荐

社会心态蓝皮书
中国社会心态研究报告（2017）
王俊秀　杨宜音/主编　2017年12月出版　估价：89.00元

◆ 本书是中国社会科学院社会学研究所社会心理研究中心"社会心态蓝皮书课题组"的年度研究成果，运用社会心理学、社会学、经济学、传播学等多种学科的方法进行了调查和研究，对于目前我国社会心态状况有较广泛和深入的揭示。

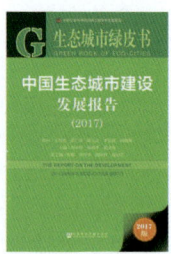

生态城市绿皮书
中国生态城市建设发展报告（2017）
刘举科　孙伟平　胡文臻/主编　2017年7月出版　估价：118.00元

◆ 报告以绿色发展、循环经济、低碳生活、民生宜居为理念，以更新民众观念、提供决策咨询、指导工程实践、引领绿色发展为宗旨，试图探索一条具有中国特色的城市生态文明建设新路。

城市生活质量蓝皮书
中国城市生活质量报告（2017）
中国经济实验研究院/主编　2017年7月出版　估价：89.00元

◆ 本书对全国35个城市居民的生活质量主观满意度进行了电话调查，同时对35个城市居民的客观生活质量指数进行了计算，为我国城市居民生活质量的提升，提出了针对性的政策建议。

公共服务蓝皮书
中国城市基本公共服务力评价（2017）
钟君　吴正杲/主编　2017年12月出版　估价：89.00元

◆ 中国社会科学院经济与社会建设研究室与华图政信调查组成联合课题组，从2010年开始对基本公共服务力进行研究，研创了基本公共服务力评价指标体系，为政府考核公共服务与社会管理工作提供了理论工具。

行 业 报 告 类

行业报告类皮书立足重点行业、新兴行业领域，
提供及时、前瞻的数据与信息

企业社会责任蓝皮书
中国企业社会责任研究报告（2017）

黄群慧　钟宏武　张蒽　翟利峰/著　2017年10月出版　估价：89.00元

◆ 本书剖析了中国企业社会责任在2016~2017年度的最新发展特征，详细解读了省域国有企业在社会责任方面的阶段性特征，生动呈现了国内外优秀企业的社会责任实践。对了解中国企业社会责任履行现状、未来发展，以及推动社会责任建设有重要的参考价值。

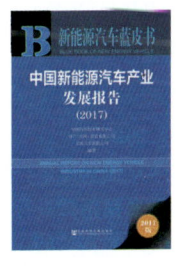

新能源汽车蓝皮书
中国新能源汽车产业发展报告（2017）

黄中国汽车技术研究中心　日产（中国）投资有限公司
东风汽车有限公司/编著　2017年7月出版　估价：98.00元

◆ 本书对我国2016年新能源汽车产业发展进行了全面系统的分析，并介绍了国外的发展经验。有助于相关机构、行业和社会公众等了解中国新能源汽车产业发展的最新动态，为政府部门出台新能源汽车产业相关政策法规、企业制定相关战略规划，提供必要的借鉴和参考。

杜仲产业绿皮书
中国杜仲橡胶资源与产业发展报告（2016~2017）

杜红岩　胡文臻　俞锐/主编　2017年1月出版　估价：85.00元

◆ 本书对2016年来的杜仲产业的发展情况、研究团队在杜仲研究方面取得的重要成果、部分地区杜仲产业发展的具体情况、杜仲新标准的制定情况等进行了较为详细的分析与介绍，使广大关心杜仲产业发展的读者能够及时跟踪产业最新进展。

企业蓝皮书
中国企业绿色发展报告 No.2（2017）

李红玉　朱光辉 / 主编　　2017 年 8 月出版　　估价：89.00 元

◆ 本书深入分析中国企业能源消费、资源利用、绿色金融、绿色产品、绿色管理、信息化、绿色发展政策及绿色文化方面的现状，并对目前存在的问题进行研究，剖析因果，谋划对策。为企业绿色发展提供借鉴，为我国生态文明建设提供支撑。

中国上市公司蓝皮书
中国上市公司发展报告（2017）

张平　王宏淼 / 主编　　2017 年 10 月出版　　估价：98.00 元

◆ 本书由中国社会科学院上市公司研究中心组织编写的，着力于全面、真实、客观反映当前中国上市公司财务状况和价值评估的综合性年度报告。本书详尽分析了 2016 年中国上市公司情况，特别是现实中暴露出的制度性、基础性问题，并对资本市场改革进行了探讨。

资产管理蓝皮书
中国资产管理行业发展报告（2017）

智信资产管理研究院 / 编著　　2017 年 6 月出版　　估价：89.00 元

◆ 中国资产管理行业刚刚兴起，未来将中国金融市场最有看点的行业。本书主要分析了 2016 年度资产管理行业的发展情况，同时对资产管理行业的未来发展做出科学的预测。

体育蓝皮书
中国体育产业发展报告（2017）

阮伟　钟秉枢 / 主编　　2017 年 12 月出版　　估价：89.00 元

◆ 本书运用多种研究方法，在对于体育竞赛业、体育用品业、体育场馆业、体育传媒业等传统产业研究的基础上，紧紧围绕 2016 年体育领域内的各种热点事件进行研究和梳理，进一步拓宽了研究的广度、提升了研究的高度、挖掘了研究的深度。

皮书系列 重点推荐   国别与地区类

国别与地区类

国别与地区类皮书关注全球重点国家与地区，
提供全面、独特的解读与研究

美国蓝皮书
美国研究报告（2017）

郑秉文　黄平／主编　2017年6月出版　估价：89.00元

◆ 本书是由中国社会科学院美国所主持完成的研究成果，它回顾了美国2016年的经济、政治形势与外交战略，对2017年以来美国内政外交发生的重大事件及重要政策进行了较为全面的回顾和梳理。

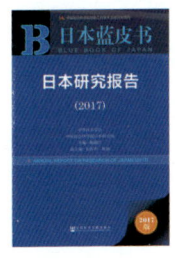

日本蓝皮书
日本研究报告（2017）

杨伯江／主编　2017年5月出版　估价：89.00元

◆ 本书对2016年拉丁美洲和加勒比地区诸国的政治、经济、社会、外交等方面的发展情况做了系统介绍，对该地区相关国家的热点及焦点问题进行了总结和分析，并在此基础上对该地区各国2017年的发展前景做出预测。

亚太蓝皮书
亚太地区发展报告（2017）

李向阳／主编　2017年3月出版　估价：89.00元

◆ 本书是中国社会科学院亚太与全球战略研究院的集体研究成果。2016年的"亚太蓝皮书"继续关注中国周边环境的变化。该书盘点了2016年亚太地区的焦点和热点问题，为深入了解2016年及未来中国与周边环境的复杂形势提供了重要参考。

德国蓝皮书
德国发展报告（2017）

郑春荣 / 主编　2017 年 6 月出版　估价：89.00 元

◆ 本报告由同济大学德国研究所组织编撰，由该领域的专家学者对德国的政治、经济、社会文化、外交等方面的形势发展情况，进行全面的阐述与分析。

日本经济蓝皮书
日本经济与中日经贸关系研究报告（2017）

王洛林 / 张季风 / 编著　2017 年 5 月出版　估价：89.00 元

◆ 本书系统、详细地介绍了 2016 年日本经济以及中日经贸关系发展情况，在进行了大量数据分析的基础上，对 2017 年日本经济以及中日经贸关系的大致发展趋势进行了分析与预测。

俄罗斯黄皮书
俄罗斯发展报告（2017）

李永全 / 编著　2017 年 7 月出版　估价：89.00 元

◆ 本书系统介绍了 2016 年俄罗斯经济政治情况，并对 2016 年该地区发生的焦点、热点问题进行了分析与回顾；在此基础上，对该地区 2017 年的发展前景进行了预测。

非洲黄皮书
非洲发展报告 No.19（2016～2017）

张宏明 / 主编　2017 年 8 月出版　估价：89.00 元

◆ 本书是由中国社会科学院西亚非洲研究所组织编撰的非洲形势年度报告，比较全面、系统地分析了 2016 年非洲政治形势和热点问题，探讨了非洲经济形势和市场走向，剖析了大国对非洲关系的新动向；此外，还介绍了国内非洲研究的新成果。

地方发展类

地方发展类皮书关注中国各省份、经济区域，
提供科学、多元的预判与资政信息

北京蓝皮书
北京公共服务发展报告（2016~2017）

施昌奎 / 主编　2017年2月出版　估价：89.00元

◆ 本书是由北京市政府职能部门的领导、首都著名高校的教授、知名研究机构的专家共同完成的关于北京市公共服务发展与创新的研究成果。

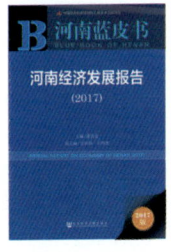

河南蓝皮书
河南经济发展报告（2017）

张占仓 / 编著　2017年3月出版　估价：89.00元

◆ 本书以国内外经济发展环境和走向为背景，主要分析当前河南经济形势，预测未来发展趋势，全面反映河南经济发展的最新动态、热点和问题，为地方经济发展和领导决策提供参考。

广州蓝皮书
2017年中国广州经济形势分析与预测

庾建设　陈浩钿　谢博能 / 主编　2017年7月出版　估价：85.00元

◆ 本书由广州大学与广州市委政策研究室、广州市统计局联合主编，汇集了广州科研团体、高等院校和政府部门诸多经济问题研究专家、学者和实际部门工作者的最新研究成果，是关于广州经济运行情况和相关专题分析、预测的重要参考资料。

文化传媒类

皮书系列
重点推荐

文化传媒类

文化传媒类皮书透视文化领域、文化产业，
探索文化大繁荣、大发展的路径

新媒体蓝皮书

中国新媒体发展报告 No.8（2017）

唐绪军 / 主编　2017年6月出版　估价：89.00元

◆ 本书是由中国社会科学院新闻与传播研究所组织编写的关于新媒体发展的最新年度报告，旨在全面分析中国新媒体的发展现状，解读新媒体的发展趋势，探析新媒体的深刻影响。

移动互联网蓝皮书

中国移动互联网发展报告（2017）

官建文 / 编著　2017年6月出版　估价：89.00元

◆ 本书着眼于对中国移动互联网2016年度的发展情况做深入解析，对未来发展趋势进行预测，力求从不同视角、不同层面全面剖析中国移动互联网发展的现状、年度突破及热点趋势等。

传媒蓝皮书

中国传媒产业发展报告（2017）

崔保国 / 主编　2017年5月出版　估价：98.00元

◆ "传媒蓝皮书"连续十多年跟踪观察和系统研究中国传媒产业发展。本报告在对传媒产业总体以及各细分行业发展状况与趋势进行深入分析基础上，对年度发展热点进行跟踪，剖析新技术引领下的商业模式，对传媒各领域发展趋势、内体经营、传媒投资进行解析，为中国传媒产业正在发生的变革提供前瞻行参考。

皮书系列 2017全品种 — 经济类

经济类

"三农"互联网金融蓝皮书
中国"三农"互联网金融发展报告（2017）
著（编）者：李勇坚 王弢　2017年8月出版 / 估价：98.00元
PSN B-2016-561-1/1

G20国家创新竞争力黄皮书
二十国集团（G20）国家创新竞争力发展报告（2016~2017）
著（编）者：李建平 李闽榕 赵新力　周天勇
2017年8月出版 / 估价：158.00元
PSN Y-2011-229-1/1

产业蓝皮书
中国产业竞争力报告（2017）No.7
著（编）者：张其仔　2017年12月出版 / 估价：98.00元
PSN B-2010-175-1/1

城市创新蓝皮书
中国城市创新报告（2017）
著（编）者：周天勇 旷建伟　2017年11月出版 / 估价：89.00元
PSN B-2013-340-1/1

城市蓝皮书
中国城市发展报告No.10
著（编）者：潘家华 单菁菁　2017年9月出版 / 估价：89.00元
PSN B-2007-091-1/1

城乡一体化蓝皮书
中国城乡一体化发展报告（2016～2017）
著（编）者：汝信 付崇兰　2017年7月出版 / 估价：85.00元
PSN B-2011-226-1/2

城镇化蓝皮书
中国新型城镇化健康发展报告（2017）
著（编）者：张占斌　2017年8月出版 / 估价：89.00元
PSN B-2014-396-1/1

创新蓝皮书
创新型国家建设报告（2016～2017）
著（编）者：詹正茂　2017年12月出版 / 估价：89.00元
PSN B-2009-140-1/1

创业蓝皮书
中国创业发展报告（2016～2017）
著（编）者：黄群慧 赵卫星 钟宏武等
2017年11月出版 / 估价：89.00元
PSN B-2016-578-1/1

低碳发展蓝皮书
中国低碳发展报告（2016~2017）
著（编）者：齐晔 张希良　2017年3月出版 / 估价：98.00元
PSN B-2011-223-1/1

低碳经济蓝皮书
中国低碳经济发展报告（2017）
著（编）者：薛进军 赵忠秀　2017年6月出版 / 估价：85.00元
PSN B-2011-194-1/1

东北蓝皮书
中国东北地区发展报告（2017）
著（编）者：朱宇 张新颖　2017年12月出版 / 估价：89.00元
PSN B-2006-067-1/1

发展与改革蓝皮书
中国经济发展和体制改革报告No.8
著（编）者：邹东涛 王再文　2017年1月出版 / 估价：98.00元
PSN B-2008-122-1/1

工业化蓝皮书
中国工业化进程报告（2017）
著（编）者：黄群慧　2017年12月出版 / 估价：158.00元
PSN B-2007-095-1/1

管理蓝皮书
中国管理发展报告（2017）
著（编）者：张晓东　2017年10月出版 / 估价：98.00元
PSN B-2014-416-1/1

国际城市蓝皮书
国际城市发展报告（2017）
著（编）者：屠启宇　2017年2月出版 / 估价：89.00元
PSN B-2012-260-1/1

国家创新蓝皮书
中国创新发展报告（2017）
著（编）者：陈劲　2017年12月出版 / 估价：89.00元
PSN B-2014-370-1/1

金融蓝皮书
中国金融发展报告（2017）
著（编）者：李杨 王国刚　2017年12月出版 / 估价：89.00元
PSN B-2004-031-1/6

京津冀金融蓝皮书
京津冀金融发展报告（2017）
著（编）者：王爱俭 李向前
2017年3月出版 / 估价：89.00元
PSN B-2016-528-1/1

京津冀蓝皮书
京津冀发展报告（2017）
著（编）者：文魁 祝尔娟　2017年4月出版 / 估价：89.00元
PSN B-2012-262-1/1

经济蓝皮书
2017年中国经济形势分析与预测
著（编）者：李扬　2016年12月出版 / 定价：89.00元
PSN B-1996-001-1/1

经济蓝皮书·春季号
2017年中国经济前景分析
著（编）者：李扬　2017年6月出版 / 估价：89.00元
PSN B-1999-008-1/1

经济蓝皮书·夏季号
中国经济增长报告（2016～2017）
著（编）者：李扬　2017年9月出版 / 估价：98.00元
PSN B-2010-176-1/1

经济信息绿皮书
中国与世界经济发展报告（2017）
著（编）者：杜平　2017年12月出版 / 估价：89.00元
PSN G-2003-023-1/1

就业蓝皮书
2017年中国本科生就业报告
著（编）者：麦可思研究院　2017年6月出版 / 估价：98.00元
PSN B-2009-146-1/2

皮书系列
2017全品种

经济类

就业蓝皮书
2017年中国高职高专生就业报告
著(编)者：麦可思研究院　2017年6月出版 / 估价：98.00元
PSN B-2015-472-2/2

科普能力蓝皮书
中国科普能力评价报告（2017）
著(编)者：任富　强李群　2017年8月出版 / 估价：89.00元
PSN B-2016-556-1/1

临空经济蓝皮书
中国临空经济发展报告（2017）
著(编)者：连玉明　2017年9月出版 / 估价：89.00元
PSN B-2014-421-1/1

农村绿皮书
中国农村经济形势分析与预测（2016~2017）
著(编)者：魏后凯　杜志雄　黄秉信
2017年4月出版 / 估价：89.00元
PSN G-1998-003-1/1

农业应对气候变化蓝皮书
气候变化对中国农业影响评估报告 No.3
著(编)者：矫梅燕　2017年8月出版 / 估价：98.00元
PSN B-2014-413-1/1

气候变化绿皮书
应对气候变化报告（2017）
著(编)者：王伟光　郑国光　2017年6月出版 / 估价：89.00元
PSN G-2009-144-1/1

区域蓝皮书
中国区域经济发展报告（2016~2017）
著(编)者：赵弘　2017年6月出版 / 估价：89.00元
PSN B-2004-034-1/1

全球环境竞争力绿皮书
全球环境竞争力报告（2017）
著(编)者：李建平　李闽榕　王金南
2017年12月出版 / 估价：198.00元
PSN G-2013-363-1/1

人口与劳动绿皮书
中国人口与劳动问题报告 No.18
著(编)者：蔡昉　张车伟　2017年11月出版 / 估价：89.00元
PSN G-2000-012-1/1

商务中心区蓝皮书
中国商务中心区发展报告 No.3（2016）
著(编)者：李国红　单菁菁　2017年1月出版 / 估价：89.00元
PSN B-2015-444-1/1

世界经济黄皮书
2017年世界经济形势分析与预测
著(编)者：张宇燕　2016年12月出版 / 定价：89.00元
PSN Y-1999-006-1/1

世界旅游城市绿皮书
世界旅游城市发展报告（2017）
著(编)者：宋宇　2017年1月出版 / 估价：128.00元
PSN G-2014-400-1/1

土地市场蓝皮书
中国农村土地市场发展报告（2016~2017）
著(编)者：李光荣　2017年3月出版 / 估价：89.00元
PSN B-2016-527-1/1

西北蓝皮书
中国西北发展报告（2017）
著(编)者：高建龙　2017年3月出版 / 估价：89.00元
PSN B-2012-261-1/1

西部蓝皮书
中国西部发展报告（2017）
著(编)者：姚慧琴　徐璋勇　2017年9月出版 / 估价：89.00元
PSN B-2005-039-1/1

新型城镇化蓝皮书
新型城镇化发展报告（2017）
著(编)者：李伟　宋敏　沈体雁　2017年3月出版 / 估价：98.00元
PSN B-2014-431-1/1

新兴经济体蓝皮书
金砖国家发展报告（2017）
著(编)者：林跃勤　周文　2017年12月出版 / 估价：89.00元
PSN B-2011-195-1/1

长三角蓝皮书
2017年新常态下深化一体化的长三角
著(编)者：王庆五　2017年12月出版 / 估价：88.00元
PSN B-2005-038-1/1

中部竞争力蓝皮书
中国中部经济社会竞争力报告（2017）
著(编)者：教育部人文社会科学重点研究基地
　　　　　南昌大学中国中部经济社会发展研究中心
2017年12月出版 / 估价：89.00元
PSN B-2012-276-1/1

中部蓝皮书
中国中部地区发展报告（2017）
著(编)者：宋亚平　2017年12月出版 / 估价：88.00元
PSN B-2007-089-1/1

中国省域竞争力蓝皮书
中国省域经济综合竞争力发展报告（2017）
著(编)者：李建平　李闽榕　高燕京
2017年2月出版 / 估价：198.00元
PSN B-2007-088-1/1

中三角蓝皮书
长江中游城市群发展报告（2017）
著(编)者：秦尊文　2017年9月出版 / 估价：89.00元
PSN B-2014-417-1/1

中小城市绿皮书
中国中小城市发展报告（2017）
著(编)者：中国城市经济学会中小城市经济发展委员会
　　　　　中国城镇化促进会中小城市发展委员会
　　　　　《中国中小城市发展报告》编纂委员会
　　　　　中小城市发展战略研究院
2017年11月出版 / 估价：128.00元
PSN G-2010-161-1/1

中原蓝皮书
中原经济区发展报告（2017）
著(编)者：李英杰　2017年6月出版 / 估价：88.00元
PSN B-2011-192-1/1

自贸区蓝皮书
中国自贸区发展报告（2017）
著(编)者：王力　2017年7月出版 / 估价：89.00元
PSN B-2016-559-1/1

社会政法类

北京蓝皮书
中国社区发展报告（2017）
著(编)者：于燕燕　　2017年2月出版 / 估价：89.00元
PSN B-2007-083-5/8

殡葬绿皮书
中国殡葬事业发展报告（2017）
著(编)者：李伯森　　2017年4月出版 / 估价：158.00元
PSN G-2010-180-1/1

城市管理蓝皮书
中国城市管理报告（2016~2017）
著(编)者：刘林　刘承水　2017年5月出版 / 估价：158.00元
PSN B-2013-336-1/1

城市生活质量蓝皮书
中国城市生活质量报告（2017）
著(编)者：中国经济实验研究院
2017年7月出版 / 估价：89.00元
PSN B-2013-326-1/1

城市政府能力蓝皮书
中国城市政府公共服务能力评估报告（2017）
著(编)者：何艳玲　　2017年4月出版 / 估价：89.00元
PSN B-2013-338-1/1

慈善蓝皮书
中国慈善发展报告（2017）
著(编)者：杨团　　2017年6月出版 / 估价：89.00元
PSN B-2009-142-1/1

党建蓝皮书
党的建设研究报告 No.2（2017）
著(编)者：崔建民　陈东平　2017年2月出版 / 估价：89.00元
PSN B-2016-524-1/1

地方法治蓝皮书
中国地方法治发展报告 No.3（2017）
著(编)者：李林　田禾　2017年3月出版 / 估价：108.00元
PSN B-2015-442-1/1

法治蓝皮书
中国法治发展报告 No.15（2017）
著(编)者：李林　田禾　2017年3月出版 / 估价：118.00元
PSN B-2004-027-1/1

法治政府蓝皮书
中国法治政府发展报告（2017）
著(编)者：中国政法大学法治政府研究院
2017年2月出版 / 估价：98.00元
PSN B-2015-502-1/2

法治政府蓝皮书
中国法治政府评估报告（2017）
著(编)者：中国政法大学法治政府研究院
2016年11月出版 / 估价：98.00元
PSN B-2016-577-2/2

反腐倡廉蓝皮书
中国反腐倡廉建设报告 No.7
著(编)者：张英伟　　2017年12月出版 / 估价：89.00元
PSN B-2012-259-1/1

非传统安全蓝皮书
中国非传统安全研究报告（2016~2017）
著(编)者：余潇枫　魏志江　2017年6月出版 / 估价：89.00元
PSN B-2012-273-1/1

妇女发展蓝皮书
中国妇女发展报告 No.7
著(编)者：王金玲　　2017年9月出版 / 估价：148.00元
PSN B-2006-069-1/1

妇女教育蓝皮书
中国妇女教育发展报告 No.4
著(编)者：张李玺　　2017年10月出版 / 估价：78.00元
PSN B-2008-121-1/1

妇女绿皮书
中国性别平等与妇女发展报告（2017）
著(编)者：谭琳　　2017年12月出版 / 估价：99.00元
PSN G-2006-073-1/1

公共服务蓝皮书
中国城市基本公共服务力评价（2017）
著(编)者：钟君　吴正杲　2017年12月出版 / 估价：89.00元
PSN B-2011-214-1/1

公民科学素质蓝皮书
中国公民科学素质报告（2016~2017）
著(编)者：李群　陈雄　马宗文
2017年1月出版 / 估价：89.00元
PSN B-2014-379-1/1

公共关系蓝皮书
中国公共关系发展报告（2017）
著(编)者：柳斌杰　　2017年11月出版 / 估价：89.00元
PSN B-2016-580-1/1

公益蓝皮书
中国公益慈善发展报告（2017）
著(编)者：朱健刚　　2017年4月出版 / 估价：118.00元
PSN B-2012-283-1/1

国际人才蓝皮书
海外华侨华人专业人士报告（2017）
著(编)者：王辉耀　苗绿　2017年8月出版 / 估价：89.00元
PSN B-2012-409-4/4

国际人才蓝皮书
中国国际移民报告（2017）
著(编)者：王辉耀　　2017年2月出版 / 估价：89.00元
PSN B-2012-304-3/4

国际人才蓝皮书
中国留学发展报告（2017）No.5
著(编)者：王辉耀　苗绿　2017年10月出版 / 估价：89.00元
PSN B-2012-244-2/4

海洋社会蓝皮书
中国海洋社会发展报告（2017）
著(编)者：崔凤　宋宁而　2017年7月出版 / 估价：89.00元
PSN B-2015-478-1/1

社会政法类

皮书系列 2017全品种

行政改革蓝皮书
中国行政体制改革报告（2017）No.6
著(编)者：魏礼群　2017年5月出版／估价：98.00元
PSN B-2011-231-1/1

华侨华人蓝皮书
华侨华人研究报告（2017）
著(编)者：贾益民　2017年12月出版／估价：128.00元
PSN B-2011-204-1/1

环境竞争力绿皮书
中国省域环境竞争力发展报告（2017）
著(编)者：李建平　李闽榕　王金南
2017年11月出版／估价：198.00元
PSN G-2010-165-1/1

环境绿皮书
中国环境发展报告（2017）
著(编)者：刘鉴强　2017年11月出版／估价：89.00元
PSN G-2006-048-1/1

基金会蓝皮书
中国基金会发展报告（2016~2017）
著(编)者：中国基金会发展报告课题组
2017年4月出版／估价：85.00元
PSN B-2013-368-1/1

基金会绿皮书
中国基金会发展独立研究报告（2017）
著(编)者：基金会中心网　中央民族大学基金会研究中心
2017年4月出版／估价：88.00元
PSN G-2011-213-1/1

基金会透明度蓝皮书
中国基金会透明度发展研究报告（2017）
著(编)者：基金会中心网　清华大学廉政与治理研究中心
2017年12月出版／估价：89.00元
PSN B-2015-509-1/1

家庭蓝皮书
中国"创建幸福家庭活动"评估报告（2017）
国务院发展研究中心"创建幸福家庭活动评估"课题组著
2017年8月出版／估价：89.00元
PSN B-2012-261-1/1

健康城市蓝皮书
中国健康城市建设研究报告（2017）
著(编)者：王鸿春　解继江　盛继洪
2017年9月出版／估价：89.00元
PSN B-2016-565-2/2

教师蓝皮书
中国中小学教师发展报告（2017）
著(编)者：曾晓东　鱼霞　2017年6月出版／估价：89.00元
PSN B-2012-289-1/1

教育蓝皮书
中国教育发展报告（2017）
著(编)者：杨东平　2017年4月出版／估价：89.00元
PSN B-2006-047-1/1

科普蓝皮书
中国基层科普发展报告（2016~2017）
著(编)者：赵立　新陈玲　2017年9月出版／估价：89.00元
PSN B-2016-569-3/3

科普蓝皮书
中国科普基础设施发展报告（2017）
著(编)者：任福君　2017年6月出版／估价：89.00元
PSN B-2010-174-1/3

科普蓝皮书
中国科普人才发展报告（2017）
著(编)者：郑念　任嵘嵘　2017年4月出版／估价：98.00元
PSN B-2015-513-2/3

科学教育蓝皮书
中国科学教育发展报告（2017）
著(编)者：罗晖　王康友　2017年10月出版／估价：89.00元
PSN B-2015-487-1/1

劳动保障蓝皮书
中国劳动保障发展报告（2017）
著(编)者：刘燕斌　2017年9月出版／估价：188.00元
PSN B-2014-415-1/1

老龄蓝皮书
中国老年宜居环境发展报告（2017）
著(编)者：党俊武　周燕珉　2017年1月出版／估价：89.00元
PSN B-2013-320-1/1

连片特困区蓝皮书
中国连片特困区发展报告（2017）
著(编)者：游俊　冷志明　丁建军
2017年3月出版／估价：98.00元
PSN B-2013-321-1/1

民间组织蓝皮书
中国民间组织报告（2017）
著(编)者：黄晓勇　2017年12月出版／估价：89.00元
PSN B-2008-118-1/1

民调蓝皮书
中国民生调查报告（2017）
著(编)者：谢耘耕　2017年12月出版／估价：98.00元
PSN B-2014-398-1/1

民族发展蓝皮书
中国民族发展报告（2017）
著(编)者：郝时远　王延中　王希恩
2017年4月出版／估价：98.00元
PSN B-2006-070-1/1

女性生活蓝皮书
中国女性生活状况报告 No.11（2017）
著(编)者：韩湘景　2017年10月出版／估价：98.00元
PSN B-2006-071-1/1

汽车社会蓝皮书
中国汽车社会发展报告（2017）
著(编)者：王俊秀　2017年1月出版／估价：89.00元
PSN B-2011-224-1/1

皮书系列 2017全品种

社会政法类

青年蓝皮书
中国青年发展报告（2017）No.3
著（编）者：廉思 等　2017年4月出版 / 估价：89.00元
PSN B-2013-333-1/1

青少年蓝皮书
中国未成年人互联网运用报告（2017）
著（编）者：李文革　沈杰　季为民
2017年11月出版 / 估价：89.00元
PSN B-2010-156-1/1

青少年体育蓝皮书
中国青少年体育发展报告（2017）
著（编）者：郭建军　杨桦　2017年9月出版 / 估价：89.00元
PSN B-2015-482-1/1

群众体育蓝皮书
中国群众体育发展报告（2017）
著（编）者：刘国永　杨桦　2017年12月出版 / 估价：89.00元
PSN B-2016-519-2/3

人权蓝皮书
中国人权事业发展报告 No.7（2017）
著（编）者：李君如　2017年9月出版 / 估价：98.00元
PSN B-2011-215-1/1

社会保障绿皮书
中国社会保障发展报告（2017）No.9
著（编）者：王延中　2017年4月出版 / 估价：89.00元
PSN G-2001-014-1/1

社会风险评估蓝皮书
风险评估与危机预警评估报告（2017）
著（编）者：唐钧　2017年8月出版 / 估价：85.00元
PSN B-2016-521-1/1

社会工作蓝皮书
中国社会工作发展报告（2017）
著（编）者：民政部社会工作研究中心
2017年8月出版 / 估价：89.00元
PSN B-2009-141-1/1

社会管理蓝皮书
中国社会管理创新报告 No.5
著（编）者：连玉明　2017年11月出版 / 估价：89.00元
PSN B-2012-300-1/1

社会蓝皮书
2017年中国社会形势分析与预测
著（编）者：李培林　陈光金　张翼
2016年12月出版 / 定价：89.00元
PSN B-1998-002-1/1

社会体制蓝皮书
中国社会体制改革报告No.5（2017）
著（编）者：龚维斌　2017年4月出版 / 估价：89.00元
PSN B-2013-330-1/1

社会心态蓝皮书
中国社会心态研究报告（2017）
著（编）者：王俊秀　杨宜音　2017年12月出版 / 估价：89.00元
PSN B-2011-199-1/1

社会组织蓝皮书
中国社会组织评估发展报告（2017）
著（编）者：徐家良　廖鸿　2017年12月出版 / 估价：89.00元
PSN B-2013-366-1/1

生态城市绿皮书
中国生态城市建设发展报告（2017）
著（编）者：刘举科　孙伟平　胡文臻
2017年9月出版 / 估价：118.00元
PSN G-2012-269-1/1

生态文明绿皮书
中国省域生态文明建设评价报告（ECI 2017）
著（编）者：严耕　2017年12月出版 / 估价：98.00元
PSN G-2010-170-1/1

体育蓝皮书
中国公共体育服务发展报告（2017）
著（编）者：戴健　2017年12月出版 / 估价：89.00元
PSN B-2013-367-2/4

土地整治蓝皮书
中国土地整治发展研究报告 No.4
著（编）者：国土资源部土地整治中心
2017年7月出版 / 估价：89.00元
PSN B-2014-401-1/1

土地政策蓝皮书
中国土地政策研究报告（2017）
著（编）者：高延利　李宪文
2017年12月出版 / 估价：89.00元
PSN B-2015-506-1/1

医改蓝皮书
中国医药卫生体制改革报告（2017）
著（编）者：文学国　房志武　2017年11月出版 / 估价：98.00元
PSN B-2014-432-1/1

医疗卫生绿皮书
中国医疗卫生发展报告 No.7（2017）
著（编）者：申宝忠　韩玉珍　2017年4月出版 / 估价：85.00元
PSN G-2004-033-1/1

应急管理蓝皮书
中国应急管理报告（2017）
著（编）者：宋英华　2017年9月出版 / 估价：98.00元
PSN B-2016-563-1/1

政治参与蓝皮书
中国政治参与报告（2017）
著（编）者：房宁　2017年9月出版 / 估价：118.00元
PSN B-2011-200-1/1

中国农村妇女发展蓝皮书
农村流动女性城市生活发展报告（2017）
著（编）者：谢丽华　2017年12月出版 / 估价：89.00元
PSN B-2014-434-1/1

宗教蓝皮书
中国宗教报告（2017）
著（编）者：邱永辉　2017年4月出版 / 估价：89.00元
PSN B-2008-117-1/1

行业报告类

SUV蓝皮书
中国SUV市场发展报告（2016~2017）
著(编)者：靳军　2017年9月出版／估价：89.00元
PSN B-2016-572-1/1

保健蓝皮书
中国保健服务产业发展报告 No.2
著(编)者：中国保健协会　中共中央党校
2017年7月出版／估价：198.00元
PSN B-2012-272-3/3

保健蓝皮书
中国保健食品产业发展报告 No.2
著(编)者：中国保健协会
　　　　中国社会科学院食品药品产业发展与监管研究中心
2017年7月出版／估价：198.00元
PSN B-2012-271-2/3

保健蓝皮书
中国保健用品产业发展报告 No.2
著(编)者：中国保健协会
　　　　国务院国有资产监督管理委员会研究中心
2017年3月出版／估价：198.00元
PSN B-2012-270-1/3

保险蓝皮书
中国保险业竞争力报告（2017）
著(编)者：项俊波　2017年12月出版／估价：99.00元
PSN B-2013-311-1/1

冰雪蓝皮书
中国滑雪产业发展报告（2017）
著(编)者：孙承华　伍斌　魏庆华　张鸿俊
2017年8月出版／估价：89.00元
PSN B-2016-560-1/1

彩票蓝皮书
中国彩票发展报告（2017）
著(编)者：益彩基金　2017年4月出版／估价：98.00元
PSN B-2015-462-1/1

餐饮产业蓝皮书
中国餐饮产业发展报告（2017）
著(编)者：邢颖　2017年6月出版／估价：98.00元
PSN B-2009-151-1/1

测绘地理信息蓝皮书
新常态下的测绘地理信息研究报告（2017）
著(编)者：库热西·买合苏提
2017年12月出版／估价：118.00元
PSN B-2009-145-1/1

茶业蓝皮书
中国茶产业发展报告（2017）
著(编)者：杨江帆　李闽榕　2017年10月出版／估价：88.00元
PSN B-2010-164-1/1

产权市场蓝皮书
中国产权市场发展报告（2016～2017）
著(编)者：曹和平　2017年5月出版／估价：89.00元
PSN B-2009-147-1/1

产业安全蓝皮书
中国出版传媒产业安全报告（2016~2017）
著(编)者：北京印刷学院文化产业安全研究院
2017年3月出版／估价：89.00元
PSN B-2014-384-13/14

产业安全蓝皮书
中国文化产业安全报告（2017）
著(编)者：北京印刷学院文化产业安全研究院
2017年12月出版／估价：89.00元
PSN B-2014-378-12/14

产业安全蓝皮书
中国新媒体产业安全报告（2017）
著(编)者：北京印刷学院文化产业安全研究院
2017年12月出版／估价：89.00元
PSN B-2015-500-14/14

城投蓝皮书
中国城投行业发展报告（2017）
著(编)者：王晨艳　丁伯康　2017年11月出版／估价：300.00元
PSN B-2016-514-1/1

电子政务蓝皮书
中国电子政务发展报告（2016~2017）
著(编)者：李季　杜平　2017年7月出版／估价：89.00元
PSN B-2003-022-1/1

杜仲产业绿皮书
中国杜仲橡胶资源与产业发展报告（2016～2017）
著(编)者：杜红岩　胡文臻　俞锐
2017年1月出版／估价：85.00元
PSN G-2013-350-1/1

房地产蓝皮书
中国房地产发展报告 No.14（2017）
著(编)者：李春华　王业强　2017年5月出版／估价：89.00元
PSN B-2004-028-1/1

服务外包蓝皮书
中国服务外包产业发展报告（2017）
著(编)者：王晓红　刘德军
2017年6月出版／估价：89.00元
PSN B-2013-331-2/2

服务外包蓝皮书
中国服务外包竞争力报告（2017）
著(编)者：王力　刘春生　黄育华
2017年11月出版／估价：85.00元
PSN B-2011-216-1/2

工业和信息化蓝皮书
世界网络安全发展报告（2016~2017）
著(编)者：洪京一　2017年4月出版／估价：89.00元
PSN B-2015-452-5/5

工业和信息化蓝皮书
世界信息化发展报告（2016~2017）
著(编)者：洪京一　2017年4月出版／估价：89.00元
PSN B-2015-451-4/5

皮书系列 2017全品种

行业报告类

工业和信息化蓝皮书
世界信息技术产业发展报告（2016~2017）
著(编)者：洪京一　2017年4月出版 / 估价：89.00元
PSN B-2015-449-2/5

工业和信息化蓝皮书
移动互联网产业发展报告（2016~2017）
著(编)者：洪京一　2017年4月出版 / 估价：89.00元
PSN B-2015-448-1/5

工业和信息化蓝皮书
战略性新兴产业发展报告（2016~2017）
著(编)者：洪京一　2017年4月出版 / 估价：89.00元
PSN B-2015-450-3/5

工业设计蓝皮书
中国工业设计发展报告（2017）
著(编)者：王晓红　于炜　张立群
2017年9月出版 / 估价：138.00元
PSN B-2014-420-1/1

黄金市场蓝皮书
中国商业银行黄金业务发展报告（2016~2017）
著(编)者：平安银行　2017年3月出版 / 估价：98.00元
PSN B-2016-525-1/1

互联网金融蓝皮书
中国互联网金融发展报告（2017）
著(编)者：李东荣　2017年9月出版 / 估价：128.00元
PSN B-2014-374-1/1

互联网医疗蓝皮书
中国互联网医疗发展报告（2017）
著(编)者：宫晓东　2017年9月出版 / 估价：89.00元
PSN B-2016-568-1/1

会展蓝皮书
中外会展业动态评估年度报告（2017）
著(编)者：张敏　2017年1月出版 / 估价：88.00元
PSN B-2013-327-1/1

金融监管蓝皮书
中国金融监管报告（2017）
著(编)者：胡滨　2017年6月出版 / 估价：89.00元
PSN B-2012-281-1/1

金融蓝皮书
中国金融中心发展报告（2017）
著(编)者：王力　黄育华　2017年11月出版 / 估价：85.00元
PSN B-2011-186-6/6

建筑装饰蓝皮书
中国建筑装饰行业发展报告（2017）
著(编)者：刘晓一　葛顺道　2017年7月出版 / 估价：198.00元
PSN B-2016-554-1/1

客车蓝皮书
中国客车产业发展报告（2016~2017）
著(编)者：姚蔚　2017年10月出版 / 估价：85.00元
PSN B-2013-361-1/1

旅游安全蓝皮书
中国旅游安全报告（2017）
著(编)者：郑向敏　谢朝武　2017年5月出版 / 估价：128.00元
PSN B-2012-280-1/1

旅游绿皮书
2016~2017年中国旅游发展分析与预测
著(编)者：张广瑞　刘德谦　2017年4月出版 / 估价：89.00元
PSN G-2002-018-1/1

煤炭蓝皮书
中国煤炭工业发展报告（2017）
著(编)者：岳福斌　2017年12月出版 / 估价：85.00元
PSN B-2008-123-1/1

民营企业社会责任蓝皮书
中国民营企业社会责任报告（2017）
著(编)者：中华全国工商业联合会
2017年12月出版 / 估价：89.00元
PSN B-2015-511-1/1

民营医院蓝皮书
中国民营医院发展报告（2017）
著(编)者：庄一强　2017年10月出版 / 估价：85.00元
PSN B-2012-299-1/1

闽商蓝皮书
闽商发展报告（2017）
著(编)者：李闽榕　王日根　林琛
2017年12月出版 / 估价：89.00元
PSN B-2012-298-1/1

能源蓝皮书
中国能源发展报告（2017）
著(编)者：崔民选　王军生　陈义和
2017年10月出版 / 估价：98.00元
PSN B-2006-049-1/1

农产品流通蓝皮书
中国农产品流通产业发展报告（2017）
著(编)者：贾敬敦　张东科　张玉玺　张鹏毅　周伟
2017年1月出版 / 估价：89.00元
PSN B-2012-288-1/1

企业公益蓝皮书
中国企业公益研究报告（2017）
著(编)者：钟宏武　汪杰　顾一　黄晓娟　等
2017年12月出版 / 估价：89.00元
PSN B-2015-501-1/1

企业国际化蓝皮书
中国企业国际化报告（2017）
著(编)者：王辉耀　2017年11月出版 / 估价：98.00元
PSN B-2014-427-1/1

企业蓝皮书
中国企业绿色发展报告 No.2（2017）
著(编)者：李红玉　朱光辉　2017年8月出版 / 估价：89.00元
PSN B-2015-481-2/2

企业社会责任蓝皮书
中国企业社会责任研究报告（2017）
著(编)者：黄群慧　钟宏武　张蒽　翟利峰
2017年11月出版 / 估价：89.00元
PSN B-2009-149-1/1

汽车安全蓝皮书
中国汽车安全发展报告（2017）
著(编)者：中国汽车技术研究中心
2017年7月出版 / 估价：89.00元
PSN B-2014-385-1/1

行业报告类
皮书系列 2017全品种

汽车电子商务蓝皮书
中国汽车电子商务发展报告（2017）
著(编)者： 中华全国工商业联合会汽车经销商商会
　　　　　北京易观智库网络科技有限公司
2017年10月出版 / 估价：128.00元
PSN B-2015-485-1/1

汽车工业蓝皮书
中国汽车工业发展年度报告（2017）
著(编)者： 中国汽车工业协会 中国汽车技术研究中心
　　　　　丰田汽车（中国）投资有限公司
2017年4月出版 / 估价：128.00元
PSN B-2015-463-1/2

汽车工业蓝皮书
中国汽车零部件产业发展报告（2017）
著(编)者： 中国汽车工业协会 中国汽车工程研究院
2017年10月出版 / 估价：98.00元
PSN B-2016-515-2/2

汽车蓝皮书
中国汽车产业发展报告（2017）
著(编)者： 国务院发展研究中心产业经济研究部
　　　　　中国汽车工程学会 大众汽车集团（中国）
2017年8月出版 / 估价：98.00元
PSN B-2008-124-1/1

人力资源蓝皮书
中国人力资源发展报告（2017）
著(编)者： 余兴安　2017年11月出版 / 估价：89.00元
PSN B-2012-287-1/1

融资租赁蓝皮书
中国融资租赁业发展报告（2016～2017）
著(编)者： 李光荣 王力　2017年8月出版 / 估价：89.00元
PSN B-2015-443-1/1

商会蓝皮书
中国商会发展报告No.5（2017）
著(编)者： 王钦敏　2017年7月出版 / 估价：89.00元
PSN B-2008-125-1/1

输血服务蓝皮书
中国输血行业发展报告（2017）
著(编)者： 朱永明 耿鸿武　2016年8月出版 / 估价：89.00元
PSN B-2016-583-1/1

上市公司蓝皮书
中国上市公司社会责任信息披露报告（2017）
著(编)者： 张旺 张杨　2017年11月出版 / 估价：89.00元
PSN B-2011-234-1/1

社会责任管理蓝皮书
中国上市公司社会责任能力成熟度报告（2017）No.2
著(编)者： 肖红军 李晓光 李伟阳
2017年12月出版 / 估价：98.00元
PSN B-2015-507-2/2

社会责任管理蓝皮书
中国企业公众透明度报告(2017)No.3
著(编)者： 黄速建 熊梦 李晓光 肖红军
2017年1月出版 / 估价：98.00元
PSN B-2015-440-1/2

食品药品蓝皮书
食品药品安全与监管政策研究报告（2016～2017）
著(编)者： 唐民皓　2017年6月出版 / 估价：89.00元
PSN B-2009-129-1/1

世界能源蓝皮书
世界能源发展报告（2017）
著(编)者： 黄晓勇　2017年6月出版 / 估价：99.00元
PSN B-2013-349-1/1

水利风景区蓝皮书
中国水利风景区发展报告（2017）
著(编)者： 谢婵才 兰思仁　2017年5月出版 / 估价：89.00元
PSN B-2015-480-1/1

私募市场蓝皮书
中国私募股权市场发展报告（2017）
著(编)者： 曹和平　2017年12月出版 / 估价：89.00元
PSN B-2010-162-1/1

碳市场蓝皮书
中国碳市场报告（2017）
著(编)者： 定金彪　2017年11月出版 / 估价：89.00元
PSN B-2014-430-1/1

体育蓝皮书
中国体育产业发展报告（2017）
著(编)者： 阮伟 钟秉枢　2017年12月出版 / 估价：89.00元
PSN B-2010-179-1/4

网络空间安全蓝皮书
中国网络空间安全发展报告（2017）
著(编)者： 惠志斌 唐涛　2017年4月出版 / 估价：89.00元
PSN B-2015-466-1/1

西部金融蓝皮书
中国西部金融发展报告（2017）
著(编)者： 李忠民　2017年8月出版 / 估价：85.00元
PSN B-2010-160-1/1

协会商会蓝皮书
中国行业协会商会发展报告（2017）
著(编)者： 景朝阳 李勇　2017年4月出版 / 估价：99.00元
PSN B-2015-461-1/1

新能源汽车蓝皮书
中国新能源汽车产业发展报告（2017）
著(编)者： 中国汽车技术研究中心
　　　　　日产（中国）投资有限公司 东风汽车有限公司
2017年7月出版 / 估价：98.00元
PSN B-2013-347-1/1

新三板蓝皮书
中国新三板市场发展报告（2017）
著(编)者： 王力　2017年6月出版 / 估价：89.00元
PSN B-2016-534-1/1

信托市场蓝皮书
中国信托业市场报告（2016～2017）
著(编)者： 用益信托工作室
2017年1月出版 / 估价：198.00元
PSN B-2014-371-1/1

皮书系列 2017全品种
行业报告类

信息化蓝皮书
中国信息化形势分析与预测（2016~2017）
著(编)者：周宏仁　2017年8月出版 / 估价：98.00元
PSN B-2010-168-1/1

信用蓝皮书
中国信用发展报告（2017）
著(编)者：章政　田侃　2017年4月出版 / 估价：99.00元
PSN B-2013-328-1/1

休闲绿皮书
2017年中国休闲发展报告
著(编)者：宋瑞　2017年10月出版 / 估价：89.00元
PSN G-2010-158-1/1

休闲体育蓝皮书
中国休闲体育发展报告（2016~2017）
著(编)者：李相如　钟炳枢　2017年10月出版 / 估价：89.00元
PSN G-2016-516-1/1

养老金融蓝皮书
中国养老金融发展报告（2017）
著(编)者：董克用　姚余栋
2017年6月出版 / 估价：89.00元
PSN B-2016-584-1/1

药品流通蓝皮书
中国药品流通行业发展报告（2017）
著(编)者：佘鲁林　温再兴　2017年8月出版 / 估价：158.00元
PSN B-2014-429-1/1

医院蓝皮书
中国医院竞争力报告（2017）
著(编)者：庄一强　曾益新　2017年3月出版 / 估价：128.00元
PSN B-2016-529-1/1

医药蓝皮书
中国中医药产业园战略发展报告（2017）
著(编)者：裴长洪　房书亭　吴滌心
2017年8月出版 / 估价：89.00元
PSN B-2012-305-1/1

邮轮绿皮书
中国邮轮产业发展报告（2017）
著(编)者：汪泓　2017年10月出版 / 估价：89.00元
PSN G-2014-419-1/1

智能养老蓝皮书
中国智能养老产业发展报告（2017）
著(编)者：朱勇　2017年10月出版 / 估价：89.00元
PSN B-2015-488-1/1

债券市场蓝皮书
中国债券市场发展报告（2016~2017）
著(编)者：杨农　2017年10月出版 / 估价：89.00元
PSN B-2016-573-1/1

中国节能汽车蓝皮书
中国节能汽车发展报告（2016~2017）
著(编)者：中国汽车工程研究院股份有限公司
2017年9月出版 / 估价：98.00元
PSN B-2016-566-1/1

中国上市公司蓝皮书
中国上市公司发展报告（2017）
著(编)者：张平　王宏淼
2017年10月出版 / 估价：98.00元
PSN B-2014-414-1/1

中国陶瓷产业蓝皮书
中国陶瓷产业发展报告（2017）
著(编)者：左和平　黄速建　2017年10月出版 / 估价：98.00元
PSN B-2016-574-1/1

中国总部经济蓝皮书
中国总部经济发展报告（2016~2017）
著(编)者：赵弘　2017年9月出版 / 估价：89.00元
PSN B-2005-036-1/1

中医文化蓝皮书
中国中医药文化传播发展报告（2017）
著(编)者：毛嘉陵　2017年7月出版 / 估价：89.00元
PSN B-2015-468-1/1

装备制造业蓝皮书
中国装备制造业发展报告（2017）
著(编)者：徐东华　2017年12月出版 / 估价：148.00元
PSN B-2015-505-1/1

资本市场蓝皮书
中国场外交易市场发展报告（2016~2017）
著(编)者：高峦　2017年3月出版 / 估价：89.00元
PSN B-2009-153-1/1

资产管理蓝皮书
中国资产管理行业发展报告（2017）
著(编)者：智信资产管理研究院
2017年6月出版 / 估价：89.00元
PSN B-2014-407-2/2

文化传媒类

传媒竞争力蓝皮书
中国传媒国际竞争力研究报告（2017）
著（编）者：李本乾 刘强
2017年11月出版 / 估价：148.00元
PSN B-2013-356-1/1

传媒蓝皮书
中国传媒产业发展报告（2017）
著（编）者：崔保国 2017年5月出版 / 估价：98.00元
PSN B-2005-035-1/1

传媒投资蓝皮书
中国传媒投资发展报告（2017）
著（编）者：张向东 谭云明
2017年6月出版 / 估价：128.00元
PSN B-2015-474-1/1

动漫蓝皮书
中国动漫产业发展报告（2017）
著（编）者：卢斌 郑玉明 牛兴侦
2017年9月出版 / 估价：89.00元
PSN B-2011-198-1/1

非物质文化遗产蓝皮书
中国非物质文化遗产发展报告（2017）
著（编）者：陈平 2017年5月出版 / 估价：98.00元
PSN B-2015-469-1/1

广电蓝皮书
中国广播电影电视发展报告（2017）
著（编）者：国家新闻出版广电总局发展研究中心
2017年7月出版 / 估价：98.00元
PSN B-2006-072-1/1

广告主蓝皮书
中国广告主营销传播趋势报告 No.9
著（编）者：黄升民 杜国清 邵华冬 等
2017年10月出版 / 估价：148.00元
PSN B-2005-041-1/1

国际传播蓝皮书
中国国际传播发展报告（2017）
著（编）者：胡正荣 李继东 姬德强
2017年11月出版 / 估价：89.00元
PSN B-2014-408-1/1

纪录片蓝皮书
中国纪录片发展报告（2017）
著（编）者：何苏六 2017年9月出版 / 估价：89.00元
PSN B-2011-222-1/1

科学传播蓝皮书
中国科学传播报告（2017）
著（编）者：詹正茂 2017年7月出版 / 估价：89.00元
PSN B-2008-120-1/1

两岸创意经济蓝皮书
两岸创意经济研究报告（2017）
著（编）者：罗昌智 林咏能
2017年10月出版 / 估价：98.00元
PSN B-2014-437-1/1

两岸文化蓝皮书
两岸文化产业合作发展报告（2017）
著（编）者：胡惠林 李保宗 2017年7月出版 / 估价：89.00元
PSN B-2012-285-1/1

媒介与女性蓝皮书
中国媒介与女性发展报告(2016~2017)
著（编）者：刘利群 2017年9月出版 / 估价：118.00元
PSN B-2013-345-1/1

媒体融合蓝皮书
中国媒体融合发展报告（2017）
著（编）者：梅宁华 宋建武 2017年7月出版 / 估价：89.00元
PSN B-2015-479-1/1

全球传媒蓝皮书
全球传媒发展报告（2017）
著（编）者：胡正荣 李继东 唐晓芬
2017年11月出版 / 估价：89.00元
PSN B-2012-237-1/1

少数民族非遗蓝皮书
中国少数民族非物质文化遗产发展报告（2017）
著（编）者：肖远平（彝）柴立（满）
2017年8月出版 / 估价：98.00元
PSN B-2015-467-1/1

视听新媒体蓝皮书
中国视听新媒体发展报告（2017）
著（编）者：国家新闻出版广电总局发展研究中心
2017年7月出版 / 估价：98.00元
PSN B-2011-184-1/1

文化创新蓝皮书
中国文化创新报告（2017）No.7
著（编）者：于平 傅才武 2017年7月出版 / 估价：98.00元
PSN B-2009-143-1/1

文化建设蓝皮书
中国文化发展报告（2016~2017）
著（编）者：江畅 孙伟平 戴茂堂
2017年6月出版 / 估价：116.00元
PSN B-2014-392-1/1

文化科技蓝皮书
文化科技创新发展报告（2017）
著（编）者：于平 李凤亮 2017年11月出版 / 估价：89.00元
PSN B-2013-342-1/1

文化蓝皮书
中国公共文化服务发展报告（2017）
著（编）者：刘新成 张永新 张旭
2017年12月出版 / 估价：98.00元
PSN B-2007-093-2/10

文化蓝皮书
中国公共文化投入增长测评报告（2017）
著（编）者：王亚南 2017年4月出版 / 估价：89.00元
PSN B-2014-435-10/10

皮书系列 2017全品种　文化传媒类·地方发展类

文化蓝皮书
中国少数民族文化发展报告（2016~2017）
著(编)者：武翠英 张晓明 任乌晶
2017年9月出版 / 估价：89.00元
PSN B-2013-369-9/10

文化蓝皮书
中国文化产业发展报告（2016~2017）
著(编)者：张晓明 王家新 章建刚
2017年2月出版 / 估价：89.00元
PSN B-2002-019-1/10

文化蓝皮书
中国文化产业供需协调检测报告（2017）
著(编)者：王亚南　2017年2月出版 / 估价：89.00元
PSN B-2013-323-8/10

文化蓝皮书
中国文化消费需求景气评价报告（2017）
著(编)者：王亚南　2017年4月出版 / 估价：89.00元
PSN B-2011-236-4/10

文化品牌蓝皮书
中国文化品牌发展报告（2017）
著(编)者：欧阳友权　2017年5月出版 / 估价：98.00元
PSN B-2012-277-1/1

文化遗产蓝皮书
中国文化遗产事业发展报告（2017）
著(编)者：苏杨 张颖岚 王宇飞
2017年8月出版 / 估价：98.00元
PSN B-2008-119-1/1

文学蓝皮书
中国文情报告（2016~2017）
著(编)者：白烨　2017年5月出版 / 估价：49.00元
PSN B-2011-221-1/1

新媒体蓝皮书
中国新媒体发展报告No.8（2017）
著(编)者：唐绪军　2017年6月出版 / 估价：89.00元
PSN B-2010-169-1/1

新媒体社会责任蓝皮书
中国新媒体社会责任研究报告（2017）
著(编)者：钟瑛　2017年11月出版 / 估价：89.00元
PSN B-2014-423-1/1

移动互联网蓝皮书
中国移动互联网发展报告（2017）
著(编)者：官建文　2017年6月出版 / 估价：89.00元
PSN B-2012-282-1/1

舆情蓝皮书
中国社会舆情与危机管理报告（2017）
著(编)者：谢耘耕　2017年9月出版 / 估价：128.00元
PSN B-2011-235-1/1

影视风控蓝皮书
中国影视舆情与风控报告（2017）
著(编)者：司若　2017年4月出版 / 估价：138.00元
PSN B-2016-530-1/1

地方发展类

安徽经济蓝皮书
合芜蚌国家自主创新综合示范区研究报告（2016~2017）
著(编)者：王开玉　2017年11月出版 / 估价：89.00元
PSN B-2014-383-1/1

安徽蓝皮书
安徽社会发展报告（2017）
著(编)者：程桦　2017年4月出版 / 估价：89.00元
PSN B-2013-325-1/1

安徽社会建设蓝皮书
安徽社会建设分析报告（2016~2017）
著(编)者：黄家海 王开玉 蔡宪
2016年4月出版 / 估价：89.00元
PSN B-2013-322-1/1

澳门蓝皮书
澳门经济社会发展报告（2016~2017）
著(编)者：吴志良 郝雨凡　2017年6月出版 / 估价：98.00元
PSN B-2009-138-1/1

北京蓝皮书
北京公共服务发展报告（2016~2017）
著(编)者：施昌奎　2017年2月出版 / 估价：89.00元
PSN B-2008-103-7/8

北京蓝皮书
北京经济发展报告（2016~2017）
著(编)者：杨松　2017年6月出版 / 估价：89.00元
PSN B-2006-054-2/8

北京蓝皮书
北京社会发展报告（2016~2017）
著(编)者：李伟东　2017年6月出版 / 估价：89.00元
PSN B-2006-055-3/8

北京蓝皮书
北京社会治理发展报告（2016~2017）
著(编)者：殷星辰　2017年5月出版 / 估价：89.00元
PSN B-2014-391-8/8

北京蓝皮书
北京文化发展报告（2016~2017）
著(编)者：李建盛　2017年4月出版 / 估价：89.00元
PSN B-2007-082-4/8

北京律师绿皮书
北京律师发展报告No.3（2017）
著(编)者：王隽　2017年7月出版 / 估价：88.00元
PSN G-2012-301-1/1

皮书系列 2017全品种 — 地方发展类

北京旅游蓝皮书
北京旅游发展报告（2017）
著(编)者：北京旅游学会　2017年1月出版 / 估价：88.00元
PSN B-2011-217-1/1

北京人才蓝皮书
北京人才发展报告（2017）
著(编)者：于淼　2017年12月出版 / 估价：128.00元
PSN B-2011-201-1/1

北京社会心态蓝皮书
北京社会心态分析报告（2016～2017）
著(编)者：北京社会心理研究所
2017年8月出版 / 估价：89.00元
PSN B-2014-422-1/1

北京社会组织管理蓝皮书
北京社会组织发展与管理（2016～2017）
著(编)者：黄江松　2017年4月出版 / 估价：88.00元
PSN B-2015-446-1/1

北京体育蓝皮书
北京体育产业发展报告（2016～2017）
著(编)者：钟秉枢　陈杰　杨铁黎
2017年9月出版 / 估价：89.00元
PSN B-2015-475-1/1

北京养老产业蓝皮书
北京养老产业发展报告（2017）
著(编)者：周明明　冯喜良　2017年8月出版 / 估价：89.00元
PSN B-2015-465-1/1

滨海金融蓝皮书
滨海新区金融发展报告（2017）
著(编)者：王爱俭　张锐钢　2017年12月出版 / 估价：89.00元
PSN B-2014-424-1/1

城乡一体化蓝皮书
中国城乡一体化发展报告·北京卷（2016～2017）
著(编)者：张宝秀　黄序　2017年5月出版 / 估价：89.00元
PSN B-2012-258-2/2

创意城市蓝皮书
北京文化创意产业发展报告（2017）
著(编)者：张京成　王国华　2017年10月出版 / 估价：89.00元
PSN B-2012-263-1/7

创意城市蓝皮书
青岛文化创意产业发展报告（2017）
著(编)者：马达　张丹妮　2017年8月出版 / 估价：89.00元
PSN B-2011-235-1/1

创意城市蓝皮书
天津文化创意产业发展报告（2016～2017）
著(编)者：谢思全　2017年6月出版 / 估价：89.00元
PSN B-2016-537-7/7

创意城市蓝皮书
无锡文化创意产业发展报告（2017）
著(编)者：谭军　张鸣年　2017年10月出版 / 估价：89.00元
PSN B-2013-346-3/7

创意城市蓝皮书
武汉文化创意产业发展报告（2017）
著(编)者：黄永林　陈汉桥　2017年9月出版 / 估价：99.00元
PSN B-2013-354-4/7

创意上海蓝皮书
上海文化创意产业发展报告（2016～2017）
著(编)者：王慧敏　王兴全　2017年8月出版 / 估价：89.00元
PSN B-2016-562-1/1

福建妇女发展蓝皮书
福建省妇女发展报告（2017）
著(编)者：刘群英　2017年11月出版 / 估价：88.00元
PSN B-2011-220-1/1

福建自贸区蓝皮书
中国（福建）自由贸易实验区发展报告（2016～2017）
著(编)者：黄茂兴　2017年4月出版 / 估价：108.00元
PSN B-2017-532-1/1

甘肃蓝皮书
甘肃经济发展分析与预测（2017）
著(编)者：朱智文　罗哲　2017年1月出版 / 估价：89.00元
PSN B-2013-312-1/6

甘肃蓝皮书
甘肃社会发展分析与预测（2017）
著(编)者：安文华　包晓霞　谢增虎
2017年1月出版 / 估价：89.00元
PSN B-2013-313-2/6

甘肃蓝皮书
甘肃文化发展分析与预测（2017）
著(编)者：安文华　周小华　2017年1月出版 / 估价：89.00元
PSN B-2013-314-3/6

甘肃蓝皮书
甘肃县域和农村发展报告（2017）
著(编)者：刘进军　柳民　王建兵
2017年1月出版 / 估价：89.00元
PSN B-2013-316-5/6

甘肃蓝皮书
甘肃舆情分析与预测（2017）
著(编)者：陈双梅　郝树声　2017年1月出版 / 估价：89.00元
PSN B-2013-315-4/6

甘肃蓝皮书
甘肃商贸流通发展报告（2017）
著(编)者：杨志武　王福生　王晓芳
2017年1月出版 / 估价：89.00元
PSN B-2016-523-6/6

广东蓝皮书
广东全面深化改革发展报告（2017）
著(编)者：周林生　涂成林　2017年12月出版 / 估价：89.00元
PSN B-2015-504-3/3

广东蓝皮书
广东社会工作发展报告（2017）
著(编)者：罗观翠　2017年6月出版 / 估价：89.00元
PSN B-2014-402-2/3

广东蓝皮书
广东省电子商务发展报告（2017）
著(编)者：程晓　邓顺国　2017年7月出版 / 估价：89.00元
PSN B-2013-360-1/3

皮书系列 2017全品种

地方发展类

广东社会建设蓝皮书
广东省社会建设发展报告（2017）
著(编)者：广东省社会工作委员会
2017年12月出版 / 估价：99.00元
PSN B-2014-436-1/1

广东外经贸蓝皮书
广东对外经济贸易发展研究报告（2016~2017）
著(编)者：陈万灵　2017年8月出版 / 估价：98.00元
PSN B-2012-286-1/1

广西北部湾经济区蓝皮书
广西北部湾经济区开放开发报告（2017）
著(编)者：广西北部湾经济区规划建设管理委员会办公室
广西社会科学院广西北部湾发展研究院
2017年2月出版 / 估价：89.00元
PSN B-2010-181-1/1

巩义蓝皮书
巩义经济社会发展报告（2017）
著(编)者：丁同民　朱军　2017年4月出版 / 估价：58.00元
PSN B-2016-533-1/1

广州蓝皮书
2017年中国广州经济形势分析与预测
著(编)者：庾建设　陈浩钿　谢博能
2017年7月出版 / 估价：85.00元
PSN B-2011-185-9/14

广州蓝皮书
2017年中国广州社会形势分析与预测
著(编)者：张强　陈怡霓　杨秦　2017年6月出版 / 估价：85.00元
PSN B-2008-110-5/14

广州蓝皮书
广州城市国际化发展报告（2017）
著(编)者：朱名宏　2017年8月出版 / 估价：79.00元
PSN B-2012-246-11/14

广州蓝皮书
广州创新型城市发展报告（2017）
著(编)者：尹涛　2017年7月出版 / 估价：79.00元
PSN B-2012-247-12/14

广州蓝皮书
广州经济发展报告（2017）
著(编)者：朱名宏　2017年7月出版 / 估价：79.00元
PSN B-2005-040-1/14

广州蓝皮书
广州农村发展报告（2017）
著(编)者：朱名宏　2017年8月出版 / 估价：79.00元
PSN B-2010-167-8/14

广州蓝皮书
广州汽车产业发展报告（2017）
著(编)者：杨再高　冯兴亚　2017年7月出版 / 估价：79.00元
PSN B-2006-066-3/14

广州蓝皮书
广州青年发展报告（2016~2017）
著(编)者：徐柳　张强　2017年9月出版 / 估价：79.00元
PSN B-2013-352-13/14

广州蓝皮书
广州商贸业发展报告（2017）
著(编)者：李江涛　肖振宇　荀振英
2017年7月出版 / 估价：79.00元
PSN B-2012-245-10/14

广州蓝皮书
广州社会保障发展报告（2017）
著(编)者：蔡国萱　2017年8月出版 / 估价：79.00元
PSN B-2014-425-14/14

广州蓝皮书
广州文化创意产业发展报告（2017）
著(编)者：徐咏虹　2017年7月出版 / 估价：79.00元
PSN B-2008-111-6/14

广州蓝皮书
中国广州城市建设与管理发展报告（2017）
著(编)者：董皞　陈小钢　李江涛
2017年7月出版 / 估价：85.00元
PSN B-2007-087-4/14

广州蓝皮书
中国广州科技创新发展报告（2017）
著(编)者：邹采荣　马正勇　陈爽
2017年7月出版 / 估价：79.00元
PSN B-2006-065-2/14

广州蓝皮书
中国广州文化发展报告（2017）
著(编)者：徐俊忠　陆志强　顾涧清
2017年7月出版 / 估价：79.00元
PSN B-2009-134-7/14

贵阳蓝皮书
贵阳城市创新发展报告No.2（白云篇）
著(编)者：连玉明　2017年10月出版 / 估价：89.00元
PSN B-2015-491-3/10

贵阳蓝皮书
贵阳城市创新发展报告No.2（观山湖篇）
著(编)者：连玉明　2017年10月出版 / 估价：89.00元
PSN B-2011-235-1/1

贵阳蓝皮书
贵阳城市创新发展报告No.2（花溪篇）
著(编)者：连玉明　2017年10月出版 / 估价：89.00元
PSN B-2015-490-2/10

贵阳蓝皮书
贵阳城市创新发展报告No.2（开阳篇）
著(编)者：连玉明　2017年10月出版 / 估价：89.00元
PSN B-2015-492-4/10

贵阳蓝皮书
贵阳城市创新发展报告No.2（南明篇）
著(编)者：连玉明　2017年10月出版 / 估价：89.00元
PSN B-2015-496-8/10

贵阳蓝皮书
贵阳城市创新发展报告No.2（清镇篇）
著(编)者：连玉明　2017年10月出版 / 估价：89.00元
PSN B-2015-489-1/10

地方发展类

皮书系列 2017全品种

贵阳蓝皮书
贵阳城市创新发展报告No.2（乌当篇）
著（编）者：连玉明　2017年10月出版／估价：89.00元
PSN B-2015-495-7/10

贵阳蓝皮书
贵阳城市创新发展报告No.2（息烽篇）
著（编）者：连玉明　2017年10月出版／估价：89.00元
PSN B-2015-493-5/10

贵阳蓝皮书
贵阳城市创新发展报告No.2（修文篇）
著（编）者：连玉明　2017年10月出版／估价：89.00元
PSN B-2015-494-6/10

贵阳蓝皮书
贵阳城市创新发展报告No.2（云岩篇）
著（编）者：连玉明　2017年10月出版／估价：89.00元
PSN B-2015-498-10/10

贵州房地产蓝皮书
贵州房地产发展报告No.4（2017）
著（编）者：武廷方　2017年7月出版／估价：89.00元
PSN B-2014-426-1/1

贵州蓝皮书
贵州册亨经济社会发展报告(2017)
著（编）者：黄德林　2017年3月出版／估价：89.00元
PSN B-2016-526-8/9

贵州蓝皮书
贵安新区发展报告（2016~2017）
著（编）者：马长青　吴大华　2017年6月出版／估价：89.00元
PSN B-2015-459-4/9

贵州蓝皮书
贵州法治发展报告（2017）
著（编）者：吴大华　2017年5月出版／估价：89.00元
PSN B-2012-254-2/9

贵州蓝皮书
贵州国有企业社会责任发展报告（2016~2017）
著（编）者：郭丽　周航　马强
2017年12月出版／估价：89.00元
PSN B-2015-512-6/9

贵州蓝皮书
贵州民航业发展报告（2017）
著（编）者：申振东　吴大华　2017年10月出版／估价：89.00元
PSN B-2015-471-5/9

贵州蓝皮书
贵州民营经济发展报告（2017）
著（编）者：杨静　吴大华　2017年3月出版／估价：89.00元
PSN B-2016-531-9/9

贵州蓝皮书
贵州人才发展报告（2017）
著（编）者：于杰　吴大华　2017年9月出版／估价：89.00元
PSN B-2014-382-3/9

贵州蓝皮书
贵州社会发展报告（2017）
著（编）者：王兴骥　2017年6月出版／估价：89.00元
PSN B-2010-166-1/9

贵州蓝皮书
贵州国家级开放创新平台发展报告（2017）
著（编）者：申晓庆　吴大华　李泓
2017年6月出版／估价：89.00元
PSN B-2016-518-1/9

海淀蓝皮书
海淀区文化和科技融合发展报告（2017）
著（编）者：陈名杰　孟景伟　2017年5月出版／估价：85.00元
PSN B-2013-329-1/1

杭州都市圈蓝皮书
杭州都市圈发展报告（2017）
著（编）者：沈翔　戚建国　2017年5月出版／估价：128.00元
PSN B-2012-302-1/1

杭州蓝皮书
杭州妇女发展报告（2017）
著（编）者：魏颖　2017年6月出版／估价：89.00元
PSN B-2014-403-1/1

河北经济蓝皮书
河北省经济发展报告（2017）
著（编）者：马树强　金浩　张贵
2017年4月出版／估价：89.00元
PSN B-2014-380-1/1

河北蓝皮书
河北经济社会发展报告（2017）
著（编）者：郭金平　2017年1月出版／估价：89.00元
PSN B-2014-372-1/1

河北食品药品安全蓝皮书
河北食品药品安全研究报告（2017）
著（编）者：丁锦霞　2017年6月出版／估价：89.00元
PSN B-2015-473-1/1

河南经济蓝皮书
2017年河南经济形势分析与预测
著（编）者：胡五岳　2017年2月出版／估价：89.00元
PSN B-2007-086-1/1

河南蓝皮书
2017年河南社会形势分析与预测
著（编）者：刘道兴　牛苏林　2017年4月出版／估价89.00元
PSN B-2005-043-1/8

河南蓝皮书
河南城市发展报告（2017）
著（编）者：张占仓　王建国　2017年5月出版／估价：89.00元
PSN B-2009-131-3/8

河南蓝皮书
河南法治发展报告（2017）
著（编）者：丁同民　张林海　2017年5月出版／估价：89.00元
PSN B-2014-376-6/8

河南蓝皮书
河南工业发展报告（2017）
著（编）者：张占仓　丁同民　2017年5月出版／估价：89.00元
PSN B-2013-317-5/8

河南蓝皮书
河南金融发展报告（2017）
著（编）者：河南省社会科学院
2017年6月出版／估价：89.00元
PSN B-2014-390-7/8

皮书系列 重点推荐

地方发展类

河南蓝皮书
河南经济发展报告（2017）
著(编)者：张占仓　　2017年3月出版 / 估价：89.00元
PSN B-2010-157-4/8

河南蓝皮书
河南农业农村发展报告（2017）
著(编)者：吴海峰　　2017年4月出版 / 估价：89.00元
PSN B-2015-445-8/8

河南蓝皮书
河南文化发展报告（2017）
著(编)者：卫绍生　　2017年3月出版 / 估价：88.00元
PSN B-2008-106-2/8

河南商务蓝皮书
河南商务发展报告（2017）
著(编)者：焦锦淼　穆荣国　2017年6月出版 / 估价：88.00元
PSN B-2014-399-1/1

黑龙江蓝皮书
黑龙江经济发展报告（2017）
著(编)者：朱宇　　2017年1月出版 / 估价：89.00元
PSN B-2011-190-2/2

黑龙江蓝皮书
黑龙江社会发展报告（2017）
著(编)者：谢宝禄　　2017年1月出版 / 估价：89.00元
PSN B-2011-189-1/2

湖北文化蓝皮书
湖北文化发展报告（2017）
著(编)者：吴成国　　2017年10月出版 / 估价：95.00元
PSN B-2016-567-1/1

湖南城市蓝皮书
区域城市群整合
著(编)者：童中贤　韩未名
2017年12月出版 / 估价：89.00元
PSN B-2006-064-1/1

湖南蓝皮书
2017年湖南产业发展报告
著(编)者：梁志峰　　2017年5月出版 / 估价：128.00元
PSN B-2011-207-2/8

湖南蓝皮书
2017年湖南电子政务发展报告
著(编)者：梁志峰　　2017年5月出版 / 估价：128.00元
PSN B-2014-394-6/8

湖南蓝皮书
2017年湖南经济展望
著(编)者：梁志峰　　2017年5月出版 / 估价：128.00元
PSN B-2011-206-1/8

湖南蓝皮书
2017年湖南两型社会与生态文明发展报告
著(编)者：梁志峰　　2017年5月出版 / 估价：128.00元
PSN B-2011-208-3/8

湖南蓝皮书
2017年湖南社会发展报告
著(编)者：梁志峰　　2017年5月出版 / 估价：128.00元
PSN B-2014-393-5/8

湖南蓝皮书
2017年湖南县域经济社会发展报告
著(编)者：梁志峰　　2017年5月出版 / 估价：128.00元
PSN B-2014-395-7/8

湖南蓝皮书
湖南城乡一体化发展报告（2017）
著(编)者：陈文胜　王文强　陆福兴　邝奕轩
2017年6月出版 / 估价：89.00元
PSN B-2015-477-8/8

湖南县域绿皮书
湖南县域发展报告 No.3
著(编)者：袁准　周小毛　2017年9月出版 / 估价：89.00元
PSN G-2012-274-1/1

沪港蓝皮书
沪港发展报告（2017）
著(编)者：尤安山　　2017年9月出版 / 估价：89.00元
PSN B-2013-362-1/1

吉林蓝皮书
2017年吉林经济社会形势分析与预测
著(编)者：马克　　2015年12月出版 / 估价：89.00元
PSN B-2013-319-1/1

吉林省城市竞争力蓝皮书
吉林省城市竞争力报告（2017）
著(编)者：崔岳春　张磊　　2017年3月出版 / 估价：89.00元
PSN B-2015-508-1/1

济源蓝皮书
济源经济社会发展报告（2017）
著(编)者：喻新安　　2017年4月出版 / 估价：89.00元
PSN B-2014-387-1/1

健康城市蓝皮书
北京健康城市建设研究报告（2017）
著(编)者：王鸿春　　2017年8月出版 / 估价：89.00元
PSN B-2015-460-1/2

江苏法治蓝皮书
江苏法治发展报告 No.6（2017）
著(编)者：蔡道通　龚廷泰　2017年8月出版 / 估价：98.00元
PSN B-2012-290-1/1

江西蓝皮书
江西经济社会发展报告（2017）
著(编)者：张勇　姜玮　梁勇　2017年10月出版 / 估价：89.00元
PSN B-2015-484-1/2

江西蓝皮书
江西设区市发展报告（2017）
著(编)者：姜玮　梁勇　　2017年10月出版 / 估价：79.00元
PSN B-2016-517-2/2

江西文化蓝皮书
江西文化产业发展报告（2017）
著(编)者：张圣才　汪春翔
2017年10月出版 / 估价：128.00元
PSN B-2015-499-1/1

地方发展类 — 皮书系列 重点推荐

街道蓝皮书
北京街道发展报告No.2（白纸坊篇）
著(编)者：连玉明　2017年8月出版 / 估价：98.00元
PSN B-2016-544-7/15

街道蓝皮书
北京街道发展报告No.2（椿树篇）
著(编)者：连玉明　2017年8月出版 / 估价：98.00元
PSN B-2016-548-11/15

街道蓝皮书
北京街道发展报告No.2（大栅栏篇）
著(编)者：连玉明　2017年8月出版 / 估价：98.00元
PSN B-2016-552-15/15

街道蓝皮书
北京街道发展报告No.2（德胜篇）
著(编)者：连玉明　2017年8月出版 / 估价：98.00元
PSN B-2016-551-14/15

街道蓝皮书
北京街道发展报告No.2（广安门内篇）
著(编)者：连玉明　2017年8月出版 / 估价：98.00元
PSN B-2016-540-3/15

街道蓝皮书
北京街道发展报告No.2（广安门外篇）
著(编)者：连玉明　2017年8月出版 / 估价：98.00元
PSN B-2016-547-10/15

街道蓝皮书
北京街道发展报告No.2（金融街篇）
著(编)者：连玉明　2017年8月出版 / 估价：98.00元
PSN B-2016-538-1/15

街道蓝皮书
北京街道发展报告No.2（牛街篇）
著(编)者：连玉明　2017年8月出版 / 估价：98.00元
PSN B-2016-545-8/15

街道蓝皮书
北京街道发展报告No.2（什刹海篇）
著(编)者：连玉明　2017年8月出版 / 估价：98.00元
PSN B-2016-546-9/15

街道蓝皮书
北京街道发展报告No.2（陶然亭篇）
著(编)者：连玉明　2017年8月出版 / 估价：98.00元
PSN B-2016-542-5/15

街道蓝皮书
北京街道发展报告No.2（天桥篇）
著(编)者：连玉明　2017年8月出版 / 估价：98.00元
PSN B-2016-549-12/15

街道蓝皮书
北京街道发展报告No.2（西长安街篇）
著(编)者：连玉明　2017年8月出版 / 估价：98.00元
PSN B-2016-543-6/15

街道蓝皮书
北京街道发展报告No.2（新街口篇）
著(编)者：连玉明　2017年8月出版 / 估价：98.00元
PSN B-2016-541-4/15

街道蓝皮书
北京街道发展报告No.2（月坛篇）
著(编)者：连玉明　2017年8月出版 / 估价：98.00元
PSN B-2016-539-2/15

街道蓝皮书
北京街道发展报告No.2（展览路篇）
著(编)者：连玉明　2017年8月出版 / 估价：98.00元
PSN B-2016-550-13/15

经济特区蓝皮书
中国经济特区发展报告（2017）
著(编)者：陶一桃　2017年12月出版 / 估价：98.00元
PSN B-2009-139-1/1

辽宁蓝皮书
2017年辽宁经济社会形势分析与预测
著(编)者：曹晓峰　梁启东
2017年1月出版 / 估价：79.00元
PSN B-2006-053-1/1

洛阳蓝皮书
洛阳文化发展报告（2017）
著(编)者：刘福兴　陈启明　2017年7月出版 / 估价：89.00元
PSN B-2015-476-1/1

南京蓝皮书
南京文化发展报告（2017）
著(编)者：徐宁　2017年10月出版 / 估价：89.00元
PSN B-2014-439-1/1

南宁蓝皮书
南宁经济发展报告（2017）
著(编)者：胡建华　2017年9月出版 / 估价：79.00元
PSN B-2016-570-2/3

南宁蓝皮书
南宁社会发展报告（2017）
著(编)者：胡建华　2017年9月出版 / 估价：79.00元
PSN B-2016-571-3/3

内蒙古蓝皮书
内蒙古反腐倡廉建设报告 No.2
著(编)者：张志华　无极　2017年12月出版 / 估价：79.00元
PSN B-2013-365-1/1

浦东新区蓝皮书
上海浦东经济发展报告（2017）
著(编)者：沈开艳　周奇　2017年1月出版 / 估价：89.00元
PSN B-2011-225-1/1

青海蓝皮书
2017年青海经济社会形势分析与预测
著(编)者：陈玮　2015年12月出版 / 估价：79.00元
PSN B-2012-275-1/1

人口与健康蓝皮书
深圳人口与健康发展报告（2017）
著(编)者：陆杰华　罗乐宣　苏杨
2017年11月出版 / 估价：89.00元
PSN B-2011-228-1/1

皮书系列 重点推荐 　　地方发展类

山东蓝皮书
山东经济形势分析与预测（2017）
著(编)者：李广杰　　2017年7月出版 / 估价：89.00元
PSN B-2014-404-1/4

山东蓝皮书
山东社会形势分析与预测（2017）
著(编)者：张华　唐洲雁　2017年6月出版 / 估价：89.00元
PSN B-2014-405-2/4

山东蓝皮书
山东文化发展报告（2017）
著(编)者：涂可国　　2017年11月出版 / 估价：98.00元
PSN B-2014-406-3/4

山西蓝皮书
山西资源型经济转型发展报告（2017）
著(编)者：李志强　　2017年7月出版 / 估价：89.00元
PSN B-2011-197-1/1

陕西蓝皮书
陕西经济发展报告（2017）
著(编)者：任宗哲　白宽犁　裴成荣
2015年12月出版 / 估价：89.00元
PSN B-2009-135-1/5

陕西蓝皮书
陕西社会发展报告（2017）
著(编)者：任宗哲　白宽犁　牛昉
2015年12月出版 / 估价：89.00元
PSN B-2009-136-2/5

陕西蓝皮书
陕西文化发展报告（2017）
著(编)者：任宗哲　白宽犁　王长寿
2015年12月出版 / 估价：89.00元
PSN B-2009-137-3/5

上海蓝皮书
上海传媒发展报告（2017）
著(编)者：强荧　焦雨虹　　2017年1月出版 / 估价：89.00元
PSN B-2012-295-5/7

上海蓝皮书
上海法治发展报告（2017）
著(编)者：叶青　　2017年6月出版 / 估价：89.00元
PSN B-2012-296-6/7

上海蓝皮书
上海经济发展报告（2017）
著(编)者：沈开艳　　2017年1月出版 / 估价：89.00元
PSN B-2006-057-1/7

上海蓝皮书
上海社会发展报告（2017）
著(编)者：杨雄　周海旺　　2017年1月出版 / 估价：89.00元
PSN B-2006-058-2/7

上海蓝皮书
上海文化发展报告（2017）
著(编)者：荣跃明　　2017年1月出版 / 估价：89.00元
PSN B-2006-059-3/7

上海蓝皮书
上海文学发展报告（2017）
著(编)者：陈圣来　　2017年6月出版 / 估价：89.00元
PSN B-2012-297-7/7

上海蓝皮书
上海资源环境发展报告（2017）
著(编)者：周冯琦　汤庆合　任文伟
2017年1月出版 / 估价：89.00元
PSN B-2006-060-4/7

社会建设蓝皮书
2017年北京社会建设分析报告
著(编)者：宋贵伦　冯虹　　2017年10月出版 / 估价：89.00元
PSN B-2010-173-1/1

深圳蓝皮书
深圳法治发展报告（2017）
著(编)者：张骁儒　　2017年6月出版 / 估价：89.00元
PSN B-2015-470-6/7

深圳蓝皮书
深圳经济发展报告（2017）
著(编)者：张骁儒　　2017年7月出版 / 估价：89.00元
PSN B-2008-112-3/7

深圳蓝皮书
深圳劳动关系发展报告（2017）
著(编)者：汤庭芬　　2017年6月出版 / 估价：89.00元
PSN B-2007-097-2/7

深圳蓝皮书
深圳社会建设与发展报告（2017）
著(编)者：张骁儒　陈东平　2017年7月出版 / 估价：89.00元
PSN B-2008-113-4/7

深圳蓝皮书
深圳文化发展报告(2017)
著(编)者：张骁儒　　2017年7月出版 / 估价：89.00元
PSN B-2016-555-7/7

四川法治蓝皮书
丝绸之路经济带发展报告（2016～2017）
著(编)者：任宗哲　白宽犁　谷孟宾
2017年12月出版 / 估价：85.00元
PSN B-2014-410-1/1

四川法治蓝皮书
四川依法治省年度报告 No.3（2017）
著(编)者：李林　杨天宗　田禾
2017年3月出版 / 估价：108.00元
PSN B-2015-447-1/1

四川蓝皮书
2017年四川经济形势分析与预测
著(编)者：杨钢　　2017年1月出版 / 估价：98.00元
PSN B-2007-098-2/7

四川蓝皮书
四川城镇化发展报告（2017）
著(编)者：侯水平　陈炜　2017年4月出版 / 估价：85.00元
PSN B-2015-456-7/7

皮书系列 重点推荐

地方发展类·国际问题类

四川蓝皮书
四川法治发展报告（2017）
著（编）者：郑泰安　2017年1月出版／估价：89.00元
PSN B-2015-441-5/7

四川蓝皮书
四川企业社会责任研究报告（2016~2017）
著（编）者：侯水平　盛毅　翟刚
2017年4月出版／估价：89.00元
PSN B-2014-386-4/7

四川蓝皮书
四川社会发展报告（2017）
著（编）者：李羚　2017年5月出版／估价：89.00元
PSN B-2008-127-3/7

四川蓝皮书
四川生态建设报告（2017）
著（编）者：李晟之　2017年4月出版／估价：85.00元
PSN B-2015-455-6/7

四川蓝皮书
四川文化产业发展报告（2017）
著（编）者：向宝云　张立伟
2017年4月出版／估价：89.00元
PSN B-2006-074-1/7

体育蓝皮书
上海体育产业发展报告（2016~2017）
著（编）者：张林　黄海燕
2017年10月出版／估价：89.00元
PSN B-2015-454-4/4

体育蓝皮书
长三角地区体育产业发展报告（2016~2017）
著（编）者：张林　2017年4月出版／估价：89.00元
PSN B-2015-453-3/4

天津金融蓝皮书
天津金融发展报告（2017）
著（编）者：王爱俭　孔德昌
2017年12月出版／估价：98.00元
PSN B-2014-418-1/1

图们江区域合作蓝皮书
图们江区域合作发展报告（2017）
著（编）者：李铁　2017年6月出版／估价：98.00元
PSN B-2015-464-1/1

温州蓝皮书
2017年温州经济社会形势分析与预测
著（编）者：潘忠强　王春光　金浩
2017年4月出版／估价：89.00元
PSN B-2008-105-1/1

西咸新区蓝皮书
西咸新区发展报告（2016~2017）
著（编）者：李扬　王军　2017年6月出版／估价：89.00元
PSN B-2016-535-1/1

扬州蓝皮书
扬州经济社会发展报告（2017）
著（编）者：丁纯　2017年12月出版／估价：98.00元
PSN B-2011-191-1/1

长株潭城市群蓝皮书
长株潭城市群发展报告（2017）
著（编）者：张萍　2017年12月出版／估价：89.00元
PSN B-2008-109-1/1

中医文化蓝皮书
北京中医文化传播发展报告（2017）
著（编）者：毛嘉陵　2017年5月出版／估价：79.00元
PSN B-2015-468-1/2

珠三角流通蓝皮书
珠三角商圈发展研究报告（2017）
著（编）者：王先庆　林至颖
2017年7月出版／估价：98.00元
PSN B-2012-292-1/1

遵义蓝皮书
遵义发展报告（2017）
著（编）者：曾征　龚永育　雍思强
2017年12月出版／估价：89.00元
PSN B-2014-433-1/1

国际问题类

"一带一路"跨境通道蓝皮书
"一带一路"跨境通道建设研究报告（2017）
著（编）者：郭业洲　2017年8月出版／估价：89.00元
PSN B-2016-558-1/1

"一带一路"蓝皮书
"一带一路"建设发展报告（2017）
著（编）者：孔丹　李永全　2017年7月出版／估价：89.00元
PSN B-2016-553-1/1

阿拉伯黄皮书
阿拉伯发展报告（2016~2017）
著（编）者：罗林　2017年11月出版／估价：89.00元
PSN Y-2014-381-1/1

北部湾蓝皮书
泛北部湾合作发展报告（2017）
著（编）者：吕余生　2017年12月出版／估价：85.00元
PSN B-2008-114-1/1

大湄公河次区域蓝皮书
大湄公河次区域合作发展报告（2017）
著（编）者：刘稚　2017年8月出版／估价：89.00元
PSN B-2011-196-1/1

大洋洲蓝皮书
大洋洲发展报告（2017）
著（编）者：喻常森　2017年10月出版／估价：89.00元
PSN B-2013-341-1/1

皮书系列重点推荐　国际问题类

德国蓝皮书
德国发展报告（2017）
著(编)者：郑春荣　2017年6月出版 / 估价：89.00元
PSN B-2012-278-1/1

东盟黄皮书
东盟发展报告（2017）
著(编)者：杨晓强　庄国土
2017年3月出版 / 估价：89.00元
PSN Y-2012-303-1/1

东南亚蓝皮书
东南亚地区发展报告（2016～2017）
著(编)者：厦门大学东南亚研究中心　王勤
2017年12月出版 / 估价：89.00元
PSN B-2012-240-1/1

俄罗斯黄皮书
俄罗斯发展报告（2017）
著(编)者：李永全　2017年7月出版 / 估价：89.00元
PSN Y-2006-061-1/1

非洲黄皮书
非洲发展报告 No.19（2016～2017）
著(编)者：张宏明　2017年8月出版 / 估价：89.00元
PSN Y-2012-239-1/1

公共外交蓝皮书
中国公共外交发展报告（2017）
著(编)者：赵启正　雷蔚真
2017年4月出版 / 估价：89.00元
PSN B-2015-457-1/1

国际安全蓝皮书
中国国际安全研究报告（2017）
著(编)者：刘慧　2017年7月出版 / 估价：98.00元
PSN B-2016-522-1/1

国际形势黄皮书
全球政治与安全报告（2017）
著(编)者：李慎明　张宇燕
2016年12月出版 / 估价：89.00元
PSN Y-2001-016-1/1

韩国蓝皮书
韩国发展报告（2017）
著(编)者：牛林杰　刘宝全
2017年11月出版 / 估价：89.00元
PSN B-2010-155-1/1

加拿大蓝皮书
加拿大发展报告（2017）
著(编)者：仲伟合　2017年9月出版 / 估价：89.00元
PSN B-2014-389-1/1

拉美黄皮书
拉丁美洲和加勒比发展报告（2016～2017）
著(编)者：吴白乙　2017年6月出版 / 估价：89.00元
PSN Y-1999-007-1/1

美国蓝皮书
美国研究报告（2017）
著(编)者：郑秉文　黄平　2017年6月出版 / 估价：89.00元
PSN B-2011-210-1/1

缅甸蓝皮书
缅甸国情报告（2017）
著(编)者：李晨阳　2017年12月出版 / 估价：86.00元
PSN B-2013-343-1/1

欧洲蓝皮书
欧洲发展报告（2016～2017）
著(编)者：黄平　周弘　江时学
2017年6月出版 / 估价：89.00元
PSN B-1999-009-1/1

葡语国家蓝皮书
葡语国家发展报告（2017）
著(编)者：王成安　张敏　2017年12月出版 / 估价：89.00元
PSN B-2015-503-1/2

葡语国家蓝皮书
中国与葡语国家关系发展报告·巴西（2017）
著(编)者：张曙光　2017年8月出版 / 估价：89.00元
PSN B-2016-564-2/2

日本经济蓝皮书
日本经济与中日经贸关系研究报告（2017）
著(编)者：张季风　2017年5月出版 / 估价：89.00元
PSN B-2008-102-1/1

日本蓝皮书
日本研究报告（2017）
著(编)者：杨柏江　2017年5月出版 / 估价：89.00元
PSN B-2002-020-1/1

上海合作组织黄皮书
上海合作组织发展报告（2017）
著(编)者：李进峰　吴宏伟　李少捷
2017年6月出版 / 估价：89.00元
PSN Y-2009-130-1/1

世界创新竞争力黄皮书
世界创新竞争力发展报告（2017）
著(编)者：李闽榕　李建平　赵新力
2017年1月出版 / 估价：148.00元
PSN Y-2013-318-1/1

泰国蓝皮书
泰国研究报告（2017）
著(编)者：庄国土　张禹东
2017年8月出版 / 估价：118.00元
PSN B-2016-557-1/1

土耳其蓝皮书
土耳其发展报告（2017）
著(编)者：郭长刚　刘义　2017年9月出版 / 估价：89.00元
PSN B-2014-412-1/1

亚太蓝皮书
亚太地区发展报告（2017）
著(编)者：李向阳　2017年3月出版 / 估价：89.00元
PSN B-2001-015-1/1

印度蓝皮书
印度国情报告（2017）
著(编)者：吕昭义　2017年12月出版 / 估价：89.00元
PSN B-2012-241-1/1

印度洋地区蓝皮书
印度洋地区发展报告（2017）
著(编)者：汪戎　　2017年6月出版 / 估价：89.00元
PSN B-2013-334-1/1

英国蓝皮书
英国发展报告（2016~2017）
著(编)者：王展鹏　　2017年11月出版 / 估价：89.00元
PSN B-2015-486-1/1

越南蓝皮书
越南国情报告（2017）
著(编)者：广西社会科学院　罗梅　李碧华
2017年12月出版 / 估价：89.00元
PSN B-2006-056-1/1

以色列蓝皮书
以色列发展报告（2017）
著(编)者：张倩红　　2017年8月出版 / 估价：89.00元
PSN B-2015-483-1/1

伊朗蓝皮书
伊朗发展报告（2017）
著(编)者：冀开远　　2017年10月出版 / 估价：89.00元
PSN B-2016-575-1/1

中东黄皮书
中东发展报告 No.19（2016~2017）
著(编)者：杨光　　2017年10月出版 / 估价：89.00元
PSN Y-1998-004-1/1

中亚黄皮书
中亚国家发展报告（2017）
著(编)者：孙力　吴宏伟　　2017年7月出版 / 估价：98.00元
PSN Y-2012-238-1/1

皮书序列号是社会科学文献出版社专门为识别皮书、管理皮书而设计的编号。皮书序列号是出版皮书的许可证号，是区别皮书与其他图书的重要标志。

它由一个前缀和四部分构成。这四部分之间用连字符"-"连接。前缀和这四部分之间空半个汉字（见示例）。

《国际人才蓝皮书：中国留学发展报告》序列号示例

从示例中可以看出，《国际人才蓝皮书：中国留学发展报告》的首次出版年份是2012年，是社科文献出版社出版的第244个皮书品种，是"国际人才蓝皮书"系列的第2个品种（共4个品种）。

社会科学文献出版社　　**皮书系列**

✦ 皮书起源 ✦

"皮书"起源于十七、十八世纪的英国，主要指官方或社会组织正式发表的重要文件或报告，多以"白皮书"命名。在中国，"皮书"这一概念被社会广泛接受，并被成功运作、发展成为一种全新的出版形态，则源于中国社会科学院社会科学文献出版社。

✦ 皮书定义 ✦

皮书是对中国与世界发展状况和热点问题进行年度监测，以专业的角度、专家的视野和实证研究方法，针对某一领域或区域现状与发展态势展开分析和预测，具备原创性、实证性、专业性、连续性、前沿性、时效性等特点的公开出版物，由一系列权威研究报告组成。

✦ 皮书作者 ✦

皮书系列的作者以中国社会科学院、著名高校、地方社会科学院的研究人员为主，多为国内一流研究机构的权威专家学者，他们的看法和观点代表了学界对中国与世界的现实和未来最高水平的解读与分析。

✦ 皮书荣誉 ✦

皮书系列已成为社会科学文献出版社的著名图书品牌和中国社会科学院的知名学术品牌。2016年，皮书系列正式列入"十三五"国家重点出版规划项目；2012~2016年，重点皮书列入中国社会科学院承担的国家哲学社会科学创新工程项目；2017年，55种院外皮书使用"中国社会科学院创新工程学术出版项目"标识。

中国皮书网
www.pishu.cn

发布皮书研创资讯,传播皮书精彩内容
引领皮书出版潮流,打造皮书服务平台

栏目设置

关于皮书:何谓皮书、皮书分类、皮书大事记、皮书荣誉、
皮书出版第一人、皮书编辑部

最新资讯:通知公告、新闻动态、媒体聚焦、网站专题、视频直播、下载专区

皮书研创:皮书规范、皮书选题、皮书出版、皮书研究、研创团队

皮书评奖评价:指标体系、皮书评价、皮书评奖

互动专区:皮书说、皮书智库、皮书微博、数据库微博

所获荣誉

2008年、2011年,中国皮书网均在全国新闻出版业网站荣誉评选中获得"最具商业价值网站"称号;

2012年,获得"出版业网站百强"称号。

网库合一

2014年,中国皮书网与皮书数据库端口合一,实现资源共享。更多详情请登录www.pishu.cn。

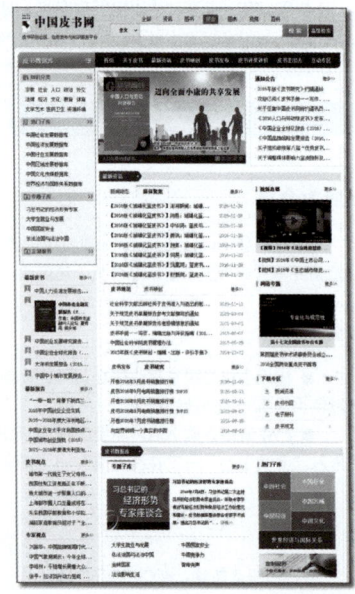

权威报告·热点资讯·特色资源

皮书数据库
ANNUAL REPORT(YEARBOOK) DATABASE

当代中国与世界发展高端智库平台

所获荣誉

- 2016年，入选"国家'十三五'电子出版物出版规划骨干工程"
- 2015年，荣获"搜索中国正能量 点赞2015""创新中国科技创新奖"
- 2013年，荣获"中国出版政府奖·网络出版物奖"提名奖
- 连续多年荣获中国数字出版博览会"数字出版·优秀品牌"奖

成为会员

通过网址www.pishu.com.cn或使用手机扫描二维码进入皮书数据库网站，进行手机号码验证或邮箱验证即可成为皮书数据库会员（建议通过手机号码快速验证注册）。

会员福利

- 使用手机号码首次注册会员可直接获得100元体验金，不需充值即可购买和查看数据库内容（仅限使用手机号码快速注册）。
- 已注册用户购书后可免费获赠100元皮书数据库充值卡。刮开充值卡涂层获取充值密码，登录并进入"会员中心"—"在线充值"—"充值卡充值"，充值成功后即可购买和查看数据库内容。

数据库服务热线：400-008-6695
数据库服务QQ：2475522410
数据库服务邮箱：database@ssap.cn

图书销售热线：010-59367070/7028
图书服务QQ：1265056568
图书服务邮箱：duzhe@ssap.cn

权威 · 现状 · 前沿

"十二五""十三五"国家重点图书出版规划项目
皮书系列

权威报告·热点资讯·特色资源

皮书数据库
ANNUAL REPORT(YEARBOOK)
DATABASE

当代中国与世界发展高端智库平台

所获荣誉

- 2016年，入选"国家'十三五'电子出版物出版规划骨干工程"
- 2015年，荣获"搜索中国正能量 点赞2015""创新中国科技创新奖"
- 2013年，荣获"中国出版政府奖·网络出版物奖"提名奖
- 连续多年荣获中国数字出版博览会"数字出版·优秀品牌"奖

成为会员

通过网址www.pishu.com.cn或使用手机扫描二维码进入皮书数据库网站，进行手机号码验证或邮箱验证即可成为皮书数据库会员（建议通过手机号码快速验证注册）。

会员福利

- 使用手机号码首次注册会员可直接获得100元体验金，不需充值即可购买和查看数据库内容（仅限使用手机号码快速注册）。
- 已注册用户购书后可免费获赠100元皮书数据库充值卡。刮开充值卡涂层获取充值密码，登录并进入"会员中心"—"在线充值"—"充值卡充值"，充值成功后即可购买和查看数据库内容。

数据库服务热线：400-008-6695
数据库服务QQ：2475522410
数据库服务邮箱：database@ssap.cn
图书销售热线：010-59367070/7028
图书服务QQ：1265056568
图书服务邮箱：duzhe@ssap.cn

城市生活质量蓝皮书
BLUE BOOK OF
QUALITY OF LIFE IN CITIES

REPORT ON THE QUALITY
OF LIFE IN CHINESE CITIES
（2016）

Expected Stability，Existing Challenges

Zhang Liancheng　Zhang Ping
Yang Chunxue　Lang Lihua
Zhao Jiazhang　Zhang Ziran

NATIONAL INSTITUTE FOR ECONOMIC EXPERIMENTATION

社会科学文献出版社
SOCIAL SCIENCES ACADEMIC PRESS（CHINA）

"Blue Book of Quality of Life in Cities" Editorial Committee

Zhang Liancheng; Zhang Ping; Yang Chunxue;
Lang Lihua; Zhao Jiazhang; Zhang Ziran

Co-authors of the Report

Zhang Liancheng; Zhang Ping; Yang Chunxue; Lang Lihua; Zhao Jiazhang;
Zhang Ziran; Wang Yin; He Yubiao; Chen Jianxian; Wang Yu

Organizers / Planners of the Survey

Zhang Ping; Zhang Liancheng; Yang Chunxue; Ji Hong; Liu Xiahui;
Lang Lihua; Xu Xue; Wang Cheng; Zhang Xiaojing; Tian Xinmin;
Yuan Fuhua; Zhang Ziran; Zhao Jiazhang; Wang Yin; Cai Bin

National Institute for Economic Experimentation (NIEE)

Since the reform and opening up, especially after the establishment of socialist market economic system, China's economic development has entered a new stage. China has become the world's second largest economy; its per capita income has reached the level of middle-income countries. Meanwhile, China's reform is changing from the "shallow water area" into "deep water area", the reform will face more difficult and complex situation, the "practice trial and error" of China reform must change from "feeling the stones" policy toward the "experimental trial and error" by the use of modern means of simulation and evaluation. On the other hand, from the perspective of academic development, current scientific research is directing to cooperative study and cross-disciplinary collaborative research. This situation requires China's universities, research institutions to break the disciplinary boundaries and sectoral boundaries, integrating all available resources, cooperate and innovate together, so as to face new challenges in China's society. In this context, after a long term investigation, demonstration and carefully prepared, Capital University of Economics and Business (CUEB) and Institute of Economics of Chinese Academy of Social Sciences (CASS) decide to set up the "National Institute for Economic Experimentation" jointly.

Early in the year of 2006, CUEB has set up "Research Center of China Economic Growth and Business Cycle" together with Institute of Economics of CASS. Since 2007, this Center has successfully held six sessions of "Forum on China Economic Growth and Business Cycle" with Hong Kong Economic Herald. This Forum has become an important platform for

academic exchanges for well-known economists whose research field focus on macroeconomics. In 2010, CUEB established "Research Center of China City Life Quality" together with Institute of Economics of CASS. After months of research on the city's life quality index, the center firstly released life quality index of 30 capital cities in China in the fifth session of the "Forum on China Economic Growth and Business Cycle" in 2011, which caused a great response, and attracted the attention of international counterparts including the World Bank and other international bodies. NIEE is based on the above research institute.

Currently, the Institute has set up "Research Center of China Economic Growth and Business Cycle" "Research Center of China City Life Quality" "Research Center of Quantitative Economics" and "WTO Research Center", and the Economic Operation and International Trade Laboratory, Economic Warning Laboratories, Economic Data Processing and Computer Simulation Lab and Digital Investigations Center.

After integration of the original institutions and laboratories, NIEE proposed the following institutions:

1. Experts Committee of National Institute for Economic Experimentation;

2. Research Center of China Economic Growth and Business Cycle;

3. Research Center of China City Life Quality;

4. Research Center of Quantitative Economics;

5. Post-doctoral Stations;

6. Forum on China Economic Growth and Business Cycle;

7. Research Center for Beijing Economic Transition and Development;

8. Economic Operation and Warning Laboratories, Computer Simulation Laboratories.

The recent tasks of NIEE are as follows.

Firstly, we will continue the research on the economic growth and business cycle of China, and we will try our best to make the forum better and better, and to make it an international forum.

Secondly, we will expand research on life quality index, gradually extended

from the capital cities to medium-sized cities, from domestic to international cities, while normalizing the release of the indexe. In addition, life quality is only part of economic growth quality, so after the Institute was founded, the quality of the whole economic growth will gradually be incorporated into the institute's research horizon and strive for a group of high-quality scientific research.

Thirdly, the institute will continue to expand the scope of research on economic experiments, carry out experiments for economic reform, policies effect and economic growth pressure, and provide quantitative decision support for China's reform, government agencies and relevant departments, as well as the whole society.

Fourthly, we will establish a graduates guidance team with international features, closely cooperate with foreign universities, co-direct master and doctoral students, and enroll post doctors for the benefits of talent construction for Capital University of Economics and Business.

Finally, NIEE have a close working relationship with more than 20 universities abroad, after the Institute was founded, it will carry out extensive international cooperation and academic exchanges, joint research, collaborative innovation, which further international character of the institute.

The purpose of National Institute for Economic Experimentation (NIEE) is: Promote economic experimentation research, prosper science and economic, push forward China's economic system reform, improve the quality of economic growth, and promote economic development. The objective of NIEE is: Through our unremitting efforts, NIEE will become an internationally first class research institute in this field in the future.

Abstract

In 2016, the Quality of Urban Life Research Center under the National Institute for Economic Experimentation (NIEE) continued with its survey of the quality of life (QOL) in 35 Chinese cities. Subjective satisfaction indexes and objective (social and economic data) indexes of 2016 were obtained after careful calculation. Same as before, the last several digits of the interviewees' telephone numbers were still chosen randomly to ensure reasonable and stochastic spatial distribution of the samples. 14, 193 effective random samples were produced as a result. As is shown by the survey, in 2016, the subjective indexes of the 35 cities average 55.82–above the satisfaction level and slightly higher than that of 2015. And all the 35 cities score over 50 (the critical point between the satisfaction and the dissatisfaction intervals) in the subjective index. As for the objective indexes (social and economic data indexes), eastern cities still perform better than central and western cities, despite contrasts between the subjective and the objective indexes of some cities. In 2016, the objective indexes of the 35 cities average 54.75 – lower than the 2015 average of 55.84. Results of the special surveys show that: in the eyes of the residents in all the 35 cities, air quality is the most influential factor of QOL, followed by commodity prices, food safety and then transportation; house prices are expected to fall over the next one or two years; and the residents are generally optimistic about their job prospects. All in all, at present the Chinese economy

is at a critical stage of reform and transformation. Challenges and risks still exist during the course of economic and social development. Compared to that of last year, the objectiveindexeshave declined slightly, while the subjective indexes have generally remained stable. At the same time however, we are still faced with severe challenges, such as high living costs, a fast pace of life, unstable house prices and worrying job prospects. Therefore, in the process of future economic and social development and transformation, the Central Government and the local governments should continue to work on life-related systems, stabilize economic growth and further improve urban residents'quality of life.

Keywords: Quality of Urban Life (QOUL); Subjective Satisfaction Index; Objective Index; House Price Expectation; Employment Expectation

CONTENTS

BⅠ General Reports

B.1　**The 2016 Survey on the Quality of Urban Life**　/ 001

　　1.1　Introduction　/ 001

　　1.2　Main Findings　/ 002

　　1.3　Report Outline　/ 004

B.2　**Research Overview of Quality of Urban Life**　/ 006

　　2.1　Research Process　/ 006

　　2.2　Concept　/ 008

　　2.3　Related Theories　/ 009

　　2.4　Relationship between Government Quality and

　　　　 Quality of Residents' Life　/ 011

　　2.5　Quality-of-life Indicator System　/ 017

BⅡ Analysis Reports

B.3　**Introduction to the 2016 Survey**　/ 021

Blue Book of Quality of Life in Cities

B.4　The 2016 Quality-of-life Indexes of the 35 Chinese Cities　　/ 025

B.5　Quality-of-life Subindexes of the 35 Chinese Cities　　/ 035

BⅢ　Special Surveys

B.6　Survey on House Price Expectation　　/ 129

B.7　Survey on Primary Concern: Air Quality Comes First,

　　Followed by Commodity Prices　　/ 134

B.8　Survey on Employment Satisfaction　　/ 138

BⅣ　Conclusions

B.9　Conclusions and Enlightenments　　/ 144

General Reports

B.1
The 2016 Survey on the Quality of Urban Life

1.1   Introduction

The Quality of Urban Life Research Center under NIEE conducted a tracking survey of the quality of life (QOL) in 35 Chinese cities from March to May, 2016. It was the 6th annual survey since 2011. Related subjective satisfaction indexes and objective indexes of QLICC (Quality-of-life Index of Chinese Cities) were obtained through statistical analysis and calculation for the evaluation of China's urban quality of life in 2016. The indexes were released on the 10th Forum on China Economic Growth and Business Cycle (2016). The subjective survey lasted for over two months and produced14, 193 effective random samples. The standard error of the overall subjective indexes

Blue Book of Quality of Life in Cities

was 0.179. In addition, besides the surveys on urban house price expectation and residents'primary concern, a survey on residents'employment expectation was newly added to the subjective telephone interview. The objective (social and economic data) indexes, on the other hand, were calculated based on the social and economic data of the 35 cities released by the authorities, which ensured both the objectivity and the authority of the indexes.

1.2   Main Findings

As is shown by the survey, in 2016, the subjective indexes of the 35 cities average 55.82 —above the satisfaction level and slightly higher than that of 2015. All the 35 cities score over 50 (the critical point between the satisfaction and the dissatisfaction intervals) in the satisfaction index. And the 5 related subindexes average, respectively: living standard (60.44), living cost (39.74), human capital (62.20), social security (60.66) and living experience (56.05). Compared to those of 2015, all the subindexes have somewhat improved, but the satisfaction subindex of living cost is still below the satisfaction level. In addition, the pace of life indicator of the living experiencesubindexaverage 44.07 which is also below satisfaction.

Cities ranked top 10 in the list of satisfaction indexes are: Ningbo (1), Hangzhou (2), Kunming (3), Nanning (4), Chongqing (5), Chengdu (6), Dalian (7), Jinan (8), Xining (9) and Hohhot (10). And the bottom 10 cities are: Guiyang (26), Nanjing (27), Zhengzhou (28), Fuzhou (29), Shanghai (30), Shenzhen (31), Changchun (32), Xi'an (33), Lanzhou (34) and Xiamen (35).

As for objective (social and economic data) indexes, eastern cities still perform better than central and western cities, although contrasts exist between the subjective and the objective indexes of some cities. In 2016, the

002

The 2016 Survey on the Quality of Urban Life

objective indexes of the 35 cities average 54.75, lower than the 2015 average of 55.84. 32out of the 35 cities score 50 or above– 1 more than that of 2015. The 5 objective subindexes average respectively: living cost (58.74), living experience (57.54), human capital (56.98), social security (50.43) and living standard (50.07). Compared to those of 2015, the objective subindexes of living standard, human capital and social security have somewhat dropped, while the objective subindexes of living cost and living experience have slightly improved. Cities ranked top 10 in the list of objective indexes are: Beijing (1), Shenzhen (2), Nanjing (3), Guangzhou (4), Hangzhou (5), Shanghai (6), Kunming (7), Wuhan (8), Xi'an (9) and Guiyang (10). And the bottom 10 cities are: Hefei (26), Harbin (27), Nanchang (28), Haikou (29), Lanzhou (30), Nanning (31), Fuzhou (32), Chongqing (33), Xining (34) and Zhengzhou (35).

The three special surveys were also conducted this year on the basis of the subjective satisfaction survey and the objective index investigation. The survey on primary concern indicates that, among the four given choices, residents of all the 35 cities regard air quality as the most influential factor of their QOL (46.33%). Commodity prices (23.94%) comes second, followed by food safety (20.87%) and then transportation (8.86%). Different from the result of last year, this year urban residents pay more attention to commodity prices than to food safety. In the special survey on house price expectation, the house price expectation indexes of the 35 cities average 40.16–lower than the 2015 average of 43.86, which means house prices are expected to decline over the next one or two years. As for the newly-added survey on employmentexpectation, the indexes of the 35 cities average 57.41. And all the cities score over 50. Although the score is comparatively low, the index of job prospects is still above the optimistic level.

003

Blue Book of Quality of Life in Cities

At present, the Chinese economy is at a critical stage of reform and transformation. Challenges and risks still exist during the course of economic and social development. Compared to that of last year, the objective indexes have declined slightly, while the subjective indexes have generally remained stable. At the same time, however, we are still faced with severe challenges, such as high living costs, a fast pace of life, unstable house prices and worrying job prospects. Therefore, in the process of future economic and social development and transformation, the central and local governments should continue to work on life-related systems, stabilized economic growth and further improve urban residents' quality of life.

1.3   Report Outline

The second report of this book is a comprehensive report of QOUL. Researches on quality of life are sorted out and summed up here from the aspect of research progresses, concept, related theories and indicator systems.

The third report is an introduction to the 2016 survey, which explains the survey techniques of the subjective data, the design of the objective data indicators and the sources of the objective data.

The fourth report presents the 2016 quality-of-life indexes of the 35 cities, including rankings and descriptions of their subjective and objective indexes. For the convenience of dynamic analysis, the score and the ranking of each city's general index are listed out in this part and compared with the result of the previous surveys. Meanwhile, histograms of the 2012-2016 subjective and objective indexes are also provided, as well as related index bar charts.

The fifth report is about the 2016 subindexes of the 35 cities. The subindexes and their respective rankings are listed out here one by one, along

004

with their primary indicator radar charts. Subindexhistogramsand bar charts are also provided for the sake of dynamic comparison.

The third part "Special Surveys" is an introduction to the three special surveys on house price expectation, residents'primary concern and employment satisfaction.

The forth part "Conclusions" is about main findings and enlightenments of the survey, along with suggestions on policies.

B.2
Research Overview of Quality of Urban Life

Since the reform and opening-up of China, as the economy develops, profound changes have taken place in people's lives. The pursuit of life has shifted from survival to a comprehensive quality life. Improving people's quality of life is an important advertisement of the "people-oriented" scientific development concept. And if we are to build China into a moderately prosperous society in an all-round way, it should also be one of our essential goals. Therefore, the study on quality of life is of vital significance. QOL research requires the clarification of related concepts, theories and evidences, which can only be achieved by sorting out previous literatures.

2.1 Research Process

Residents'quality of life is a subject of global importance. Researches in this field are mainly conducted in the United States and other developed countries, but the Soviet Union also made its contribution. Scholars such as Hoffmann & Suttner in 1976 and Szalai & Andrews in 1980 compared and summarized the research status and achievements of different countries.

Modern QOL study originated in the United States and is closely related to the rise of development economics. With the changes of history and social environment, and as people's welfare consciousness progresses, QOL research

Research Overview of Quality of Urban Life —

has also been extended to more fields and deeper topics. In 1933, sociologists started to pay attention to the study of QOL, and William Ogburn published his book *Recent Social Trends*. Gurin et al. (1957) conducted the first survey on social quality among American residents, in order to analyze their mental state and feeling of well-being. It is noteworthy that Galbraith (1958), a leader of the institutional school, made the first definition of "quality of life". Since then, the concept of QOL has been constantly enriched and improved. Bauer (1966) used the term "quality of life" in his book *Social Indicators*. And the study on "quality of life" started to separate from "social indicators", and became noticed by the academics as an independent subject which discusses people's psychological feeling of the economy, the society and their living environment. In his book *Politics and the Stages of Growth*, Rostow (1971) put "quality of life" into a theoretical research framework. He believed that the pursuit of "quality of life"was the final stage of social development. Obviously, to him, QOL was more of a psychological feeling of happiness after material needs were met. In the 1990s, Perroux, Milesi and Cummins et al. stated that the ultimate goal of economic development was to improve human welfare.

In the 1970s, Chinese scholars began to carry out preliminary studies on the quality of life. And large-scale surveys and empirical analysis started to appear after the 1980s. In the 1990s, the National Bureau of Statistics (NBS) and other departments developed related indicator systems and quantitative criteria which specified the quality of life for a moderately prosperous society. And in the new century, some universities and research institutions began to set up quality of life research centers and published relative survey reports. Since then, QOL study has entered a new stage of development.

Blue Book of Quality of Life in Cities

2.2 Concept

Quality of life is a concept of broad connotations, concerning both subjective content and objective reality. American economist Galbraith was the first one to study the quality of life systematically. He found that socially and psychologically speaking, the strong economy of the United States did not bring a better sense of happiness and satisfaction. Later, Galbraith and Ball coined the term "quality of life"in 1960. From then on, the academics began to pay attention to the study of "quality of life". After five decades, there is still no consensus on its definition. The understanding and requirements of different social groups may vary greatly. To people of lower incomes, the basic need for food and clothing is not yet met, thus quality of life can be defined as how well the basic needs are met, their quality of life generally depends on materials. To people of higher incomes however, it refers to a quality life, and their quality of life is determined mainly by spiritual matters.

According to some economists, differences in preference have led to differences in the understanding of QOL. To the lower-income people of less living materials and higher marginal utility, increasing materials can improve total utility and enhance their sense of happiness. To the higher-income people on the other hand, living materials are of low marginal utility, while spiritual products are of higher utility, therefore, increasing spiritual products may promote their sense of happiness. Some sociologists think material QOL refers to needs, and spiritual QOL refers to desires. The former meets the most basic survival and physiological needs, while the latter satisfies various high-level desires for ideals, beliefs and esteem. At the phase of needs, without the support of materials, even if high-level desires exist,

Research Overview of Quality of Urban Life

they cannot be realized. Only after material needs are met, can desires be possibly satisfied. There is no clear boundary between "needs" and "desires". They may occur simultaneously in the same person. But on the other hand, they are also different and should not be confused with. As Veehoven (1991) pointed out, "needs" is an absolute concept. Needs are instinctive and limited. However, "desires" are relative concepts. They are spiritual and endless.

At present, there are two modes of QOL study. One is the Scandinavian mode which emphasizes objective living conditions. The quality of life is regarded as a personal control of resources. For example, Rostow (1971) stated that"the quality of life involves the beautification of the natural environment and the improvement of the social environment". The other is the American mode which focuses on the subjective quality of life.

To sum up, quality of life involves a set of concepts, including both tangible material life and intangible spiritual life. In my opinion, Zhou Changcheng's definition (2001) is more accurate. He thought quality of life depends on"how well the society improves people's life and how well residents'needs are met. It refers to the sense of identity each member of the society has toward oneself and one's social environment based on a certain level of material conditions".

2.3 Related Theories

QOL study is an interdisciplinary subject which involves economics, sociology, psychology, demography and resources & environment science. Different disciplines approach QOL from different perspectives, with different emphases, and have their own concepts, methodologies and theoretical systems. These systems help to enrich and extend the research of QOL.

Blue Book of Quality of Life in Cities

2.3.1 Economics perspective

Economics emphasizes the optimal allocation of resources under constraint conditions. When connected with QOL research, economics studies how to use effective resources to maximize the quality of life of the behavior subject. In economics, the purpose of consumer behaviors is to maximize utility. Here, utility refers to a psychological feeling – the sense of happiness and satisfaction that consumers obtain through commodity consumption. Therefore, there is a positive correlation between utility and QOL. Under the income constraint, consumers may choose between material and spiritual products and improve their own quality of life according to the equimarginal principle. Producers can better their quality of life by maximizing their profits under constraint conditions. And governments may achieve the maximization of social welfare through tax and property rights systems, so as to enhance the QOL of the entire society. In 1976, B.C. Liu tried to put quality of life into a micro analysis framework. Jester et al. (1981) combined both tangible and intangible resources when considering the allocation of resources and the maximization of QOL. And in 1986, Li Yining introduced welfare economics into QOL study in his book *Socialist Political Economics*. He believed that the quality of life was closely related to social welfare; under the same income level, Pareto Improvement could be achieved by bettering the natural and the social environment, and thus enhance the QOL of the entire society.

2.3.2 Social psychology perspective

Campbell, Schiller, Geisen and Lin Nan are the principal social psychologists in QOL study. Campbell (1981) mainly analyzed the sense of happiness

010

from a psychological perspective. Different from economists' hypotheses, psychologists believe reducing one's needs can enhance the sense of happiness. But when needs are not satisfied, one's sense of happiness will turn negative. Schiller (1974) thought that QOL depended on one's self-evaluation and one's relationship with others; the quality of life was subjective, complicated and interactive. Geisen regarded QOL as a part of one's self-perception which changed with the relationship between one's self and the society. And according to Lin Nan (1987), QOL was the "evaluation and summary of life and other related aspects", which emphasized one's sense of satisfaction over the economic and the social environment. Generally speaking, QOL consists of three aspects: the satisfaction over life, the sense of happiness and public-benefit payback activities.

2.3.3 Ecology perspective

Milbrath analyzed the quality of life from an ecologicalperspective. He believed that the quality of life was not independent from the ecosystem, but a part of it and an important factor of the ecological features. Changes in the natural environment can affect the quality of life. And similarly, upgrading the quality of life also helps to improve the natural environment. QOL is dynamic, not static. Obviously, ecology emphasizes the relationship between different matters. And the quality of life is interrelated and interacts with other factors of the environment.

2.4 Relationship between Government Quality and Quality of Residents' Life

The academics have long paid attention to the influence of economic and

Blue Book of Quality of Life in Cities

social factors on residents' quality of life. The economic factors include economic growth, income gap, inflation and unemployment rate, while the social factors involves gender, age, marital status and social class (Dolan et al., 2008). In recent years, it has been found that government quality is also an important variable of QOL (Chen Gang and Li Shu, 2012; Zhang Kezhong and He Lingyun, 2012). Government quality is a multi-dimensional concept, concerning factors such as efficiency, rule of law, governance, supply of public goods, property rights protection and level of corruption.

2.4.1　Direct mechanism of government quality on quality of residents' life

The government executes the power entrusted by its people, manages social and public affairs and takes charge of resource management and policy-making, so as to enhance national welfare and improve citizens' objective and subjective quality of life. A crucial criterion for assessing government quality is how well the government meets the needs of residents' subjective and objective QOL.

Helliwell and Huang (2008) divided government quality into democratic quality and technical quality both of which can directly affect residents' quality of life. On one hand, high democratic quality helps to improve QOL. According to Frey and Stutzer's research (2002), the subjective QOL of Swedish residents has a significant positive correlation with the democratic level. In a highly democratic society, residents can fully participate in policy-making and thus obtain the "procedural utility" which enhances their sense of happiness. Moreover, since the governor is elected by the people, the residents are more likely to agree with his/her governing philosophy. Such resonance may also enhance residents' subjective quality of life. On the other hand, good

technical quality also has a positive impact on residents' quality of life. After studying the European countries and their residents, Tavits (2008) found that corruption could significantly influence residents' quality of life. The worse the corruption, the lower the sense of happiness, and vice versa. In a corrupted country, public goods were only provided to the highest bidders or persons with relationships, and were excluded from all the other people. As a result, the total quality of life declined. Since the ones involved incorruption lost their independence, they became unhappy as well. Corruption would also destroy interpersonal relationships, and thereby lower residents'subjective quality of life.

In countries of different income and development levels, government quality has different impacts on residents' quality of life. Technical quality is of more importance to underdeveloped countries of lower income level, while democratic quality is of more significance to developed countries of higher income level (Helliwell and Huang, 2008; Otter, 2008). In a developing country, residents usually prefer the government to improve its technical quality by providing social stability, mature systems and fine public goods. For example, to the residents in most developing countries of Southeast Asia, improvements in medical and housing conditions may bring much stronger sense of happiness than progresses in democracy. Some factors can serve as solid material or institutional foundation for the enhancement of residents' subjective and objective quality of life, such as advancement in administrative efficiency or the rule of law, a fair and equitable social environment and astable political environment. As the economy develops and incomes increase, the basic needs of life will be satisfied. And then the need for political democracy and participation will begin to rise, while the democratic quality will start to play an increasingly important role in residents' quality of life.

 Blue Book of Quality of Life in Cities

High democratic quality can ensure people's participation in the political process, and thus improve both the "political utility" and their sense of happiness.

Technical quality and democratic quality of a government can influence residents' quality of life in different ways. Good governance itself is a source of happiness (Zhang Kezhong and He Lingyun, 2012). High government quality provides the economic, social and political environment as well as mature systems for residents' QOL, and brings a strong sense of security and happiness.

2.4.2 Indirect mechanism of government quality on quality of residents' life

Government quality is a complicated and multi-dimensional concept which is assessed with different criteria. Early literature stated that government quality depended on the level of corruption. The World Bank assesses government quality from six aspects, including citizen expression, government accountability, political stability and low violence, government efficiency, management quality and the rule of law. The Freedom House pays more attention to the extent of citizens' liberty and government's power. And University of Gothenburg focuses on the justice of the government. Despite the differences in the evaluation criteria of government quality, most parties have reached an agreement on the following indicators: government efficiency, the level of corruption and the rule of law. Generally speaking, the improvement of government efficiency, the decrease of corruption and fair, equitable systems can enhance residents' subjective quality of life.

Government quality may influence residents' quality of life in five indirect ways. Firstly, high government quality can promote economic growth which in turn improves residents'quality of life. On one hand, the government can

push forward the reform of various systems with its administrative power, and thus encourages economic development. According to Zhang Wuchang (2009), the main reason for China's rapid economic development is that the Chinese government had pushed forward the reform of fiscal decentralization with a strong hand. As a result, fierce competition started to appear among the counties, which helped to promoted regional economic growth. As was found by Zhang Derong (2013), the institutional dividend of the reform was an important driver of China's economic growth. On the other hand, the government has to raise governance costs in order to maintain social stability. When economic growth reaches a certain stage and starts to decelerate, deep-seated contradictions will build up, and unstable factors will increase. Then the government will have to raise its governance costs, resulting in the increase of total social costs and the slowdown of economic growth. North (1981) stated that government quality could well explain the rise and fall of the European countries in the past millennium. Mauro (1995) also pointed out that government quality was an important reason for the differences of economic growth among the countries. And economic growth can directly affect residents' objective quality of life. As was found by Xing Zhanjun (2011), economic growth was a crucial reason for the subjective QOL improvement among Chinese residents. Economic growth helps to increase residents' incomes, improve their material life, and fill people with hope for the future. All this can enhance the quality of life.

Secondly, government quality can influence the extent of income distribution and inequality, which in turn affects residents' quality of life. A corrupted government may aggravate income inequality. The more corrupted the government is, the more rent-seeking behaviors prevail. Under a distorted tax and expenditure structure, the unfairness of income distribution will be exacerbated (Alesina et al., 2004). Moreover, corruption will further intensify

the inequality of opportunities, resulting in the solidification of social classes and the instability of life (Alesina et al., 2005). When social and income inequality worsens, the quality of life will be unlikely to rise, and the sense of happiness will be reduced. Researches in China found that high government quality could significantly decrease income distribution inequality (Chen Gang, 2011), and that less income inequality could enhance residents' sense of happiness (He Lixin and Pan Chunyang, 2011).

Thirdly, high government quality can increase residents' sense of happiness by means of mature judicial systems. On one hand, with a set of mature and efficient judicial systems, a good government can ensure both procedural and result justice. When residents obtain the "procedural utility", their quality of life will be improved as well. On the other hand, mature judicial systems can protect residents' safety and property rights, and increase their sense of security, which will in turn enhance the sense of happiness (Bjornskov et al., 2010).

Fourthly, government quality can affect the social trust system, which in turn influences residents' quality of life. In a trusting society, interpersonal relationships tend to be more harmonious, which may lead to a better quality of life (Helliwell and Putnam, 2004). Moreover, the trust system helps to cultivate and create social capitals, and can therefore lower transaction costs and solve the free rider problem. As a result, residents' quality of life may be improved (Hudson, 2006). On the contrary, Rothstein and Eek (2009) stated that if a government was highly corrupted, and all the market participants were rent-seeking, then social trust would be hard to form, and the creation of social capitals would be hindered. Then the residents would tend to be unhappy, and their quality of life would decline.

Finally, government quality can influence the structure of fiscal expenditure, which will in turn affect residents' quality of life. The quality of

Research Overview of Quality of Urban Life

a government is reflected in the behavior and structure of its expenditure. And the expenditure structure has a significant impact on residents' sense of happiness. According to Hessami (2010) and Kotakorpi & Laamanen (2010), both educational and medical expenditures help to improve residents' quality of life. Under a highly corrupted government, there are less rent-seeking opportunities in education and health care and more opportunities in the war industry. In the pursuit of more benefits, the government may cut down educational and medical expenditure, so as to increase military expenditure. Such behaviors may lead to the decline of residents' quality of life (Mauro, 1998). Government investment in China is comparatively low in education and health care and high in administration. Such a distorted structure of fiscal expenditure will not help to enhance residents' sense of happiness. And as was found by Chen Gang and Li Shu (2010), the improvement of government quality would significantly increase the expenditure for social uses as well as its efficiency, and thus enhance residents' quality of life.

Government quality may influence residents' QOL through a variety of mechanisms. High government quality can improve residents'quality of life and raise residents' sense of happiness. Poor government quality will lower residents' quality of life. Therefore, government quality is an important driver of QOL improvement. By raising the quality of the government, residents' QOL can be greatly upgraded.

2.5 Quality-of-life Indicator System

2.5.1 Research progresses abroad

Generally speaking, there are three research modes on QOL indicator systems: the GDP account expansion mode, the social indicator mode and the

 Blue Book of Quality of Life in Cities

subjective psychological mode.

1. GDP account expansion mode

There are some defects in the traditional GDP accounting system. GDP is no perfect indicator of social welfare. It cannot reveal the health of children, the quality of education or the beauty of poems. To make up for its defects, some scholars put forward the GDP account expansion mode, including the "Genuine Progress Index" and the "Index of Sustainable Economic Welfare". GDP is the basic unit of evaluation. And the QOL indicator system is formed by studying individual consumption and capital accounts. This mode not only reveals the improvement of QOL, such as how happy people are, how good the environment condition is and how advanced education is, but also reflects the decline of QOL caused by environment deterioration or the gap between the rich and the poor.

2. Social indicator mode

From the 1960s to the 1980s, the "Social Indicator Movement" arose in the West. As reflections of residents' quality of life, social indicators include economic, social, political and other indicators, concerning housing, education, environment, health care and social security, as well as political freedom and freedom of speech. The Nordic countries have divided living standards into two indicators: the quality of material life and the progresses of life. The United Nations has also proposed the "Human Development Index".

3. Subjective psychological mode

The subjective psychological mode pays more attention to the quality of residents' spiritual life and the psychological feelings of individuals. Gurin (1957) was the first one to use this mode, mainly on the analysis of individual mental illnesses. Later scholars expanded on the mode by paying attention to personal emotions and psychological health, as well as the sense of social

018

Research Overview of Quality of Urban Life

identity and the sense of belonging. For example, Campbell and Professor Lin Nan analyzed the quality of life from emotion, cognition and behavior, and created three indicators: the indicator of satisfaction, the indicator of well-being and the indicator of social activity enthusiasm.

2.5.2　Research progresses in China

Following the preliminary study on QOL in the 1970s, another wave of research appeared in the 1980s. Li Yining and Lu Hanlong were among the leading researchers. Li Yining (1986) believed that the quality of life could reflect people's life and social welfare. Lu Hanlong and Professor Lin Nan of the United Statesmeasuredresidents' quality of life from emotion, cognition and behavior (Lin Nan and Lu Hanlong, 1987). Lu Shuhua and Wei Luying's QOL indicators included not only objective indicators such as the basic necessities of life, but also subjective indicators of satisfaction and well-being. Zhou Changcheng divided the quality of life into four areas, namely the capacity of the environment, the utility of life, the ability of survival and the individual evaluation of life (Zhou Changcheng, 2001). Luo Ping and Yin Yanmin et al. (2000) created 8 factors and 38 specific indicators for the measurement of residents' quality of life. The 8 factors included income status, consumption structure, housing condition, family life, social services, health condition, culture&education and economic environment. Based on the IMD indicator system, Zhao Yanyun and Wang Zuocheng (2003) designed a QOL indicator system of 11 factors, including economic development, income distribution, level of consumption, transportation condition, level of information, level of health assurance, employment security, level of education, public order, status of urbanization and living standards. Ji Zhusun (2003) measured the quality of life from five aspects, namely material living

019

Blue Book of Quality of Life in Cities

standards, spiritual and cultural life, social life, physical and mental health&
emotional life & space of personality development, and national QOL
improvements. Zhang Runqing and Xie Yanhui (2004) studied the QOL of
rural residents, and chose two major indicators — the quality of material
life and the quality of spiritual life. The quality of material life consisted of
9 indicators: GDP per capita, proportion of non-agricultural labor force,
educational programs, number of doctors per 10,000 residents, average life
expectancy, rate of natural population growth and Engel coefficient; while
the quality of spiritual life is made up of 7 indicators such as the extent of
satisfaction over government rural policies, individual living conditions and
one's own marriage. Jia Haiwei (2005) established a quality-of-work-and-life
assessment indicator system, and studied the QOL of university and college
teachers. Wang Yudong et al. (2001) learned more about the QOL of older
people through a survey conducted among the elderly. Liao Xiangyue and He
Chunlin (2002) measured residents' quality of life from four dimensions: the
sense of security, the sense of control, the sense of harmony and the sense
of autonomy.

Analysis Reports

B.3

Introduction to the 2016 Survey

To ensure the continuity and comparability of survey results, the 2015 survey retained the whole set of adopted techniques, indicator system constitution and sample choosing method used in the previous three years, while making small adjustments and improvements.

3.1   Overall Introduction to the Survey

The Quality of Urban Life Research Center under NIEE conducted a tracking survey of the QOL in 35 Chinese cities from March to May, 2016. It was the 6th annual survey since 2011. Related subjective satisfaction indexes and

Blue Book of Quality of Life in Cities

objective economic data indexes of QLICC were obtained through statistical analysis and calculation for the evaluation of China's urban quality of life in 2016. The indexes were released on the 10th Forum on China Economic Growth and Business Cycle (2016). The subjective satisfaction survey lasted for over two months and produced 14,193 effective random samples. The standard error of the overall subjective indexes was 0.179. Besides, in addition to the surveys on urban house price expectation and residents' primary concern, a survey on residents' employment expectation was newly added to the subjective satisfaction telephone interview.

3.2 Constitution of the Subjective and the Objective Indicator Systems and Special Surveys

Based on our understanding and the reality of China, NIEE established the QLICC index (Quality-of-life Index of Chinese Cities) system in 2011. The system consists of two parts: the subjective satisfaction index system and the objective (social and economic data) index system. In 2016, the constitution of the subjective and the objective indicator systems is a continuation of the practice since 2012 (See Table 1 and Table 2).

Table 1 The QLICC Subjective Indicator System

Satisfaction index (subjective index)	Subjective questions	Answers and Values				
		100	75	50	25	0
Satisfaction index of living standard	Income status (50%)	Very satisfied	Satisfied	Average	Dissatisfied	Very dissatisfied
	Income expectation (50%)	Very optimistic	Optimistic	Average	Pessimistic	Very pessimistic
Satisfaction index of living cost	Living cost	Very low	Low	Average	High	Very high

022

Introduction to the 2016 Survey —

Continued table

Satisfaction index (subjective index)	Subjective questions	Answers and Values				
		100	75	50	25	0
Satisfaction index of human capital	Human capital	Very satisfied	Satisfied	Average	Dissatisfied	Very dissatisfied
Satisfaction index of social security	Health care and elderly support (50%)	Very satisfied	Satisfied	Average	Dissatisfied	Very dissatisfied
	Public order (50%)	Very satisfied	Satisfied	Average	Dissatisfied	Very dissatisfied
Satisfaction index of living experience	Pace of life (50%)	Very slow	Slow	Average	Quick	Very quick
	Living convenience (50%)	Very convenient	Convenient	Average	Inconvenient	Very inconvenient

In 2016, besides the surveys on urban house price expectation and residents' primary concern, a survey on employment was newly added to the subjective satisfaction telephone interview, in order to learn more about the impact of Internet consumption on urban residents' quality of life. Results of the three special surveys are still not calculated in the QLICC system, but they may serve as references in understanding residents'extent of satisfaction over living cost and living experience.

Table 2　The QLICC Objective Indicator System

Social and economic data (objective) index	Primary Indicator	Secondary indicator	Impact on the Quality of Urban Life*
Objective index of living standard	Income level	Consumption rate (consumption/income)	+
		Per capita wealth (including per capita savings and per capita housing wealth)	+
		Per capita disposable income	+
	Life improvements	Per capita consumption growth	+
		Per capita wealth growth	+
		Per capita disposable income growth	+

023

 Blue Book of Quality of Life in Cities

Continued table

Social and economic data (objective) index	Primary Indicator	Secondary indicator	Impact on the Quality of Urban Life*
Objective index of living cost	Living cost	House price index	−
		Inflation rate	−
		House-price-to-income ratio	−
Objective index of human capital	Human capital	Educational provision index (including number of schools per 10,000 residents and number of teachers per 10,000 residents)	+
		Ratio of educational, cultural and entertainment expenditures	+
Objective index of social security	Social security	Social security coverage	+
		Basic medical insurance coverage	+
		Unemployment insurance coverage	+
Objective index of living experience	Living convenience	Transportation capacity (including per capita road area, number of public transportation vehicles per 10,000 residents and number of taxies per 10,000 residents)	+
		Number of cinemas and theaters per 10,000 residents	+
		Medical care capacity (including number of hospital beds per 10,000 residents, number of hospitals per 10,000 residents and number of doctors per 10,000 residents)	+
	Eco-environment	Per capita green area	+
		Air quality	+
	Perception of income disparities	Gini coefficient	−

* In the Table, "+" = positive impact; "−" = negative impact.

B.4
The 2016 Quality-of-life Indexes of the 35 Chinese Cities

The QOL indexes and rankings were obtained on the basis of the 2016 QLICC survey, and compared with previous survey results since 2012.

4.1 Subjective Satisfaction Indexes have Risen Slightly but at a Slower Rate

According to the survey result, as is shown in Table 1, the national weighted average of subjective indexes is 55.82 this year, which has remained above the satisfaction level and kept rising ever since the first survey in 2011. Since the values assigned to the satisfaction interval is between 50 and 75, residents seem to be generally satisfied with their quality of life. From 2012 to 2016, the national weighted averages of satisfaction indexes are50.88, 50.87, 51.57, 55.38 and 55.82 respectively. The lowest score has continued to rise as well: Guiyang scored 47.33 in 2012; Lanzhou scored 48.57 in 2013; Shenzhen scored 49.51 in 2014; Lanzhou scored 53.30 in 2015; and Xiamen scores53.98 in 2016. That is to say, in both 2015 and 2016, the satisfaction indexes of all the 35 cities have been over 50 — above the satisfaction level.

Blue Book of Quality of Life in Cities

Table 1 The 2016 Subjective Satisfaction Indexes of the 35 Chinese Cities

City	2016			2015		2014		2013		2012	
	Score	Ranking	Places risen	Score	Ranking	Score	Ranking	Score	Ranking	Score	Ranking
Ningbo	57.36	1	2	57.24	3	52.63	8	52.17	7	52.51	7
Hangzhou	56.75	2	-1	57.58	1	52.83	4	52.05	10	54.04	2
Kunming	56.63	3	2	57.03	5	49.63	34	48.73	33	48.72	32
Nanning	56.59	4	14	55.24	18	50.00	32	49.81	28	49.60	27
Chongqing	56.56	5	12	55.26	17	52.69	7	51.01	19	52.28	11
Chengdu	56.51	6	7	55.46	13	52.14	10	51.40	13	52.13	12
Dalian	56.42	7	5	55.49	12	50.61	26	50.10	26	50.37	18
Jinan	56.41	8	3	55.73	11	52.57	9	53.68	1	53.78	4
Xining	56.40	9	16	54.72	25	51.94	13	52.21	6	51.57	14
Hohhot	56.38	10	17	54.64	27	50.62	25	50.37	22	50.14	22
Taiyuan	56.30	11	23	53.32	34	50.90	23	49.90	27	49.38	29
Wuhan	56.23	12	4	55.34	16	50.45	28	49.07	32	49.95	24
Hefei	56.19	13	-7	56.85	6	51.94	12	52.34	5	53.20	5
Haikou	56.09	14	-10	57.09	4	51.83	16	51.80	11	50.05	23
Nanchang	56.00	15	-1	55.41	14	51.31	21	50.35	23	48.41	33
Yinchuan	55.99	16	16	53.81	32	51.90	15	51.07	18	52.29	10
Harbin	55.95	17	-8	56.59	9	51.05	22	49.79	29	48.78	31
Guangzhou	55.91	18	3	55.00	21	50.05	31	49.21	31	49.74	25
Urumqi	55.89	19	10	54.48	29	50.76	24	50.38	21	50.23	21
Shenyang	55.80	20	-5	55.40	15	52.85	3	51.25	16	49.73	26
Shijiazhuang	55.74	21	1	54.95	22	51.75	18	52.17	8	53.86	3
Qingdao	55.73	22	-3	55.18	19	53.06	1	53.05	2	52.31	8
Beijing	55.64	23	5	54.49	28	51.78	17	50.16	24	49.47	28
Changsha	55.63	24	0	54.89	24	50.37	29	50.15	25	50.29	19
Tianjin	55.61	25	5	54.22	30	52.81	6	51.35	14	52.07	13
Guiyang	55.61	26	7	53.77	33	49.94	33	49.58	30	47.33	35
Nanjing	55.39	27	-20	56.70	7	51.43	20	51.70	12	50.75	16
Zhengzhou	55.25	28	-8	55.03	20	50.25	30	51.28	15	50.76	15
Fuzhou	55.20	29	-6	54.92	23	51.90	14	52.06	9	52.60	6

The 2016 Quality-of-life Indexes of the 35 Chinese Cities

Continued table

City	2016			2015		2014		2013		2012	
	Score	Ranking	Places risen	Score	Ranking	Score	Ranking	Score	Ranking	Score	Ranking
Shanghai	55.20	30	-20	55.74	10	51.94	11	50.53	20	50.24	20
Shenzhen	54.67	31	0	54.06	31	49.51	35	48.68	34	49.16	30
Changchun	54.48	32	-24	56.60	8	52.88	2	52.34	4	54.51	1
Xi'an	54.47	33	-7	54.65	26	50.58	27	51.16	17	50.40	17
Lanzhou	54.07	34	1	53.30	35	51.50	19	48.57	35	47.95	34
Xiamen	53.98	35	-33	57.57	2	52.82	5	53.00	3	52.30	9
average	55.82			55.38		51.57		50.87		50.88	

Viewed by index ranking changes, only Hangzhou and Ningbo have ranked among the top 10 five years in a row since 2012, while Guiyang and Shenzhen have ranked among the bottom 10 over the past five years. This is the first time for Nanning, Dalian and Hohhot to enter the top 10 list. Compared to that of 2015, the rankings of Taiyuan, Hohhot and Xining have experienced the most obvious rises, going up 23, 17 and 16 places respectively; while the rankings of Xiamen, Changchun, Shanghai and Nanjing have seen the most dramatic drops, falling 33, 24, 20 and 20 places. From 2012 to 2016, the ranking of Beijing has been No.28, No.24, No.17, No.28 and No.23, generally in the lower range.

The weighted averages of the five satisfaction subindexes are: human capital (62.20), social security (60.66), living standard (60.44), living experience (56.05) and living cost (39.74). Compared to those of 2015, the weighted averages of all the 5 subindexes have somewhat improved. The highest is the human capital index, and the lowest is the living cost index.

As is shown in the general subjective index histogram (Figure 1), the overall improvement in satisfaction results from the rise and concentration of index scores.

Blue Book of Quality of Life in Cities

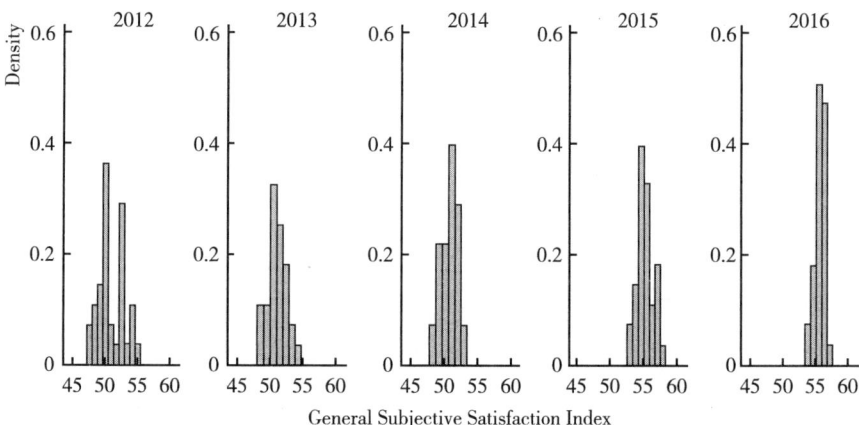

General Subjective Satisfaction Index

Figure 1   A Histogram of the 2012–2016 Subjective Satisfaction Indexes of the 35 Cities

Such trends are also clearly seen in the result of statistical analysis. In 2012, the highest scorer of general subjective index was Changchun (54.51), while the lowest was Guiyang (47.33). There was a difference of 7.18 in between. And the standard deviation was 1.81. In 2013, the highest scorer was Jinan (53.68), while the lowest was Lanzhou (48.57). The difference was 5.11, and the standard deviation was 1.31. In 2014, the highest scorer was Qingdao (53.06), while the lowest was Shenzhen (49.51). The difference was 3.55, and the standard deviation was 1.05. In 2015, the highest scorer was Hangzhou (57.58), while the lowest was Lanzhou (53.30). The difference was 4.28, and the standard deviation was 1.15. In 2016, the highest scorer is Ningbo (57.36), while the lowest is Xiamen (53.98). The difference is 3.38, and the standard deviation is 0.76. Obviously, the highest score has seen little change, but the lowest score has climbed up quickly. In 2016, the index experienced the greatest rise. And the standard deviation among cities has been reduced from 1.81 (in 2012) to 0.76.

From the perspective of cities, from 2012 to 2016, the general subjective indexes of most cities have improved. As is shown in Figure 2, the

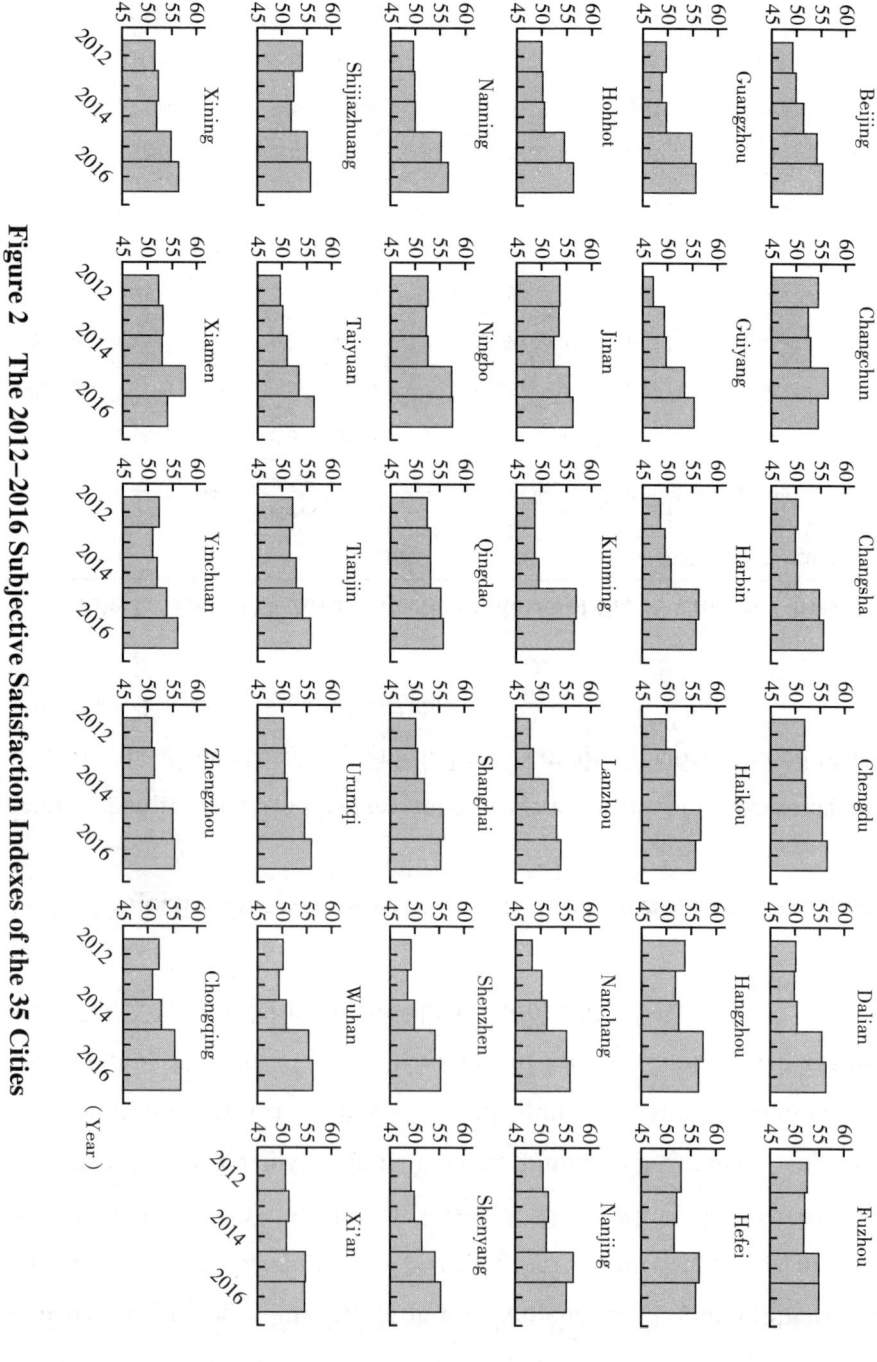

Figure 2　The 2012–2016 Subjective Satisfaction Indexes of the 35 Cities

indexes of Beijing, Guiyang, Hohhot, Nanchang, Qingdao, Shenyang, Taiyuan, Urumqi, Lanzhou and Nanning have kept rising. The indexes of Changsha, Chengdu, Dalian, Fuzhou, Guangzhou, Jinan, Ningbo, Shenzhen, Shijiazhuang, Tianjin, Wuhan, Xining, Yinchuan, Zhengzhou and Chongqing have fluctuated but still gone up. And the indexes of Changchun, Harbin, Haikou, Hangzhou, Hefei, Kunming, Nanjing, Shanghai, Xi'an and Xiamen have slightly dropped.

4.2　Objective Indexes have Declined due to Economic Pressure

Same as before, the 2016 objective indexes were obtained by calculating and analyzing the 20 objective economic indicators of the 35 cities released by the authorities. The result is shown in Table 2.

Table 2　The 2012–2016 Objective Indexes of the 35 Chinese Cities

City	2016			2015		2014		2013		2012	
	Score	Ranking	Places Risen	Score	Ranking	Score	Ranking	Score	Ranking	Score	Ranking
Beijing	64.42	1	0	67.41	1	68.78	1	69.80	1	68.72	1
Shenzhen	64.00	2	5	59.87	7	63.25	4	63.93	5	64.24	3
Nanjing	62.79	3	-1	63.37	2	65.52	3	66.65	3	62.38	5
Guangzhou	60.76	4	1	61.08	5	66.39	2	66.85	2	64.87	2
Hangzhou	59.60	5	-1	61.70	4	59.49	13	59.54	12	59.09	8
Shanghai	58.93	6	0	59.95	6	61.30	7	61.78	8	62.72	4
Kunming	58.23	7	1	59.69	8	60.61	10	58.05	15	54.08	14
Wuhan	57.95	8	1	58.87	9	60.33	12	58.93	13	56.61	10
Xi'an	57.93	9	-6	62.39	3	61.61	5	64.65	4	61.59	6
Guiyang	57.20	10	4	56.92	14	56.46	18	52.45	29	50.98	25

030

The 2016 Quality-of-life Indexes of the 35 Chinese Cities —

Continued table

City	2016			2015		2014		2013		2012	
	Score	Ranking	Places Risen	Score	Ranking	Score	Ranking	Score	Ranking	Score	Ranking
Hohhot	57.17	11	0	58.16	11	60.99	9	62.22	6	59.55	7
Shenyang	57.04	12	0	57.22	12	60.41	11	59.99	10	56.59	11
Yinchuan	55.72	13	0	57.19	13	56.77	17	57.68	16	52.45	18
Ningbo	54.88	14	1	55.70	15	61.11	8	61.47	9	55.21	12
Changchun	54.49	15	1	55.22	16	57.63	15	59.64	11	52.29	19
Shijiazhuang	54.03	16	4	54.00	20	54.44	25	54.78	24	50.49	28
Xiamen	53.91	17	2	54.32	19	61.58	6	61.89	7	58.86	9
Urumqi	53.74	18	3	53.53	21	54.42	26	54.59	26	49.73	32
Changsha	53.56	19	-9	58.48	10	59.15	14	58.36	14	53.53	16
Taiyuan	53.53	20	6	52.15	26	51.62	31	55.45	21	52.15	20
Qingdao	53.16	21	-4	55.03	17	55.87	21	54.76	25	54.05	15
Dalian	52.69	22	-4	54.38	18	56.15	19	55.64	20	52.00	21
Jinan	52.50	23	1	52.72	24	56.10	20	56.84	17	53.22	17
Chengdu	52.48	24	-2	53.35	22	54.89	23	55.96	19	51.15	24
Tianjin	52.35	25	5	51.25	30	55.48	22	55.42	22	54.30	13
Hefei	52.23	26	-1	52.69	25	56.83	16	56.73	18	50.92	26
Harbin	52.03	27	1	51.45	28	53.80	28	51.86	30	50.44	29
Nanchang	51.99	28	-5	52.88	23	51.29	32	53.03	27	49.03	34
Haikou	51.64	29	0	51.28	29	53.72	29	51.50	31	51.17	23
Lanzhou	50.73	30	1	51.22	31	54.79	24	55.22	23	50.08	31
Nanning	50.25	31	1	49.79	32	52.93	30	50.00	33	50.69	27
Fuzhou	50.12	32	-5	51.55	27	53.96	27	52.66	28	51.37	22
Chongqing	49.17	33	2	47.93	35	51.04	33	47.83	35	49.40	33
Xining	48.19	34	-1	49.08	33	50.15	34	49.29	34	45.21	35
Zhengzhou	46.93	35	-1	48.68	34	48.39	35	50.54	32	50.26	30
Average	54.75			55.84		57.87		57.75		54.56	

Blue Book of Quality of Life in Cities

The averages of the objective indexes of the surveyed 35 cities are 54.56, 57.75, 57.87, 55.84 and 54.75 respectively from 2012 to 2016. From dynamic changes, the objective index started to drop in 2015 and continues to decline in 2016, although it is still above the satisfaction level.

Horizontally speaking, Beijing has topped the list five years in a row. Shenzhen, Nanjing, Guangzhou, Shanghai and Xi'an have all ranked among the top 10 in the past five years. Harbin, Nanning, Xining, Zhengzhou and Chongqing have stayed among the bottom 10 during the same period. Guiyang has entered the top 10 list for the first time. And Changsha has experienced the greatest drop. It was ranked top 10 in 2015 and quickly goes down to No.19 in 2016. Zhengzhou, Nanning, Xining and Chongqing scored below 50 in 2015. But in 2016, the index of Nanning goes back up to 50.25. The lowest scorer is Zhengzhou (46.93). According to the QLICC system, below 50 (the critical point between the satisfaction and the dissatisfaction intervals) means below the satisfaction level. Therefore, from the perspective of objective index, the QOL of Xining, Chongqing and Zhengzhou is unsatisfactory. Figure 3 is a histogram of the 2012-2016 objective indexes of the 35 cities.

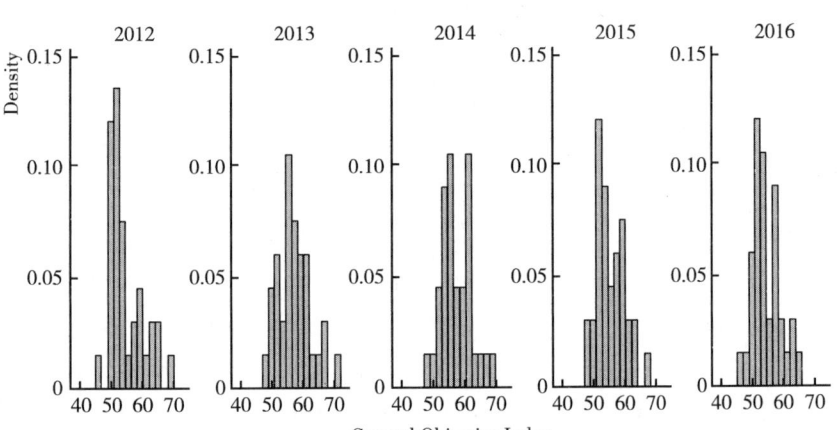

Figure 3   A Histogram of the 2012–2016 Objective Indexes of the 35 Cities

The 2016 Quality-of-life Indexes of the 35 Chinese Cities —

Among the 35 cities, the objective indexes of Beijing, Nanjing, Guangzhou and Shanghai have experienced slight drops 3 years in a row, and the indexes of Hohhot, Ningbo, Changchun, Xiamen, Chengdu, Jinan and Lanzhou have also declined. Together, they account for nearly 1/3 of the cities. However, the index of Guiyang has climbed up in the past five years, rising from 50.98 in 2012 to 57.20 in 2016 (See Figure 4).

Viewed from the result of statistical analysis, Beijing has been the highest scorer (68.72, 69.80, 68.78, 67.41 and 64.42) in general objective index from 2012 to 2016, while Xining (45.21), Chongqing (47.83), Zhengzhou (48.39), Chongqing (47.93) and Zhengzhou (46.93) have been the lowest scorers of each year. The differences between the highest and the lowest scores are23.51, 21.97, 20.39, 19.48 and 17.49 respectively. And the corresponding standard deviations are 5.32, 5.22, 4.68, 4.55 and 4.22. Obviously, both the highest and the lowest scores have kept declining, but the difference between them has gradually reduced. The objective indexes of most cities had improved slightly in 2013 and 2014, and then started to drop again in 2015 and 2016.

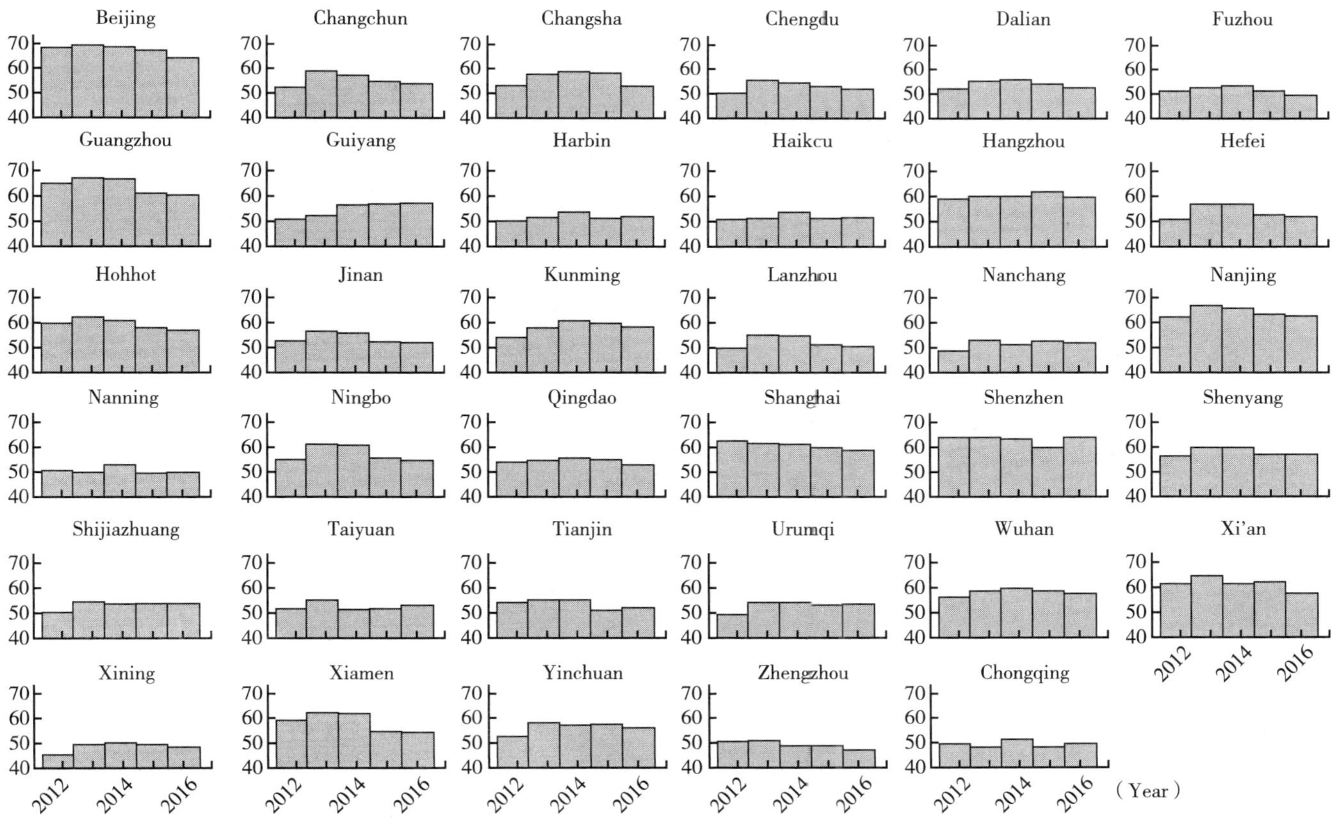

Figure 4 The 2012–2016 Objective Indexes of the 35 Cities

B.5
Quality-of-life Subindexes of the 35 Chinese Cities

Scores and rankings of the satisfaction indexes and the objective indexes (social and economic data indexes) can be explained by their subindexes [1] which will be compared and analyzed in this part.

5.1　Living Standard Index

Living standard index consists of a satisfaction index and an objective index. The former was obtained through a telephone survey by assigning values to survey answers, and the latter by calculating the social economic indicators of the 35 cities.

5.1.1　Satisfaction Index of Living Standard

According to the QLICC system, the satisfaction index of living standard comes from the weighted average of income status and income expectation satisfaction subindexes. Table 1 lists the 2016 survey result of living standard satisfaction. As can be seen from Table 1, the indexes of all the 35 cities are

---

[1]　Same as in the previous surveys, the subindexes supporting the general indexes of the 35 cities are: living standard, living costs, human capital, social security and living experience subindexes. And each subindex consists of a subjective satisfaction index and an objective index (social and economic data indexes).

035

Blue Book of Quality of Life in Cities

above 50 (the critical point between the satisfaction and the dissatisfaction intervals), and 23 cities score over 60. From 2012 to 2016, the weighted averages of the living standard satisfaction index are 51.28, 52.51, 54.32, 60.07 and 60.44 respectively– above the satisfaction level five years in a row and growing; The growth rates are 2.4%, 3.4%, 10.6% and 0.6%, which indicates that its growth has started to slow down.

Table 1　The 2012–2016 Living Standard Satisfaction Indexes of the 35 Cities

City	2016			2015		2014		2013		2012	
	Score	Ranking	Places Risen	Score	Ranking	Score	Ranking	Score	Ranking	Score	Ranking
Ningbo	62.06	1	0	63.16	1	54.58	12	54.62	6	52.77	8
Beijing	61.99	2	10	60.43	12	58.68	1	52.19	22	50.37	23
Nanning	61.62	3	27	58.58	30	51.89	31	51.48	28	51.47	16
Kunming	61.55	4	-1	62.28	3	52.91	23	52.84	17	52.32	11
Dalian	61.33	5	19	59.74	24	52.84	24	50.28	32	50.69	22
Chongqing	61.26	6	21	59.00	27	56.63	2	52.11	24	52.64	9
Haikou	61.21	7	-5	62.78	2	56.03	4	56.46	1	54.75	3
Hangzhou	61.11	8	-2	62.04	6	54.97	10	54.10	10	56.49	1
Chengdu	61.11	9	13	59.91	22	55.02	8	53.30	15	51.39	18
Hefei	60.88	10	-6	62.27	4	53.99	17	54.14	9	55.76	2
Jinan	60.84	11	6	60.27	17	54.28	16	54.29	8	51.43	17
Hohhot	60.81	12	20	58.14	32	54.43	14	54.31	7	50.36	24
Harbin	60.81	13	-5	61.31	8	52.27	27	49.86	33	48.89	30
Xining	60.75	14	6	60.04	20	51.99	30	55.00	4	52.31	12
Nanjing	60.60	15	-4	60.65	11	52.69	26	52.34	19	49.23	29
Guangzhou	60.59	16	-7	61.09	9	52.77	25	52.32	20	50.97	21
Qingdao	60.50	17	-7	60.97	10	55.37	6	55.81	2	52.59	10
Nanchang	60.49	18	3	60.00	21	53.48	21	52.18	23	48.27	32
Taiyuan	60.31	19	6	59.25	25	51.84	32	50.42	30	48.27	33
Tianjin	60.26	20	14	57.89	34	54.98	9	52.24	21	51.27	19
Zhengzhou	60.14	21	5	59.08	26	50.98	35	48.00	35	52.86	7
Changsha	60.10	22	-8	60.31	14	54.53	13	53.44	14	50.29	25
Urumqi	60.01	23	-8	60.29	15	54.90	11	54.10	11	50.99	20

036

Quality-of-life Subindexes of the 35 Chinese Cities

Continued table

City	2016			2015		2014		2013		2012	
	Score	Ranking	Places Risen	Score	Ranking	Score	Ranking	Score	Ranking	Score	Ranking
Shenzhen	59.98	24	-11	60.41	13	53.49	20	51.65	26	52.08	14
Fuzhou	59.94	25	-2	59.76	23	54.40	15	54.64	5	53.76	4
Wuhan	59.75	26	-7	60.07	19	53.25	22	50.39	31	49.95	26
Shanghai	59.75	27	-9	60.16	18	56.60	3	52.59	18	51.65	15
Shijiazhuang	59.63	28	3	58.46	31	51.69	33	51.79	25	53.38	6
Changchun	59.38	29	-22	61.64	7	55.32	7	53.07	16	53.74	5
Guiyang	59.14	30	5	57.58	35	53.61	19	53.74	13	49.40	28
Shenyang	58.85	31	-2	58.89	29	53.65	18	51.54	27	46.95	34
Lanzhou	58.74	32	1	58.04	33	51.42	34	49.72	34	46.88	35
Yinchuan	58.22	33	-17	60.29	16	52.16	29	51.1	29	49.74	27
Xiamen	57.66	34	-29	62.26	5	55.78	5	55.69	3	52.18	13
Xi'an	57.58	35	-7	58.94	28	52.26	28	53.88	12	48.79	31
Average	60.44			60.07		54.32		52.51		51.28	

As is shown in the histogram, the scores of the 35 cities have generally improved and concentrated. Most cities have gone up from the interval of 50-55 to 55-65 (See the Figure 1).

And from statistical analysis, the gaps among cities have been narrowed. In 2012, the highest scorer of living standard subjective index was Hangzhou (56.49), while the lowest scorer was Lanzhou (46.88). There was a difference of 9.61, and the standard deviation of the 35 cities was 2.21. In 2013, the highest scorer was Haikou (56.46), while the lowest scorer was Zhengzhou (48.00). The difference was 8.46, and the standard deviation was 1.88. In 2014, the highest scorer was Beijing (58.68), while the lowest scorer was Zhengzhou (50.98). The difference was 7.70, and the standard deviation was 1.70. In 2015, the highest scorer was Ningbo (63.16), while the lowest scorer was Guiyang (57.58). The difference was 5.58, and the standard deviation was 1.42. In 2016, the highest scorer is

Blue Book of Quality of Life in Cities

Ningbo (62.06), while the lowest scorer is Xi'an (57.58). The difference is 4.48, and the standard deviation is 1.09. The gap between the highest and the lowest scores has been reduced by over 50%, from 9.61 in 2012 to 4.48 in 2016. The standard deviation has also dropped by 50%, from 2.21 in 2012 to 1.09 in 2016. Obviously, the lowest score has been rising faster than the highest score.

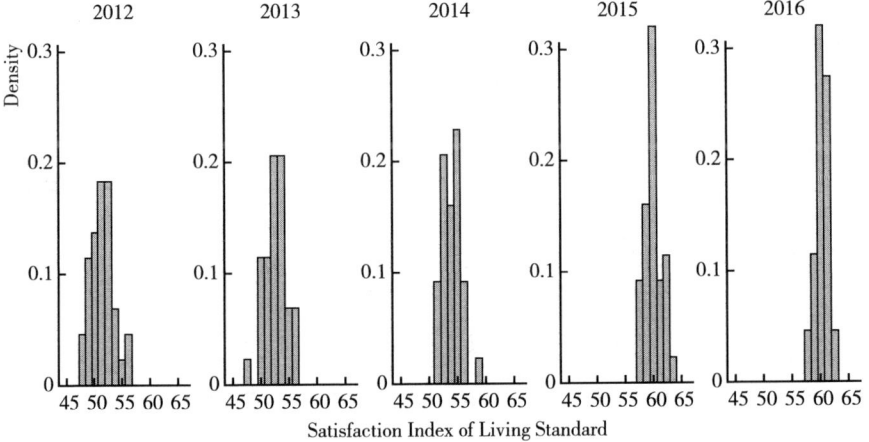

Figure 1 A Histogram of the 2012–2016 Living Standard Satisfaction Indexes of the 35 Cities

Cities ranked top 10 in the list of living standard satisfaction indexes are: Ningbo (1), Beijing (2), Nanning (3), Kunming (4), Dalian (5), Chongqing (6), Haikou (7), Hangzhou (8), Chengdu (9) and Hefei (10), including 5eastern cities, 1central city and 4western cities. And the bottom 10cities are: Wuhan (26), Shanghai (27), Shijiazhuang (28), Changchun (29), Guiyang (30), Shenyang (31), Lanzhou (32), Yinchuan (33), Xiamen (34) and Xi'an (35), including 4 eastern cities, 2 central cities and 4 western cities. Haikou and Hangzhou have ranked among the top 10 five years in a row, while Lanzhou

Quality-of-life Subindexes of the 35 Chinese Cities

has remained among the bottom 10 during the same period. From the distribution of the top 10 and the bottom 10 cities, the indexes of the western cities are generally even with that of the eastern cities.

Among the top 10cities, the rankings of Beijing, Nanning, Dalian, Chongqing and Chengdu have seen the greatest improvementscompared to the result of 2015. According to the places risen, the cities can be sequenced as follows: Nanning (+27), Chongqing (+21), Dalian (+19), Chengdu (+13) and Beijing (+10). Among the bottom 10cities, the rankings of Wuhan, Shanghai, Changchun, Shenyang, Yinchuan, Xiamen and Xi'an have somewhat declined. And the ranking changes are as follows: Wuhan (-7), Shanghai (-9), Changchun (-22), Shenyang (-2), Yinchuan (-17), Xiamen (-29) and Xi'an (-7).

Viewed by cities, as is shown in Figure 2, the scores of 8 cities (Beijing, Nanning, Chengdu, Hohhot, Nanchang, Taiyuan, Tianjin and Lanzhou) have risen 4 years in a row. Compared to the result of 2015, although the 2016average is slightly higher than the 2015 average of 60.07, the satisfaction indexes of only 16 cities have improved. Nanning is of the greatest rise, from 58.58 to 61.62, and from No.30 to No.3. The satisfaction of 19 cities is lower than that of last year. Xiamen was of the quickest drop, from 62.26 to 57.66, and from No.5 to No.34.

The satisfaction index of living standard comes from the weighted average of the income status and the income expectation satisfaction indexes. According to the survey result, as is shown in Table 2, from 2012 to 2016, the weighted averages of the income status satisfaction indexes are 51.52, 52.54, 52.92, 59.65 and 60.66 respectively—above the satisfaction level five years in a row and growing. The average annual growth rates are 1.98%, 0.72%, 12.71% and 1.69%. Obviously, the growth has fluctuated greatly.

039

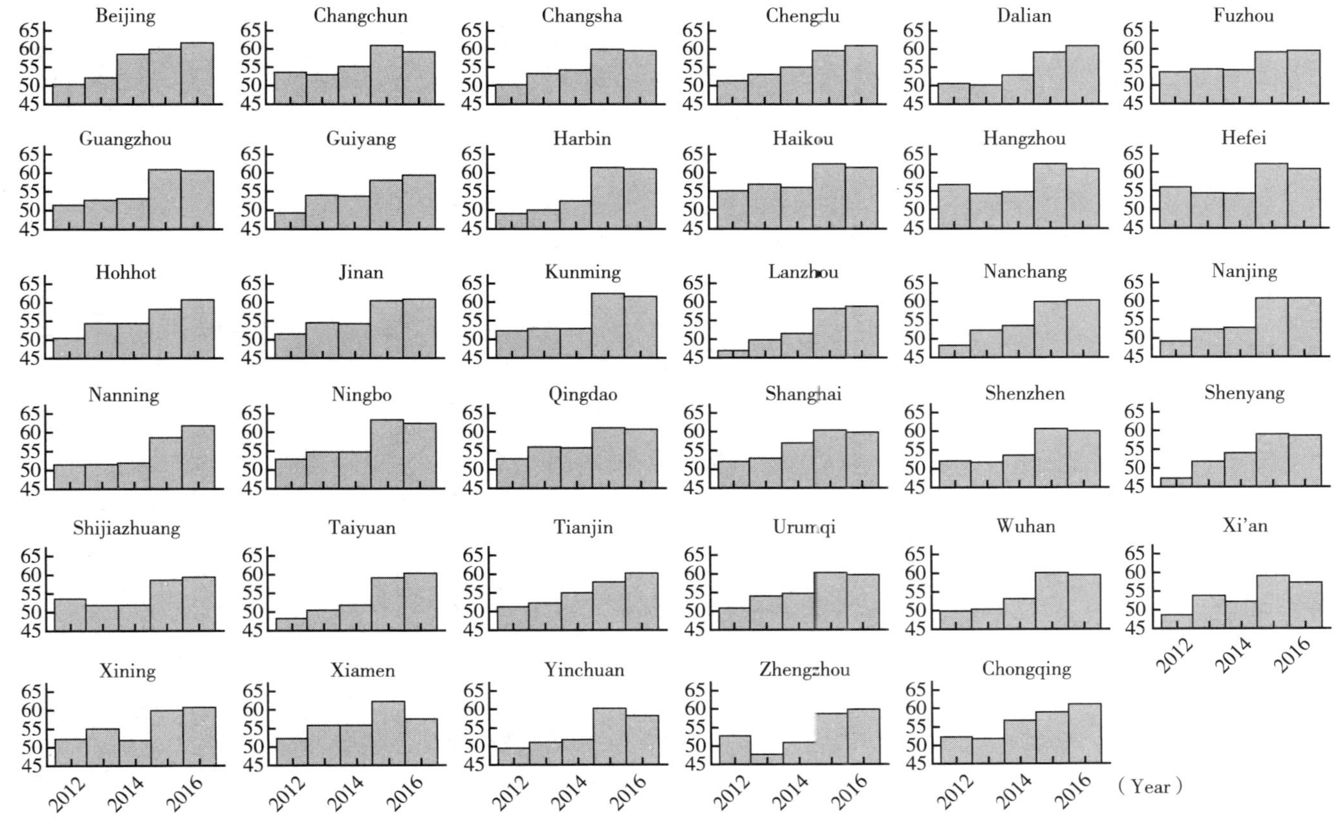

Figure 2 The 2012–2016 Living Standard Satisfaction Indexes of the 35 Cities (The scores are shown on the vertical axis)

Quality-of-life Subindexes of the 35 Chinese Cities

Table 2　The 2012–2016 Income Status Satisfaction Indexes of the 35 Cities

City	2016			2015		2014		2013		2012	
	Score	Ranking	Places Risen	Score	Ranking	Score	Ranking	Score	Ranking	Score	Ranking
Jinan	63.01	1	10	60.72	11	52.52	19	54.15	11	52.11	14
Kunming	62.41	2	6	61.05	8	52.05	22	53.17	16	51.76	16
Guangzhou	62.19	3	9	60.65	12	51.20	25	52.94	17	50.57	21
Beijing	62.11	4	12	59.80	16	56.56	2	51.65	24	50.10	22
Chongqing	62.00	5	23	58.57	28	55.58	5	51.38	25	53.45	7
Ningbo	61.91	6	-4	63.28	2	54.58	10	55.21	6	53.65	6
Haikou	61.73	7	-4	62.86	3	56.83	1	56.87	1	57.50	2
Nanning	61.49	8	21	58.45	29	50.05	31	51.20	27	50.00	23
Chengdu	61.43	9	17	58.99	26	53.39	14	53.82	12	50.88	19
Dalian	61.31	10	8	59.68	18	51.86	23	50.46	30	49.69	24
Xining	61.29	11	2	60.57	13	52.72	18	54.44	8	52.78	13
Qingdao	61.28	12	-2	60.77	10	54.85	8	56.58	2	53.18	10
Zhengzhou	61.18	13	10	59.08	23	49.44	33	48.42	34	53.10	12
Hefei	61.14	14	-10	62.09	4	54.15	11	54.42	9	55.04	3
Hangzhou	61.04	15	-14	63.38	1	55.67	4	56.25	5	58.25	1
Changchun	60.86	16	-9	61.49	7	54.12	12	54.52	7	54.01	5
Changsha	60.74	17	5	59.37	22	52.83	17	52.62	18	48.10	30
Hohhot	60.53	18	15	56.89	33	53.13	15	53.80	13	48.21	29
Lanzhou	60.46	19	16	56.12	35	49.03	35	48.87	33	44.60	35
Shijiazhuang	60.42	20	12	57.22	32	49.95	32	51.85	22	53.43	8
Nanchang	60.33	21	-4	59.68	17	51.49	24	51.18	28	48.58	26
Harbin	60.17	22	-17	62.09	5	50.52	30	49.33	32	47.78	33
Urumqi	60.08	23	1	59.08	24	55.92	3	54.38	10	53.29	9
Fuzhou	60.04	24	3	58.90	27	53.00	16	56.39	4	54.19	4
Yinchuan	59.94	25	-19	61.65	6	49.28	34	51.37	26	53.13	11
Shanghai	59.94	26	-6	59.54	20	55.33	6	52.60	19	51.43	17
Guiyang	59.70	27	7	56.33	34	51.17	26	51.98	21	47.86	32
Wuhan	59.62	28	-13	59.80	15	52.17	21	50.39	31	49.68	25
Tianjin	59.39	29	2	57.34	31	54.67	9	52.15	20	50.79	20
Shenzhen	59.06	30	-9	59.37	21	50.98	27	51.12	29	51.39	18
Taiyuan	58.76	31	-12	59.55	19	50.78	28	48.32	35	48.51	27
Nanjing	58.54	32	-7	59.01	25	52.46	20	53.42	14	48.08	31
Shenyang	57.90	33	-3	58.12	30	53.40	13	51.75	23	46.57	34
Xi'an	57.83	34	-20	60.07	14	50.73	29	53.25	15	48.30	28
Xiamen	56.81	35	-26	60.83	9	54.92	7	56.39	3	52.03	15
Average	60.66			59.65		52.92		52.54		51.52	

041

  Blue Book of Quality of Life in Cities

From the distribution of the scores, as is shown in Figure 3, both the lowest and the highest scores of income status satisfaction have greatly improved. The lowest score has moved up gradually from the interval of 40-45 (in 2012) to the interval of 45-50, 50-55 and 55-60, while the highest score has gone up from the interval of 55-60 to 60-65. And the gap between the lowest and the highest scores has been reduced from about 20 in 2012 to less than 10 in 2016. To be specific, in 2012, the highest scorer was Hangzhou (58.25), while the lowest scorer was Lanzhou (44.60). The difference was 13.65, and the standard deviation was 2.90. In 2013, the highest scorer was Haikou (56.87), while the lowest scorer was Taiyuan (48.32). The difference was 8.55, and the standard deviation was 2.26. In 2014, the highest scorer was Haikou (56.83), while the lowest scorer was Lanzhou (49.03). The difference was 7.80, and the standard deviation was 2.12. In 2015, the highest scorer was Hangzhou (63.38), while the lowest scorer was Lanzhou (56.12). The difference was 7.26, and the standard deviation was 1.78. In 2016, the highest scorer is Jinan (63.01), while the lowest scorer is Xiamen (56.81). The difference is 6.20, and the standard deviation is 1.36.

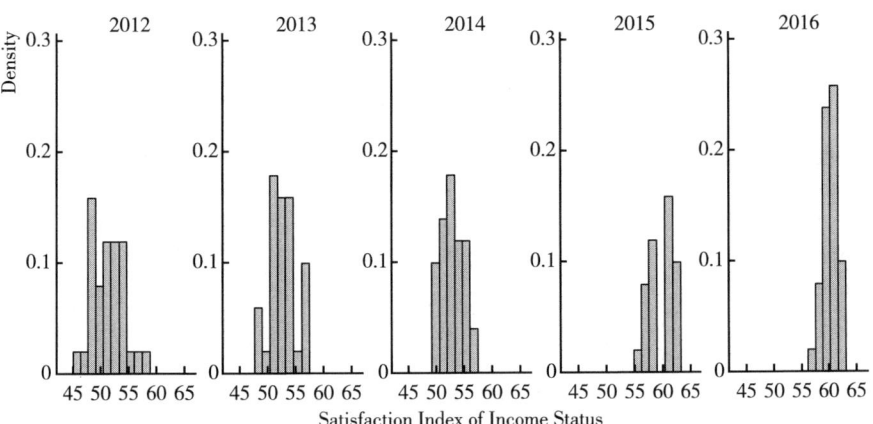

Figure 3   A Histogram of the 2012–2016 Income Status Satisfaction Indexes of the 35 Cities

Quality-of-life Subindexes of the 35 Chinese Cities ── ⟨↵

Viewed by cities, as is shown in Figure 4, Beijing, Changsha, Chengdu, Dalian, Lanzhou, Nanchang, Shanghai, Tianjin and Urumqi (25% of the surveyed cities) have experienced an improvement in the index for four years. The income status satisfaction indexes of Fuzhou, Guangzhou, Guiyang, Hohhot, Jinan, Kunming, Nanning, Qingdao, Shijiazhuang, Xining, Zhengzhou and Chongqing have fluctuated but still gone up. And the indexes of Changchun, Harbin, Haikou, Hangzhou, Hefei, Nanjing, Ningbo, Shenzhen, Shenyang, Taiyuan, Wuhan, Xi'an, Xiamen and Yinchuan have slightly dropped compared to the result of 2015.

Cities ranked top 10 in the list of income status satisfaction indexes are: Jinan (1), Kunming (2), Guangzhou (3), Beijing (4), Chongqing (5), Ningbo (6), Haikou (7), Nanning (8), Chengdu (9) and Dalian (10). And the bottom 10cities are: Shanghai (26), Guiyang (27), Wuhan (28), Tianjin (29), Shenzhen (30), Taiyuan (31), Nanjing (32), Shenyang (33), Xi'an (34) and Xiamen (35). Among the top 10 cities, Chongqing (+23), Nanning (+21), Chengdu (+17), Beijing (+12), Jinan (+10), Guangzhou (+9), Dalian (+8) and Kunming (+6) have seen a great advancement in the ranking, while Ningbo (-4) and Haikou (-4) have experienced a slight decline compared to the result of 2015. Among the bottom 10cities, the rankings of Guiyang (+7) and Tianjin (+2) have risen, while the rankings of Xiamen (-26), Xi'an (-20), Wuhan (-13), Taiyuan (-12), Shenzhen (-9), Nanjing (-7), Shanghai (-6) and Shenyang (-3) have dropped. In the top 10 list, Chongqing has made the greatest improvement. And in the bottom 10list, Xiamen has encountered the biggest decline. Regionally speaking, there are 6 eastern cities and 4 western cities in the top 10 list; and 6 eastern cities, 2 central cities and 2 western cities in the bottom 10 list.

As is shown by the survey result in Table 3, the weighted averages of the

043

Figure 4　The 2012–2016 Income Status Satisfaction Indexes of the 35 Cities (The scores are shown on the vertical axis)

Quality-of-life Subindexes of the 35 Chinese Cities

income expectation satisfaction indexes are 51.36, 52.48, 55.50, 60.50 and 60.23 from 2012 to 2016. The average annual growth rates are 2.18%, 5.75%, 9.01% and -0.45% respectively. Obviously, the index had kept improving at an accelerating rate before 2015 and starts to drop in 2016.

Table 3   The 2012–2016 Income Expectation Satisfaction Indexes of the 35 Cities

City	2016			2015		2014		2013		2012	
	Score	Ranking	Places Risen	Score	Ranking	Score	Ranking	Score	Ranking	Score	Ranking
Nanjing	62.66	1	5	62.28	6	52.91	32	51.26	29	50.38	26
Ningbo	62.22	2	1	63.03	3	54.58	18	54.03	10	51.89	16
Beijing	61.88	3	10	61.05	13	60.79	1	52.74	17	50.63	25
Taiyuan	61.86	4	26	58.95	30	52.90	33	52.51	19	48.02	32
Nanning	61.76	5	28	58.70	33	53.72	30	51.76	24	52.93	6
Harbin	61.45	6	12	60.53	18	54.03	22	50.39	32	50.00	28
Dalian	61.35	7	16	59.80	23	53.81	26	50.09	34	51.69	21
Hangzhou	61.18	8	8	60.69	16	54.27	21	51.94	23	54.72	2
Tianjin	61.14	9	25	58.45	34	55.29	15	52.34	21	51.75	20
Hohhot	61.10	10	18	59.40	28	55.73	13	54.82	6	52.50	10
Shenzhen	60.90	11	-1	61.46	10	55.99	10	52.18	22	52.78	8
Chengdu	60.79	12	2	60.84	14	56.65	4	52.78	16	51.90	15
Haikou	60.69	13	-9	62.70	4	55.22	16	56.04	1	52.00	14
Kunming	60.68	14	-12	63.52	2	53.77	29	52.50	20	52.88	7
Nanchang	60.66	15	5	60.31	20	55.46	14	53.18	13	47.97	33
Hefei	60.63	16	-11	62.45	5	53.83	25	53.85	11	56.47	1
Chongqing	60.52	17	10	59.43	27	57.67	3	52.84	15	51.82	19
Xining	60.22	18	8	59.51	26	51.27	35	55.56	2	51.85	18
Urumqi	59.95	19	-10	61.51	9	53.87	24	53.81	12	48.68	31
Wuhan	59.89	20	-1	60.34	19	54.33	20	50.39	33	50.21	27
Fuzhou	59.85	21	-4	60.61	17	55.80	12	52.90	14	53.32	5
Shenyang	59.80	22	3	59.67	25	53.90	23	51.33	28	47.34	34
Qingdao	59.71	23	-11	61.17	12	55.89	11	55.04	4	52.00	13
Shanghai	59.56	24	-9	60.79	15	57.87	2	52.57	18	51.88	17

Blue Book of Quality of Life in Cities

Continued table

City	2016			2015		2014		2013		2012	
	Score	Ranking	Places Risen	Score	Ranking	Score	Ranking	Score	Ranking	Score	Ranking
Changsha	59.46	25	-14	61.25	11	56.23	7	54.26	9	52.49	11
Zhengzhou	59.11	26	3	59.08	29	52.51	34	47.58	35	52.62	9
Guangzhou	58.99	27	-19	61.53	8	54.34	19	51.71	26	51.38	22
Shijiazhuang	58.83	28	-4	59.70	24	53.43	31	51.74	25	53.33	4
Jinan	58.68	29	-7	59.82	22	56.04	9	54.43	8	50.75	24
Guiyang	58.58	30	2	58.83	32	56.05	8	55.51	3	50.95	23
Xiamen	58.51	31	-30	63.69	1	56.63	5	55.00	5	52.33	12
Changchun	57.89	32	-25	61.80	7	56.52	6	51.62	27	53.48	3
Xi'an	57.33	33	2	57.81	35	53.79	28	54.50	7	49.27	29
Lanzhou	57.02	34	-13	59.97	21	53.80	27	50.56	31	49.15	30
Yinchuan	56.49	35	-4	58.93	31	55.05	17	50.82	30	46.35	35
Average	60.23			60.5		55.50		52.48		51.36	

From the distribution of the indexes, in 2012, the highest scorer of the income expectation satisfaction index was Hefei (56.47), while the lowest scorer was Yinchuan (46.35). In 2013, the highest scorer was Haikou (56.04), while the lowest scorer was Zhengzhou (47.58). In 2014, the highest scorer was Beijing (60.79), while the lowest scorer was Xining (51.27). In 2015, the highest scorer was Xiamen (63.69), while the lowest scorer was Xi'an (57.81). And in 2016, the highest scorer is Nanjing (62.66), while the lowest scorer is Yinchuan (56.49). The differences between the highest and the lowest scores are 10.12, 8.46, 9.52, 5.88 and 6.17 from 2012 to 2016, and the standard deviations are 2.04, 1.80, 1.74, 1.43 and 1.45 respectively. Obviously, the differences among cities have been narrowed.

As is shown in Figure 5, the distribution of the lowest scores has gone up from the interval of 45-50 to 55-60, while that of the highest scores has improved from 55-60 to 60-65.

Quality-of-life Subindexes of the 35 Chinese Cities —— ↙

Cities ranked top 10 in the list of income expectation satisfaction indexes are: Nanjing (1), Ningbo (2), Beijing (3), Taiyuan (4), Nanning (5), Harbin (6), Dalian (7), Hangzhou (8), Tianjin (9) and Hohhot (10). And the bottom 10cities are: Zhengzhou (26), Guangzhou (27), Shijiazhuang (28), Jinan (29), Guiyang (30), Xiamen (31), Changchun (32), Xi'an (33), Lanzhou (34) and Yinchuan (35). Compared to that of 2015, the rankings of the top 10cities have all improved. The specific changes are as follows: Nanjing (+5), Ningbo (+1), Beijing (+10), Taiyuan (+26), Nanning (+28), Harbin (+12), Dalian (+16), Hangzhou (+8), Tianjin (+25) and Hohhot (+18). The ranking changes of the bottom 10 cities are: Zhengzhou (3), Guangzhou (-19), Shijiazhuang (-4), Jinan (-7), Guiyang (+2), Xiamen (-30), Changchun (-25), Xi'an (+2), Lanzhou (-13) and Yinchuan (-4). Regionally speaking, there are 6 eastern cities, 2 central cities and 2 western cities in the top 10 list; and 4 eastern cities, 2 central cities and 4 western cities in the bottom 10 list.

Viewed by cities, as is shown in Figure 6, the income expectation

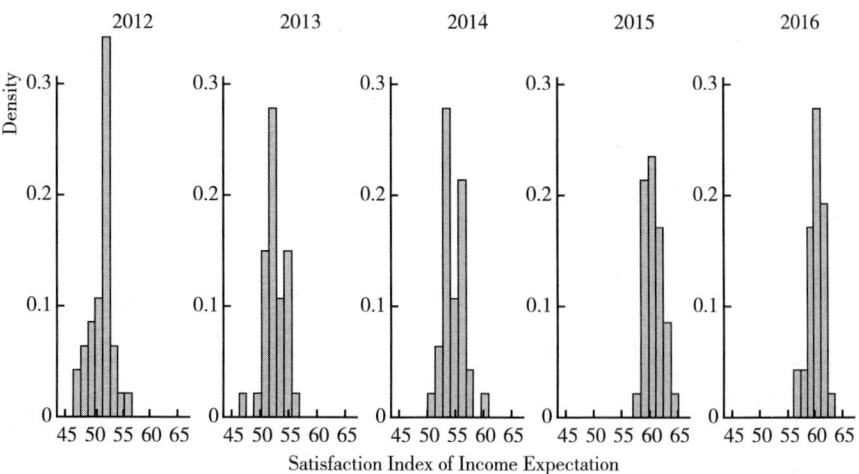

Figure 5   A Histogram of the 2012–2016 Income Expectation Satisfaction Indexes of the 35 Cities

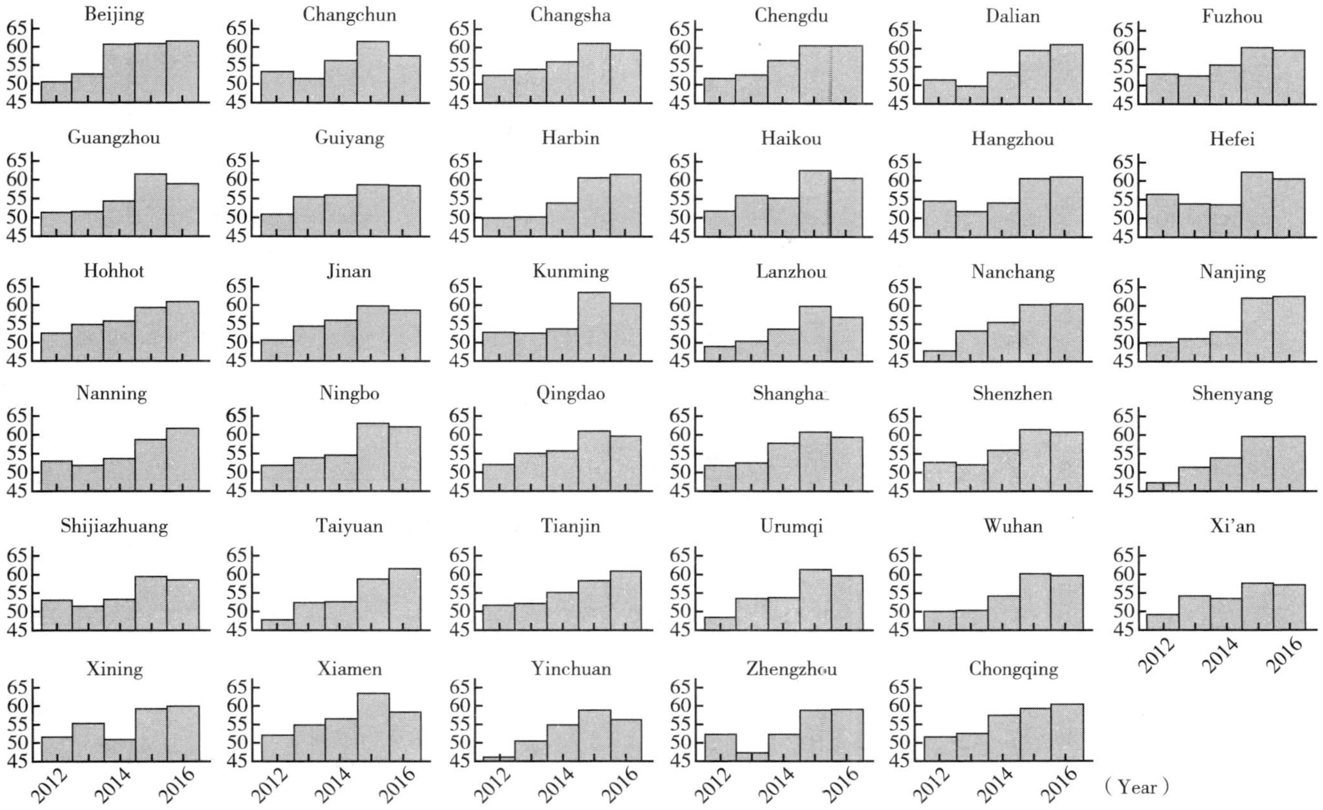

Figure 6 The 2012–2016 Income Expectation Satisfaction Indexes of the 35 Cities (The scores are shown on the vertical axis)

Quality-of-life Subindexes of the 35 Chinese Cities

satisfaction indexes of the 35 cities have generally improved from 2012 to 2016. Among them, Beijing, Harbin, Hohhot, Nanchang, Nanjing, Shenyang, Taiyuan, Tianjin and Chongqing (26% of the surveyed cities) have seen an increase 4 years in a row. The indexes of Dalian, Hangzhou, Nanning, Xining and Zhengzhou (14% of the surveyed cities) have fluctuated but still risen. And the indexes of most cities (60% of the surveyed cities), such as Changchun, Changsha, Chengdu, Fuzhou, Guangzhou, Guiyang, Haikou, Hefei, Jinan, Kunming, Lanzhou, Ningbo, Qingdao, Shanghai, Shenzhen, Shijiazhuang, Urumqi, Wuhan, Xi'an, Xiamen and Yinchuan, dropped slightly in 2016.

5.1.2 Objective Index of Living Standard

According to the QLICC system, the objective index of living standard consists of two primary indicators (income level and life improvements) which are in turn made up of six secondary indicators (consumption rate, per capita wealth, per capita disposable income, per capita consumption growth, per capita wealth growth and per capita disposable income growth). The objective indexes were obtained by calculating these indicators.

The result of calculation is shown in Table 4. The weighted averages of the indexes are 56.28, 63.39, 68.06, 59.83 and 50.07 respectively from 2012 to 2016. The objective index peaked in 2014, then started to drop, and reaches 50.07 (the lowest score since 2012) in 2016. It is mainly because that the scores of the index are closely related to economic growth. As China's economic development slows down to the medium-high speed stage, the index also drops down to the base line this year. Figure 7 is a histogram of the 2012-2016 living standard objective indexes of the 35 cities.

Blue Book of Quality of Life in Cities

Table 4   The 2012–2016 Living Standard Objective Indexes of the 35 Cities

City	2016			2015		2014		2013		2012	
	Score	Ranking	Places Risen	Score	Ranking	Score	Ranking	Score	Ranking	Score	Ranking
Shenzhen	80.00	1	13	59.30	14	75.18	8	78.91	3	64.78	7
Shanghai	70.73	2	0	79.02	2	79.45	2	73.93	6	77.84	2
Beijing	61.55	3	-2	80.00	1	80.00	1	77.84	5	80.03	1
Hangzhou	60.55	4	-1	76.42	3	72.60	10	73.83	7	76.79	3
Nanjing	59.44	5	0	69.77	5	77.90	4	80.00	1	66.33	6
Guangzhou	56.76	6	4	60.71	10	75.76	6	70.24	11	72.14	4
Ningbo	53.77	7	1	62.08	8	75.54	7	72.47	8	68.70	5
Tianjin	52.58	8	15	55.56	23	68.39	14	60.42	23	57.02	13
Chengdu	52.22	9	-3	62.62	6	71.21	13	72.13	10	58.80	11
Xiamen	52.12	10	2	60.56	12	79.43	3	79.22	2	52.40	23
Guiyang	51.37	11	0	60.58	11	62.79	26	49.09	32	47.86	27
Jinan	51.14	12	13	55.16	25	71.92	11	72.27	9	57.43	12
Urumqi	50.72	13	2	59.11	15	63.78	24	58.61	26	47.54	28
Wuhan	49.53	14	-1	59.72	13	71.82	12	60.51	22	50.81	25
Nanchang	49.07	15	1	58.46	16	52.77	34	60.59	21	46.60	31
Harbin	48.15	16	15	50.58	31	63.60	25	49.04	33	55.47	18
Shenyang	47.68	17	13	52.73	30	66.32	17	57.82	27	48.84	26
Changchun	47.64	18	0	57.86	18	66.77	16	63.27	16	53.67	20
Haikou	47.41	19	5	55.30	24	64.21	23	69.40	12	59.80	10
Hohhot	47.27	20	9	52.83	29	65.87	18	68.67	13	55.87	16
Qingdao	47.21	21	-12	61.36	9	65.47	19	56.06	28	64.76	8
Shijiazhuang	46.97	22	4	53.79	26	60.53	27	58.80	25	53.09	21
Hefei	46.72	23	-1	55.80	22	74.09	9	67.04	14	55.75	17
Fuzhou	46.20	24	-7	57.98	17	67.16	15	61.51	17	60.75	9
Chongqing	45.96	25	9	44.60	34	58.86	30	40.00	35	53.90	19
Zhengzhou	45.14	26	-5	56.44	21	57.00	32	61.4	18	56.11	14
Changsha	44.69	27	-23	70.09	4	76.15	5	60.91	20	50.97	24
Lanzhou	43.67	28	4	50.15	32	64.84	21	65.59	15	46.30	32
Yinchuan	43.62	29	-10	57.45	19	54.12	33	60.00	24	45.55	33
Kunming	43.45	30	-2	53.32	28	57.07	31	55.27	29	40.76	34
Dalian	42.95	31	-11	57.17	20	64.56	22	61.23	19	47.14	29
Xi'an	42.78	32	-25	62.55	7	64.90	20	78.59	4	56.07	15

050

Quality-of-life Subindexes of the 35 Chinese Cities

Continued table

City	2016			2015		2014		2013		2012	
	Score	Ranking	Places Risen	Score	Ranking	Score	Ranking	Score	Ranking	Score	Ranking
Xining	41.95	33	-6	53.61	27	59.10	28	54.92	30	40.00	35
Nanning	41.55	34	-1	45.35	33	59.04	29	41.04	34	52.98	22
Taiyuan	40.00	35	0	40.00	35	40.00	35	52.32	31	46.87	30
Average	50.07			59.83		68.06		63.39		56.28	

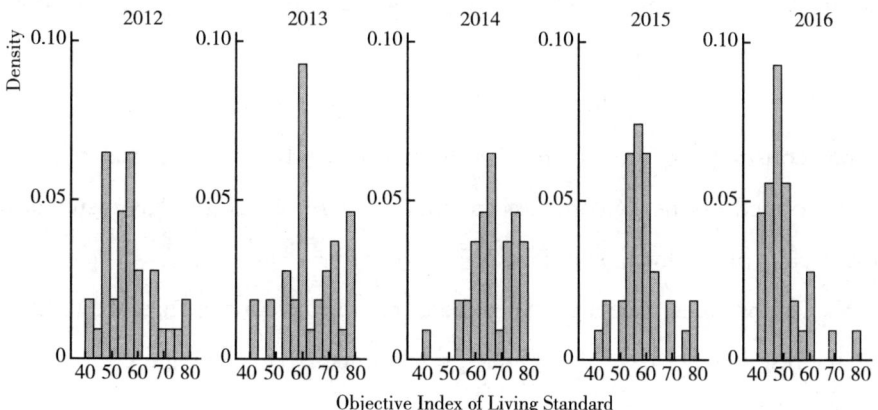

Figure 7　A Histogram of the 2012–2016 Living Standard Objective Indexes of the 35 Cities

Cities ranked top 10 in the list of living standard objective indexes are: Shenzhen (1), Shanghai (2), Beijing (3), Hangzhou (4), Nanjing (5), Guangzhou (6), Ningbo (7), Tianjin (8), Chengdu (9) and Xiamen (10). And the bottom 10cities are: Zhengzhou (26), Changsha (27), Lanzhou (28), Yinchuan (29), Kunming (30), Dalian (31), Xi'an (32), Xining (33), Nanning (34) and Taiyuan (35). Only 13 out of the 35 cities score over 50 in 2016, whereas in 2015, there were 32 cities. Since 2012, Beijing, Shanghai, Hangzhou, Nanjing and Ningbo have ranked among the top 10 five years in a row; while Taiyuan, Kunming and Xining have remained among the bottom 10 during the same period. In the top 10 list, Tianjin (15) and Shenzhen

051

Blue Book of Quality of Life in Cities

(13) have seen the greatest improvements. And in the bottom 10list, Xi'an (-25), Changsha (-23), Dalian (-11) and Yinchuan (-10) have experienced the most drastic drops. Regionally speaking, there are 9 eastern cities and 1 western city among the top 10 cities; and 1eastern city, 3 central cities and 6 western cities among the bottom 10 cities. Beijing had topped the list in the past. But in 2016, Shenzhen takes its place and ranks No.1, whose score also rises from 59.3 (2015) to 80. Taiyuan ranks No.35, and the score is only 40. All this shows that there are significant regional differences in the objective index of living standard. As for secondary indicators, the per capita consumption growth and the per capita wealth growth indexes of 2015 had dropped drastically compared to that of 2014, which directly resulted in the decline of the living standard objective index.

Viewed by cities, except for Shenzhen, the objective living standard indexes of the rest 34 cities have all declined greatly since 2015 (See Figure 8).

5.2　Living Cost Index

Living cost index consists of a subjective satisfaction index and an objective (social economic data) index. The former was obtained through telephone survey by assigning values to survey answers, and the latter by calculating social economic indicators.

5.2.1　Satisfaction Index of Living Cost

As is shown by the indexes and rankings listed in Table 5.None of the cities scores over 50 in 2016. It shows that residents of all the surveyed cities are unsatisfied with their living costs. Although the living cost index stays below satisfaction, dynamically speaking, 2012-2016, the weighted averages of the

052

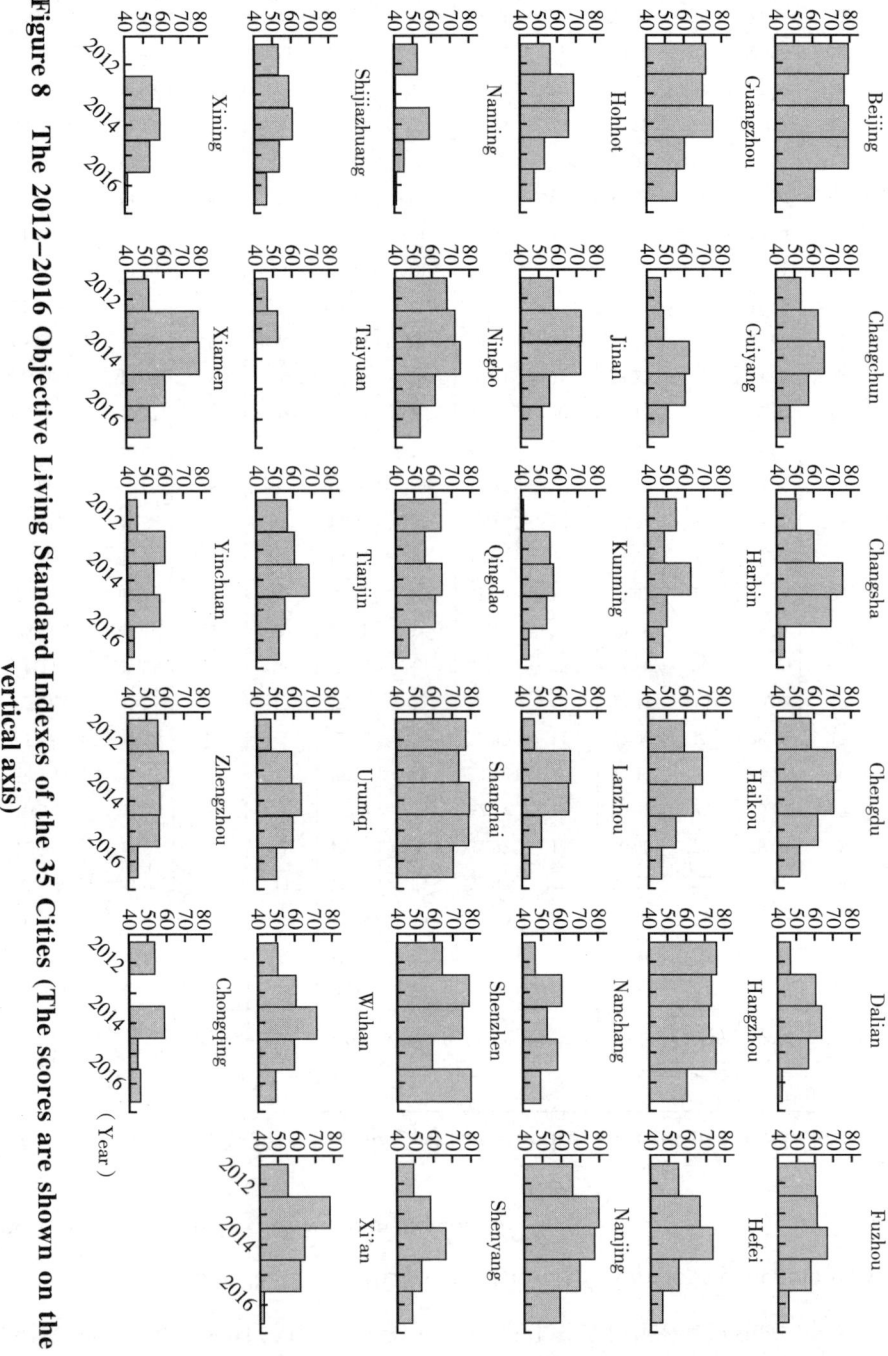

Figure 8   The 2012–2016 Objective Living Standard Indexes of the 35 Cities (The scores are shown on the vertical axis)

Blue Book of Quality of Life in Cities

index which are 28.91, 31.22, 31.81, 38.94 and 39.74, have climbed up five years in a row, from 28.91 in 2012 to 39.74 in 2016. Obviously, people now become less unsatisfied with the living costs.

Table 5   The 2012–2016 Living Cost Satisfaction Indexes of the 35 Cities

City	2016			2015		2014		2013		2012	
	Score	Ranking	Places Risen	Score	Ranking	Score	Ranking	Score	Ranking	Score	Ranking
Yinchuan	45.30	1	28	36.56	29	30.29	28	27.47	31	27.60	22
Jinan	43.45	2	8	41.33	10	35.72	2	36.16	3	35.39	2
Hohhot	43.40	3	27	36.15	30	30.99	23	30.85	20	26.43	28
Nanchang	41.97	4	11	39.68	15	33.87	7	33.18	12	28.66	14
Kunming	41.93	5	-1	42.97	4	31.82	16	30.00	22	28.04	18
Ningbo	41.83	6	3	41.49	9	32.21	13	29.03	25	26.62	27
Shijiazhuang	41.63	7	5	40.26	12	34.92	4	39.13	1	34.27	4
Harbin	41.26	8	-1	42.21	7	32.33	11	32.06	17	28.38	17
Chengdu	41.26	9	13	37.93	22	32.12	14	32.41	15	30.92	12
Haikou	41.23	10	-4	42.28	6	28.25	35	33.96	8	26.00	29
Guiyang	41.17	11	20	35.71	31	30.19	29	29.38	23	25.71	30
Nanning	41.15	12	1	40.15	13	31.72	18	33.45	10	27.16	24
Hefei	40.90	13	-11	43.82	2	35.02	3	34.40	6	35.43	1
Dalian	40.84	14	0	40.06	14	29.70	30	27.04	32	25.15	33
Chongqing	40.66	15	4	38.76	19	32.27	12	32.94	14	30.98	10
Xi'an	40.48	16	4	38.19	20	32.98	9	33.03	13	31.92	6
Hangzhou	40.41	17	-9	42.19	8	31.58	20	29.10	24	28.42	16
Urumqi	40.05	18	7	37.10	25	29.23	31	28.53	28	24.67	34
Changsha	39.90	19	-2	38.93	17	30.49	26	31.08	19	27.63	21
Shenyang	39.89	20	-9	40.45	11	37.48	1	36.31	2	31.73	7
Fuzhou	39.78	21	-3	38.87	18	31.70	19	33.65	9	31.21	9
Taiyuan	39.69	22	12	35.32	34	33.04	8	34.22	7	30.94	11
Zhengzhou	39.41	23	-7	39.66	16	31.75	17	35.03	5	31.67	8
Wuhan	39.22	24	-1	37.81	23	32.44	10	31.96	18	30.57	13
Qingdao	39.13	25	2	36.80	27	30.75	24	28.78	27	27.12	25
Guangzhou	38.98	26	6	35.58	32	30.39	27	28.46	29	27.79	20
Nanjing	38.80	27	-22	42.50	5	31.55	21	30.10	21	27.95	19
Xining	38.44	28	5	35.48	33	30.62	25	28.89	26	27.31	23

Quality-of-life Subindexes of the 35 Chinese Cities ——

Continued table

City	2016			2015		2014		2013		2012	
	Score	Ranking	Places Risen	Score	Ranking	Score	Ranking	Score	Ranking	Score	Ranking
Shanghai	37.81	29	-8	37.96	21	28.58	32	25.59	35	25.45	31
Xiamen	37.70	30	-27	43.34	3	31.25	22	32.36	16	28.49	15
Shenzhen	37.58	31	-5	37.03	26	28.42	34	26.56	33	25.30	32
Tianjin	37.28	32	-8	37.77	24	34.82	6	33.32	11	32.62	5
Changchun	37.24	33	-32	43.86	1	34.89	5	36.02	4	34.36	3
Lanzhou	35.97	34	-6	36.79	28	31.84	15	27.82	30	26.70	26
Beijing	35.50	35	0	33.76	35	28.53	33	26.13	34	23.06	35
Average	39.74			38.94		31.81		31.22		28.91	

Viewed by cities, in 2012, the highest scorer of the living cost satisfaction index was Hefei (35.42), while the lowest scorer was Beijing (23.06). The difference in between was 12.36. In 2013, the highest scorer was Shijiazhuang (39.13), while the lowest scorer was Shanghai (25.59). The difference was 13.54. In 2014, the highest scorer was Shenyang (37.48), while the lowest scorer was Haikou (28.25). The difference was 9.23. In 2015, the highest scorer was Changchun (43.86), while the lowest scorer was Beijing (33.76). The difference was 10.10. And in 2016, the highest scorer is Yinchuan (45.30), while the lowest scorer is Beijing (35.50). The difference is 9.80. Obviously, the distribution of the living cost satisfaction indexes has been improving and concentrating from 2012 to 2016. As is shown in Figure 9, the lowest score of the index has gone up from the interval of 20-30 to 30-40, and the highest score from 30-40 to 40-50. 2012-2016, the standard deviations are 3.14, 13.54, 9.23, 10.1 and 9.8 respectively.

In 2016, cities ranked top 10 in the list of living cost satisfaction indexes are: Yinchuan (1), Jinan (2), Hohhot (3), Nanchang (4), Kunming (5), Ningbo (6), Shijiazhuang (7), Harbin (8), Chengdu (9) and Haikou (10). And the

Blue Book of Quality of Life in Cities

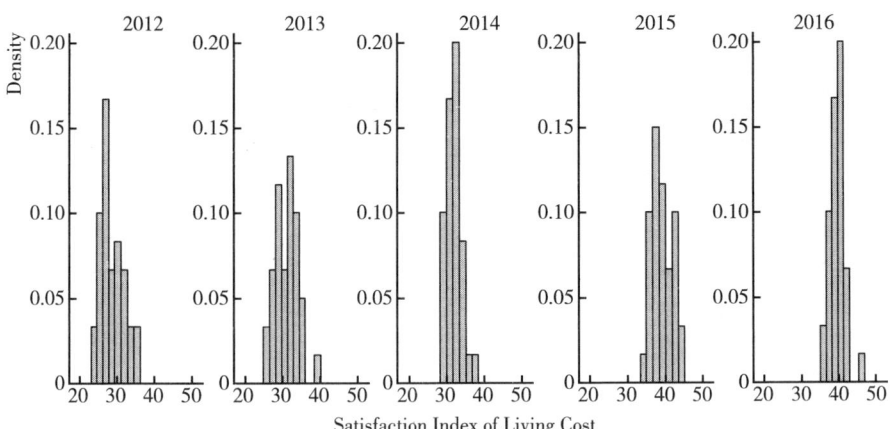

Figure 9 A Histogram of the 2012–2016 Living Cost Satisfaction Indexes of the 35 Cities

bottom 10 cities are: Guangzhou (26), Nanjing (27), Xining (28), Shanghai (29), Xiamen (30), Shenzhen (31), Tianjin (32), Changchun (33), Lanzhou (34) and Beijing (35). Among the top 10 cities, Yinchuan (+28) and Hohhot (+27) have seen the greatest rises in the ranking, followed by Chengdu (+13), Nanchang (+11), Jinan (+8), Shijiazhuang (+5) and Ningbo (+3). Among the bottom 10cities, Changchun (-32), Xiamen (-27) and Nanjing (-22) have experienced the quickest drops. The rankings of Yinchuan and Hohhot have risen from No.29 and No.30 in 2015 to No.1 and No.3 in 2016; while those of Changchun and Xiamen have dropped from No.1 and No.3 to No.33 and No.30. The ranking of Beijing remains unchanged, but its residents are the most unsatisfied with living costs. Beijing has stayed among the bottom 3 for five years, while Shenzhen and Guangzhou have remained among the bottom 10 for five and four years respectively. Shanghai has generally ranked after the 20th. All this shows that as a whole, residents of first-tier cities are the most unsatisfied with living costs. And Jinan has stayed in the top 10 list in the past five years, with a low and stable level of dissatisfaction.

056

Quality-of-life Subindexes of the 35 Chinese Cities —

Overall, the subjective living cost indexes of the 35 cities have kept rising from 2012 to 2016, which shows that the residents have become more and more satisfied with their living costs. The indexes of Beijing, Dalian, Guangzhou, Guiyang, Hohhot, Nanchang, Ningbo, Qingdao, Shenzhen, Urumqi, Wuhan, Xi'an and Xining have experienced continuous improvements. The indexes of Changsha, Chengdu, Fuzhou, Jinan, Nanning, Shijiazhuang, Taiyuan, Chongqing and Yinchuan have fluctuated but still gone up. And the indexes of Changchun, Harbin, Haikou, Hangzhou, Hefei, Kunming, Lanzhou, Nanjing, Shanghai, Shenyang, Tianjin, Xiamen and Zhengzhou had dropped slightly in 2016 (See Figure 10).

5.2.2 Objective Index of Living Cost

According to the QLICC system, the living cost objective index of each city was obtained by calculating its secondary indicators — house price index, inflation rate and house-price-to-income ratio. Table 6 list the 2016 living cost objective indexes of the 35 cities, along with their respective rankings.

Table 6 The 2012–2016 Living Cost Objective Indexes of the 35 Cities

City	2016			2015		2014		2013		2012	
	Score	Ranking	Places Risen	Score	Ranking	Score	Ranking	Score	Ranking	Score	Ranking
Kunming	80.00	1	0	80.00	1	80.00	1	80.00	1	74.00	2
Changsha	71.45	2	0	72.10	2	68.58	3	71.79	3	69.57	3
Hohhot	70.39	3	1	69.49	4	72.25	2	77.96	2	79.97	1
Xi'an	66.37	4	-1	71.13	3	63.89	4	65.27	6	61.38	9
Yinchuan	65.40	5	0	61.74	5	60.96	7	65.18	7	59.38	14
Xining	65.19	6	2	60.30	8	61.08	6	66.05	5	60.51	10
Nanchang	63.26	7	0	61.35	7	59.61	8	64.81	8	63.36	5
Shijiazhuang	62.99	8	-2	61.45	6	62.30	5	66.75	4	64.74	4
Qingdao	62.54	9	0	60.11	9	58.38	11	63.40	10	62.34	8

057

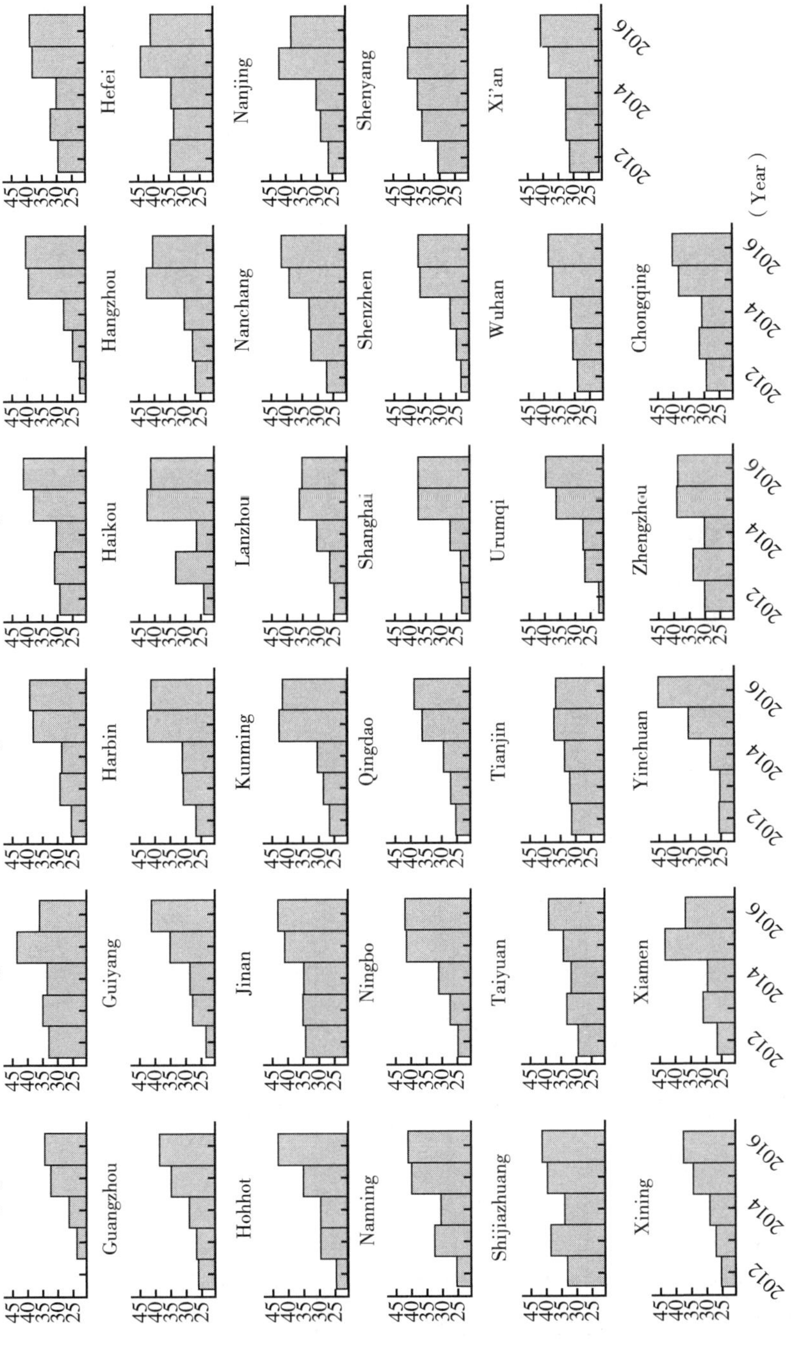

Figure 10 The 2012–2016 Living Cost Satisfaction Indexes of the 35 Cities (The scores are shown on the vertical axis)

Quality-of-life Subindexes of the 35 Chinese Cities ——

Continued table

City	2016			2015		2014		2013		2012	
	Score	Ranking	Places Risen	Score	Ranking	Score	Ranking	Score	Ranking	Score	Ranking
Shenyang	62.07	10	1	59.19	11	56.66	15	62.89	12	60.11	11
Chongqing	61.46	11	2	58.35	13	58.89	10	63.36	11	63.34	6
Wuhan	60.94	12	-2	59.73	10	57.75	12	62.61	13	59.68	13
Chengdu	60.71	13	1	57.21	14	55.97	16	61.68	15	60.06	12
Urumqi	60.67	14	5	54.76	19	52.94	23	58.33	22	46.58	29
Jinan	60.40	15	-3	58.94	12	59.29	9	64.59	9	59.19	16
Guiyang	60.38	16	-1	56.32	15	56.67	14	61.67	16	58.21	17
Lanzhou	60.35	17	1	55.20	18	55.50	17	59.93	19	52.63	22
Changchun	59.24	18	3	53.84	21	54.10	19	59.57	20	53.58	20
Zhengzhou	59.16	19	-3	55.75	16	56.88	13	62.30	14	63.02	7
Dalian	59.05	20	-3	55.35	17	52.44	24	57.15	24	56.00	18
Nanning	58.38	21	-1	54.44	20	54.83	18	60.61	18	54.24	19
Harbin	58.05	22	0	53.71	22	53.87	21	58.67	21	52.46	23
Hefei	56.91	23	0	52.21	23	53.89	20	58.17	23	51.49	26
Xiamen	53.93	24	2	49.57	26	53.86	22	60.70	17	59.22	15
Nanjing	53.80	25	-1	50.60	24	50.28	26	55.70	25	52.18	24
Fuzhou	53.62	26	-1	50.26	25	49.00	28	55.43	26	51.01	27
Tianjin	53.26	27	1	48.50	28	51.02	25	54.63	28	51.83	25
Ningbo	52.77	28	2	47.78	30	49.75	27	55.19	27	46.16	30
Taiyuan	52.70	29	2	47.17	31	46.66	30	53.84	29	46.09	31
Haikou	52.57	30	2	46.31	32	47.74	29	40.00	35	39.97	35
Hangzhou	51.12	31	-4	48.89	27	44.41	32	48.73	32	42.50	33
Guangzhou	51.10	32	-3	48.16	29	46.32	31	53.15	30	53.24	21
Shanghai	48.30	33	0	45.57	33	43.59	33	50.00	31	44.50	32
Beijing	47.49	34	0	42.99	34	40.00	35	45.17	34	40.80	34
Shenzhen	40.00	35	0	40.00	35	40.87	34	45.82	33	50.14	28
Average	58.74			54.58		53.84		58.67		56.10	

From 2012 to 2016, the weighted averages of the living cost objective index are 56.10, 58.67, 53.84, 54.58 and 58.74 respectively. The averages have risen for two years, which shows that the actual living costs have continued to decline. Correspondingly, the satisfaction indexes of living cost have kept

Blue Book of Quality of Life in Cities

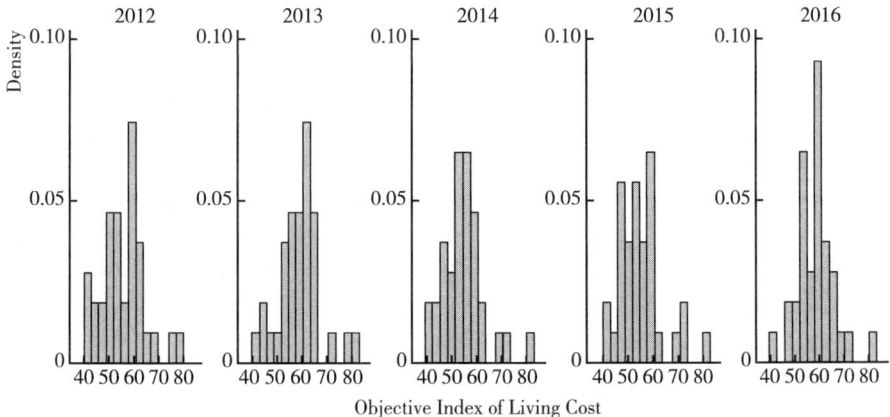

Figure 11   A Histogram of the 2012–2016 Living Cost Objective Indexes of the 35 Cities

improving. However, since the subjective index of living cost remains below 50, the residents are still not satisfied with their living costs.

Viewed by cities, in 2016, cities ranked top 10 in the list of living cost objective indexes are: Kunming (1), Changsha (2), Hohhot (3), Xi'an (4), Yinchuan (5), Xining (6), Nanchang (7), Shijiazhuang (8), Qingdao (9) and Shenyang (10). And the bottom 10 cities are: Fuzhou (26), Tianjin (27), Ningbo (28), Taiyuan (29), Haikou (30), Hangzhou (31), Guangzhou (32), Shanghai (33), Beijing (34) and Shenzhen (35). Regionally speaking, there are 3 eastern cities, 2 central cities and 5 western cities in the top 10 list; and 9 eastern cities, 1 central city and no western city in the bottom 10 list. Kunming, Changsha, Xi'an, Hohhot, Shijiazhuang, Nanchang and Xining have ranked among the top 10 five years in a row, which indicates a comparatively low living cost in these cities. Shenzhen, Beijing, Shanghai, Haikou, Taiyuan, Ningbo and Hangzhou have ranked among the bottom 10 during the same period, which shows that the living costs in such cities have been relatively high. It should be noted that in 2016, only Shenzhen, Beijing and Shanghai

060

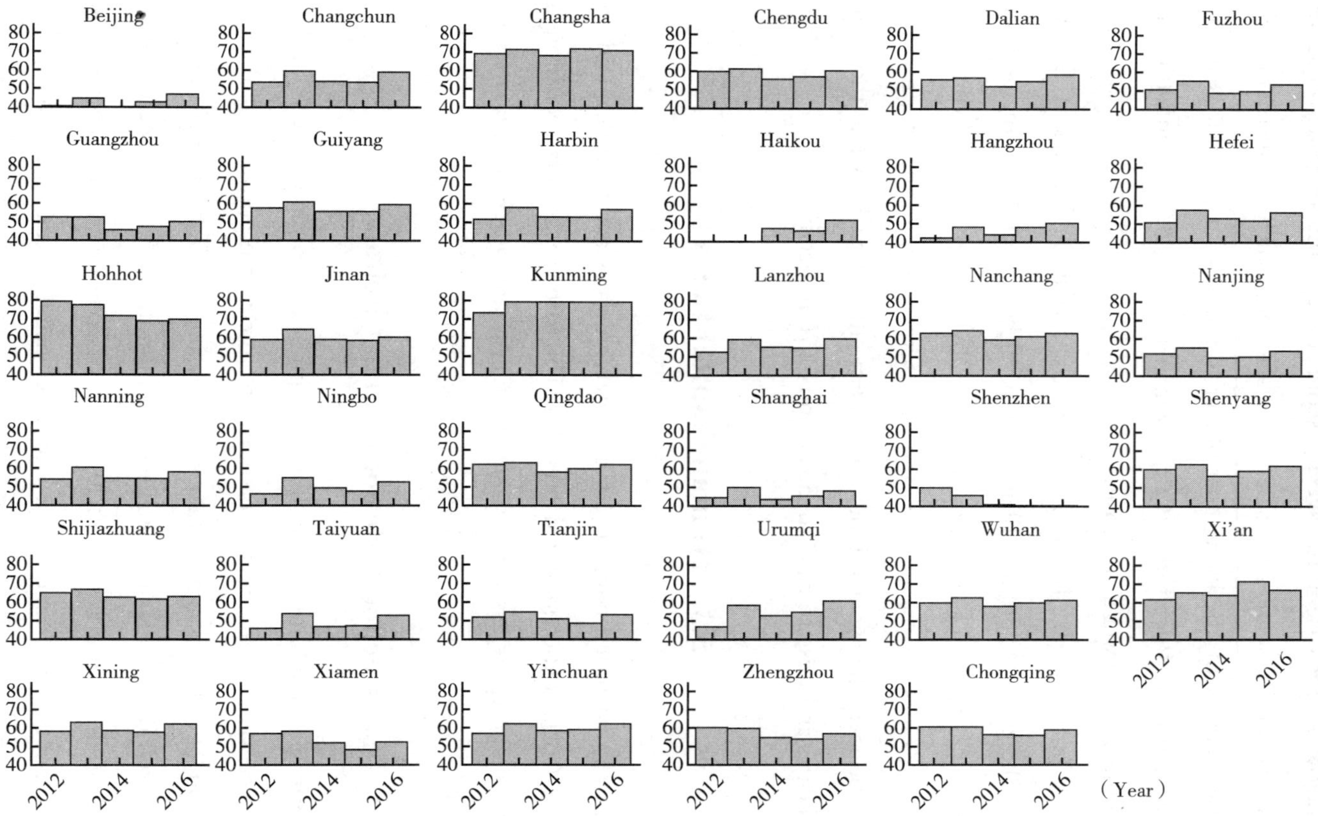

Figure 12 The 2012–2016 Living Cost Objective Indexes of the 35 Cities (The scores are shown on the vertical axis)

Blue Book of Quality of Life in Cities

score below 50. Increase in the average score suggests the lowering of urban living costs and the rising of residents' satisfaction, which is consistent with the improvement of the living cost objective indexes. In the past year, the national Consumer Price Index (CPI) is generally about 2% (low inflation). It has also helped to lower living costs.

As is shown in Figure 12, among the 35 cities, only the indexes of Beijing (43.29), Shenzhen (43.36) and Shanghai (46.39) have been lower than 50 for five years. Guangzhou scores merely 50.39. Obviously, the actual living costs in first-tier cities are the highest, and the corresponding satisfaction is the lowest. Besides, the average index of eastern cities is 52.47, while those of central cities and western cities are58.80 and 62.76 respectively.

5.3 Human Capital Index

Human capital index consists of a subjective satisfaction index and an objective (social and economic data) index. The former was obtained through telephone survey by assigning values to survey answers, and the latter by calculating social economic indicators of the 35 cities.

5.3.1 Satisfaction Index of Human Capital

The satisfaction subindexes of human capital were obtained by inquiring of interviewees about the satisfaction over their own and their children's education, and then assigning values to their answers. Table 7 lists the 2016 survey result of the human capital satisfaction indexes. In 2016, the weighted average of the subindexes is 62.20, which has continued to improve for 4 years. 33 out of the 35 cities score over 60. Generally speaking, the indexes of most cities are going up steadily.

062

Quality-of-life Subindexes of the 35 Chinese Cities —

Table 7   The 2012–2016 Human Capital Satisfaction Indexes of the 35 Cities

City	2016			2015		2014		2013		2012	
	Score	Ranking	Places Risen	Score	Ranking	Score	Ranking	Score	Ranking	Score	Ranking
Wuhan	64.22	1	8	62.43	9	57.67	26	57.09	31	58.09	26
Xining	63.98	2	5	62.48	7	61.59	4	60.09	10	58.80	21
Hangzhou	63.89	3	0	63.43	3	60.57	6	59.24	16	62.38	6
Beijing	63.60	4	6	62.36	10	60.47	7	59.68	11	59.33	16
Ningbo	63.40	5	-3	64.32	2	60.24	8	60.14	9	64.19	1
Chongqing	63.25	6	10	61.70	16	59.56	13	57.74	27	58.83	20
Tianjin	63.16	7	17	61.10	24	60.20	9	59.30	14	61.27	9
Shenyang	63.15	8	3	62.36	11	59.78	11	57.79	26	57.61	28
Guangzhou	62.95	9	-4	63.03	5	57.71	23	57.59	28	59.43	14
Hefei	62.84	10	-4	62.90	6	58.50	20	61.37	6	59.71	13
Taiyuan	62.76	11	24	58.34	35	57.70	24	53.49	35	55.20	35
Changsha	62.72	12	19	59.76	31	57.26	32	58.20	24	60.38	12
Nanning	62.70	13	5	61.52	18	57.69	25	58.73	21	58.18	25
Chengdu	62.57	14	1	61.86	15	57.66	27	58.17	25	59.14	18
Haikou	62.28	15	-11	63.37	4	61.69	3	59.11	17	58.00	27
Harbin	62.12	16	-3	62.10	13	58.01	22	57.23	29	56.76	30
Urumqi	62.10	17	10	60.80	27	58.54	18	61.86	3	61.18	10
Dalian	62.07	18	4	61.20	22	57.45	29	61.67	4	59.20	17
Shanghai	62.00	19	-11	62.44	8	61.26	5	60.35	8	58.79	22
Zhengzhou	61.82	20	1	61.29	21	57.51	28	61.54	5	58.45	24
Guiyang	61.69	21	11	59.50	32	56.98	33	59.60	12	55.48	33
Jinan	61.67	22	-2	61.39	20	58.98	16	61.99	2	62.20	7
Fuzhou	61.64	23	2	61.02	25	60.13	10	59.60	13	62.72	4
Shenzhen	61.56	24	6	60.54	30	56.75	34	57.03	32	57.34	29
Kunming	61.46	25	-2	61.19	23	56.15	35	54.33	34	55.45	34
Nanjing	61.33	26	-14	62.27	12	58.10	21	59.29	15	59.36	15
Lanzhou	61.10	27	6	59.09	33	61.74	2	57.20	30	58.52	23
Qingdao	61.07	28	-14	61.91	14	61.84	1	62.61	1	62.62	5
Hohhot	60.96	29	0	60.63	29	57.29	30	60.96	7	61.07	11
Changchun	60.86	30	-13	61.58	17	59.48	14	58.90	19	63.37	2
Shijiazhuang	60.73	31	-5	60.99	26	58.67	17	58.86	20	63.31	3
Nanchang	60.57	32	-4	60.78	28	58.51	19	58.45	23	56.10	32
Yinchuan	60.08	33	1	58.63	34	59.13	15	58.52	22	61.98	8
Xi'an	59.65	34	-15	61.46	19	57.29	31	56.65	33	56.19	31
Xiamen	58.38	35	-34	65.60	1	59.75	12	59.03	18	59.01	19
Average	62.20			61.73		58.98		58.89		59.42	

063

Blue Book of Quality of Life in Cities

The improvement of the human capital satisfaction indexes is also reflected in Figure 13. The distribution of the lowest score has gone up from the interval of 50-55 (in 2012) to 55-60. And the highest score has remained within 60-65, except in 2015. In 2012, the highest scorer was Ningbo (64.19), while the lowest scorer was Taiyuan (55.20). In 2013, the highest scorer was Qingdao (62.61), while the lowest scorer was Taiyuan (53.49). In 2014, the highest scorer was Qingdao (61.84), while the lowest scorer was Kunming (56.15). In 2015, the highest scorer was Xiamen (65.60), while the lowest scorer was Taiyuan (58.34). And in 2016, the highest scorer is Wuhan (64.22), while the lowest scorer is Xiamen (58.38). The differences between the highest and the lowest scores are 8.99, 9.12, 5.69, 7.26 and 5.84 respectively. It shows that the human capital satisfaction of the 35 cities has generally improved, and that the gaps has narrowed.

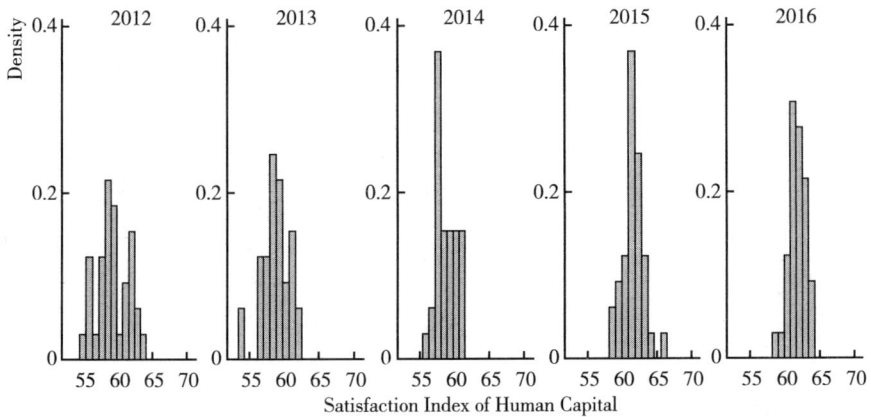

Figure 13   A Histogram of the 2012–2016 Human Capital Satisfaction Indexes of the 35 Cities

Viewed by cities, in 2016, cities ranked top 10 in the list of human capital satisfaction indexes are: Wuhan (1), Xining (2), Hangzhou (3), Beijing (4), Ningbo (5), Chongqing (6), Tianjin (7), Shenyang (8), Guangzhou (9)

064

and Hefei (10). And the bottom 10 cities are: Nanjing (26), Lanzhou (27), Qingdao (28), Hohhot (29), Changchun (30), Shijiazhuang (31), Nanchang (32), Yinchuan (33), Xi'an (34) and Xiamen (35). Xining, Hangzhou and Beijing have ranked among the top 10 three years in a row, while Ningbo has stayed in the top 10 list for five years. Shenzhen, Hohhot and Nanchang, on the other hand, have fallen behind over the past three years, which indicates a lower satisfaction over their education status. It should be noted that Xiamen ranked No.1 in 2015 and falls right down to the last place this year. And its score drops from 65.6 to 58.38– the lowest value since 2012. Besides, regionally speaking, the ratio of eastern, central and western cities is 6:2:2 among the top 10 cities, and 3:3:4 among the bottom 10 cities.

As is shown in Figure 14, from 2012 to 2016, the indexes of Beijing, Harbin, Shenyang, Taiyuan and Xining have improved four years in a row, while those of Changsha, Chengdu, Dalian, Fuzhou, Guiyang, Hangzhou, Hohhot, Jinan, Kunming, Lanzhou, Nanning, Shenzhen, Tianjin, Urumqi, Wuhan, Yinchuan, Zhengzhou and Chongqing have fluctuated but still gone up. And the indexes of Changchun, Guangzhou, Haikou, Hefei, Nanchang, Nanjing, Ningbo, Qingdao, Shanghai, Shijiazhuang, Xi'an and Xiamen drop slightly in 2016. The result of vertical comparison also shows that the human capital satisfaction indexes of the 35 cities have kept improving. Despite the great regional differences of educational resource allocation, the gaps are narrowing among different regions.

5.3.2　Objective Index of Human Capital

According to the QLICC system, the human capital objective index of each city was obtained by calculating its two secondary indicators (educationalprovisionindex and ratio of education, culture and entertainment expenditures). Table 8 lists the 2016 human capital objective indexes of the 35 cities.

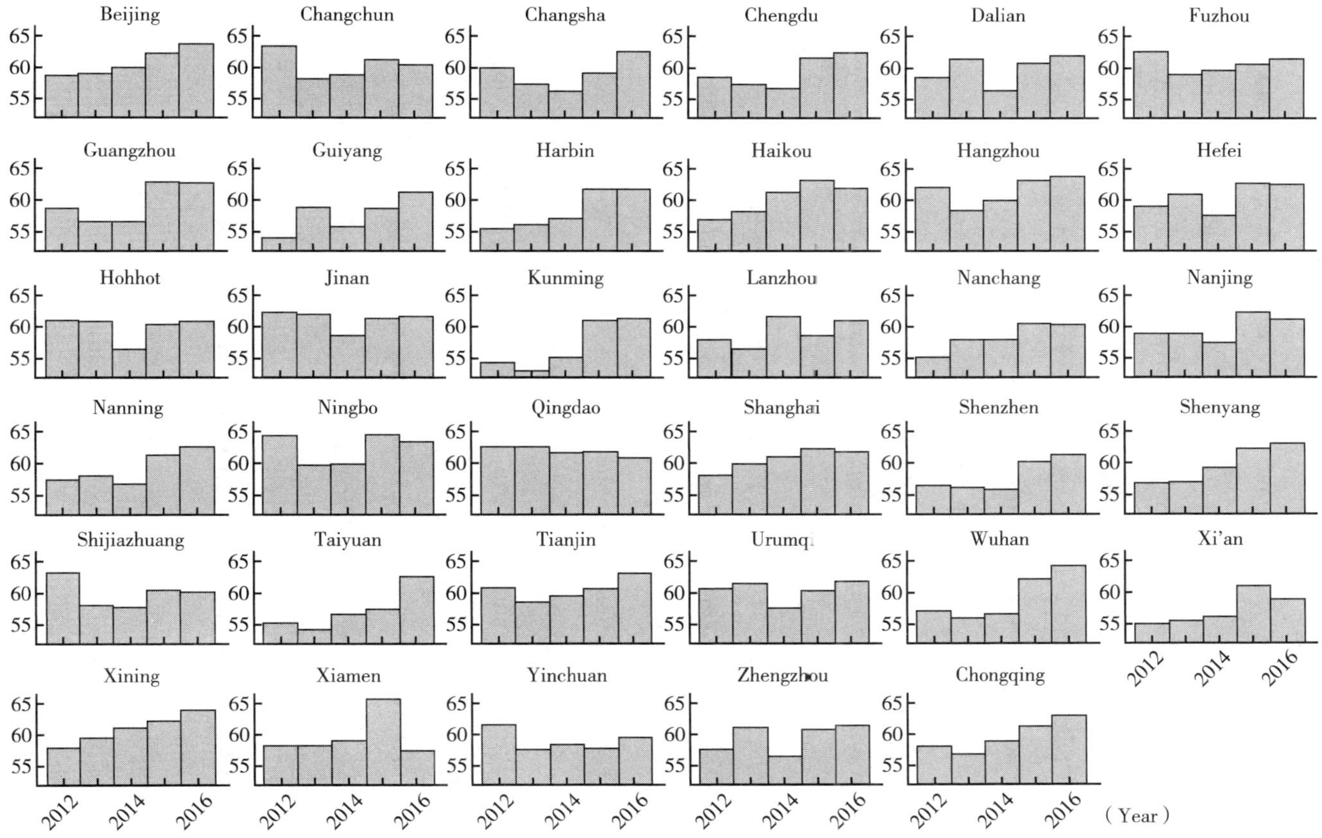

Figure 14 The 2012–2016 Human Capital Satisfaction Indexes of the 35 Cities (The scores are shown on the vertical axis)

Quality-of-life Subindexes of the 35 Chinese Cities

Table 8   The 2012– 2016 Human Capital Objective Indexes of the 35 Cities

City	2016			2015		2014		2013		2012	
	Score	Ranking	Places Risen	Score	Ranking	Score	Ranking	Score	Ranking	Score	Ranking
Nanjing	80.00	1	0	80.00	1	80.00	1	79.73	2	79.52	2
Guiyang	74.65	2	0	71.66	2	67.62	4	61.65	9	62.79	7
Wuhan	70.87	3	3	67.81	6	63.45	7	60.89	10	58.52	13
Guangzhou	69.28	4	-1	71.29	3	78.68	2	80.00	1	80.01	1
Xi'an	69.27	5	-1	70.29	4	70.94	3	72.94	3	79.42	3
Beijing	67.66	6	-1	67.89	5	67.51	5	68.76	4	70.96	4
Taiyuan	64.01	7	0	64.28	7	63.84	6	64.68	6	69.05	5
Kunming	63.53	8	1	61.64	9	59.92	10	56.19	17	57.20	17
Shanghai	62.59	9	-1	62.68	8	62.25	8	63.03	7	66.15	6
Shijiazhuang	61.62	10	1	59.99	11	57.15	15	55.22	19	47.11	33
Changchun	61.51	11	-1	61.19	10	61.22	9	61.79	8	54.72	21
Hangzhou	59.95	12	2	58.16	14	55.18	21	52.89	23	53.38	24
Yinchuan	58.67	13	0	58.23	13	57.17	14	56.57	15	57.57	16
Hohhot	58.51	14	-2	58.65	12	57.59	13	58.83	13	61.75	8
Dalian	56.95	15	3	55.84	18	53.98	22	52.62	24	52.09	27
Changsha	56.38	16	-1	57.50	15	57.92	12	66.65	5	58.80	11
Nanning	56.01	17	0	56.49	17	56.98	16	58.27	14	60.93	9
Hefei	55.97	18	-2	57.15	16	58.70	11	60.28	11	59.72	10
Jinan	55.46	19	0	55.51	19	55.33	19	55.28	18	57.66	15
Shenyang	55.02	20	1	54.56	21	55.32	20	54.67	20	55.90	20
Fuzhou	54.84	21	-1	55.01	20	56.40	18	56.38	16	51.09	28
Ningbo	52.92	22	0	54.15	22	56.55	17	59.09	12	58.62	12
Shenzhen	52.73	23	2	52.08	25	50.48	28	49.79	28	54.43	22
Tianjin	52.47	24	0	52.24	24	51.76	24	51.63	27	56.58	18
Harbin	52.23	25	-2	52.53	23	52.17	23	52.90	22	52.83	25
Nanchang	52.00	26	0	52.06	26	51.40	26	51.88	25	48.30	30
Chengdu	50.08	27	1	49.95	28	50.77	27	51.79	26	50.62	29
Lanzhou	49.63	28	-1	50.44	27	51.73	25	53.68	21	54.33	23
Urumqi	49.40	29	0	49.26	29	49.40	29	49.17	29	56.49	19
Qingdao	48.60	30	0	48.10	30	47.37	31	46.32	33	45.56	34
Zhengzhou	48.17	31	0	48.03	31	47.47	30	48.02	31	47.50	32
Haikou	47.33	32	0	47.14	32	46.59	32	46.39	32	58.08	14
Chongqing	44.59	33	0	45.26	33	46.15	33	48.03	30	48.28	31
Xiamen	41.30	34	0	41.32	34	42.54	34	43.09	34	52.32	26
Xining	40.00	35	0	40.00	35	40.00	35	40.00	35	39.99	35
Average	56.98			57.34		57.33		57.78		57.66	

067

Blue Book of Quality of Life in Cities

From 2012 to 2015, the weighted averages of the human capital objective indexes are 57.66, 57.78, 57.33 and 57.34 respectively. There are no big difference among the values. In other words, the averages have generally remained stable. In 2016, the index is 56.98, a slight drop compared to that of the previous years. But on the whole, the objective index of human capital has remained stable. As is shown in Figure 15, the distribution of the indexes has stayed roughly within the interval of 40-80. From 2012 to 2013, the highest scorer had been Guangzhou. And from 2014 to 2016, the highest scorer has been Nanjing. The difference between the highest and the lowest scores is around 40, and the standard deviations are 9.21, 9.02, 8.84, 8.77 and 8.99 respectively. Xining has been the lowest scorer in all the past five years, mainly because the growth of human capital needs long-term efforts, and both education and training take time to complete. Therefore, no big change can be achieved within a short period.

By horizontal comparison, the rankings of the cities have remained roughly unchanged. Cities ranked top 10 are: Nanjing (1), Guiyang (2), Wuhan (3),

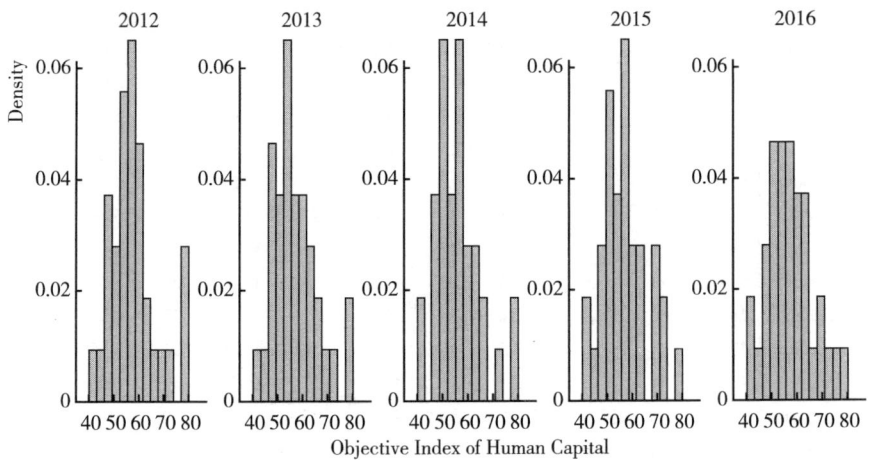

**Figure 15   A Histogram of the 2012–2016 Human Capital Objective
Indexes of the 35 Cities**

Quality-of-life Subindexes of the 35 Chinese Cities

Guangzhou (4), Xi'an (5), Beijing (6), Taiyuan (7), Kunming (8), Shanghai (9) and Shijiazhuang (10). And the bottom 10 cities are: Nanchang (26), Chengdu (27), Lanzhou (28), Urumqi (29), Qingdao (30), Zhengzhou (31), Haikou (32), Chongqing (33), Xiamen (34) and Xining (35). Nanjing, Guiyang, Guangzhou, Xi'an, Beijing, Taiyuan and Shanghai have ranked among the top 10 five years in a row, while Wuhan has remained in the list for four consecutive years. And Xining, Xiamen, Chongqing, Zhengzhou, Qingdao and Chengdu have ranked bottom 10 in the past five years, while Haikou and Urumqi have stayed in the list for four years.

From the dynamic perspective, as is shown in Figure 16, the indexes of Dalian, Qingdao, Shijiazhuang and Wuhan have kept growing for four years; while those of Lanzhou, Nanning, Xiamen, Xi'an and Chongqing have continued to decline. And the indexes of the rest cities have fluctuated during the same period.

Regionally speaking, there is no big gap among the eastern, the central and the western regions in human capital, but within the same region, there might be big differences. From the perspective of regional averages, the average of the eastern region (57.58) is similar to that of the central (57.36). And the average of the western region (54.35) falls only slightly behind. Within the same region however, there might be significant differences. Take the averages of human capital objective indexes as an example. In the eastern region, the gap between Nanjing (79.85) and Xiamen (44.11) is 35.74. And in the western region, the difference between Guiyang (67.67) and Xining (40.00) is 27.67.

Moreover, as far as human capital index is concerned, there is a significant contrast between the subjective and the objective indexes of Xining. Its subjective index ranks No.2, while the objective index ranks No.35.

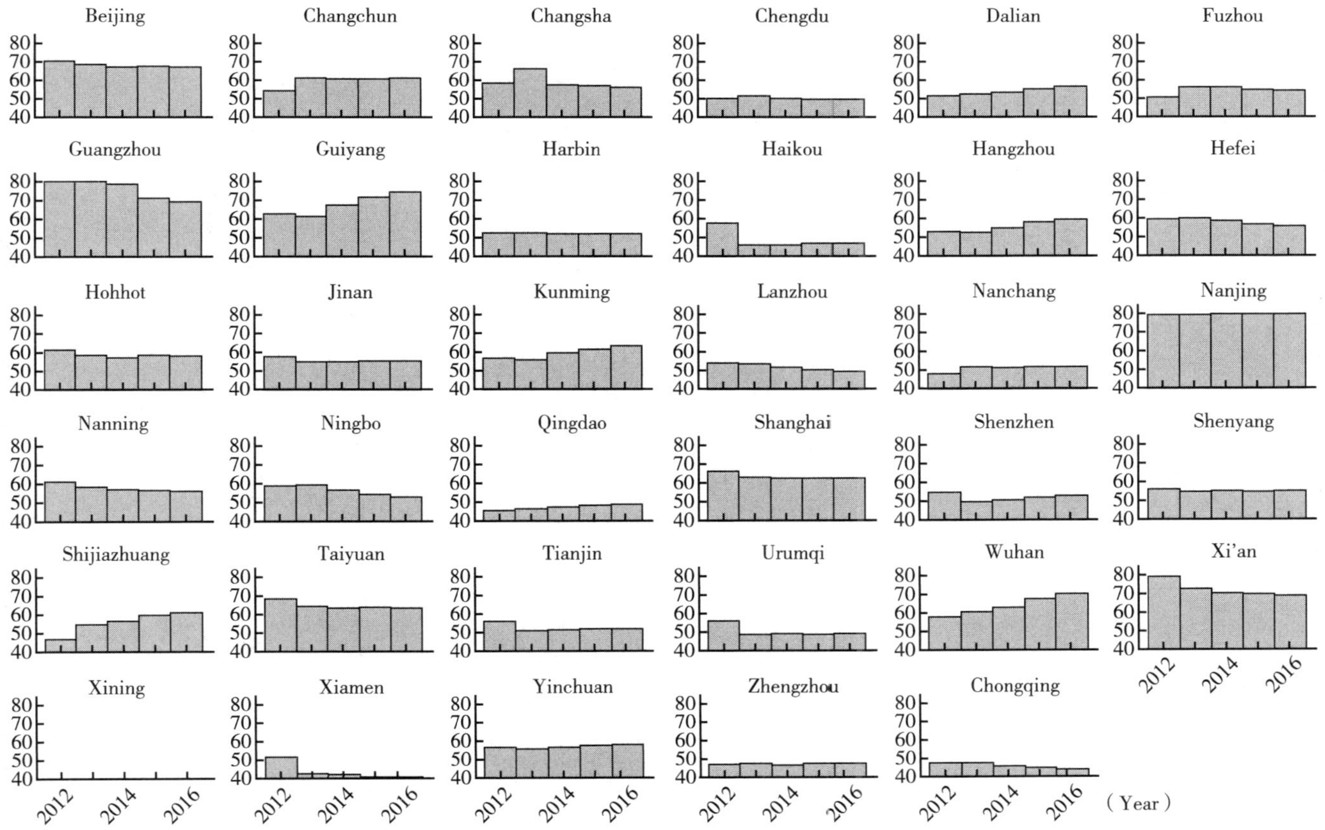

Figure 16 The 2012–2016 Human Capital Objective Indexes of the 35 Cities (The scores are shown on the vertical axis)

Quality-of-life Subindexes of the 35 Chinese Cities

5.4　Social Security Index

Social security index consists of a subjective satisfaction index and an objective (social and economic data) index.

5.4.1　Satisfaction Index of Social Security

The 2016 weighted average of the social security satisfaction indexes is60.66, while those of 2012-2015 were 59.19, 56.64, 57.87 and 60.47 respectively. The annual growth rates are-4.31%, 2.17%, 4.49% and 0.31%. Expect in 2013, the indexes of the 35 cities have remained stable and slightly improved. Table 9 lists the indexes of the 35 cities, along with their respective rankings.

Table 9　The Social Security Satisfaction Indexes of the 35 Cities

City	2016			2015		2014		2013		2012	
	Score	Ranking	Places Risen	Score	Ranking	Score	Ranking	Score	Ranking	Score	Ranking
Xining	63.04	1	4	61.38	5	57.97	16	59.31	7	62.04	9
Beijing	62.32	2	1	61.57	3	58.85	14	58.94	9	61.27	12
Ningbo	62.31	3	1	61.44	4	60.61	4	60.52	4	63.65	2
Urumqi	62.10	4	23	59.50	27	56.00	28	56.57	17	58.06	22
Wuhan	62.02	5	2	61.28	7	55.39	32	52.64	32	56.83	26
Dalian	61.57	6	12	60.49	18	58.91	13	57.18	13	61.73	10
Chongqing	61.37	7	9	60.73	16	59.14	8	55.61	24	62.78	5
Shanghai	61.33	8	-6	61.94	2	59.44	7	58.04	10	58.71	18
Hohhot	61.31	9	12	60.28	21	56.55	24	52.63	33	60.18	14
Taiyuan	61.15	10	21	59.16	31	57.03	23	56.63	16	58.66	19
Tianjin	61.05	11	18	59.36	29	58.92	12	55.14	25	58.57	21
Hangzhou	60.88	12	-11	62.60	1	61.17	1	60.76	3	64.68	1
Nanning	60.88	13	9	59.84	22	55.61	31	52.43	34	56.33	29
Chengdu	60.79	14	-1	60.81	13	57.90	17	57.05	14	61.33	11

Blue Book of Quality of Life in Cities

Continued table

City	2016			2015		2014		2013		2012	
	Score	Ranking	Places Risen	Score	Ranking	Score	Ranking	Score	Ranking	Score	Ranking
Kunming	60.76	15	-7	61.06	8	51.88	35	54.09	30	54.65	34
Guiyang	60.76	16	-1	60.76	15	55.83	30	51.98	35	52.26	35
Jinan	60.57	17	-11	61.34	6	59.13	9	59.82	6	62.65	6
Guangzhou	60.52	18	-1	60.54	17	55.03	33	54.70	27	56.81	27
Yinchuan	60.50	19	16	58.89	35	59.74	6	60.03	5	62.24	8
Qingdao	60.46	20	-11	61.04	9	60.80	3	61.87	1	62.26	7
Shenyang	60.45	21	4	59.60	25	57.26	21	56.40	18	57.04	25
Hefei	60.29	22	10	59.11	32	57.48	19	57.71	11	59.8	15
Haikou	60.25	23	-12	60.95	11	59.06	11	53.86	31	55.75	32
Zhengzhou	60.24	24	2	59.55	26	56.47	26	55.74	22	56.67	28
Xiamen	60.01	25	-15	60.95	10	61.03	2	61.25	2	62.79	4
Changchun	59.74	26	-3	59.64	23	60.47	5	57.59	12	62.83	3
Shijiazhuang	59.68	27	1	59.38	28	57.05	22	56.64	15	61.24	13
Changsha	59.65	28	-14	60.77	14	54.23	34	54.09	29	56.14	31
Harbin	59.51	29	-9	60.29	20	57.83	18	55.86	21	56.27	30
Shenzhen	59.47	30	3	59.06	33	56.48	25	55.11	26	57.04	24
Nanchang	59.43	31	-19	60.94	12	56.08	27	54.09	28	55.18	33
Nanjing	59.30	32	-13	60.47	19	59.07	10	59.22	8	59.17	17
Fuzhou	59.30	33	-9	59.60	24	58.45	15	56.23	20	58.60	20
Lanzhou	59.25	34	0	59.01	34	57.26	20	55.65	23	57.67	23
Xi'an	58.68	35	-5	59.16	30	55.84	29	56.27	19	59.65	16
Average	60.66			60.47		57.87		56.64		59.19	

In 2016, 25 out of the 35 cities score over 60 in social security satisfaction, which is slightly higher than that of 2015, but far higher than the 2014 record of 5 cities. Cities ranked top 10 are: Xining (1), Beijing (2), Ningbo (3), Urumqi (4), Wuhan (5), Dalian (6), Chongqing (7), Shanghai (8), Hohhot (9) and Taiyuan (10). And the bottom 10 cities are: Changchun (26), Shijiazhuang (27), Changsha (28), Harbin (29), Shenzhen (30), Nanchang (31), Nanjing (32), Fuzhou (33), Lanzhou (34) and Xi'an (35). Ningbo and Shanghai have ranked top 10 four years in a row. The ratio of eastern, central and western cities is 4:2:4 in the top 10 list, and 4:4:2 in the bottom 10 list.

Quality-of-life Subindexes of the 35 Chinese Cities

Compared to the past, the regional gaps of social security subjective indexes have narrowed. As is shown in Figure 17, the distribution of the indexes have concentrated from 2012 to 2016, and the interval has gone down from 50-70 (in 2012) to 55-65 (in 2016). The distribution of the highest scores has remained with the interval of 60-70, while that of the lowest scores has improved from 50-55 to 55-60. And from 2012 to 2016, the standard deviations are 2.94, 2.60, 2.07, 0.94 and 1.01 respectively.

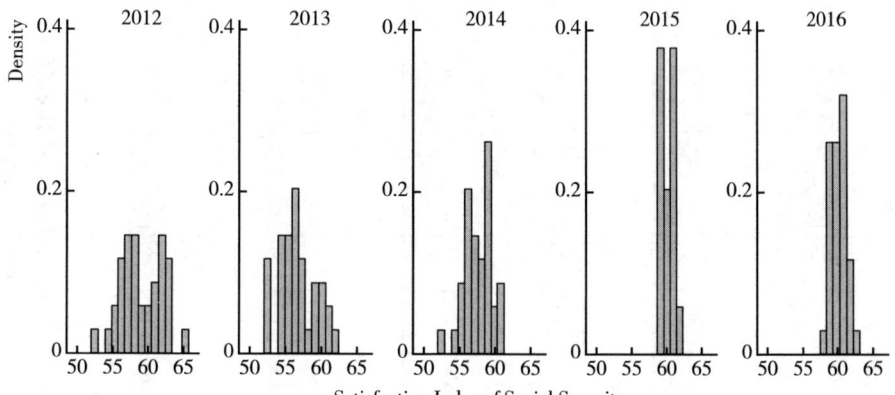

Figure 17   A Histogram of the 2012–2016 SocialSecuritySatisfaction Indexes of the 35 Cities

As is shown in Figure 18, from 2012 to 2016, except for the index of Xiamen which has dropped four years in a row, the indexes of most cities have first declined and then climbed back up. It is mainly because that since 2012, China has sped up its social security reform on the basis of established basic social security systems. Social security is a highly concerned problem, and is closely related to the interest of each member of the society. Therefore, the satisfaction over social security is influenced by a number of factors, including the implementation of reform measures, the emergence of new problems and the existence of regional

073

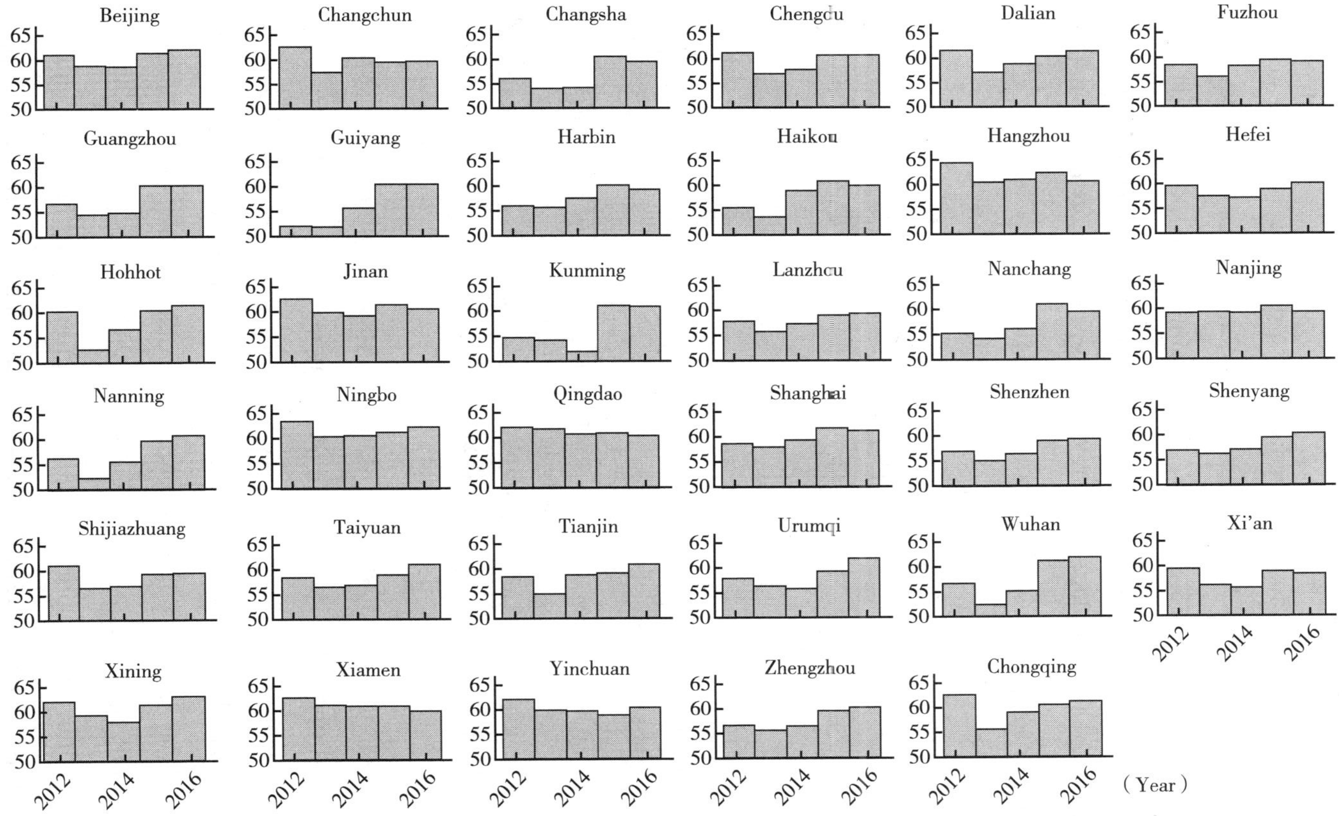

Figure 18 The 2012–2016 Social Security Satisfaction Indexes of the 35 Cities (The scores are shown on the vertical axis)

Quality-of-life Subindexes of the 35 Chinese Cities

and industrial gaps. As the reform measures are implemented, and the level of equality is improved, residents' satisfaction has continued to rise.

According to the QLICC system, the subjective satisfaction index of social security comes from the weighted average of the health care and elderly support satisfaction index and the urban security satisfaction index. Same as in the past, it was obtained through the questionnaire survey by assigning values to survey answers.

As is shown in Table10, the weighted averages of health care and elderly support satisfaction indexes are 53.61, 54.34, 54.80, 58.04 and 58.68 respectively from 2012 to 2016. The index has continued to improve.

Cities ranked top 10 are: Xining (1), Urumqi (2), Ningbo (3), Wuhan (4), Dalian (5), Kunming (6), Shanghai (7), Beijing (8), Nanning (9) and Chongqing (10). And the bottom 10 cities are: Hangzhou (26), Lanzhou (27), Harbin (28), Zhengzhou (29), Nanjing (30), Qingdao (31), Changsha (32), Changchun (33), Shenzhen (34) and Xi'an (35). From regional distribution, there are 4 eastern cities, 1 central city and 5 western cities in the top 10 list; and 4 eastern cities, 4 central cities and 2 western cities in the bottom 10 list. Compared to that of 2015, the regional distribution of the bottom 10 cities remains the same; but among the top 10 cities, the number of eastern cities decreases from 8 to 4, while the number of western cities increases from 2 to 5. It shows that the regional difference has significantly reduced. In the top 10 list, the rankings of Dalian (+21), Wuhan (+12), Nanning (+10), Chongqing (+10), Urumqi (+9), Xining (+2) and Ningbo (+1) have risen. The ranking of Kunming has remained unchanged. And the rankings of Shanghai (-6) and Beijing (-1) have dropped. In the bottom 10 list, the places of Lanzhou (+2), Harbin (+3) and Zhengzhou (+5) have improved, while those of Hangzhou (-21), Nanjing (-20), Qingdao (-16), Changsha (-18), Changchun (-9), Shenzhen (-7) and Xi'an (-2) have declined. Xining and Ningbo have stayed among the top 10 five years in a row, and none of the cities has remained among the bottom 10 in all the five years.

075

Blue Book of Quality of Life in Cities

Table 10 The Health Care and Elderly Support Satisfaction Indexes of the 35 Cities

City	2016			2015		2014		2013		2012	
	Score	Ranking	Places Risen	Score	Ranking	Score	Ranking	Score	Ranking	Score	Ranking
Xining	62.10	1	2	59.60	3	56.34	7	61.67	1	57.87	3
Urumqi	61.29	2	9	58.76	11	56.37	6	56.36	9	57.57	4
Ningbo	61.16	3	1	59.31	4	58.02	1	58.96	2	58.24	2
Wuhan	60.30	4	12	58.33	16	53.01	27	50.45	35	52.52	20
Dalian	60.21	5	21	57.22	26	52.75	30	52.13	30	53.37	18
Kunming	60.07	6	0	59.21	6	52.62	32	54.42	18	51.76	27
Shanghai	59.88	7	-6	59.79	1	55.62	14	51.96	32	48.93	35
Beijing	59.88	8	-1	59.17	7	56.15	9	57.29	5	55.71	12
Nanning	59.80	9	10	57.85	19	52.85	29	52.11	31	52.47	21
Chongqing	59.67	10	10	57.84	20	57.75	2	54.79	15	53.74	15
Taiyuan	59.28	11	24	55.72	35	53.74	22	54.05	23	57.18	7
Tianjin	59.21	12	20	56.19	32	54.33	20	51.64	33	52.06	24
Guangzhou	59.08	13	-4	59.01	9	53.32	25	52.37	29	51.38	29
Hohhot	58.85	14	11	57.34	25	55.73	12	54.53	17	57.50	5
Hefei	58.50	15	15	56.89	30	53.79	21	54.42	19	55.58	13
Jinan	58.44	16	1	58.09	17	53.44	24	54.24	22	51.96	26
Yinchuan	58.43	17	5	57.75	22	55.53	15	56.59	7	55.73	11
Shijiazhuang	58.26	18	3	57.78	21	54.79	19	56.39	8	56.55	9
Guiyang	58.21	19	4	57.60	23	54.94	17	56.64	6	53.57	16
Chengdu	58.20	20	-8	58.70	12	56.23	8	54.40	20	55.26	14
Xiamen	58.12	21	-13	59.05	8	56.06	11	55.83	12	56.40	10
Haikou	58.11	22	-20	59.65	2	57.68	3	53.11	25	49.50	34
Shenyang	58.05	23	-5	57.88	18	52.15	35	54.37	21	50.00	31
Nanchang	58.03	24	-11	58.61	13	55.36	16	55.64	13	51.63	28
Fuzhou	57.82	25	3	57.07	28	55.73	13	53.75	24	51.30	30
Hangzhou	57.47	26	-21	59.23	5	57.14	4	56.11	10	58.37	1
Lanzhou	57.40	27	2	56.98	29	54.89	18	58.33	3	52.27	23
Harbin	57.31	28	3	56.85	31	52.58	33	52.47	27	49.52	33
Zhengzhou	57.30	29	5	56.13	34	52.73	31	54.82	14	52.38	22
Nanjing	57.22	30	-20	58.83	10	53.73	23	54.61	16	49.74	32
Qingdao	57.20	31	-16	58.51	15	56.09	10	58.19	4	53.42	17
Changsha	57.10	32	-18	58.51	14	53.05	26	52.45	28	52.05	25
Changchun	56.84	33	-9	57.44	24	56.73	5	52.90	26	57.22	6
Shenzhen	56.77	34	-7	57.13	27	52.58	34	51.23	34	52.98	19
Xi'an	56.70	35	-2	56.15	33	52.90	28	55.96	11	57.04	8
Average	58.68			58.04		54.80		54.34		53.61	

076

Quality-of-life Subindexes of the 35 Chinese Cities

As is shown in the index histogram of Figure 19, the satisfaction over health care and elderly support has generally improved, whereas the gaps among cities have narrowed. In 2012, the distribution of the lowest score was below 50, while that of the highest score was within the interval of 55-60. In 2016, the distribution of the lowest score rises to 55-60, while that of the highest score goes up to 60-65. And the scores of most cities are now around 60. In 2012, the highest scorer was Hangzhou (58.37), while the lowest scorer was Shanghai (48.93). There is a difference of 9.44 in between. In 2013, the highest scorer was Xining (61.67), while the lowest scorer was Wuhan (50.45). The difference was 11.22. In 2014, the highest scorer was Ningbo (58.02), while the lowest scorer was Shenyang (52.15). The difference was 5.87. In 2015, the highest scorer was Shanghai (59.79), while the lowest scorer was Taiyuan (55.72). The difference was 4.07. And in 2016, the highest scorer is Xining (62.10), while the lowest scorer is Xi'an (56.70). The difference is 5.40.

The health care and elderly support satisfaction indexes of the 35 cities

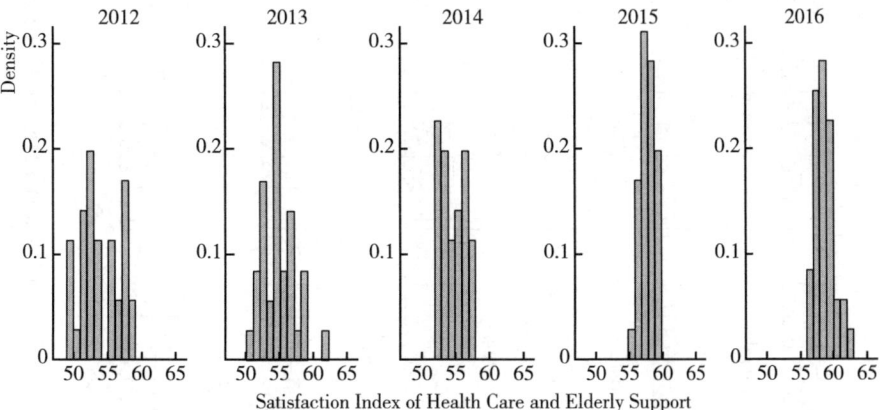

Figure 19   A Histogram of the 2012–2016 Health Care and Elderly Support Satisfaction Indexes of the 35 Cities

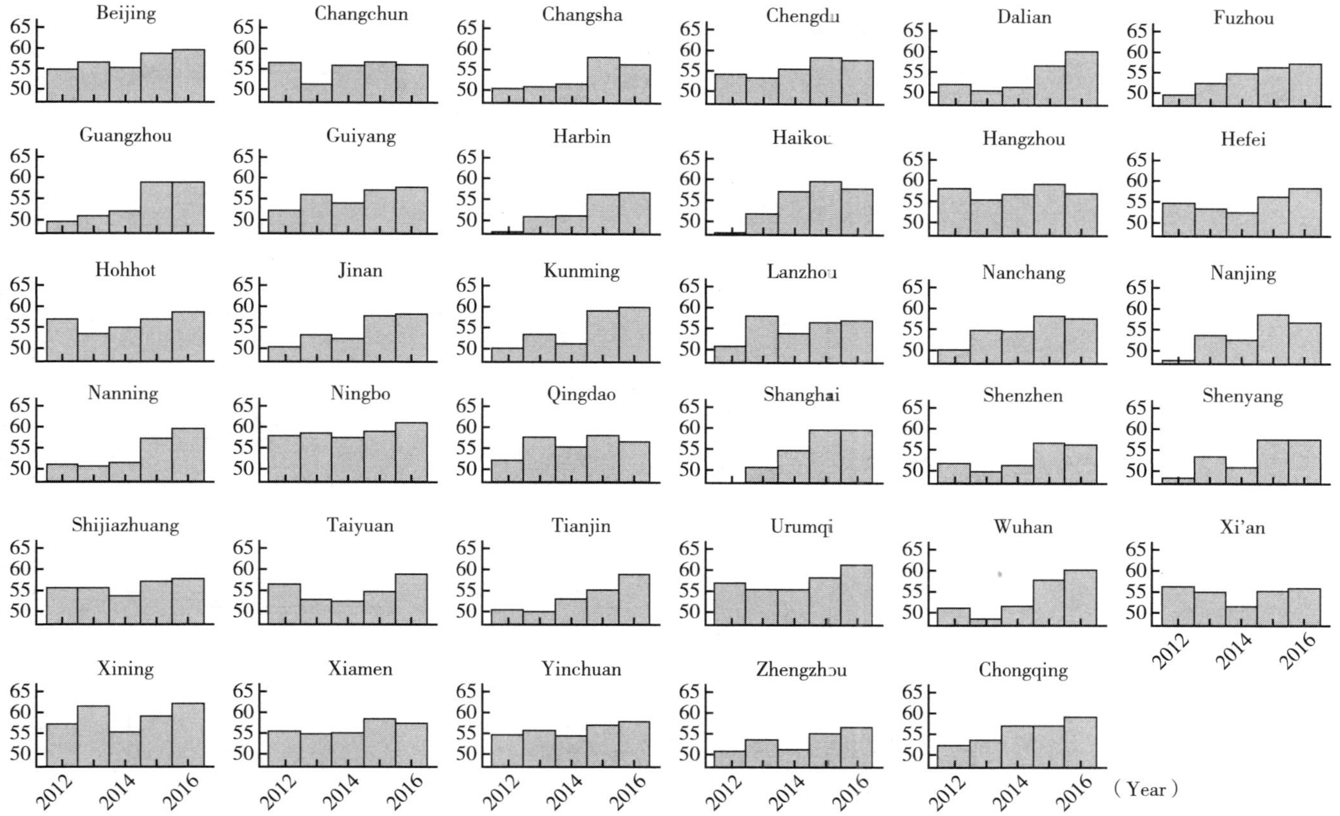

Figure 20 The 2012–2016 Health Care and Elderly Support Satisfaction Indexes of the 35 Cities (The scores are shown on the vertical axis)

Quality-of-life Subindexes of the 35 Chinese Cities — ◀◢

have generally improved from 2012 to 2016. As is shown in Figure 20, Fuzhou, Guangzhou, Harbin, Shanghai and Chongqing have experienced growth four years in a row. Compared to that of 2012, the indexes of three cities (Hangzhou, Changchun and Xi'an) have dropped.

As a whole, the surveyed 35 cities have all made progresses in health care and elderly support, and residents' satisfaction has kept improving. However, due to differences in the emphasis of the regional security systems, the mobility of the labor force and the modes of fund-raising, the rankings of many cities cannot remain stable but have changed greatly.

As is shown in Table 11, the 2016 weighted average of the urban security (public order) satisfaction indexes is 62.63 — above the satisfaction level and a slight drop compared to that of 2015. The improvement of urban public order satisfaction has come to an end. From regional distribution, there are 4 eastern cities, 2 central cities and 4 western cities among the top 10 cities; and 4 eastern cities, 2 central cities and 4 western cities in the bottom 10 list.

Table 11 The2012–2016 Urban Security (Public Order) Satisfaction Indexes of the 35 Cities

City	2016			2015		2014		2013		2012	
	Score	Ranking	Places Risen	Score	Ranking	Score	Ranking	Score	Ranking	Score	Ranking
Beijing	64.75	1	4	63.97	5	61.56	14	60.58	12	66.82	13
Hangzhou	64.29	2	-1	65.98	1	65.20	3	65.42	3	70.99	4
Xining	63.98	3	11	63.16	14	59.60	23	56.94	21	66.20	14
Hohhot	63.76	4	9	63.21	13	57.38	29	50.73	34	62.86	22
Wuhan	63.74	5	-2	64.23	3	57.77	28	54.83	28	61.13	26
Qingdao	63.72	6	4	63.57	10	65.51	2	65.55	2	71.11	3
Ningbo	63.47	7	4	63.57	11	63.21	11	62.08	10	69.05	7

079

Blue Book of Quality of Life in Cities

Continued table

City	2016			2015		2014		2013		2012	
	Score	Ranking	Places Risen	Score	Ranking	Score	Ranking	Score	Ranking	Score	Ranking
Chengdu	63.39	8	9	62.92	17	59.56	24	59.69	13	67.40	12
Guiyang	63.31	9	-3	63.92	6	56.73	32	47.32	35	50.95	35
Zhengzhou	63.18	10	6	62.96	16	60.20	21	56.66	24	60.95	28
Chongqing	63.07	11	-2	63.62	9	60.53	17	56.43	26	71.83	2
Taiyuan	63.02	12	8	62.60	20	60.32	20	59.22	15	60.15	31
Dalian	62.93	13	-6	63.75	7	65.07	4	62.22	9	70.09	5
Urumqi	62.90	14	20	60.25	34	55.63	33	56.78	23	58.55	33
Tianjin	62.89	15	6	62.54	21	63.51	9	58.64	18	65.08	17
Shenyang	62.84	16	14	61.32	30	62.37	13	58.43	19	64.09	18
Shanghai	62.78	17	-13	64.08	4	63.26	10	64.12	5	68.48	10
Jinan	62.70	18	-16	64.60	2	64.82	5	65.41	4	73.34	1
Changchun	62.63	19	8	61.84	27	64.22	7	62.29	8	68.45	11
Yinchuan	62.57	20	15	60.04	35	63.94	8	63.46	7	68.75	8
Haikou	62.39	21	1	62.24	22	60.44	18	54.61	29	62.00	25
Changsha	62.21	22	-7	63.02	15	55.42	34	55.73	27	60.23	29
Shenzhen	62.17	23	9	60.98	32	60.39	19	58.98	16	61.11	27
Hefei	62.07	24	5	61.33	29	61.18	15	61.00	11	64.03	19
Guangzhou	61.96	25	1	62.08	26	56.74	31	57.02	20	62.25	24
Nanning	61.96	26	2	61.83	28	58.37	27	52.75	32	60.19	30
Xiamen	61.91	27	-8	62.85	19	66.00	1	66.67	1	69.19	6
Harbin	61.71	28	-20	63.73	8	63.07	12	59.25	14	63.03	21
Kunming	61.46	29	-11	62.92	18	51.15	35	53.75	30	57.53	34
Nanjing	61.39	30	-5	62.11	25	64.41	6	63.83	6	68.59	9
Lanzhou	61.10	31	0	61.03	31	59.63	22	52.97	31	63.07	20
Shijiazhuang	61.09	32	1	60.97	33	59.32	25	56.89	22	65.93	15
Nanchang	60.82	33	-21	63.28	12	56.80	30	52.55	33	58.74	32
Fuzhou	60.78	34	-10	62.13	24	61.17	16	58.71	17	65.90	16
Xi'an	60.65	35	-12	62.18	23	58.78	26	56.58	25	62.26	23
Average	62.63			62.9		60.45		58.93		64.58	

Quality-of-life Subindexes of the 35 Chinese Cities

As is shown in Figure 21, from 2012 to 2016, the satisfaction over urban security (public order) has not only declined in the 35cities, but also shown a high degree of consistency. In 2012, the distribution of the index was within the interval of 50-75, while in 2015 and 2016, the index has gone down to the interval of 60-70. In 2012, the highest scorer was Jinan (73.34), while the lowest scorer was Guiyang (50.95). In 2013, the highest scorer was Xiamen (66.67), while the lowest scorer was Guiyang (47.32). In 2014, the highest scorer was Xiamen (66.00), while the lowest scorer was Kunming (51.15). In 2015, the highest scorer was Hangzhou (65.98), while the lowest scorer was Yinchuan (60.04). In 2016, the highest scorer is Beijing (64.75), while the lowest scorer is Xi'an (60.65). And the differences between the highest and the lowest scores are 22.39, 19.35, 14.85, 5.94 and 4.10 respectively.

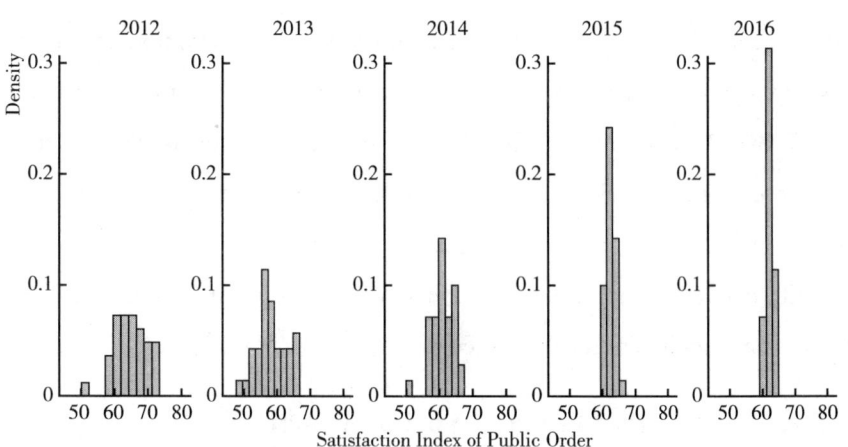

Figure 21 A Histogram of the 2012–2016 Public Order Satisfaction Indexes of the 35 Cities

As is shown in Figure 22, the public order satisfaction of the 35 cities has generally declined from 2012 to 2016. Regionally speaking, the index averages of the eastern, the central and the western regions are 63.31, 60.99

Blue Book of Quality of Life in Cities

and 60.21 respectively. That is to say, the satisfaction over urban public order is highest in the eastern region and lowest in the western region. Moreover, cities whose average indexes have stayed below 60 for five years are almost all in the western region. From the perspective of index changes however, the top 3 cities of the greater improvements are all western cities as well, namely Guiyang (+12.36), Urumqi (+4.35) and Kunming (+3.93); while the top 3 cities of the bigger declines are Jinan (-10.64), Chongqing (-8.76) and Qingdao (-7.39). Jinan and Xiamen are the only cities whose indexes have continued to drop in the past four years. And they are both in the eastern region.

The satisfaction over public order is a subjective feeling, and does not represent the actual deterioration of urban security. Such feelings can be influenced not only by events happening around us, but also and mostly by the methods and orientations of media communication. Therefore, the more advanced the economic development is, the more information channels the residents have, and the more developed minority communication is. The spread of information is much quicker in the economically developed regions than in the underdeveloped regions. From this perspective, even if the public order has actually improved in the developed regions, people's sense of security may still drop, due to residents' sensitivity toward urban security and the pessimistic direction of the media.

5.4.2 Objective Index of Social Security

According to the QLICC system, the objective index of social security was obtained by calculating the three secondary indicators: social security coverage, basic medical insurance coverage and unemployment insurance coverage. Table 12 lists the social security objective indexes of the 35 cities.

082

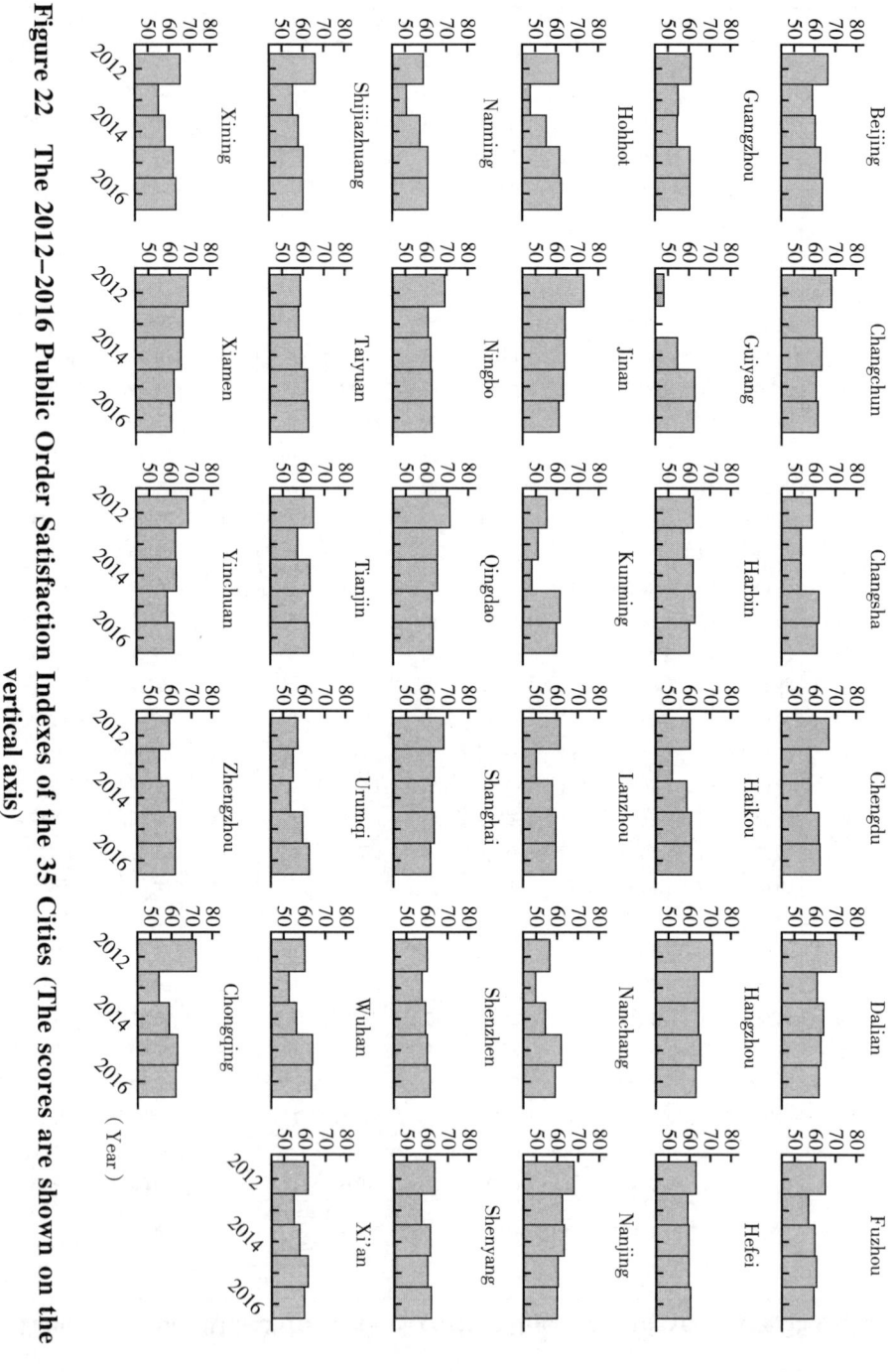

Figure 22 The 2012–2016 Public Order Satisfaction Indexes of the 35 Cities (The scores are shown on the vertical axis)

Blue Book of Quality of Life in Cities

Table 12 The 2012–2016 Social Security Objective Indexes of the 35 Cities

City	2016			2015		2014		2013		2012	
	Score	Ranking	Places Risen	Score	Ranking	Score	Ranking	Score	Ranking	Score	Ranking
Shenzhen	80.00	1	0	80.00	1	80.00	1	80.00	1	80.01	1
Hangzhou	65.76	2	1	64.23	3	65.70	5	63.84	7	58.36	7
Beijing	65.41	3	-1	66.18	2	76.39	2	77.24	2	71.82	2
Xiamen	63.87	4	0	63.40	4	73.85	3	74.37	3	71.43	3
Ningbo	60.30	5	0	61.39	5	71.22	4	72.36	4	56.19	8
Guangzhou	58.25	6	0	57.36	6	64.52	7	66.71	6	60.11	5
Shanghai	58.05	7	0	56.82	7	65.66	6	67.23	5	68.68	4
Shenyang	56.12	8	0	55.30	8	60.46	8	62.01	9	55.20	12
Nanjing	55.78	9	0	54.14	9	58.56	11	58.11	12	55.65	10
Tianjin	53.41	10	1	52.06	11	58.90	9	63.13	8	59.89	6
Dalian	53.17	11	-1	53.26	10	58.85	10	59.82	11	55.67	9
Yinchuan	51.86	12	0	50.42	12	53.28	12	51.93	16	47.15	18
Taiyuan	51.31	13	0	50.23	13	49.40	19	49.08	19	50.61	14
Xi'an	50.44	14	0	49.57	14	52.48	13	52.15	15	55.62	11
Chengdu	49.58	15	0	48.60	15	51.14	15	50.84	17	45.00	22
Urumqi	49.13	16	0	48.14	16	51.79	14	52.63	13	51.44	13
Qingdao	47.62	17	0	47.16	17	50.50	17	52.34	14	48.63	16
Jinan	47.61	18	2	46.94	20	46.71	21	47.36	20	46.08	20
Wuhan	47.44	19	2	46.69	21	50.71	16	50.48	18	49.51	15
Changchun	46.93	20	-1	46.95	19	50.17	18	59.84	10	48.23	17
Guiyang	46.52	21	1	45.70	22	45.22	24	44.95	25	44.14	24
Hohhot	46.50	22	-4	47.01	18	46.75	20	46.91	21	45.68	21
Changsha	45.33	23	0	45.20	23	45.92	23	45.97	23	43.07	27
Chongqing	44.63	24	0	44.82	24	44.97	25	44.57	26	41.48	32
Nanning	44.56	25	0	44.61	25	46.04	22	46.09	22	40.85	34
Hefei	44.13	26	2	43.49	28	44.14	30	43.72	29	44.71	23
Fuzhou	43.90	27	-1	43.76	26	44.79	27	44.06	27	42.17	31
Haikou	43.27	28	4	42.55	32	44.72	28	43.91	28	42.54	30
Lanzhou	43.17	29	-2	43.54	27	44.91	26	45.14	24	46.35	19
Kunming	42.92	30	1	42.77	31	44.52	29	41.21	33	42.85	29
Shijiazhuang	42.76	31	-1	42.89	30	41.80	32	41.77	31	40.86	33
Zhengzhou	42.17	32	-3	43.19	29	40.61	34	40.98	34	42.99	28
Nanchang	41.63	33	0	41.59	33	42.87	31	43.05	30	43.46	25
Harbin	41.37	34	0	41.04	34	41.58	33	41.73	32	43.21	26
Xining	40.00	35	0	40.00	35	40.00	35	40.00	35	39.98	35
Average	50.43			51.26		54.66		55.26		50.85	

Quality-of-life Subindexes of the 35 Chinese Cities

In 2016, the weighted average of the social security objective indexes is 50.43. From dynamic changes, the index has continued to drop after the drastic decline in 2015. Among the 35 cities, 21 cities score below 50, roughly the same as in 2015.But in 2014, there were only 17 cities. In our opinion, the main reason for the decline is that due to economic slowdown, the unemployment rate has risen, but many Chinese residents are not covered by the unemployment insurance. Besides, it should also be noted that there are big regional differences in the objective index of social security.

Cities ranked top 10are: Shenzhen (1), Hangzhou (2), Beijing (3), Xiamen (4), Ningbo (5), Guangzhou (6), Shanghai (7), Shenyang (8), Nanjing (9) and Tianjin (10). And the bottom 10 cities are: Hefei (26), Fuzhou (27), Haikou (28), Lanzhou (29), Kunming (30), Shijiazhuang (31), Zhengzhou (32), Nanchang (33), Harbin (34) and Xining (35). Among them, Shenzhen, Beijing, Hangzhou, Xiamen, Ningbo, Guangzhou and Shanghai have ranked among the top 10 five years in a row, while Shenyang and Tianjin have been in the top 10 list in four out of the five years. Fuzhou, Zhengzhou, Shijiazhuang, Kunming, Haikou, Nanchang, Harbin and Xining have stayed among the bottom 10 for five years. Shenzhen has always topped the list. Xining has come last in all the five years, but in 2016, its subjective index of social security ranks No.1. It should also be noted that there are big regional differences in the objective index of social security.

As is shown in Figure 23, there are more cities in the low score interval than in the high score interval. Among the 35 cities, all the 11 cities whose indexes has stayed above 50 for five years are all in the eastern region. It shows that economic development is the most influential factor of social security.

Figure 24 can better illustrate the great and long-existing gaps in the social security objective index among different cities. There are differences in regions and industries, in the arrangements of social security and basic medical

Blue Book of Quality of Life in Cities

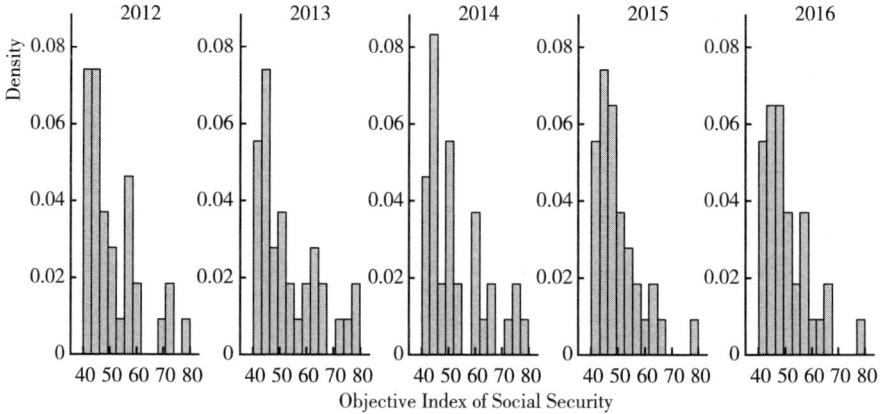

Figure 23   A Histogram of the 2012–2016 Social Security Objective Indexes of the 35 Cities

insurances, and in the related methods of payment. Since these differences cannot be overcome all at once at the national level, the gaps among regions are likely to exist for a long time. In addition, the scope and intensity of social security are closely related to income. Therefore, the coverage is certainly higher in the eastern region than in the central or the western region.

5.5   Living Experience Index

Living experience index also consists of a subjective satisfaction index and an objective (social and economic data) index.

5.5.1   Satisfaction Index of Living Experience

According to the QLICC system, the satisfaction index of living experience was obtained through the questionnaire survey by calculating the weighted average of the pace of life satisfaction index and the living conveniencesatisfaction index. Table 13 lists the 2016 living experience satisfaction indexes of the 35 cities.

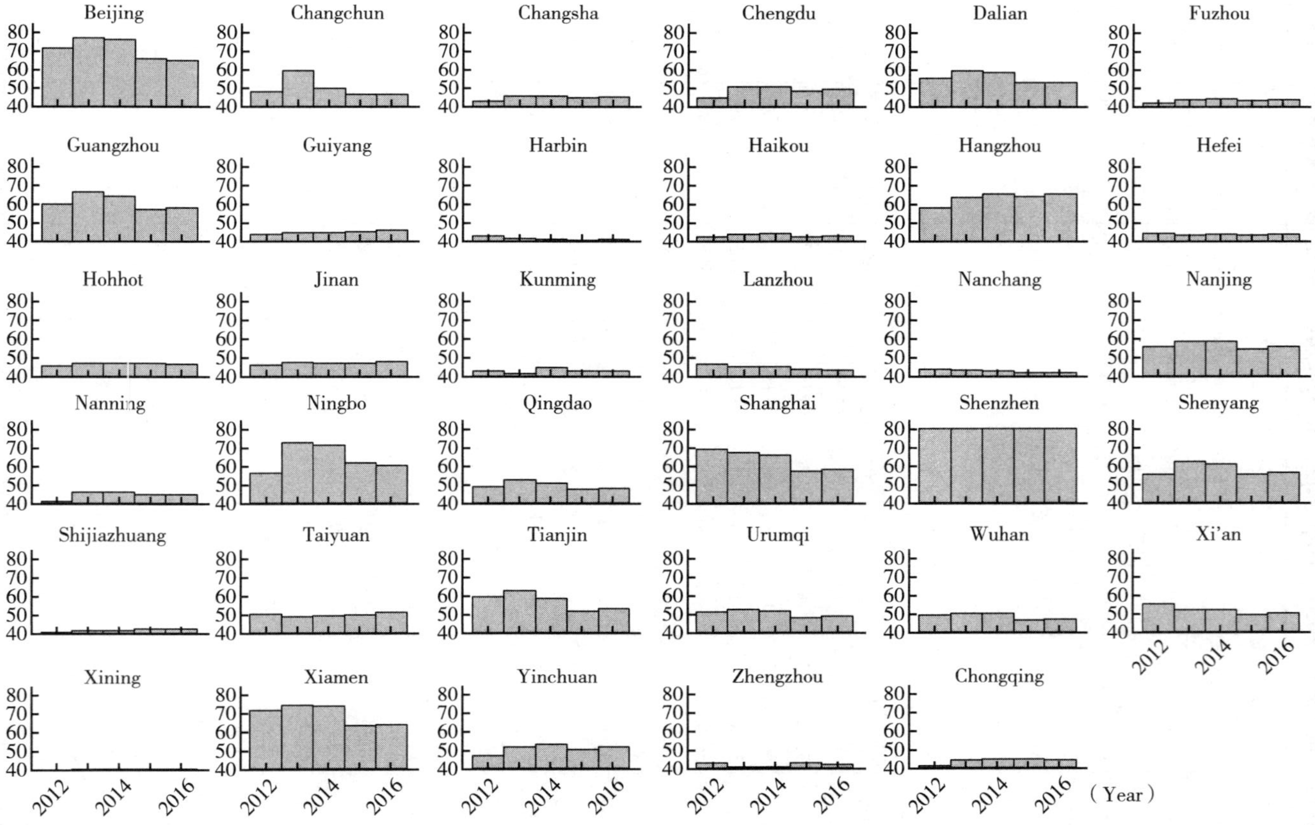

Figure 24 The 2012–2016 Social Security Objective Indexes of the 35 Cities (The scores are shown on the vertical axis)

Blue Book of Quality of Life in Cities

Table 13   The 2012–2016 Living Experience Satisfaction Indexes of the 35 Cities

City	2016			2015		2014		2013		2012	
	Score	Ranking	Places Risen	Score	Ranking	Score	Ranking	Score	Ranking	Score	Ranking
Taiyuan	57.60	1	29	54.52	30	54.91	17	54.75	18	53.84	28
Nanchang	57.54	2	16	55.66	18	54.61	22	53.84	26	53.86	27
Qingdao	57.47	3	20	55.17	23	56.54	4	56.20	9	56.96	11
Kunming	57.47	4	-1	57.63	3	55.37	12	52.40	34	53.13	33
Hangzhou	57.44	5	-3	57.65	2	55.85	9	57.05	4	58.25	3
Ningbo	57.17	6	8	55.79	14	55.49	11	56.56	8	55.34	19
Shijiazhuang	57.03	7	10	55.66	17	56.43	5	54.43	19	57.11	9
Nanjing	56.90	8	-4	57.60	4	55.75	10	57.54	3	58.08	5
Chengdu	56.81	9	-3	56.78	6	58.01	2	56.06	15	57.86	6
Shenyang	56.65	10	6	55.72	16	56.08	7	54.21	21	55.33	20
Nanning	56.59	11	-1	56.11	10	53.09	33	52.96	32	54.86	23
Guangzhou	56.52	12	14	54.76	26	54.36	25	52.99	31	53.67	30
Tianjin	56.32	13	12	54.95	25	55.13	16	56.75	5	56.63	13
Dalian	56.30	14	-1	55.97	13	54.17	27	54.35	20	55.06	22
Chongqing	56.26	15	-4	56.10	11	55.85	8	56.66	7	56.18	16
Xiamen	56.15	16	-1	55.74	15	56.30	6	56.67	6	59.01	2
Hefei	56.04	17	-8	56.17	9	54.70	21	54.09	22	55.31	21
Harbin	56.03	18	-13	57.04	5	54.83	18	53.95	23	53.62	31
Xi'an	55.95	19	1	55.48	20	54.51	24	55.96	16	55.46	18
Wuhan	55.94	20	4	55.11	24	53.48	31	53.29	27	54.31	24
Yinchuan	55.87	21	8	54.65	29	58.17	1	58.24	1	59.90	1
Xining	55.78	22	11	54.20	33	57.52	3	57.76	2	57.41	7
Changsha	55.75	23	4	54.69	27	55.33	13	53.94	24	57.02	10
Jinan	55.52	24	8	54.32	32	54.76	20	56.13	12	57.23	8
Haikou	55.48	25	-13	56.09	12	54.14	28	55.63	17	55.75	17
Hohhot	55.41	26	-25	57.98	1	53.82	30	53.07	29	52.68	34
Fuzhou	55.36	27	-6	55.36	21	54.82	19	56.20	10	56.72	12
Lanzhou	55.29	28	6	53.59	34	55.27	14	52.47	33	50.00	35
Guiyang	55.29	29	-7	55.28	22	53.12	32	53.18	28	53.81	29
Changchun	55.20	30	-23	56.25	7	54.26	26	56.14	11	58.22	4
Urumqi	55.17	31	-3	54.69	28	55.14	15	50.85	35	56.25	15
Shanghai	55.09	32	-24	56.22	8	53.84	29	56.10	13	56.58	14
Beijing	54.80	33	-2	54.35	31	52.39	35	53.87	25	53.30	32
Shenzhen	54.76	34	1	53.26	35	52.40	34	53.07	30	54.02	26
Zhengzhou	54.65	35	-16	55.59	19	54.55	23	56.09	14	54.17	25
Average	56.05			55.66		54.88		55.07		55.63	

088

Quality-of-life Subindexes of the 35 Chinese Cities

From 2012 to 2016, the index averages of the 35 cities are 55.63, 55.07, 54.88, 55.66 and 56.05 respectively. The index has stayed above the satisfaction level and continued to improve slightly two years in a row. Besides, there is no significant difference among the cities.

Cities ranked top 10 are: Taiyuan (1), Nanchang (2), Qingdao (3), Kunming (4), Hangzhou (5), Ningbo (6), Shijiazhuang (7), Nanjing (8), Chengdu (9) and Shenyang (10). And the bottom 10 cities are: Hohhot (26), Fuzhou (27), Lanzhou (28), Guiyang (29), Changchun (30), Urumqi (31), Shanghai (32), Beijing (33), Shenzhen (34) and Zhengzhou (35). Among them, Hangzhou and Nanjing have ranked among the top 10 five years in a row, while Shenzhen have stayed among the bottom 10 during the same period. Compared to the result of 2015, in the top 10 list, the rankings of Taiyuan (+29), Qingdao (+20), Nanchang (+16), Shijiazhuang (+10), Ningbo (+8) and Shenyang (+6) have climbed up, while the rankings of Kunming (-1), Hangzhou (-3), Nanjing (-4) and Chengdu (-3) have declined. In the bottom 10 list, only the rankings of Lanzhou (+6) and Shenzhen (+1) have risen, while those of Hohhot (-25), Shanghai (-24), Changchun (-23), Zhengzhou (-16), Guiyang (-7), Fuzhou (-6), Urumqi (-3) and Beijing (-2) have dropped. From 2012 to 2016, Hangzhou and Nanjing have stayed among the top 10; while Shenzhen and Guiyang have remained among the bottom 10. Beijing has ranked No.25 in one of the five years and stayed in the bottom 10 list for the rest four years. There are 5 eastern cities, 3 central cities and 2 western cities among the top 10 cities; and 4 eastern cities, 2 central cities and 4 western cities among the bottom 10 cities.

From the perspective of index distribution, the satisfaction over living experience has remained stable, and the gaps have narrowed. As is shown in Figure 25, the distribution of the indexes has further concentrated and generally stayed within the interval of 50-60 from 2012 to 2016.Yinchuan

089

(59.90, 58.24, 58.17) had been the highest scores from 2012 to 2014, while Lanzhou (50.00), Urumqi (50.85) and Beijing (52.39) had been the lowest scorers of each year. In 2015 and 2016, the highest scorers have been Hohhot (57.98) and Taiyuan (57.60), while the lowest scorers have been Shenzhen (53.26) and Zhengzhou (54.65). The differences between the highest and the lowest scores are 9.90, 7.39, 5.78, 4.72 and 2.95 respectively. The narrowing difference indicates a smaller gap of living experience satisfaction among cities.

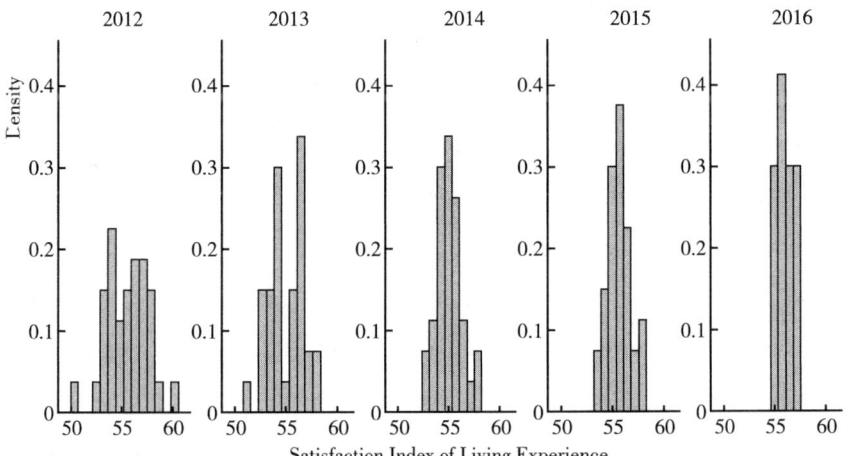

Figure 25　A Histogram of the 2012–2016 Living Experience Satisfaction Indexes of the 35 Cities

As is shown in Figure 26, although the living experience satisfaction indexes of the 35 cities have changed in different directions, they are generally on the high side. Dynamically speaking, the index of Nanchang has improved four years in a row; while those of Jinan, Xiamen and Yinchuan had continued to decline in the first four years and start to rise in 2016.

The satisfaction index of living experience consists of a pace of life satisfaction subindex and a living convenience satisfaction subindex.

As is shown in Table 14, from 2012 to 2016, the averages of the pace of

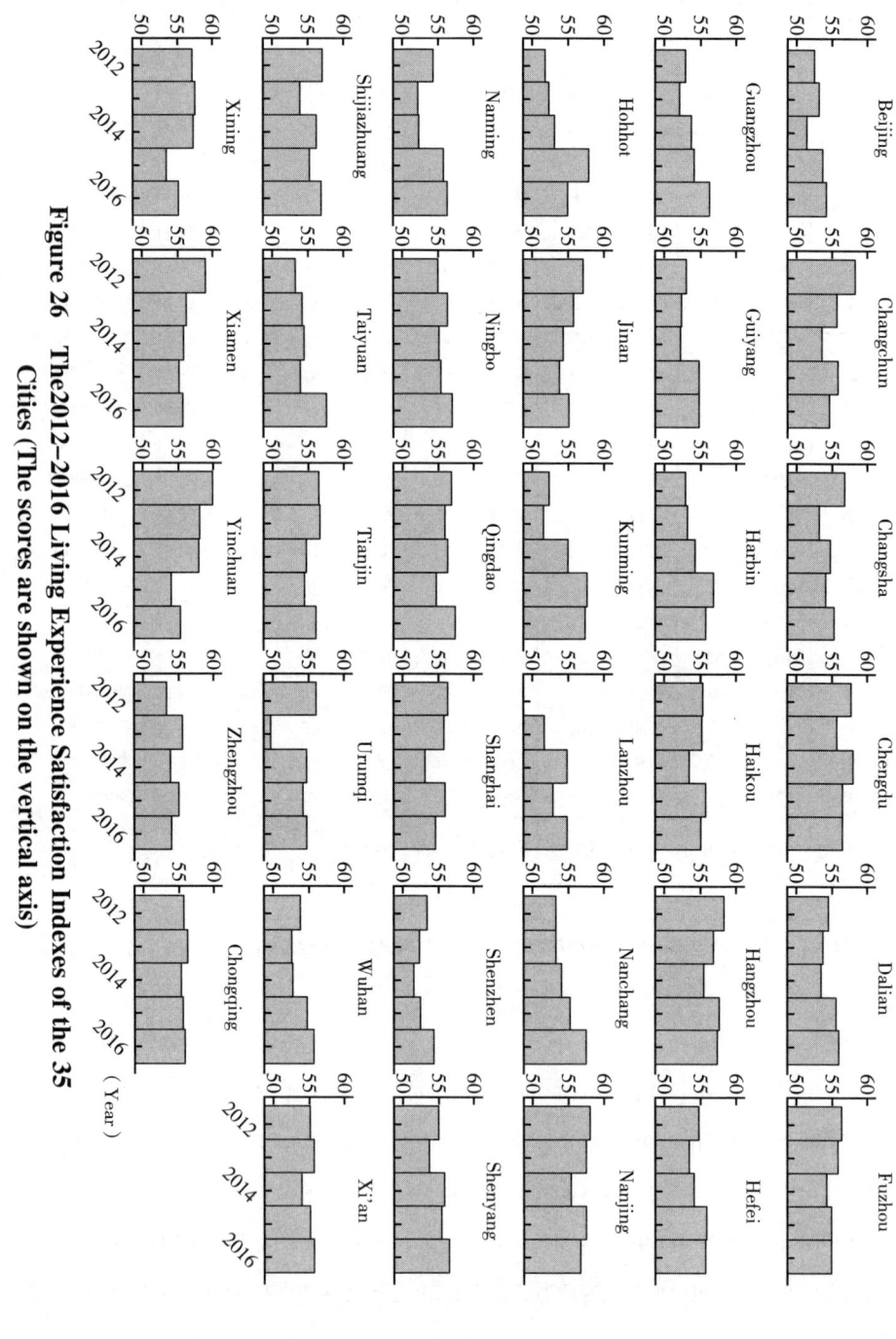

Figure 26 The 2012–2016 Living Experience Satisfaction Indexes of the 35 Cities (The scores are shown on the vertical axis)

Blue Book of Quality of Life in Cities

life satisfaction indexes are 42.87, 42.97, 41.90, 43.12 and 44.07 respectively. Generally speaking, the value of the index has remained stable. From the perspective of scores, none of the 35 cities has scored over 50 (the critical point between the satisfaction and the dissatisfaction intervals) in the pace of life satisfaction index. It shows that the fast pace of life has brought much pressure on people's lives.

Table 14   The 2012–2016 Pace of Life Satisfaction Indexes of the 35 Cities

City	2016			2015		2014		2013		2012	
	Score	Ranking	Places Risen	Score	Ranking	Score	Ranking	Score	Ranking	Score	Ranking
Kunming	48.26	1	6	45.83	7	45.32	6	44.90	13	43.27	16
Nanchang	47.21	2	17	42.63	19	43.66	9	43.62	22	43.90	13
Taiyuan	47.04	3	27	41.21	30	42.63	22	45.11	9	43.32	15
Yinchuan	46.69	4	28	39.88	32	47.36	1	45.05	10	50.00	1
Nanning	46.49	5	4	45.40	9	43.38	12	44.23	19	44.44	11
Ningbo	46.13	6	8	43.61	14	41.17	30	42.99	25	40.54	28
Shijiazhuang	46.00	7	9	43.52	16	45.48	4	43.11	23	44.35	12
Qingdao	45.99	8	21	41.25	29	41.69	29	39.22	32	40.09	29
Harbin	45.86	9	-6	46.88	3	43.29	14	42.54	28	39.96	30
Hangzhou	45.77	10	-9	47.06	1	43.63	10	45.83	8	44.93	8
Nanjing	45.57	11	-6	46.07	5	43.11	16	44.62	16	43.21	17
Dalian	45.42	12	0	44.12	12	42.20	25	42.87	26	39.57	31
Shenyang	45.36	13	2	43.56	15	43.29	13	41.81	29	40.86	27
Chongqing	45.17	14	-3	44.15	11	42.19	26	44.01	20	42.34	22
Chengdu	45.13	15	-5	45.10	10	45.98	2	47.22	4	48.39	2
Hohhot	45.08	16	-14	46.96	2	42.45	24	44.74	15	41.43	26
Jinan	44.72	17	9	41.97	26	42.45	23	45.02	11	42.92	19
Urumqi	44.35	18	-1	43.23	17	44.54	7	41.81	30	44.74	10
Xi'an	44.17	19	-1	42.79	18	42.84	17	44.32	17	42.23	24
Lanzhou	44.13	20	5	41.99	25	45.44	5	46.47	5	41.48	25
Hefei	44.05	21	-13	45.67	8	42.66	20	44.27	18	42.27	23
Wuhan	43.82	22	2	42.09	24	42.80	19	43.69	21	43.49	14
Haikou	43.75	23	-17	45.89	6	43.24	15	47.25	3	47.50	3

092

Quality-of-life Subindexes of the 35 Chinese Cities

Continued table

City	2016			2015		2014		2013		2012	
	Score	Ranking	Places Risen	Score	Ranking	Score	Ranking	Score	Ranking	Score	Ranking
Fuzhou	43.60	24	-1	42.27	23	41.90	28	44.9	14	42.49	21
Changsha	43.48	25	2	41.85	27	44.02	8	42.81	27	45.61	6
Tianjin	43.42	26	2	41.70	28	39.93	31	44.95	12	42.70	20
Guiyang	43.41	27	-5	42.31	22	42.65	21	45.90	7	45.48	7
Guangzhou	43.26	28	3	40.83	31	39.07	32	36.67	34	38.12	32
Xiamen	43.06	29	-8	42.42	21	42.80	18	43.06	24	44.77	9
Zhengzhou	41.73	30	-17	43.63	13	43.57	11	46.27	6	42.98	18
Shanghai	41.68	31	-11	42.43	20	35.69	33	38.20	33	37.05	34
Changchun	41.38	32	-28	46.35	4	42.17	27	49.88	1	45.72	5
Shenzhen	41.14	33	0	38.84	33	34.90	35	34.93	35	35.81	35
Xining	40.32	34	0	38.83	34	45.83	3	47.95	2	47.22	4
Beijing	39.25	35	0	38.72	35	35.41	34	39.32	31	37.11	33
Average	44.07			43.12		41.90		42.97		42.87	

Cities ranked top 10 are: Kunming (1), Nanchang (2), Taiyuan (3), Yinchuan (4), Nanning (5), Ningbo (6), Shijiazhuang (7), Qingdao (8), Harbin (9) and Hangzhou (10), including 4 eastern cities, 3 central cities and 3 western cities. And the bottom 10 cities are: Tianjin (26), Guiyang (27), Guangzhou (28), Xiamen (29), Zhengzhou (30), Shanghai (31), Changchun (32), Shenzhen (33), Xining (34) and Beijing (35), including 6eastern cities, 2central cities and 2western cities. In the top 10 list, Yinchuan (+28), Taiyuan (+27), Qingdao (+21), Nanchang (+17), Shijiazhuang (+9), Ningbo (+8), Kunming (+6) and Nanning (+4) have seen rises, while Hangzhou (-9) and Harbin (-6) have experienced drops. And in the bottom 10 list, the rankings of Guangzhou (+3) and Tianjin (+2) have improved. The rankings of Changchun (-28), Zhengzhou (-17), Shanghai (-11), Xiamen (-8) and Guiyang (-5) have declined.

093

The rankings of Shenzhen (0), Xining (0) and Beijing (0) have remained unchanged. Beijing, Shenzhen and Guangzhou have stayed in the bottom 10 list five years in a row. And Shanghai has ranked among the bottom 10in all the years except in 2015 when it ranked No.20. Obviously, the pace of life is rather quick in the first-tier cities.

As is shown in Figure 27, the distribution of the pace of life satisfaction indexes has concentrated and generally remained stable from 2012 to 2016. In 2012, the distribution of the indexes was within the interval of 35-50. And in 2016, the distribution is within the interval of 40-45. From 2012 to 2016, the differences between the highest and the lowest scores are 14.19, 14.95, 12.46, 8.34 and 9.01 respectively. The highest scores have no significant change, whereas the lowest scores have improved. In other words, the gaps among cities are narrowing.

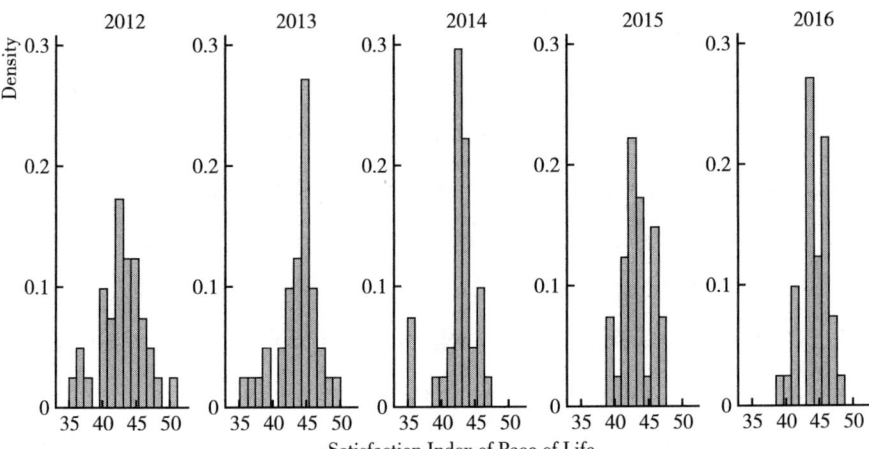

Figure 27   A Histogram of the 2012–2016 Pace of Life Satisfaction Indexes of the 35 Cities

As is shown in figure 28, viewed by cities, only Kunming and Shenyang had seen an improvement in the index three years in a row from 2012 to

Figure 28　The 2012–2016 Pace of Life Satisfaction Indexes of the 35 Cities (The scores are shown on the vertical axis)

Blue Book of Quality of Life in Cities

2015, whereas Chengdu had experienced a decline. The indexes of most the other cities had improved slightly during the same period. When comparing the index of 2012 and 2016, the average difference is only 1.49. The indexes of 10 cities have declined, while those of the rest 25 cities have all gone up. Qingdao and Harbin have seen the greatest rises (+5.9), while Xining has experienced the most drastic drop (-6.90). Regionally speaking, the index average of the western region is the highest (44.50), while that of the eastern region is the lowest (42.26). And the average of the central region is 43.88. Obviously, the pace of life is fastest in the eastern region and slowest in the western region. As a result, the satisfaction over pace of life is highest in the western region and lowest in the eastern region.

As is shown in Table 15, the 2016 average of the living convenience satisfaction index is 68.03, while the 2012-2015 index averages were 68.39, 67.18, 67.66 and 68.20 respectively. Values of the living convenience satisfaction index are higher than those of the pace of life satisfaction index, which indicates that in general, the residents of the 35 cities have been more satisfied with living convenience.

Table 15   The 2012–2016 Living Convenience Satisfaction Indexes of the 35 Cities

City	2016			2015		2014		2013		2012	
	Score	Ranking	Places Risen	Score	Ranking	Score	Ranking	Score	Ranking	Score	Ranking
Xining	71.24	1	2	69.56	3	69.20	11	67.57	14	67.59	23
Beijing	70.35	2	0	69.98	2	69.38	10	68.42	11	69.50	17
Guangzhou	69.78	3	8	68.68	11	69.65	8	69.31	9	69.23	18
Xiamen	69.24	4	4	69.05	8	69.79	7	70.28	6	73.26	3
Tianjin	69.21	5	11	68.21	16	70.33	3	68.55	10	70.56	10
Hangzhou	69.11	6	8	68.25	14	68.07	15	68.26	12	71.58	6
Changchun	69.01	7	26	66.16	33	66.35	23	62.39	29	70.72	9
Qingdao	68.95	8	-1	69.09	7	71.40	2	73.18	2	73.82	2

096

Quality-of-life Subindexes of the 35 Chinese Cities —

Continued table

City	2016			2015		2014		2013		2012	
	Score	Ranking	Places Risen	Score	Ranking	Score	Ranking	Score	Ranking	Score	Ranking
Shanghai	68.50	9	-8	70.02	1	71.98	1	73.99	1	76.12	1
Chengdu	68.49	10	2	68.46	12	70.03	4	64.90	23	67.32	24
Shenzhen	68.38	11	14	67.68	25	69.89	5	71.21	4	72.22	5
Nanjing	68.23	12	-6	69.13	6	68.39	14	70.46	5	72.95	4
Ningbo	68.20	13	7	67.97	20	69.81	6	70.14	7	70.14	12
Taiyuan	68.17	14	8	67.83	22	67.19	18	64.39	24	64.36	29
Shijiazhuang	68.07	15	9	67.80	24	67.37	17	65.75	20	69.86	14
Wuhan	68.06	16	2	68.14	18	64.17	33	62.89	28	65.13	28
Changsha	68.03	17	10	67.54	27	66.64	21	65.07	22	68.42	20
Hefei	68.03	18	12	66.68	30	66.74	20	63.91	27	68.35	21
Shenyang	67.93	19	2	67.87	21	68.86	13	66.60	17	69.80	15
Nanchang	67.87	20	-10	68.69	10	65.57	27	64.06	25	63.82	32
Xi'an	67.73	21	-4	68.18	17	66.18	24	67.59	13	68.69	19
Zhengzhou	67.57	22	4	67.54	26	65.54	28	65.91	18	65.36	26
Chongqing	67.36	23	-4	68.06	19	69.51	9	69.31	8	70.01	13
Haikou	67.21	24	8	66.29	32	65.04	32	64.01	26	64.00	30
Dalian	67.18	25	-2	67.83	23	66.13	25	65.83	19	70.55	11
Guiyang	67.16	26	-11	68.24	15	63.58	34	60.45	32	62.14	34
Fuzhou	67.12	27	-14	68.44	13	67.74	16	67.49	15	70.95	8
Nanning	66.69	28	1	66.82	29	62.81	35	61.69	30	65.28	27
Kunming	66.67	29	-25	69.44	4	65.41	29	59.90	33	62.98	33
Lanzhou	66.45	30	5	65.18	35	65.09	31	58.48	35	58.52	35
Jinan	66.32	31	0	66.67	31	67.07	19	67.25	16	71.54	7
Harbin	66.21	32	-4	67.20	28	66.37	22	65.36	21	67.28	25
Urumqi	65.99	33	1	66.16	34	65.74	26	59.89	34	67.76	22
Hohhot	65.73	34	-25	68.99	9	65.19	30	61.40	31	63.93	31
Yinchuan	65.06	35	-30	69.42	5	68.99	12	71.43	3	69.79	16
Average	68.03			68.20		67.66		67.18		68.39	

097

 Blue Book of Quality of Life in Cities

Cities ranked top 10 are: Xining (1), Beijing (2), Guangzhou (3), Xiamen (4), Tianjin (5), Hangzhou (6), Changchun (7), Qingdao (8), Shanghai (9) and Chengdu (10), including 7 eastern cities, 1 central city and 2 western cities. And the bottom 10 cities are: Guiyang (26), Fuzhou (27), Nanning (28), Kunming (29), Lanzhou (30), Jinan (31), Harbin (32), Urumqi (33), Hohhot (34) and Yinchuan (35), including 2 eastern cities, 1 central city and 7 western cities. Generally speaking, cities of high living convenience are mostly in the eastern region, while cities of low convenience are mainly in the western region. Compared to the result of 2015, the rankings of 7 out of the top 10 cities have improved in 2016, including Changchun (26), Tianjin (11), Hangzhou (8), Guangzhou (8), Xiamen (4), Xining (2) and Chengdu (2). The rankings of 2 cities—Qingdao (-1) and Shanghai (-8)— have dropped. And the ranking of Beijing has remained unchanged. Among the bottom 10 cities, the rankings of Lanzhou (+5), Nanning (+1) and Urumqi (+1) have risen, while that of Jinan has stayed the same. And the rankings of Yinchuan (-30), Kunming (-25), Hohhot (-25), Fuzhou (-14), Guiyang (-11) and Harbin (-4) have declined. Xiamen, Qingdao and Shanghai have been in the top 10 list five years in a row, while Lanzhou and Nanning have stayed in the bottom 10 list during the same period.

As is shown in Figure 29, from 2012 to 2016, the distribution of the living convenience satisfaction indexes has changed from the interval of 55-75 to 60-75.Obviously, the highest value has remained stable, while the lowest value has risen. It shows that the gaps of living convenience satisfaction have narrowed among the surveyed 35 cities.

Viewed by cities, from 2012 to 2016, the satisfaction over living convenience has continued to improve in Haikou, Xining and Taiyuan, and dropped slightly in Jinan, Ningbo, Qingdao, Shanghai, Shenzhen and Xiamen (See Figure 30).

098

Quality-of-life Subindexes of the 35 Chinese Cities —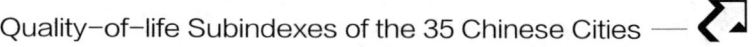

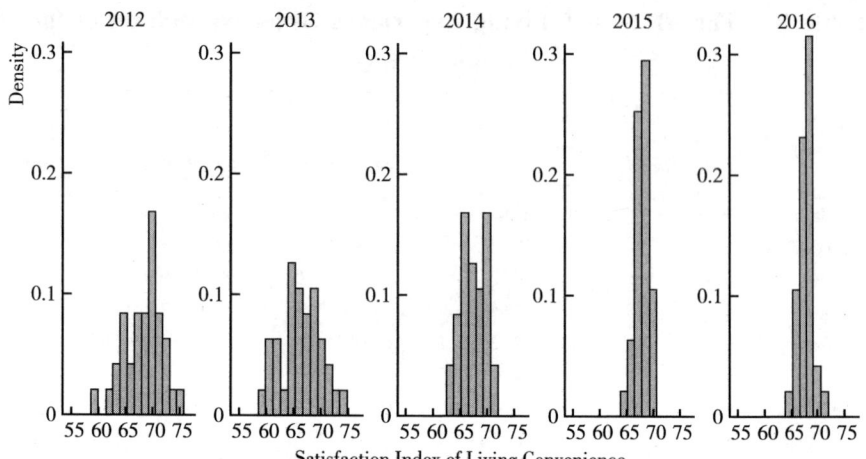

Figure 29   A Histogram of the 2012–2016 Living Convenience Satisfaction Indexes of the 35 Cities

5.5.2   Objective Index of Living Experience

According to the QLICC system, the living experience objective index of each city was obtained by calculating its three primary indicators (living convenience, Eco-environment and perception of income disparities) and six secondary indicators. Table 16 lists the 2016 living experience objective indexes of the 35 cities.

In 2016, the average of the living experience objective indexes is 57.54 which is above the satisfaction level. Overall, there is a great difference between the highest and the lowest scores. Values of the secondary indicators show that big gaps still exist in the transportation capacity, the numbers of cinemas and theatres per 10, 000 residents, the medical care capacity, the per capita green area, the air quality and the Gini coefficients of different cities.

099

Blue Book of Quality of Life in Cities

Table 16 The 2012–2016 Living Experience Objective Indexes of the 35 Chinese Cities

City	2016			2015		2014		2013		2012	
	Score	Ranking	Places Risen	Score	Ranking	Score	Ranking	Score	Ranking	Score	Ranking
Beijing	80.00	1	0	80.00	1	80.00	1	80.00	1	80.01	1
Guangzhou	68.40	2	1	67.86	3	66.66	3	64.16	3	58.88	7
Haikou	67.63	3	1	65.12	4	65.35	4	57.80	9	55.45	12
Shenzhen	67.30	4	-2	67.95	2	69.71	2	65.12	2	71.86	2
Nanjing	64.92	5	2	62.35	7	60.84	8	59.70	6	58.24	8
Shenyang	64.32	6	-1	64.32	5	63.28	5	62.56	4	62.90	5
Hohhot	63.16	7	-1	62.84	6	62.51	6	58.74	7	54.50	13
Kunming	61.27	8	1	60.70	9	61.54	7	57.57	10	55.61	10
Wuhan	60.95	9	1	60.39	10	57.93	13	60.15	5	64.52	3
Xi'an	60.78	10	3	58.43	13	55.87	18	54.32	17	55.46	11
Hangzhou	60.62	11	-3	60.82	8	59.56	9	58.41	8	64.43	4
Harbin	60.34	12	-1	59.39	11	57.77	14	56.98	12	48.25	20
Qingdao	59.85	13	1	58.42	14	57.63	15	55.68	13	48.97	19
Taiyuan	59.64	14	-2	59.08	12	58.23	11	57.34	11	48.10	21
Yinchuan	59.08	15	0	58.14	15	58.31	10	54.74	14	52.58	14
Urumqi	58.76	16	2	56.39	18	54.22	20	54.20	18	46.58	23
Xiamen	58.33	17	0	56.77	17	58.20	12	52.07	20	58.95	6
Hefei	57.40	18	3	54.81	21	53.30	21	54.46	16	42.91	31
Changchun	57.16	19	0	56.28	19	55.92	17	53.70	19	51.25	16
Lanzhou	56.85	20	-4	56.78	16	56.98	16	51.76	21	50.77	17
Shijiazhuang	55.81	21	2	51.87	23	50.43	26	51.39	22	46.63	22
Shanghai	54.99	22	-2	55.67	20	55.57	19	54.71	15	56.45	9
Ningbo	54.65	23	-1	53.10	22	52.51	22	48.24	23	46.35	24
Nanchang	53.99	24	1	50.93	25	49.82	28	44.81	30	43.40	30
Xining	53.80	25	-1	51.52	24	50.56	25	45.51	28	45.60	27
Guiyang	53.08	26	1	50.34	27	49.98	27	44.89	29	41.91	32
Fuzhou	52.02	27	-1	50.76	26	52.46	23	45.93	27	51.84	15
Dalian	51.33	28	0	50.29	28	50.90	24	47.37	24	49.07	18
Nanning	50.76	29	1	48.05	30	47.77	29	43.97	32	44.47	29
Tianjin	50.04	30	1	47.91	31	47.34	30	47.28	25	46.20	25
Changsha	49.94	31	1	47.48	32	47.20	32	46.47	26	45.23	28
Chengdu	49.79	32	-3	48.35	29	45.34	34	43.35	33	41.30	34
Chongqing	49.19	33	1	46.61	34	46.34	33	43.18	34	40.02	35
Jinan	47.87	34	-1	47.07	33	47.26	31	44.71	31	45.72	26
Zhengzhou	40.00	35	0	40.00	35	40.00	35	40.00	35	41.65	33
Average	57.54			56.17		55.57		53.67		51.89	

100

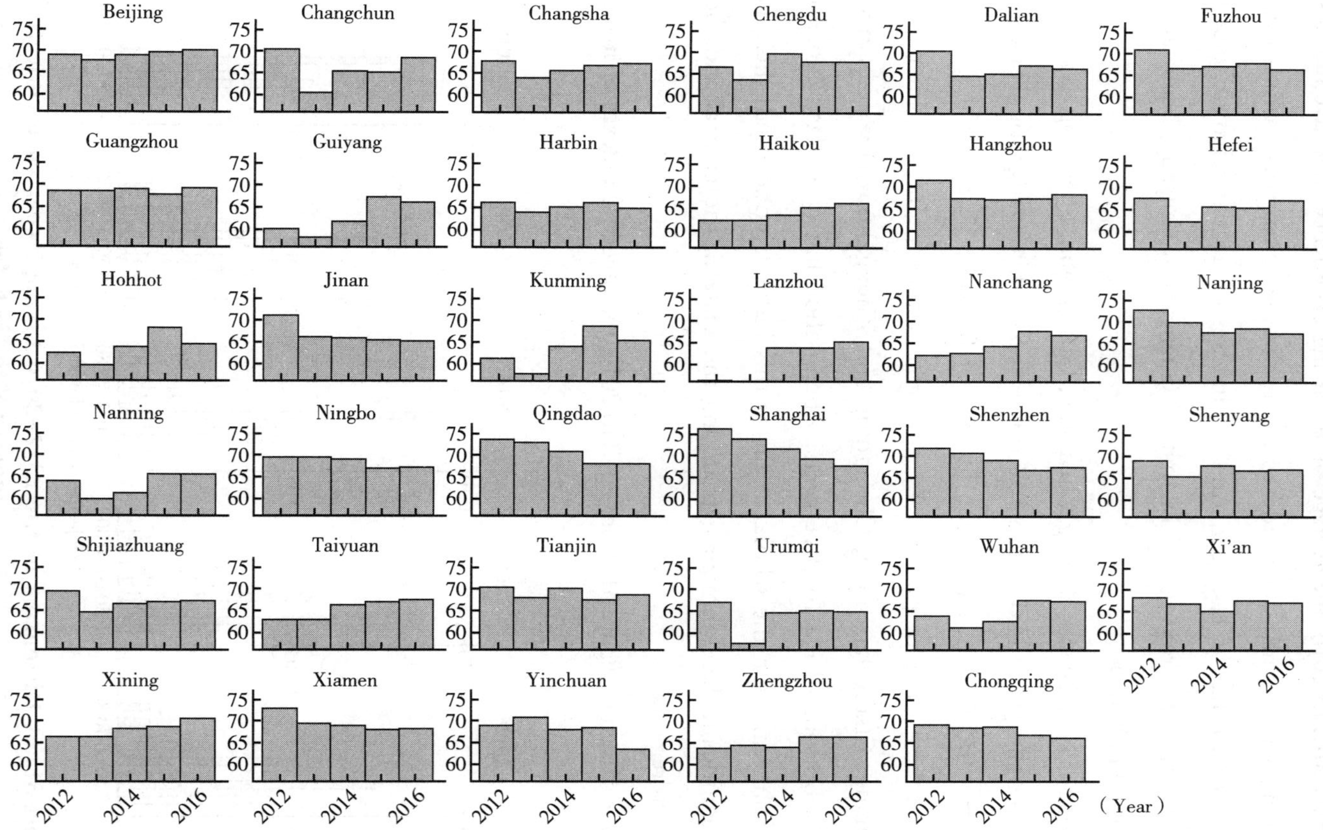

Figure 30 The 2012–2016 Living Convenience Satisfaction Indexes of the 35 Cities (The scores are shown on the vertical axis)

Blue Book of Quality of Life in Cities

From 2012 to 2016, the average of the living experience objective indexes has improved slightly. The indexes of most cities have some what risen compared to that of last year. And the indexes of 15 cities have climbed up five years in a row, especially that of Guangzhou, Guiyang, Nanchang, Urumqi and Ningbo.

Regionally speaking, Beijing, Shenzhen, Guangzhou, Shenyang, Nanjing and Kunming have ranked top 10 for five years, while Hangzhou, Haikou, Hohhot and Wuhan have been in the list for four years. Beijing have topped the list five years in a row, scoring80 or above. Guiyang, Chengdu, Nanning, Changsha, Jinan, Chongqing and Zhengzhou have remained in the bottom 10 list for five years. Zheng zhou has come last (No.35) for four years. On the whole, as far as this index is concerned, there is no significant development gap among the eastern, the central and the western regions.

As is shown in Figure 31, from 2012 to 2016, the objective indexes of living

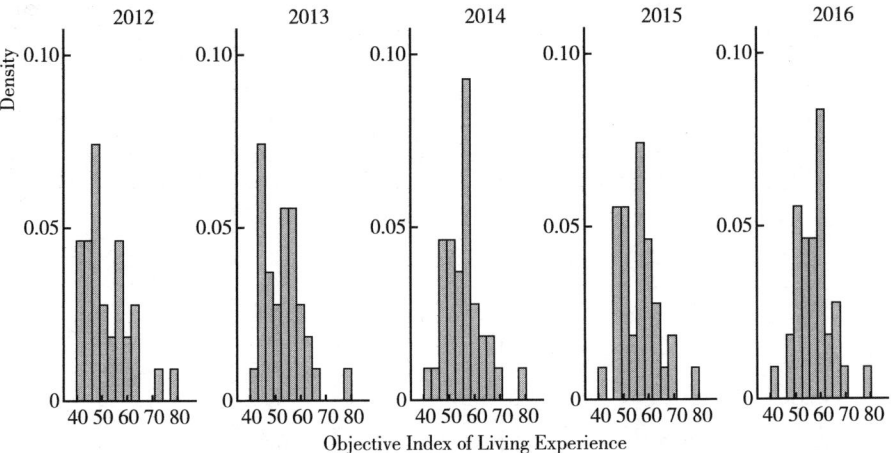

Figure 31　A Histogram of the 2012–2016 Living Experience Objective Indexes of the 35 Cities

102

Quality-of-life Subindexes of the 35 Chinese Cities

experience has generally remained stable and scattered within the interval of 40-80.But there are still big gaps among the 35 cities. The indexes of Beijing (ranked No.1 in all the five years) and Zhengzhou (ranked No.35 for five years) have remained roughly unchanged. And the indexes of all the other cities have improved, except for those of Hangzhou, Shanghai, Shenzhen, Wuhan and Xiamen (See Figure 32).

As is revealed by the above survey result, since the economic development of China entered the "New Normal", residents'satisfaction over their quality of life has continued to climb up steadily. On the other hand however, the objective indexes of QOL have kept declining since 2015, due to drastic drops in the objective indexes of living standard. To be specific, as economy growth continues to slow down, the Chinese government has decided to "adjust the mode of economic development and share the fruits of China's economic and social development", and issued a series of adjustment policies. Improvement in the satisfaction indexes shows that these policies have won the support of the general public. But the fact that the objective indexes have declined in the past two years also indicates that economic slowdown has significantly affected the life of urban residents.

5.6 Primary Indicator Radar Charts of QLICC

Figure 33 present the primary indicators of the subjective or the objective indexes of the 35 cities. Comparison can thus be made between the subjective and the objective primary indicators of the same city or that of the other cities. It can be easily discerned that living costs is still a key factor that pulls down the subjective and the objective indexes in large cities. Figure 33 are arranged according to the rankings of the objective indexes.

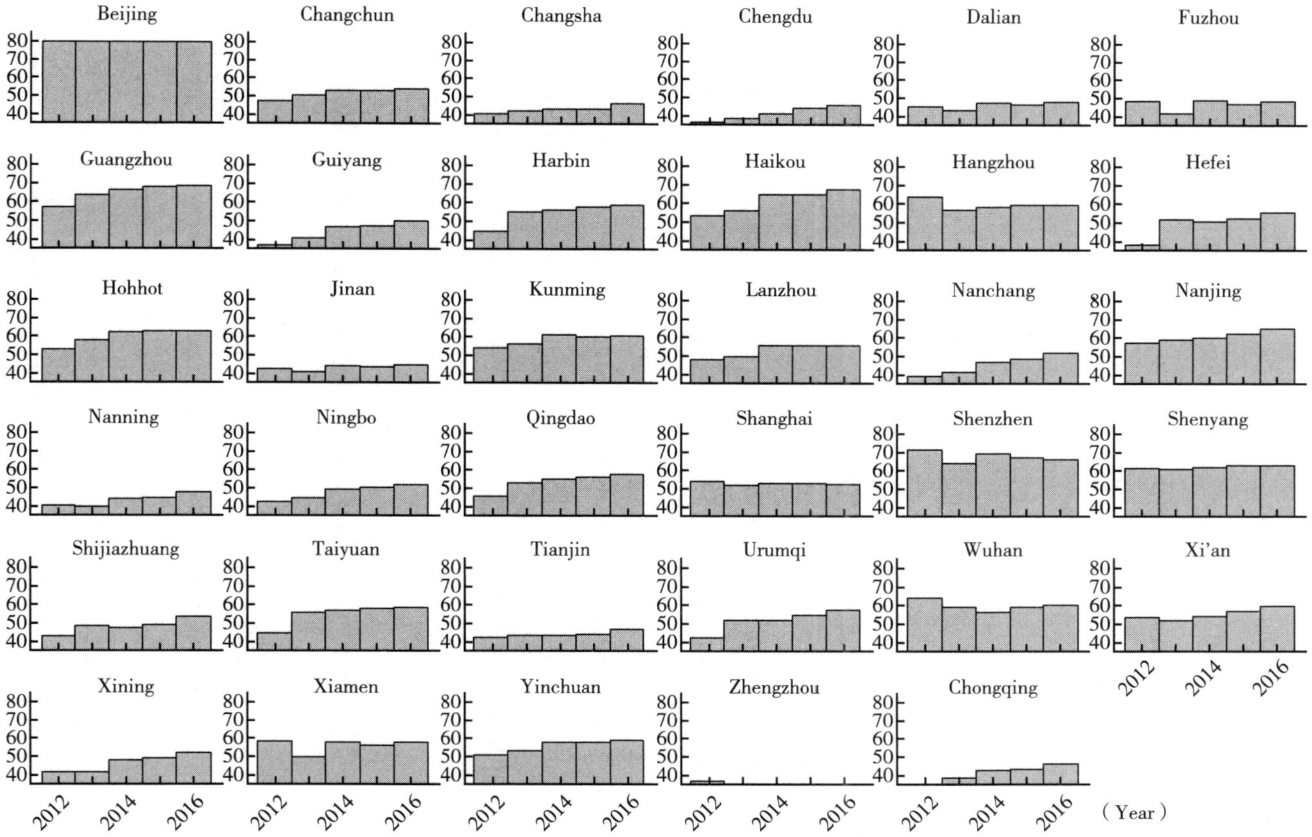

Figure 32 The 2012–2016 Living Experience Objective Indexes of the 35 Cities (The scores are shown in the vertical axis)

Quality−of−life Subindexes of the 35 Chinese Cities

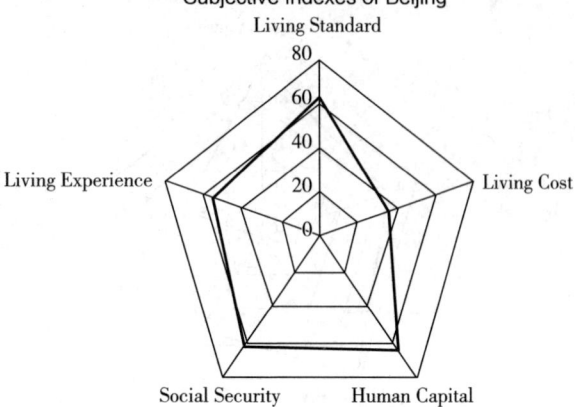

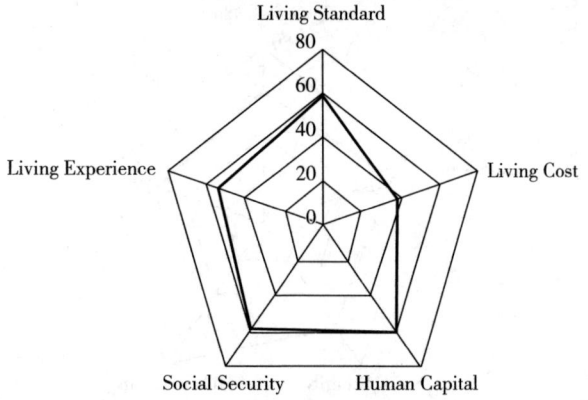

Blue Book of Quality of Life in Cities

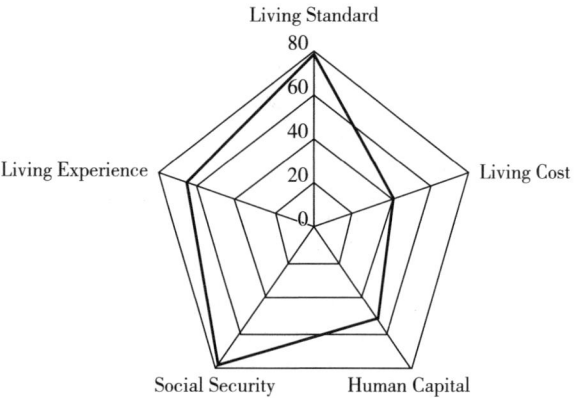

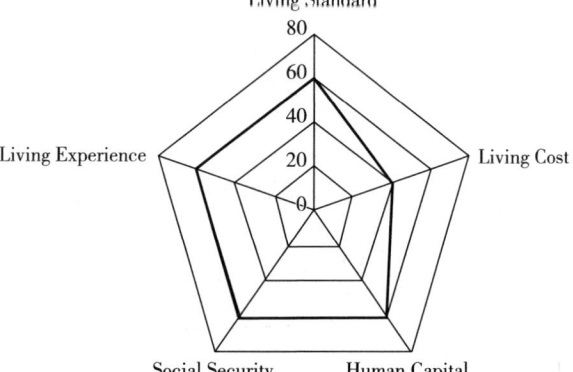

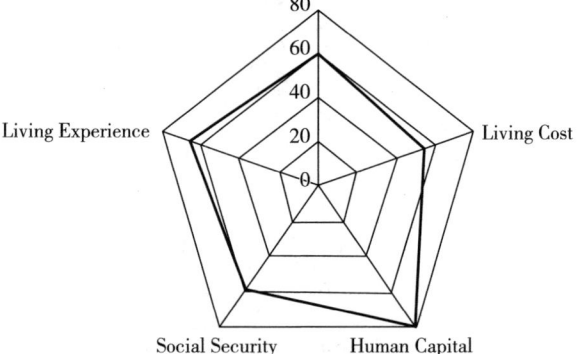

Quality-of-life Subindexes of the 35 Chinese Cities —

Subjective Indexes of Guangzhou

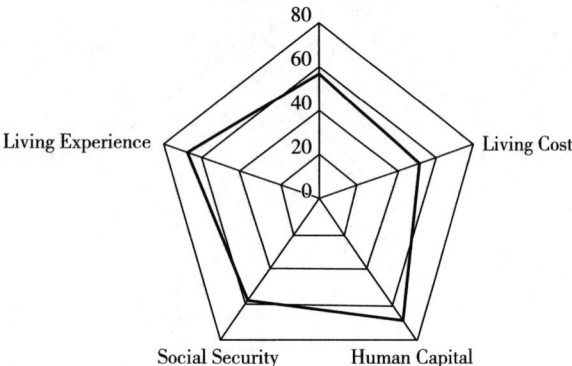

Objective Indexes of Guangzhou

Subjective Indexes of Hangzhou

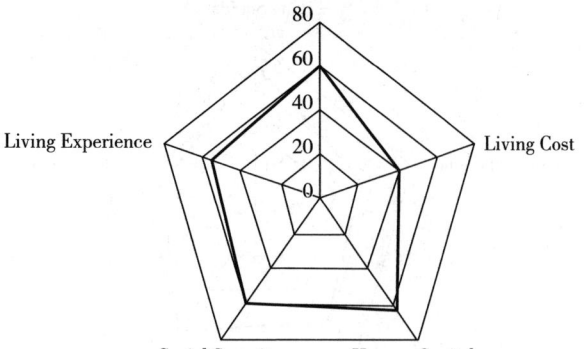

Blue Book of Quality of Life in Cities

Objective Indexes of Hangzhou

Subjective Indexes of Shanghai

Objective Indexes of Shanghai

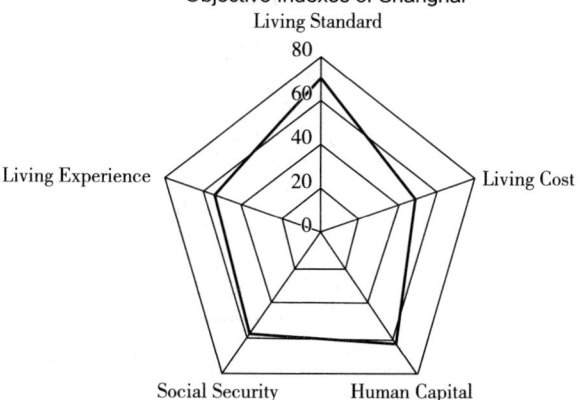

Quality-of-life Subindexes of the 35 Chinese Cities

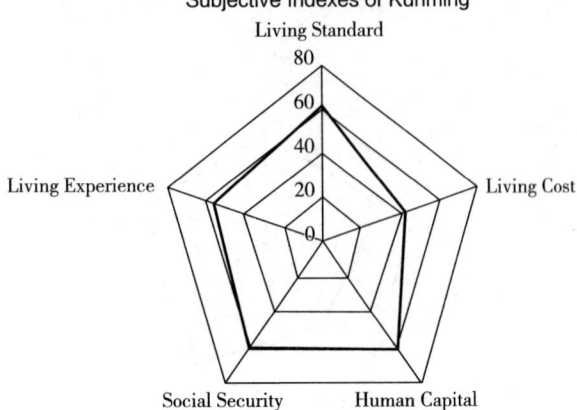

Subjective Indexes of Kunming

Objective Indexes of Kunming

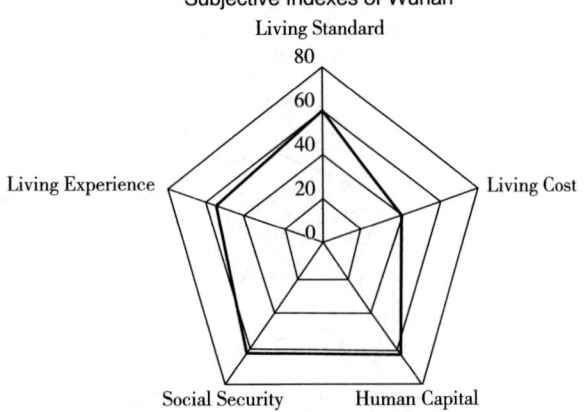

Subjective Indexes of Wuhan

109

Blue Book of Quality of Life in Cities

Objective Indexes of Wuhan

Subjective Indexes of Xi'an

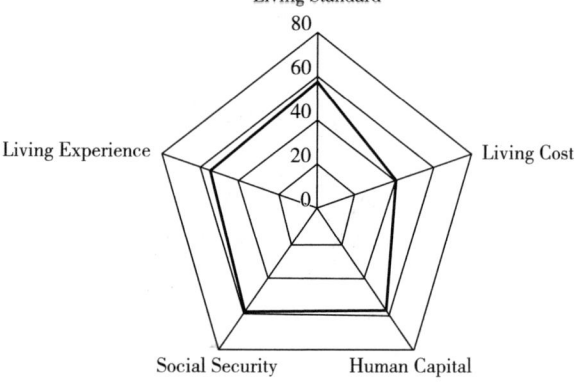

Objective Indexes of Xi'an

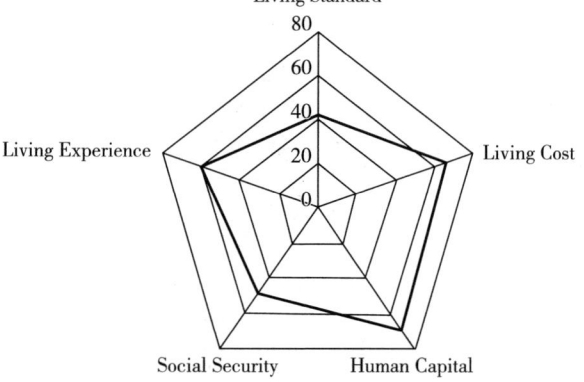

Quality-of-life Subindexes of the 35 Chinese Cities

Subjective Indexes of Guiyang

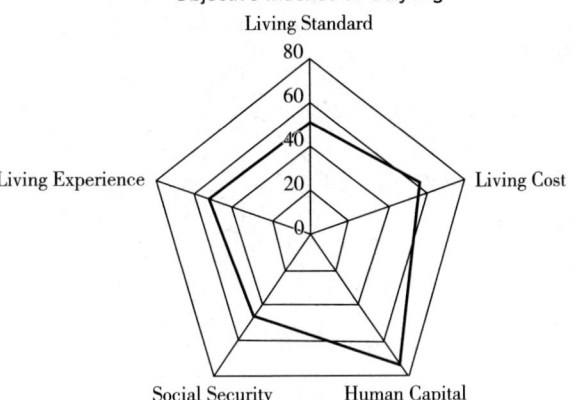

Objective Indexes of Guiyang

Subjective Indexes of Hohhot

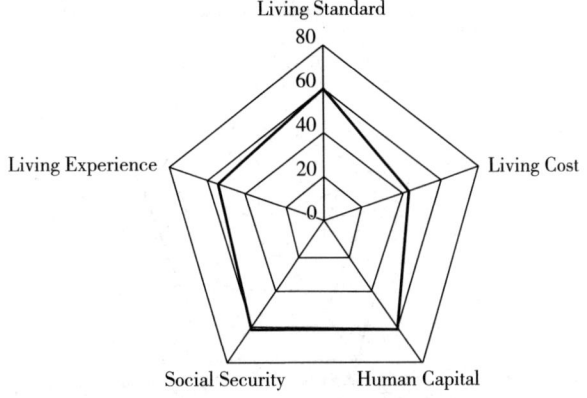

Blue Book of Quality of Life in Cities

Objective Indexes of Hohhot

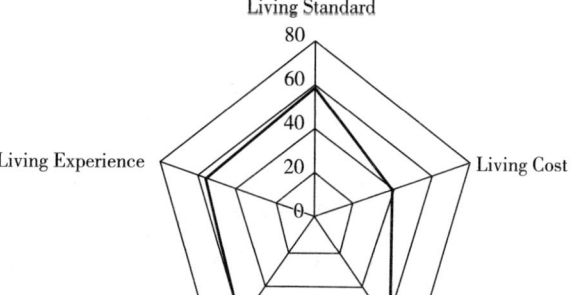

Subjective Indexes of Shenyang

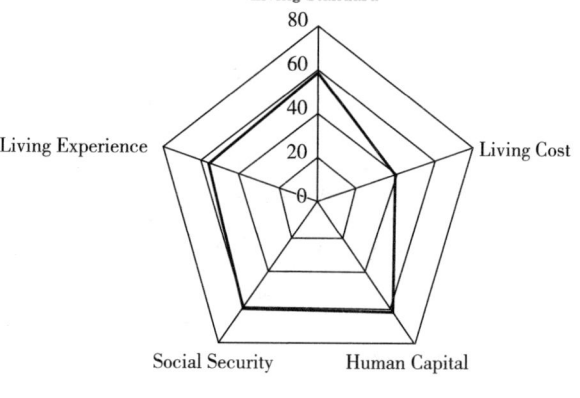

Objective Indexes of Shenyang

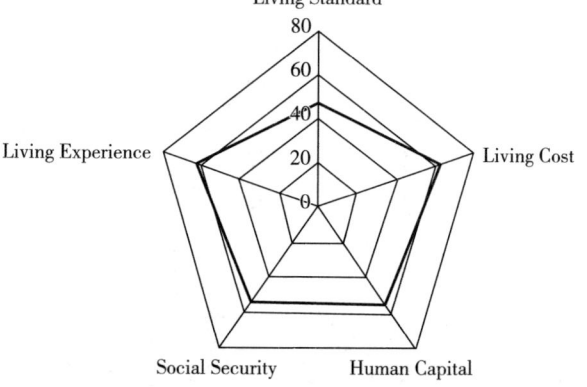

112

Quality-of-life Subindexes of the 35 Chinese Cities ── ⟨↗

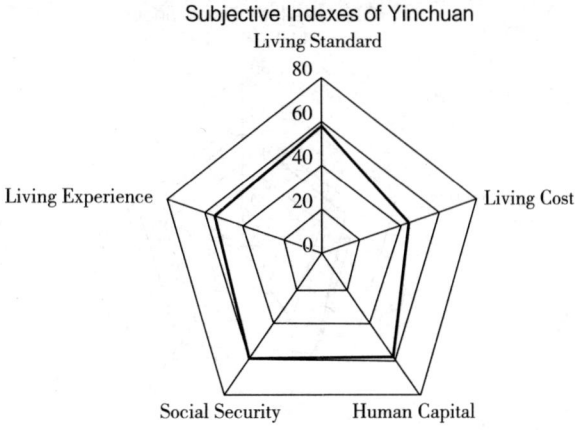

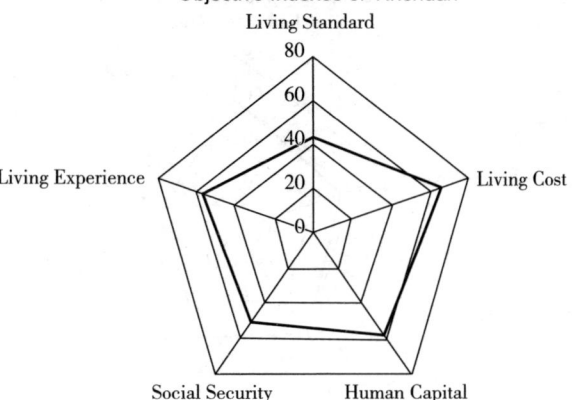

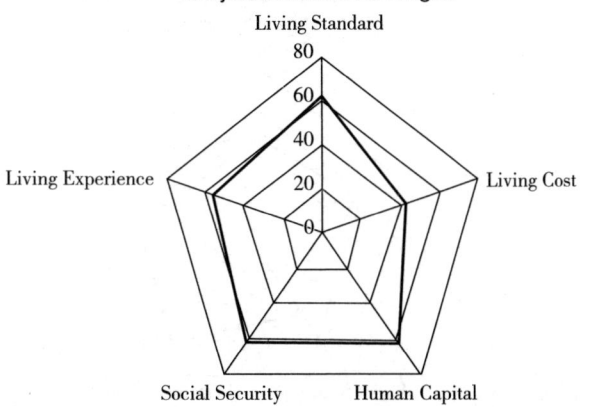

 Blue Book of Quality of Life in Cities

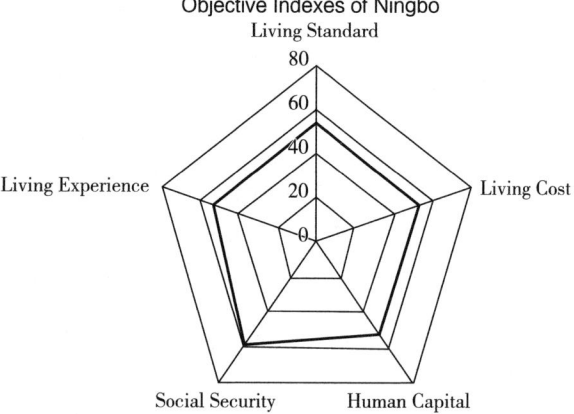

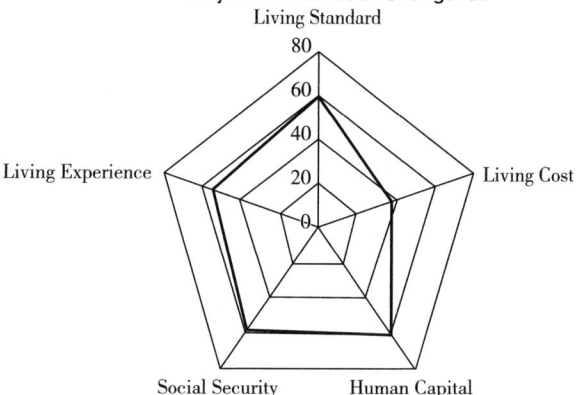

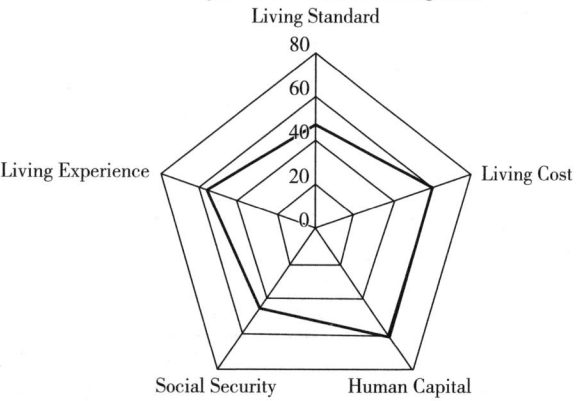

Quality-of-life Subindexes of the 35 Chinese Cities ⟵

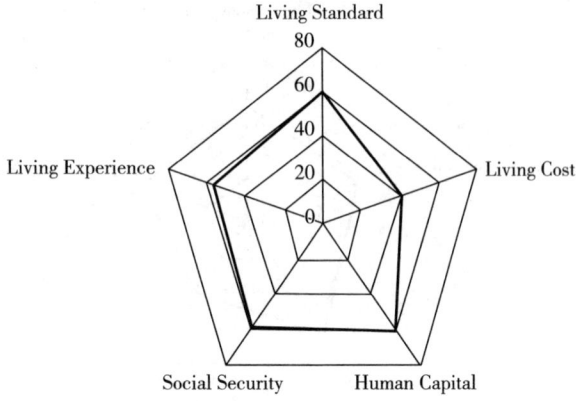

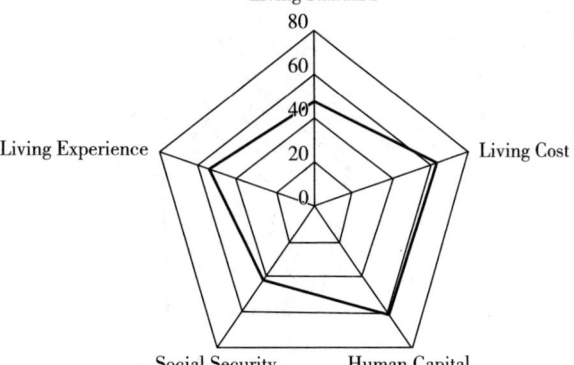

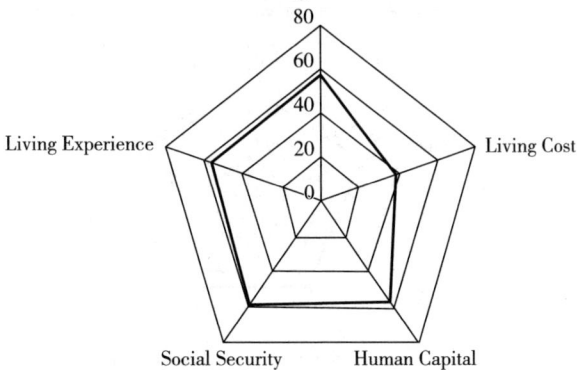

 Blue Book of Quality of Life in Cities

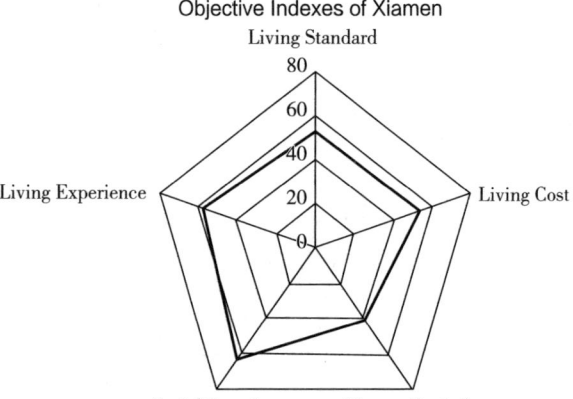

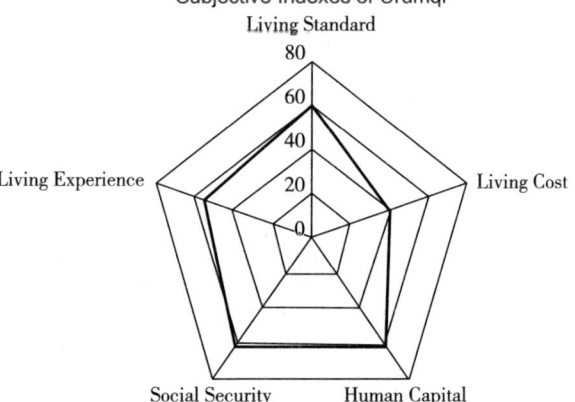

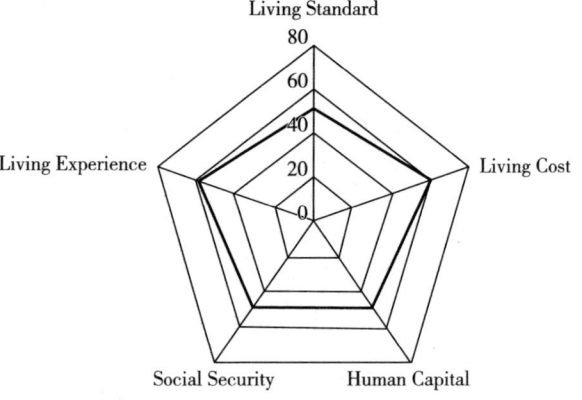

Quality-of-life Subindexes of the 35 Chinese Cities

Subjective Indexes of Changsha

Living Standard

Living Experience — Living Cost

Social Security — Human Capital

Objective Indexes of Changsha

Living Standard

Living Experience — Living Cost

Social Security — Human Capital

Subjective Indexes of Taiyuan

Living Standard

Living Experience — Living Cost

Social Security — Human Capital

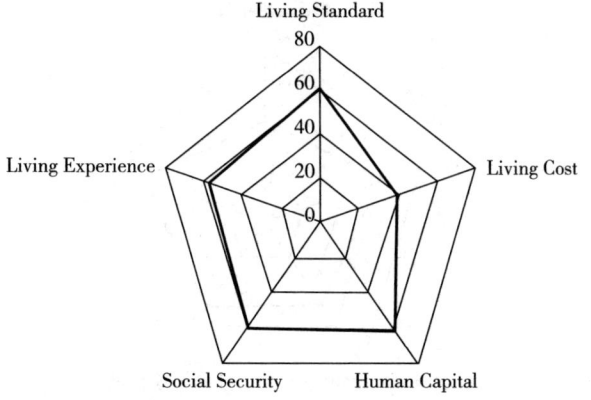

Blue Book of Quality of Life in Cities

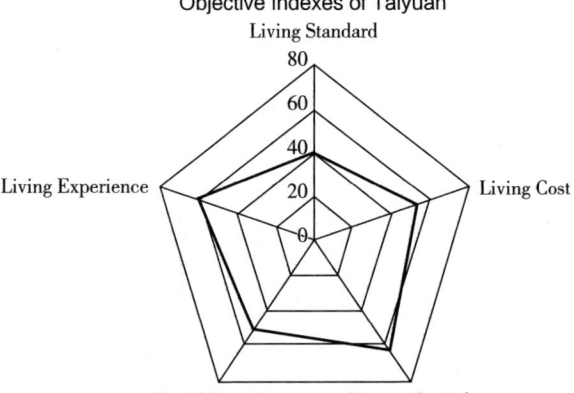

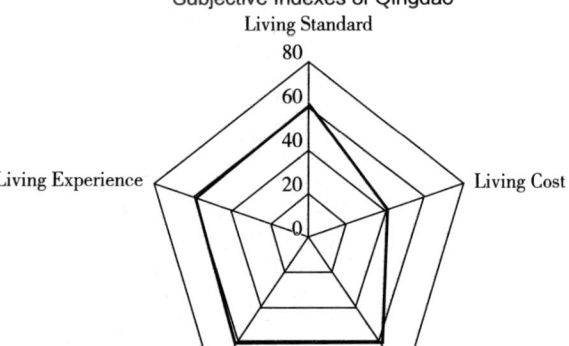

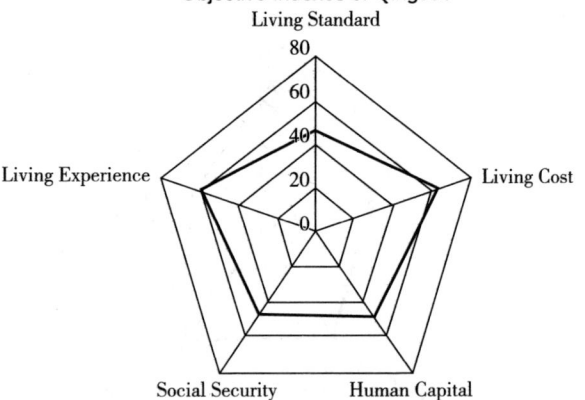

Quality-of-life Subindexes of the 35 Chinese Cities

Subjective Indexes of Dalian

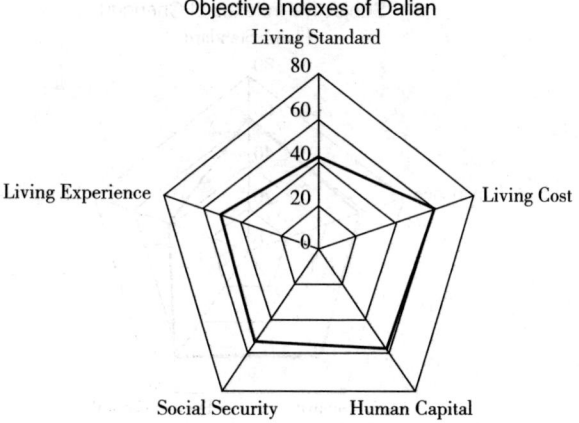

Objective Indexes of Dalian

Subjective Indexes of Jinan

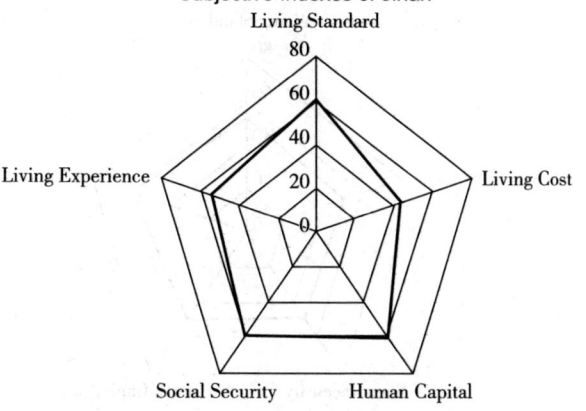

Blue Book of Quality of Life in Cities

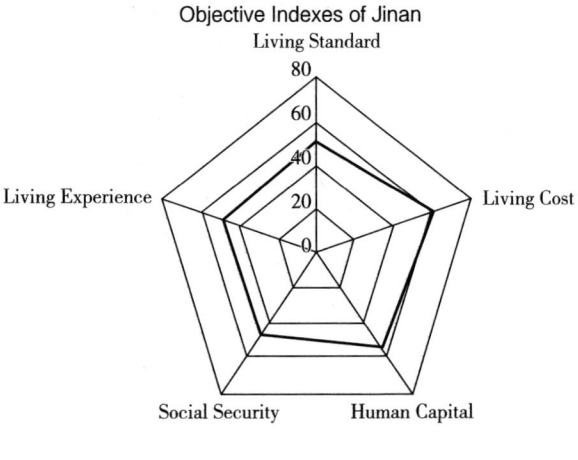

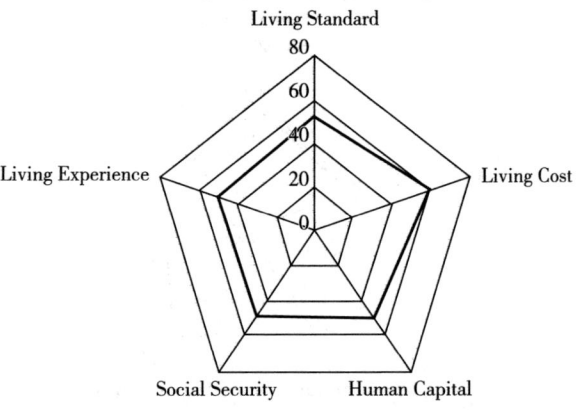

Quality-of-life Subindexes of the 35 Chinese Cities

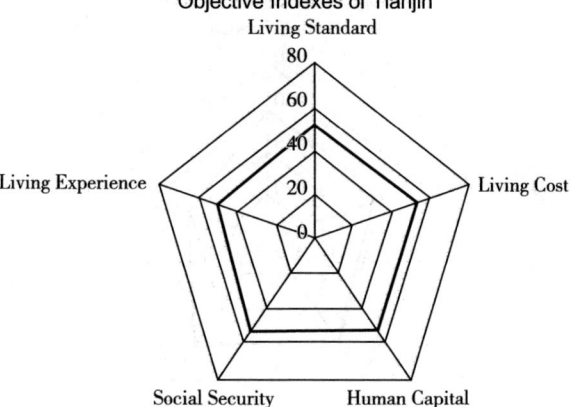

Subjective Indexes of Tianjin

Objective Indexes of Tianjin

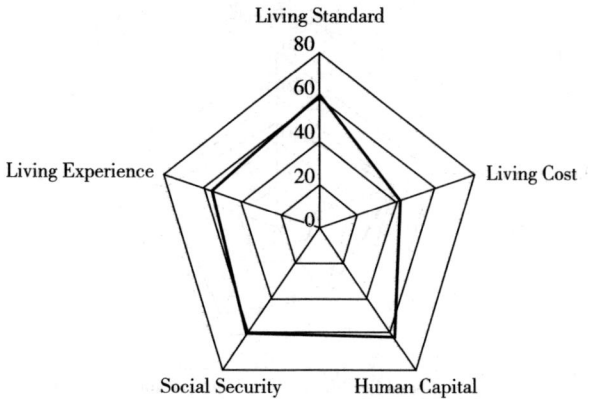

Subjective Indexes of Hefei

Blue Book of Quality of Life in Cities

Objective Indexes of Hefei

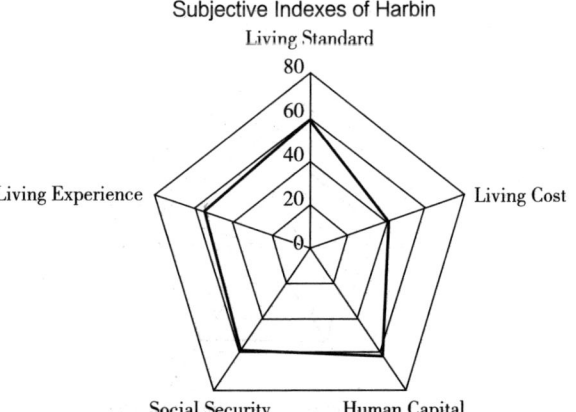

Subjective Indexes of Harbin

Objective Indexes of Harbin

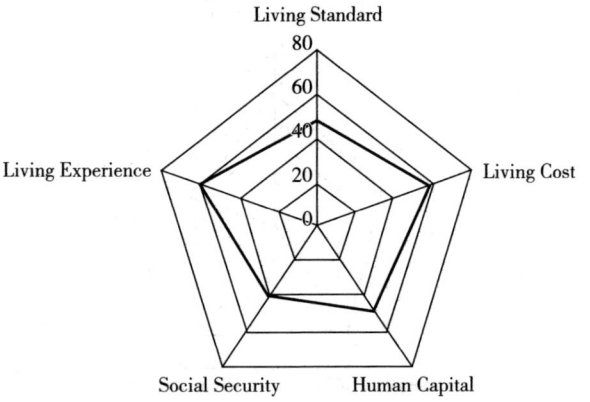

Quality-of-life Subindexes of the 35 Chinese Cities

Subjective Indexes of Nanchang

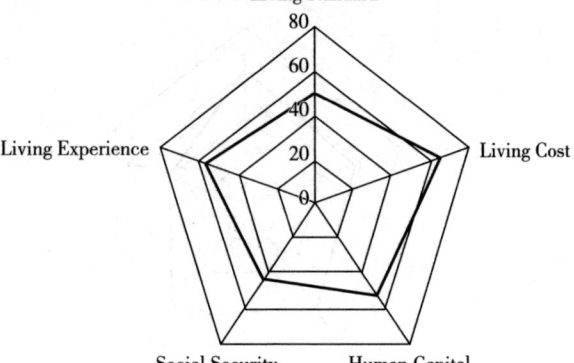

Objective Indexes of Nanchang

Subjective Indexes of Haikou

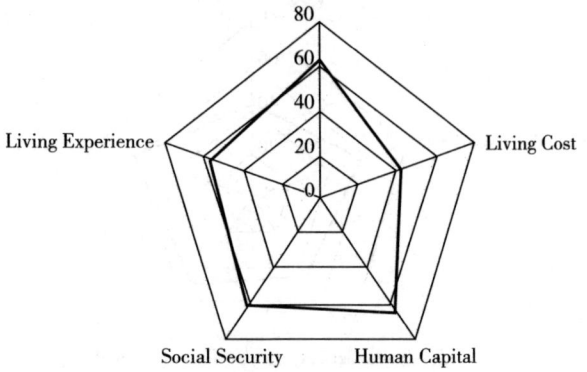

Blue Book of Quality of Life in Cities

Objective Indexes of Haikou

Living Standard

80
60
40
20
0

Living Experience

Living Cost

Social Security

Human Capital

Subjective Indexes of Lanzhou

Living Standard

80
60
40
20
0

Living Experience

Living Cost

Social Security

Human Capital

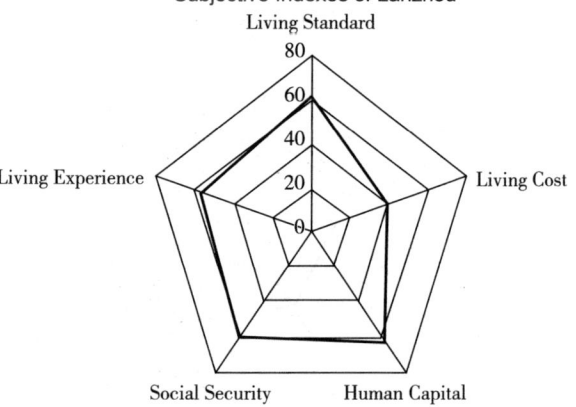

Objective Indexes of Lanzhou

Living Standard

80
60
40
20
0

Living Experience

Living Cost

Social Security

Human Capital

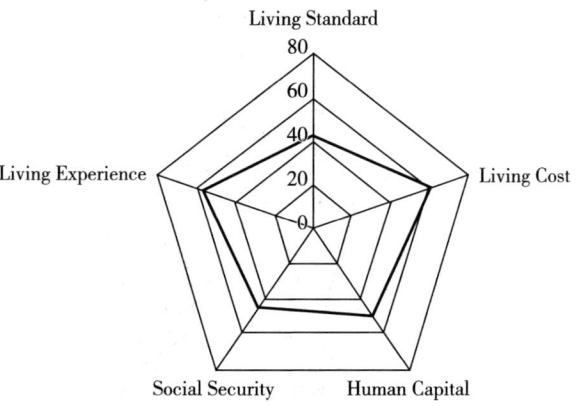

Quality-of-life Subindexes of the 35 Chinese Cities —

Subjective Indexes of Nanning

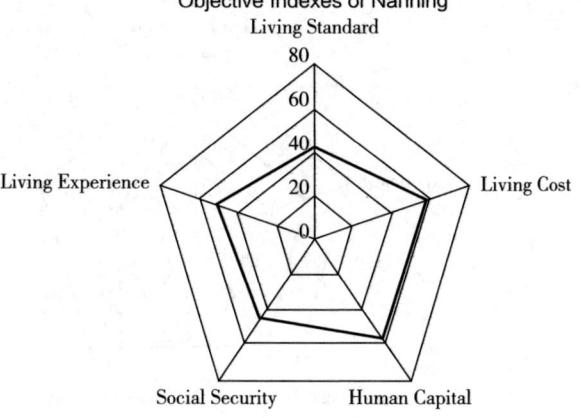

Objective Indexes of Nanning

Subjective Indexes of Fuzhou

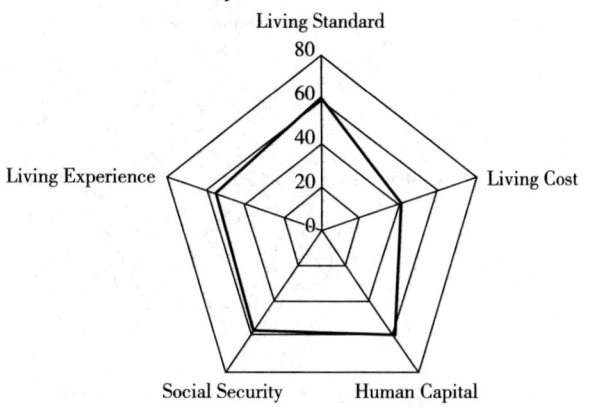

Blue Book of Quality of Life in Cities

Objective Indexes of Fuzhou

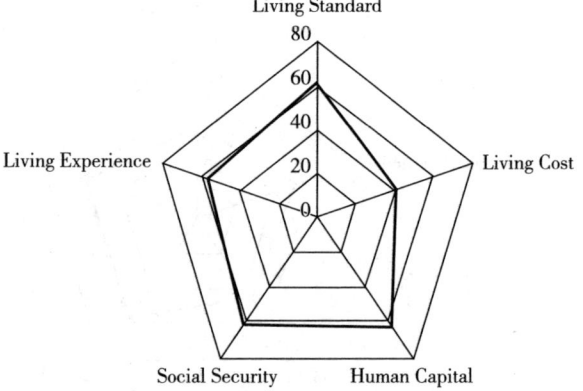

Subjective Indexes of Chongqing

Objective Indexes of Chongqing

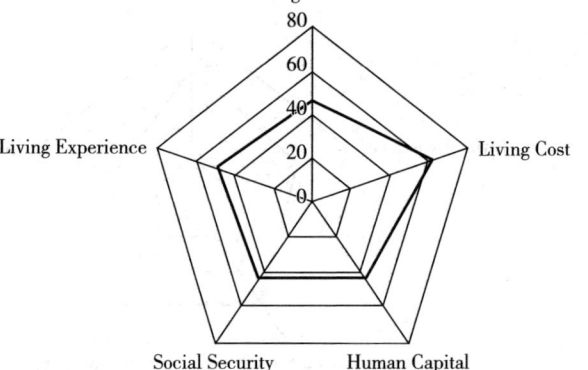

Quality-of-life Subindexes of the 35 Chinese Cities —

Subjective Indexes of Xining

Objective Indexes of Xining

Subjective Indexes of Zhengzhou

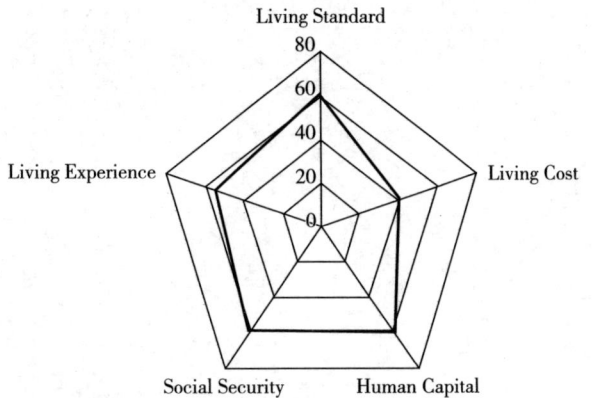

 Blue Book of Quality of Life in Cities

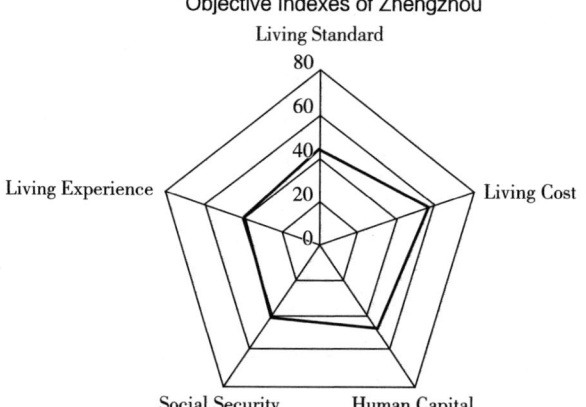

Figure 33   Primary Indicator Radar Charts of QLICC

Special Surveys

B.6

Survey on House Price Expectation

In 2016, we continued with the special survey on house price expectation. [①]
Table 1 lists the house price expectation indexes of the 35 cities.

Table 1   The 2012–2016 House Price Expectation Indexes[*] of the 35 Cities

City	2016			2015		2014		2013		2012	
	Score	ranking	Places Risen	Score	ranking	Score	ranking	Score	Ranking	Score	Ranking
Yinchuan	43.65	1	6	45.24	7	61.54	16	65.93	9	55.21	17
Hohhot	43.12	2	20	43.64	22	57.81	32	61.26	34	56.07	11

[①] The survey question was: "In your opinion, will the house process in your city of residence rise or fall in the future (1 or 2 years)?" ① Surge; ② rise; ③ even; ④ fall; and ⑤ crash. And the values assigned were: ① surge (100); ② rise (75); ③ even (50); ④ fall (25); and ⑤ crash (0).

Blue Book of Quality of Life in Cities

Continued table

City	2016			2015		2014		2013		2012	
	Score	ranking	Places Risen	Score	ranking	Score	ranking	Score	Ranking	Score	Ranking
Jinan	42.90	3	28	41.97	31	61.46	18	65.68	12	50.00	33
Shenyang	42.71	4	16	43.89	20	59.33	26	62.43	30	56.35	10
Kunming	42.62	5	14	43.98	19	60.02	24	65.38	14	55.77	13
Dalian	42.51	6	2	45.18	8	56.83	34	62.13	32	54.91	19
Guiyang	42.41	7	10	44.05	17	61.73	14	62.99	28	60.48	3
Ningbo	42.27	8	-4	45.76	4	56.74	35	62.15	31	50.68	31
Chongqing	42.24	9	3	44.41	12	59.22	27	64.46	19	55.84	12
Chengdu	42.21	10	6	44.24	16	61.80	10	63.06	27	54.53	20
Xining	41.40	11	3	44.31	14	61.05	20	68.33	2	63.89	2
Shijiazhuang	41.27	12	-2	44.62	10	61.49	17	65.19	15	54.13	23
Harbin	41.26	13	-7	45.33	6	58.63	30	60.99	35	50.39	32
Xi'an	41.23	14	9	43.61	23	60.36	22	63.64	24	55.10	18
Haikou	41.12	15	15	42.55	30	61.75	13	61.26	33	64.00	1
Urumqi	40.73	16	12	42.71	28	57.04	33	67.37	3	55.26	15
Changsha	40.28	17	-8	44.97	9	60.16	23	63.39	25	51.90	29
Hefei	40.22	18	-17	46.70	1	64.68	1	66.07	6	53.42	25
Nanning	40.20	19	-4	44.24	15	64.02	2	63.66	23	58.80	6
Qingdao	39.95	20	-7	44.39	13	61.63	15	64.57	17	46.82	35
Nanchang	39.84	21	3	43.45	24	61.13	19	66.73	4	55.28	14
Wuhan	39.84	22	10	41.74	32	61.77	11	65.40	13	54.41	21
Nanjing	39.75	23	-20	45.83	3	61.98	9	65.92	10	54.36	22
Guangzhou	39.57	24	3	43.04	27	62.28	6	68.64	1	58.55	7
Fuzhou	39.53	25	-14	44.44	11	60.61	21	64.45	20	52.75	27
Taiyuan	39.30	26	8	41.03	34	62.22	7	64.53	18	57.18	8
Changchun	39.14	27	-22	45.43	5	59.07	28	63.70	22	51.20	30
Tianjin	38.95	28	-2	43.42	26	59.49	25	63.18	26	53.65	24
Zhengzhou	38.37	29	0	42.67	29	61.77	12	66.60	5	55.24	16
Shenzhen	38.34	30	5	40.15	35	62.92	4	65.96	8	56.55	9
Shanghai	37.97	31	-10	43.66	21	62.53	5	65.97	7	53.35	26

Survey on House Price Expectation

Continued table

City	2016			2015		2014		2013		2012	
	Score	ranking	Places Risen	Score	ranking	Score	ranking	Score	Ranking	Score	Ranking
Hangzhou	37.90	32	-30	46.40	2	58.05	31	62.85	29	47.17	34
Lanzhou	37.12	33	-8	43.45	25	58.85	29	63.98	21	59.94	4
Xiamen	37.04	34	-16	43.98	18	64.02	3	65.14	16	59.59	5
Beijing	35.98	35	-2	41.43	33	62.08	8	65.71	11	52.04	28
Average	40.16			43.86		60.78		64.65		54.99	

* The higher the index, the greater the expectation of house price appreciation; the lower the index, the greater the expectation of house price decline.

According to the survey result, the 2016 weighted average of house price expectation indexes is 40.16 — lower than the 2015 average of 43.86. The fact that the index average has continued to decline for three years indicates that residents generally believe current house prices are too high and will start to drop in the near future. Besides, the indexes of all the 35 cities are below 50, which means that similar to the situation of 2015, residents of all the surveyed cities expect house prices to decline. Figure 1 illustrates the changes of the house price expectation indexes from 2012 to 2016.

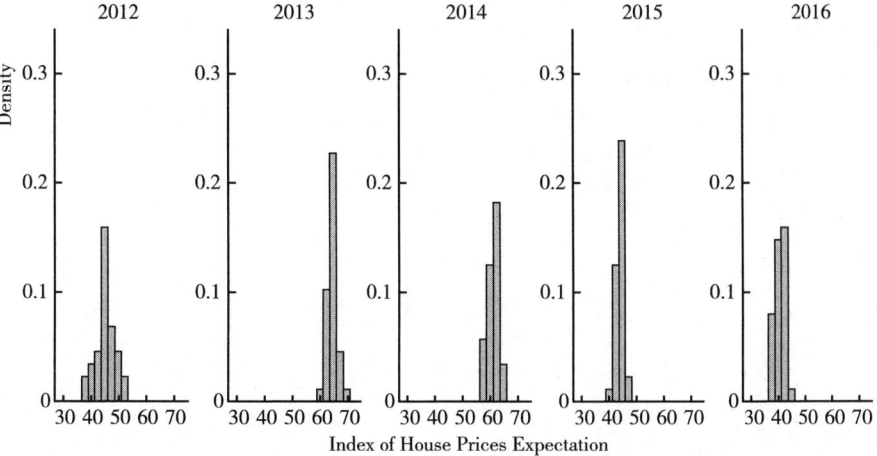

Figure 1   A Histogram of the 2012–2016 House Price Expectation Indexes

Blue Book of Quality of Life in Cities

Cities ranked top 10 in the special survey are: Yinchuan (1), Hohhot (2), Jinan (3), Shenyang (4), Kunming (5), Dalian (6), Guiyang (7), Ningbo (8), Chongqing (9) and Chengdu (10). That is to say, although the residents of these cities expect house prices to fall, they think the decline will be relatively small or the possibility will be weak. Hefei had topped the list for 2014 and 2015 two years, but in 2016 its place is taken by Yinchuan. Among the top 10 cities, the rankings of Jinan (+28), Hohhot (+20), Shenyang (+16) and Kunming (+14) have risen significantly; and only the ranking of Ningbo has somewhat dropped compared to that of the last year. The bottom 10 cities are: Taiyuan (26), Changchun (27), Tianjin (28), Zhengzhou (29), Shenzhen (30), Shanghai (31), Hangzhou (32), Lanzhou (33), Xiamen (34) and Beijing (35). That is to say, the residents of these cities expect house prices to fall drastically or think the possibility is strong. Among the bottom 10 cities, the rankings of Hangzhou (-30), Changchun (-22), Xiamen (-16) and Shanghai (-10) have gone down considerably. In actuality, there is no great difference among the index values of the 35 cities. The highest score is 43.65, while the lowest is 35.98. Therefore, residents of different cities actually have similar expectation of house prices. Figure 2 shows the 2012-2016 house price expectation indexes of the 35 cities.

132

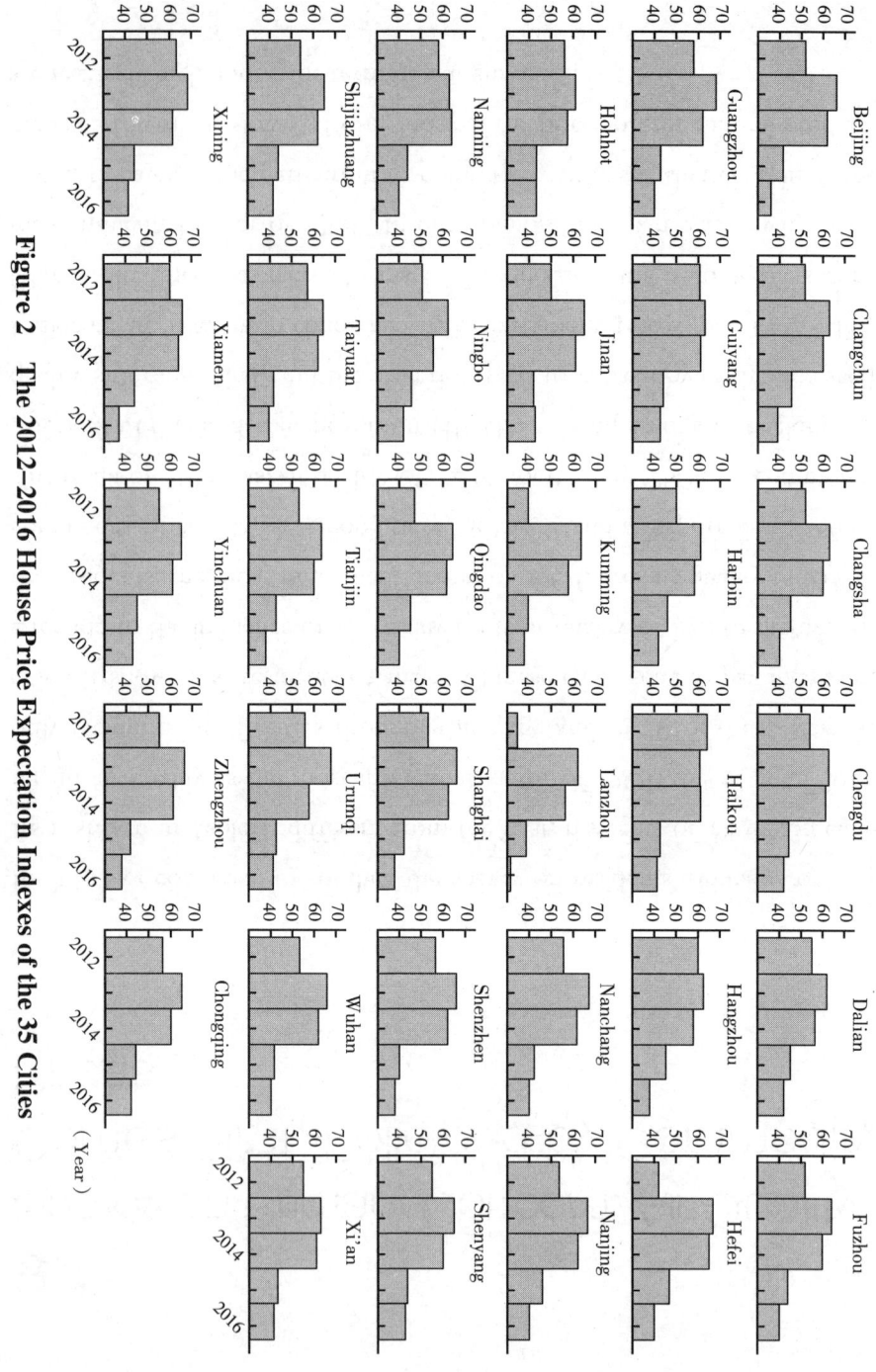

Figure 2 The 2012–2016 House Price Expectation Indexes of the 35 Cities

B.7

Survey on Primary Concern: Air Quality Comes First, Followed by Commodity Prices

In 2016, we continued to conduct the survey on residents' primary concern. As is shown in Table 1, different from the past, residents of all the 35 cities regard air quality as the most influential factor of QOL this year. In 2014, only residents of 17 cities thought this way; and in 2015, there were 32 cities. It shows that residents of major Chinese cities start to pay increasing attention to the influence of air quality on their quality of life. In the eyes of the residents, the most influential factors of QOL are: air quality (46.33%), commodity prices (23.94%), food safety (20.87%) and transportation (8.86%). The result of 2015 was: air quality (39.12%), food safety (28.77%), commodity prices (21.17%) and transportation (10.94%). Comparatively speaking, air quality still ranks first, and the attention paid to it has obviously increased. Residents are now more concerned with commodity prices than food safety. Commodity prices has taken the place of food safety and become the second most influential factor of QOL. In our opinion, the main reason why urban residents pay so much attention to commodity prices is that economic and income growth has slowed down, and that the prices of agricultural products are relatively high during the term of our survey.

134

Survey on Primary Concern: Air Quality Comes First, Followed by Commodity Prices

Table 1   Result of the Survey on Primary Concern

City	Food safety	Air quality	Commodity prices	Transportation
Beijing	17.91%	52.82%	21.96%	7.32%
Nanning	20.54%	52.16%	20.54%	6.76%
Hefei	18.37%	52.04%	21.77%	7.82%
Yinchuan	19.89%	51.38%	22.10%	6.63%
Zhengzhou	20.93%	51.16%	20.93%	6.98%
Ningbo	20.70%	50.12%	20.70%	8.48%
Jinan	19.24%	49.53%	22.40%	8.83%
Xi'an	22.56%	49.37%	18.55%	9.52%
Changsha	18.16%	48.59%	26.85%	6.39%
Urumqi	17.74%	48.39%	22.04%	11.83%
Shijiazhuang	20.53%	47.02%	23.82%	8.62%
Tianjin	19.82%	47.02%	23.68%	9.47%
Shanghai	19.76%	46.94%	23.74%	9.56%
Changchun	24.74%	46.84%	20.79%	7.63%
Qingdao	22.55%	46.74%	21.20%	9.51%
Chengdu	22.04%	46.63%	20.95%	10.38%
Fuzhou	16.50%	46.55%	29.31%	7.64%
Dalian	22.14%	46.37%	23.47%	8.02%
Nanjing	21.01%	45.57%	24.56%	8.86%
Haikou	18.86%	45.18%	25.88%	10.09%
Guangzhou	21.22%	45.14%	25.90%	7.73%
Kunming	20.83%	45.14%	24.65%	9.38%
Chongqing	21.89%	44.25%	24.72%	9.15%
Shenzhen	22.00%	44.20%	25.66%	8.15%
Hohhot	17.98%	43.82%	28.09%	10.11%
Harbin	18.81%	43.15%	27.40%	10.63%
Wuhan	24.18%	43.13%	23.63%	9.07%
Xining	27.96%	43.01%	19.35%	9.68%
Shenyang	27.05%	42.55%	22.80%	7.60%
Nanchang	22.30%	42.30%	25.25%	10.16%
Guiyang	18.41%	41.79%	27.86%	11.94%
Lanzhou	21.43%	41.33%	28.06%	9.18%

Blue Book of Quality of Life in Cities

Continued table

City	Food safety	Air quality	Commodity prices	Transportation
Xiamen	23.04%	38.74%	26.70%	11.52%
Taiyuan	21.13%	38.14%	28.35%	12.37%
Hangzhou	24.87%	37.57%	28.31%	9.26%
Average*	20.87%	46.33%	23.94%	8.86%

* The average was obtained by dividing the number of interviews choosing a certain factor by the total number of interviewees.

Residents in different regions have different understanding of the second most influential factor. People in Nanning, Zhengzhou and Ningbo think food safety and commodity prices are of same importance; while residents in Xi'an, Changchun, Qingdao, Chengdu, Wuhan, Shenyang and Xining regard food safety as the second most influential factor. And dwellers in the rest25 cities choose commodity prices instead.

Further analysis reveals that interviewees of different gender, education background, employment status or age have different concerns about air quality, food safety, commodity prices and transportation (See Table 2 and Table 3).

Table 2 Different Concerns of Residents of Different Gender, Education Background or Employment Status

Influential factor	Gender		Education		Employment	
	Male	Female	Junior college or above	Below junior college	Employed	Unemployed
Food safety	20.42%	21.29%	20.92%	20.68%	21.65%	19.67%
Air quality	46.03%	46.62%	47.65%	41.39%	46.47%	46.12%
Commodity prices	24.14%	23.75%	22.48%	29.44%	23.31%	24.91%
Transportation	9.41%	8.34%v	8.95%	8.49%	8.57%	9.30%
总计	100.00%	100.00%	100.00%	100.00%	100.00%	100.00%

Survey on Primary Concern: Air Quality Comes First, Followed by Commodity Prices

According to Table 2, residents are most concerned with air quality and commodity prices, regardless of their gender, education or employment status. Comparatively speaking, males pay more attention to commodity prices and transportation than females, while females are more concerned with food safety and air quality than males. Better-educated interviewees pay more attention to air quality, while less-educated interviewees are more concerned with commodity prices. But education has no influence on the concern of food safety and transportation. Employed residents seem to pay more attention to air quality and food safety, while unemployed residents are more concerned with commodity prices and transportation.

Table 3　Different Concerns of Different Age Groups over the Four Factors

Age	20-30	31-40	41-50	51-60	Above 60
Food safety	21.54%	19.80%	19.49%	24.39%	24.42%
Air quality	44.53%	50.29%	47.17%	39.51%	36.82%
Commodity prices	23.12%	23.14%	26.14%	29.11%	27.91%
Transportation	10.81%	6.78%	7.19%	6.99%	10.85%
Total	100.00%	100.00%	100.00%	100.00%	100.00%

Table 3 lists the different concerns of different age groups over the four factors. Air quality and commodity prices are the primary concerns of all age groups. People over 50 are the most concerned with food safety, followed by the age group of 20-30 and 31-50. The age group of 31-40 pays most attention to air quality, followed by the age group of 41-50, 20-30, 51-60 and above 60. The age group of 51-60 has the strongest interest in commodity prices, followed by the age group of above 60, 41-50 and 20-40. As for transportation, to our surprise, the age group of above 60 and 20-30 are the most concerned, followed by the age group of 41-50, 51-60 and 31-40.

B.8
Survey on Employment Satisfaction

A job is what a resident can make a living with and a basic guarantee of one's income. During the "New Normal" stage when economic growth slows down, the job market of China is faced with increasing pressure. And the expectation of job prospects becomes the most influential factor of residents' quality of life. Therefore, a special survey on employment satisfaction is newly added. The survey question was: Are you optimistic about your job prospects (in your city of residence) in the coming 2 or 3 years? And the answers given were: ① very optimistic; ② optimistic; ③ average; ④ pessimistic; and ⑤ very pessimistic. The survey result is shown in Table 1.

Table 1 The 2016 Employment Satisfaction Indexes of the 35 Cities

City	Employment satisfaction	Ranking	City	Employment satisfaction	Ranking
Taiyuan	61.47	1	Harbin	57.77	12
Dalian	59.49	2	Chengdu	57.65	13
Jinan	58.75	3	Shenzhen	57.64	14
Nanning	58.65	4	Nanjing	57.59	15
Chongqing	58.54	5	Kunming	57.55	16
Hangzhou	58.33	6	Beijing	57.35	17
Hefei	58.16	7	Qingdao	57.34	18
Yinchuan	58.15	8	Shanghai	57.28	19
Tianjin	57.89	9	Shijiazhuang	57.24	20
Hohhot	57.87	10	Shenyang	57.22	21
Ningbo	57.86	11	Haikou	57.07	22

Survey on Employment Satisfaction

Continued table

City	Employment satisfaction	Ranking	City	Employment satisfaction	Ranking
Changchun	56.91	23	Nanchang	55.98	30
Zhengzhou	56.72	24	Fuzhou	55.97	31
Guangzhou	56.65	25	Guiyang	55.85	32
Urumqi	56.59	26	Xi'an	55.08	33
Xiamen	56.28	27	Lanzhou	54.97	34
Wuhan	56.25	28	Xining	54.30	35
Changsha	56.20	29	Average	57.41	

As is revealed by the survey result, although the economic growth has slowed down over the past two years, the index average of employment satisfaction is still 57.41, near the critical point between the satisfaction and the dissatisfaction intervals. That is to say, the residents are optimistic about their job prospects in the coming 2 or 3 years. Regionally speaking, the residents of Taiyuan are the most optimistic, with a satisfaction index of 61.47. And the residents of Xining are the most pessimistic, although its satisfaction index is 54.30 – still above the satisfaction level.

Actual economic data may explain the reason for the optimism. According to the *Statistical Communiqué of the People's Republic of China on the 2015 National Economic and Social Development*, at the end of 2015, the employed population in China reached 774.51 million, of which 404.1 million were employed in urban areas. 13.12 million urban residents were newly employed around the year. And the year-end registered urban unemployment rate was 4.05%. There were 277.47 million off-farm workers in total– a 1.3% growth compared to that of last year. Among them, 168.84 million (a growth of 0.4%) worked in other places, while 108.63 million (a growth of 2.7%) worked in the local areas.

 Blue Book of Quality of Life in Cities

However, the registered unemployment rate released by NBS was somehow widely doubted both at home and abroad, and was thought of as irrelevant to the genuine unemployment situation. In this connection, a national labor force survey covering all the prefecture-level cities had its trial run in July 2015 and was formally conducted in January 2016. In February 2016, Premier Li Keqiang pointed out on the first executive meeting of the State Council after the Spring Festival that according to the survey, the national unemployment rate was 4.99% in January 2016. Compared to the rate of economic growth, the employment situation was relatively stable.

Further analysis on the survey reveals that residents of different gender, age, education background and employment status think quite differently about their job prospects (See Table 2).

Table 2　Employment Expectation of Residents of Different Gender, Age, Education Background and Employment Status

Indicator		Very pessimistic	Pessimistic	Average	Optimistic	Very optimistic
Gender	Male	1.43%	22.58%	23.61%	45.94%	6.43%
	Female	1.06%	25.61%	24.12%	44.55%	4.66%
Age	20-30	1.24%	28.10%	19.18%	45.18%	6.31%
	31-40	1.07%	17.34%	26.39%	49.71%	5.50%
	41-50	1.22%	24.11%	30.80%	40.57%	3.30%
	51-60	1.79%	30.24%	29.59%	33.98%	4.39%
	Above 60	3.10%	18.99%	32.56%	38.37%	6.98%
Education	Junior college or above	1.04%	24.08%	21.62%	47.29%	5.97%
	Below junior college	1.98%	24.37%	32.33%	37.46%	3.86%
Employment	Employed	1.17%	20.88%	24.25%	47.95%	5.75%
	Unemployed	1.35%	29.12%	23.29%	41.05%	5.19%

Survey on Employment Satisfaction

As is shown by the above table, males are more optimistic about their job prospects than females. To be specific: 52.37% of the male interviewees are either optimistic or very optimistic about the future, while merely 49.21% of the female interviewees think this way; and only 24.01% of the male residents are pessimistic or very pessimistic about their job prospects, while 26.67% of the female residents have such feelings. Since males are more competitive than females in the real job market, the survey findings are generally consistent with the current social situation.

As far as age is concerned, the age group of 31-40 is the most optimistic: 55.21% of them are either optimistic or very optimistic about the future, while only 18.41% of them are pessimistic or very pessimistic. The age group of 20-30 comes second: 51.49% of them are optimistic or very optimistic, while 29.34% of them are pessimistic or very pessimistic. The age group of above 60 comes third: 45.35 of them are optimistic or very optimistic, while 22.09% of them are pessimistic or very pessimistic. The age group of 41-50 comes fourth: 43.87% of them are optimistic or very optimistic, while 25.33% of them are pessimistic or very pessimistic. And the age group of 51-60 comes last: only 38.37% of them are optimistic or very optimistic, while up to 32.03% of them are pessimistic or very pessimistic. It should be noted that, compared to the attitude of people above 60, significant polarization of opinions appears within the age group of 20-30—some are optimistic about their job prospects, while many others are quite pessimistic.

From the perspective of education background, residents with college or university diplomas have more human capital advantages than the ones without it, and thus are more optimistic about future employment. To be specific: among the residents with diplomas, 53.26% are either optimistic or very optimistic the future, and 25.12% are pessimistic or very pessimistic;

141

Blue Book of Quality of Life in Cities

while among the residents without a diploma, only 41.32% are optimistic or very optimistic, and 26.35% are pessimistic or very pessimistic.

From the perspective of employment status, employed residents are generally more optimistic about their job prospects than the unemployed ones, considering that unemployment is a result of economic slowdown and industrial restructuring, and that employment itself is a prove of strong market competitiveness. To be specific: among the employed residents, 53.70% are either optimistic or very optimistic, and 22.05% are pessimistic or very pessimistic; while among the unemployed residents, 46.24% are optimistic or very optimistic, and up to 30.47% are pessimistic or very pessimistic.

As is shown by the survey result and related data released by NBS, unlike the situation of the end of 2015 and the first quarter of 2016, residents' employment expectation is improving at present and becomes relatively optimistic. In reality however, according to researches made by the Employment Research Center of Renmin University of China and other institutions, the China Employment Market Index (CIER index) has kept declining since the first quarter of 2015. Viewed by industries, due to the structural problems in the Chinese economy, the CIER indexes of different industries may differ greatly. The CIER of the Internet/E-commerce, funds/ securities, transportation and intermediary service industries are comparatively high; while those of the traditional service industries, the heavy industry and the mining industry (such as accounting, aviation/aerospace, energy/ mineral, electrical/electricity/water industries and cross-domain management) are relatively low. Generally speaking, since the Chinese economy is going through a transition period, the job market will also be greatly affected. Under the circumstance of structure adjustment and industrial overcapacity cutting,

Survey on Employment Satisfaction

job opportunities in the coal, steel, oil and other traditional industries have significantly decreased. Meanwhile, despite the rapid development of the "Internet+" and other new industries, they are of lessemploymentcapacity than the traditional industries. Therefore, we are currently still faced with great employment pressure. In this regard, we believe that the Central Government should on one hand take measures and release more supporting policies such as retraining programs, and on the other hand push forward the transformation of industrial structure steadily. The key to future industrial structure adjustment and development lies in the transformation and upgrading of the manufacturing industry as well as the coordinated development of producer service, finance, information and other modern service industries.

As is indicated by the 2016 quality of urban life survey, as China enters the "New Normal" and its economic development continues to slow down, challenges and risks still exist during the course of economic and social development. Compared to that of last year, the objective indexes have declined slightly, while the subjective indexes have generally remained stable. At the same time however, we are still faced with severe challenges, such as high living costs, a fast pace of life, unstable house prices and worrying job prospects. Therefore, in the process of future economic and social development and transformation, the Central Government and the local governments should continue to work on life-related systems, stabilize economic growth and further improve residents' quality of life.

Conclusions

B.9
Conclusions and Enlightenments

9.1 Contrasts Exist between Subjective and Objective Indexes; and the Quality of Life is Highly Regional

Table 1 lists the 5 subindexes of the subjective and the objective indexes, along with their changes from 2012 to 2016.

Table 1   The 2012–2016 Subjective and Objective Subindexes

	Index	2016	2015	2014	2013	2012
Subjective satisfaction index	Satisfaction index of living standard	60.44	60.07	54.32	52.51	51.28
	Satisfaction index of living cost	39.74	38.94	31.81	31.22	28.91
	Satisfaction index of human capital	62.20	61.73	58.98	58.89	59.42
	Satisfaction index of social security	60.66	60.47	57.87	56.64	59.19
	Satisfaction index of living experience	56.05	55.66	54.88	55.07	55.63

144

Conclusions and Enlightenments

Continued table

	Index	2016	2015	2014	2013	2012
	Objective index of living standard	50.07	59.83	68.06	63.39	56.28
	Objective index of living cost	58.74	54.58	53.84	58.67	56.10
Objective index	Objective index of human capital	56.98	57.34	57.33	57.78	57.66
	Objective index of social security	50.43	51.26	54.66	55.26	50.85
	Objective index of living experience	57.54	56.17	55.57	53.67	51.89

As is shown in Table 1, the subjective indexes of QOL are in obvious contrast with the objective indexes. Since 2012, and especially since 2013, the subjective indexes have generally remained stable and slightly improved. As for the objective indexes however, the living standard index had climbed up for three years and then declined drastically in the past two years. This year, the objective indexes of human capital and social security have dropped, while the objective indexes of living cost and living experience have somewhat improved. Performance of the indexes are consistent with the slowdown of economic growth in the past two years. Despite all this, the subjective index of living standard has still changed for the better. Last year, it was higher than the corresponding objective index for the first time. And this year, its score is 10.37 higher.

From 2012 to 2016, the subjective and the objective indexes, as well as their subindexes, have exhibited some regional characteristics. There has been no significant regional difference in the subjective indexes. The satisfaction indexes of the western region have improved. In the past, the indexes were high in the east and low in the west. Now it is just the opposite. As for the objective indexes, the indexes of all the three regions have declined. The index of the eastern region is higher than that of the central and the western regions. And the central and the western regions are of similar scores (See Table 2).

Blue Book of Quality of Life in Cities

Table 2 Subjective and Objective Indexes by Region

Index	Region	2016	2015	2014	2013	2012
Subjective satisfaction index	Eastern	55.74	55.71	51.90	51.44	51.44
	Central	55.75	55.50	51.14	50.65	50.66
	Western	55.92	54.76	51.06	50.39	50.24
Objective index	Eastern	56.43	56.93	59.60	59.59	57.46
	Central	52.84	53.80	54.88	55.57	51.90
	Western	53.71	54.48	55.88	55.27	52.26

Further observation of the five subjective subindexes reveals that as is shown in Table 3, in 2016, the living standard satisfaction indexes of the eastern and the central regions have declined slightly compared to that of last year, while the index of the western region has somewhat improved. As a result, the indexes of all the three regions are now of similar scores. The living cost satisfaction indexes of the eastern and the central regions have remained roughly unchanged, while that of the western region has risen and overtaken the indexes of the other two regions. The human capital satisfaction indexes of the central and western regions have all increased slightly, while the index of the eastern region has somewhat declined. The index of the central region in 2016 is the highest, followed by that of the eastern. The satisfaction indexes of social security have generally stayed the same. And the living experience satisfaction indexes of the three regions have all gone up. The index of the eastern region is the highest. And that of the central comes second.

Table 3 Subjective Subindexes by Region

Index	Region	2016	2015	2014	2013	2012
Satisfaction index of living standard	Eastern	60.39	60.56	54.55	53.28	51.91
	Central	60.23	60.49	53.21	51.44	51.00
	Western	60.07	59.37	53.38	52.87	50.57

Conclusions and Enlightenments —

Continued table

Index	Region	2016	2015	2014	2013	2012
Satisfaction index of living cost	Eastern	39.49	39.48	31.62	30.98	28.54
	Central	39.95	40.16	32.98	33.49	30.96
	Western	40.89	37.80	31.28	30.43	27.95
Satisfaction index of human capital	Eastern	62.05	62.33	59.60	59.58	60.42
	Central	62.24	61.15	58.08	58.28	58.51
	Western	61.78	60.81	58.51	58.53	58.62
Satisfaction index of social security	Eastern	60.59	60.65	58.83	57.86	60.12
	Central	60.25	60.09	56.87	55.54	57.80
	Western	60.86	60.13	56.70	55.60	58.84
Satisfaction index of living experience	Eastern	56.18	55.54	54.90	55.48	56.19
	Central	56.09	55.63	54.59	54.51	55.04
	Western	55.99	55.68	55.44	54.51	55.23

The 5 objective subindexes also exhibit obvious regional characteristics. As is shown in Table 4, the living standard objective index of the eastern region is the highest, followed by that of the central region and then the western region. Compared to that of last year, the indexes of all the three regions have declined drastically. Among them, the index of the central region has experienced the most significant drop, while the index of the western region has also come down considerably. The living cost objective indexes of the three regions have all improved, but the index of the western region is still higher than that of the eastern. The human capital objective indexes of the three regions are of similar scores and have only changed slightly compared to those of last year. The objective indexes of social security exhibit obvious regional characteristics: the index of the eastern region is the highest, followed by that of the western and then the central regions. Compared to that of last year, the indexes of the three

 Blue Book of Quality of Life in Cities

regions have all improved slightly. The living experience objective indexes of the three regions have remained stable, with the eastern region being the highest, followed by that of the western and then the central regions.

Table 4　Objective Subindexes by Region

Index	Region	2016	2015	2014	2013	2012
Objective index of living standard	Eastern	54.82	62.31	71.53	69.00	62.99
	Central	46.37	56.12	62.77	59.39	52.03
	Western	45.87	54.74	61.96	58.54	49.60
Objective index of living cost	Eastern	54.06	50.85	50.37	54.96	52.12
	Central	60.21	56.98	56.42	61.47	57.41
	Western	64.48	61.72	61.18	65.46	60.94
Objective index of human capital	Eastern	57.42	57.25	57.32	57.18	58.72
	Central	57.64	57.57	57.02	58.39	56.18
	Western	55.85	55.62	55.30	55.19	57.22
Objective index of social security	Eastern	55.95	55.47	60.16	60.89	57.08
	Central	45.04	44.80	45.67	46.86	45.72
	Western	46.30	45.92	47.37	46.95	45.50
Objective index of living experience	Eastern	59.88	58.77	58.61	55.95	56.37
	Central	54.93	53.55	52.52	51.74	48.16
	Western	56.05	54.38	53.58	50.20	48.07

9.2　House Price Expectations Are against the Actual Trends; and the Housing Regulation Systems Need to Be Improved

According to the survey result, the first-tier cities have generally ranked low in the list of house price expectation. Beijing and Shenzhen have remained in the

148

Conclusions and Enlightenments

bottom 10 list for two years, while Shanghai and Guangzhou have stayed among the bottom 15during the same period. It shows that in the eyes of urban residents, house prices in the first-tier cities are already too high and are very likely to fall in the coming future. Among the second-tier cities, Ningbo and Dalian have ranked top 10 in the past two years, while Zhengzhou has stayed among the bottom 10. And among the third-tier cities, Yinchuan has been in the top 10 list for two years, while Taiyuan has remained in the bottom 10 list. According to economic theories, price expectation is an important influential factor of price. Once consumers and investors start to have a strong inflation expectation, their consumption and investment behaviors will change accordingly, which will in turn speed up the inflation or cause the inflation to rise in a spiral; and vice versa. Nevertheless, it should be noted that China's real estate and capital markets are highly regulated by government policies. Since people cannot have accurate expectation of government policies, the impact of policies may lead to systematic bias and cause house prices to deviate from people's expectation.

For example, the survey conducted in the beginning of 2015 indicated that residents of all the 35 cities generally believed that house prices would fall. However, according to the monitoring data of E-house China R&D Institute, both the turnover and the prices of real estate in the 35 cities have continued to rise since the second half of 2015. Housing inventory has been decreasing for seven months on a month-on-month basis and for nine months on a year-on-year basis. According to the house price indexes of 70 major cities released by NBS in May 2016, the average house prices in these cities had continued to rise12months in a row on a month-on-month basis. Regionally speaking, house prices in different areas differed greatly last year. In the first-tier and the second-tier cities, the house prices rose robustly; while in the third-tier and the fourth-tier cities, housing inventory was still high, and the prices declined.

149

 Blue Book of Quality of Life in Cities

In our opinion, the robust rise of house prices was caused by the following factors: Firstly, real estate investment is one of the most important pillars of China's economic development. In order to increase investments and cut down inventory in the real estate industry, the Central Government issued a series of preferential credit policies to stimulate demands. Meanwhile, the local governments also implemented a series of easing policies, such as the adjustments of the Public Housing Fund policies, financial subsidies and tax reliefs, to increase residents' demand for houses, and especially housing improvements. Secondly, to deal with the economic slow down, the People's Bank of China has carried out an easy money policy in the past. As a result, a large number of funds flowed into the capital market during the economic down turn. Since June 2015 however, the Chinese stock market had fallen sharply, resulting in the outflow of huge credit funds from the stock market into the real estate market. Thirdly, the regional development in China is quite unbalanced. Compared to that of the second-tier or the third-tier cities, migrant workers are inevitably attracted by the employment and development opportunities, the level of public services (especially education and health care) and the convenience of infrastructure in the first-tier cities. In addition, due to the large overall inventory and the excessive house price rises happened earlier in the second-tier, the third-tier or even the fourth-tier cities, the prices of the first-tier cities rose much higher in this round than that of the second-tier or the third-tier cities.

Although house prices have continued to rise for several months, the survey result indicates that residents of the 35 major cities still expect house prices to drop in the coming one or two years. It shows that under the circumstance of economic and income growth slowdown, in the eyes of the general public, house price rises driven by the policy dividend are already beyond their reach. Therefore, it is unlikely for house prices to rise continuously at the

150

Conclusions and Enlightenments

current rate. In this regard, we believe that the nature of houses is to meet the demand for housing; and that as urbanization progresses, the government should improve the real estate regulation systems and implement consistent policies, in order to prevent drastic house price fluctuations and promote the healthy development of the real estate market.

9.3   Financial Support for Comprehensive Ecological Improvement should Be Increased to Ensure the Environmental Quality of Residents' Life

Table 5 lists the 2016 survey result of air quality satisfaction in the 35 cities.

Table 5   Air Quality[*] of the 35 Cities

City	Attention rate of air quality	PM 2.5 density	Ranking of attention rate	Ranking of PM 2.5 density	Difference in ranking
Nanning	52.16%	49.00	2	26	-24
Ningbo	50.12%	46.00	6	29	-23
Yinchuan	51.38%	53.00	4	22	-18
Fuzhou	46.55%	34.00	17	33	-16
Haikou	45.18%	23.00	20	35	-15
Shanghai	46.94%	52.00	13	24	-11
Shenzhen	44.20%	34.00	24	34	-10
Kunming	45.14%	35.00	22	32	-10
Urumqi	48.39%	61.00	10	19	-9
Guangzhou	45.14%	49.00	21	27	-6
Qingdao	46.74%	58.00	15	21	-6
Hohhot	43.82%	46.00	25	30	-5
Dalian	46.37%	53.00	18	23	-5
Beijing	52.82%	86.00	1	4	-3
Hefei	52.04%	83.00	3	5	-2
Changchun	46.84%	68.00	14	15	-1
Changsha	48.59%	74.00	9	10	-1

 Blue Book of Quality of Life in Cities

Continued table

City	Attention rate of air quality	PM 2.5 density	Ranking of attention rate	Ranking of PM 2.5 density	Difference in ranking
Xi'an	49.37%	77.00	8	8	0
Xiamen	38.74%	37.00	33	31	2
Guiyang	41.79%	48.00	31	28	3
Zhengzhou	51.16%	88.00	5	2	3
Jinan	49.53%	87.00	7	3	4
Nanchang	42.30%	52.00	30	25	5
Tianjin	47.02%	83.00	12	6	6
Chongqing	44.25%	65.00	23	16	7
Chengdu	46.63%	77.00	16	9	7
Nanjing	45.57%	74.00	19	11	8
Xining	43.01%	63.00	28	18	10
Shijiazhuang	47.02%	124.00	11	1	10
Lanzhou	41.33%	61.00	32	20	12
Harbin	43.15%	72.00	26	13	13
Shenyang	42.55%	74.00	29	12	17
Hangzhou	37.57%	65.00	35	17	18
Taiyuan	38.14%	72.00	34	14	20
Wuhan	43.13%	82.00	27	7	20

* The rankings are arranged in sequence. The higher the average PM 2.5 density, the lower the air quality.
Data source: *China Statistical Yearbook.*

When comparing the attention rates and the actual air quality of the surveyed cities, it can be found that PM 2.5 density is not in proportion to the amount of attention paid to it. In other words, air quality is not always in keeping with the attention rate. According to the relationship between air quality and the attention paid, the surveyed cities can be divided into three categories.

The first includes cities of good or excellent air quality, but the residents are still highly concerned about it. In other words, the ranking of the attention

Conclusions and Enlightenments —

rate is more than 5 places higher than that of the PM 2.5 density. In this category, there are 11 cities such as Nanning, Ningbo and Yinchuan, including 8 eastern cities and 3 western cities. It shows that as income increases, people are more and more concerned about environment quality. After the basic needs for food and clothing are met, environmental safety has become a focus of people's attention.

The second includes cities of poor or really bad air quality, but the residents pay comparatively little attention to it. In other words, the ranking of the attention rate is more than 5 places lower than that of PM 2.5 density. In this category, there are 12 cities such as Taiyuan, Shenyang and Shijiazhuang, including 4 eastern cities, 4 central cities and 4 western cities. The main reason for this is that the industrial structure in these areas is mainly made up of traditional industries. Except for a small number of cities such as Hangzhou, the environment quality of these areas has been poor all the time. Therefore, local residents do not require much of the environment quality.

The third includes cities whose rankings of air quality are inversely proportional to that of the degrees of concern. In other words, residents in cities of good air quality tend to pay little attention to environment quality, while dwellers in cities of poor air quality are highly concerned about it. And the ranking of the attention rate is (less than) 5 places higher or lower than that of PM 2.5 density. In this category, there are 12 cities such as Hohhot and Nanchang, including 4 eastern cities, 6 central cities and 2 western cities. There are cities of high environment quality and low concern, such as Hohhot, Dalian, Xiamen and Guiyang. And there are also cities of poor environment quality and high concern, such as Beijing, Hefei, Jinan and Zhengzhou. Therefore, the point is never the

153

 Blue Book of Quality of Life in Cities

amount of attention paid to environmental quality, because high concern may result from poor air quality, and low concern may come from good environmentalbackground. ①

In summary, since the reform and opening-up, China has made remarkable achievements in the economic development. On the other hand however, the attendant problem of environment pollution has not only restricted the development of the national economy, but also greatly affected people's lives. The Central Government has taken a series of legislative measures in this regard, demonstrating its firm determination to fight against pollution. Nevertheless, residents' increasing concern over air quality and the existing problems in environment protection indicate that there is still a long way to go for China's ecological improvement. According to foreign experiences, in the process of economic development, only when environmental investment accounts for 1.5% of GDP can environment deterioration be prevented; and only when it reaches 2%-3% can ecological improvement be genuinely achieved. During the "12th Five-year Plan", China's environmentalinvestmentwill account for approximately 1.5% of its GDP. But as early as 1980s, the proportions of environmental investment had already exceeded 2% in Germany and Britain, and had been up to 3.4% in Japan. Therefore, besides the strict implementation of different policies and regulations, environmental investment should also be increased in the future, so as to not only improve environment quality, but also further promote economic growth.

---

① Environmental background refers to the baseline content of chemical elements or chemical substances contained in various environmental elements in an uncontaminated natural environment.

9.4 Supervision Systems should Be Improved, Unified and Become Authoritative, in Order to Promote Residents' Satisfaction over Food Safety

According to the survey results of 2014 and 2015, air quality and food safety were the top 2 most influential factors of residents' quality of life. In the 2016 survey however, residents in only 10 out of the surveyed 35 cities choose food safety as the second most influential factor. The survey result is also corroborated by other social surveys. In the "2015 China Comprehensive Xiaokang Index" survey jointly conducted by *Xiaokang* magazine and the Media Survey Lab of Tsinghua University, food safety has topped the list of the "Top 10 Topics in Focus" four years in a row, with a public attention rate of 44.8%. But it should also be noted that residents' satisfaction over food safety is "one level higher" than that of the past. [1]

Viewed by the development history of food safety in different countries, China is currently going through a transition period between the second and the third stages. In other words, the supervision over the extensive development of food industrialization and agricultural industrialization continues to improve, but the stage of standardization and legislation is yet to come. During the third stage, the usage of various chemicals such as food additives and coloring should be strictly limited in food production. Meanwhile, relative quality systems and standards should be further improved, as well as laws and regulations. The revised *Food Safety Law* was passed by a vote of 160 in favor, 1 against and 3 abstentions on the 14th session of the 12th NPC Standing Committee held on April 24, 2015, and came into effect

---

[1] Tencent Finance: "Top 10 Topics in Focus in 2015: Food Safety is Still a Hot Topic", http://finance.qq.com/a/20151215/028601.htm.

Blue Book of Quality of Life in Cities

on October 1, 2015. In view of the defects of the original *Food Safety Law*, the revised *Food Safety Law* (the "new law") specified in the general provisions that food safety management should be carried out on the basic principles of "prevention first, risk management, in-process control and collaborative governance" under strict and scientific regulation systems.

In order to ensure strict supervision, the new law was endowed with 8 features: One was to set up a unified and authoritative regulator. Now China Food and Drug Administration is fully in charge of food safety supervision. Two was to establish strict in-process supervision systems, specifying the entire industry chain of food production and new business formats such as online food transactions. Three was to highlight prevention first and risk management. Four was to establish stringent standards and strengthen the link between standard-making and implementation. Five was to set up a formula registration system for FSMP (food for special medical purpose) and formula milk powder for infant or young children. Six was to tighten the management of pesticides. Seven was to improve risk assessment and management. And eight was to establish stringent legal liability systems and increase the civil or the criminal penalties for food safety offenses.

Six improvements were made in the new law to "correct the disorder with heavy punishments". The first was to aggravate criminal liability. The second was to add the penalty of administrative detention. Under the new law, persons who commit severe offenses, such as using nonfood raw materials in food production, selling livestock and poultry dead of diseases or using of toxic or highly toxic pesticides illegally, are now subject to administrative detention. The third was to greatly increase the amount of fines. For example, according the previous *Food Safety Law*, a fine of 10 times the value of the commodity could be charged for severe offenses such as producing or selling

156

Conclusions and Enlightenments

food containing non-food drugs or nonconforming formula milk powder for infants or young children; whereas according to the new law, the fine can be up to 30 times the value of the commodity. The fourth was to increase the penalties for repeated offenses. Under the new law, if a person commits 3 offenses in one year and is subject to administrative penalties such as fines or warnings, the production or operation should be stopped, or even the business license should be revoked. The fifth was to add the penalty for providing places for the offenses. In order to improve source and in-process supervision, the new law specifies that if a person knows about the illegal activities such as unlicensed production/operation or the use of nonfood materials, and still provides places for its production or operation, a fine of RMB 100, 000 can be imposed. And the sixth was to aggravate civil liability.

Generally speaking, both the supervision regulations of China and their implementation have been improved. These policies and measures have helped to enhance the standard of food safety. As was pointed out in the report released by China Food and Drug Administration in February 2016, among the 172, 310 batches of food samples inspected nationwide in 2015, 5541 batches were nonconforming. The qualified rate was 96.8% — 2.1 percent points higher than that of 2014.Overall, the current situation of food safety remains stable and keeps improving. In June 2016, the Ministry of Agriculture leased the result of the agricultural product inspection conducted from January to May 2016. Inspection data show that the qualified rate of inspected samples continues to improve and reaches 97.2% this year.

Nevertheless, the current food safety regulation systems can exercise little supervision over small or micro businesses which account for 80% of the total food production enterprises. In this regard, the revised *Food Safety Law* requires the local governments to work out specific regulations onthe

157

management of small workshops and vendors. And according to the new law, if a state agency is required to make provisions on a certain matter, the job should be accomplished within one year after the new law takes effect. In other words, the governments of all the provinces, autonomous regions and municipalities (directly under the Central Government) have to work out specific regulations on the management of small workshops and vendors before October 1, 2016.

9.5 Both Infrastructure and Layout should Be Stressed to Further Relieve Urban Traffic Congestion

In the survey on primary concern, transportation comes last among the four choices. And from the average of the survey samples, 8.86% of the interviewees regard transportation as the most influential factor of their quality of life—low than the 2015 value of 10.69%. The city of the lowest percentage is Yinchuan (6.63%). And the city of the highest percentage is Taiyuan (12.37%). Both the lowest and the highest percentages have declined compared to that of last year. Therefore, according to the subjective feelings of the residents, the traffic conditions of China has gradually improved.

From the perspective of objective indicators and the QLICC system, traffic conditions can be measured by two subindexes: One is the safety indicator, consisting of the death toll per 10, 000 vehicles (a relative indicator reflecting the number of accidents) and the total death toll of traffic accidents. The other is congestion conditions.

As far as traffic safety is concerned, according to the *Statistical Communique of the People's Republic of China on the 2015 National Economic and Social Development* released by NBS, the 2015 national traffic accident death toll per

Conclusions and Enlightenments

10,000 vehicles was 2.1 persons, a 5.4% drop on a year-on-year basis. When converted according to the quantity of vehicle ownership, the total traffic accident death toll of 2015 was 37,426 persons, a growth of 9.1%. The growth rate of 2015 was 0.6% higher than that of 2014. It is obvious that the situation of transportation safety is still far from satisfactory. In view of the frequent traffic accidents, we believe that: firstly, the penalties for traffic offences should be strictly imposed. Secondly, related publicity campaigns should be increased to enhance citizens' awareness of traffic safety. And thirdly, driver training systems should be further improved, and the exam requirements should be raised.

As far as residents' satisfaction is concerned, traffic congestion has already become one of the biggest headaches for people living in large or medium-sized cities. In April 2016, AMap and the Daimler Sustainable Transportation Research Center of Tsinghua University released the *2016 Q1 Traffic Analysis Report of China Major Cities*. As is pointed out in the report, compared to the first quarter of last year, traffic congestion has somewhat relieved in the 60 cities monitored by the AMap traffic big data. Among them, the traffic of nearly 1/3 of the cities is better than that of last year, especially cities in the eastern coastal areas. The congestion in another 1/3 of the cities are becoming worse, mostly of which are in the Pearl River Delta. And the traffic conditions in the rest cities have remained the same. Tianjin, Shanghai, Fuzhou and Shijiazhuang are listed in the Q1 list of better traffic, whose congestion has been reduced by 9.2%, 7.8%, 4.0% and 3.8% respectively. Meanwhile, Jinan, Changsha, Hefei, Changchun, Shenzhen and Harbin are in the Q1 list of worse traffic, whose rush hour congestion delay indexes have risen by 9.6%, 8.4%, 7.8%, 7.1%, 4.9% and 3.4%. All this shows that the management over traffic congestion has been effective.

159

 Blue Book of Quality of Life in Cities

According to foreign experiences, we need to take the following measures, in order to further relieve urban traffic congestion: First, improve urban infrastructure. As an outstanding example of the economically developed cities, the free-flow speed of Hong Kong is far higher than that of the developed mainland cities, thanks to its sophisticated infrastructure. Related data show that the freeways (there is no expressway but only freeways in Hong Kong) account for over 5.6% of the ways in Hong Kong, while freeways and expressways together constitute only less than 2.5% of the ways in Beijing and Jinan – both cities of severe congestion. In addition, the drainage systems in most mainland cities are relatively backward and will often cause water logging during rain seasons and make the traffic worse. Second, abandon the idea of mono-functional sectorization in the "Athens Charter" and further promote the idea of comprehensive functions, so as to change the job-housing imbalance. And third, increase the number of urban agglomerations (the combination of a central city and several satellite cities), in order to limit the population density of city centers and to spread people, businesses and urban functions into satellite cities. [1]

---

[1] Qian Qihu, "A Permanent Cure for Urban Traffic Congestion and Air Pollution", *Science and Technology Daily*, 21-04-2014.